GOOD AND EVIL

Reviews of the first edition

'I would not have believed that a work in moral philosophy could, in our present age, have such depth, brilliance and force.' **Norman Malcolm**

'An outstanding contribution to moral philosophy.' **Alasdair MacIntyre**

'Profound, moving ... the book is full of splendidly original and insightful discussions.' **Antony Duff,** *Philosophical Books*

'Subtle, profound and immensely valuable ...' **Paul Standish,** *Journal of Moral Education*

'... one of the deepest works of ethics I have read.' **Lars Hertzberg,** *Philosophical Investigations*

'It is a marvellous work, one which ought to change the tone as well as the focus of much contemporary moral philosophy.' **Bernadette Tobin,** *The Australian*

'... a superb, richly textured discussion which engages directly with real people and their deeply serious moral concerns.' **Brenda Almond,** *THES*

'One can only acknowledge the justice and admire the acuteness of many of its critical contributions to contemporary debates in moral philosophy.' **A. D. M. Walker,** *Journal of Applied Philosophy*

'Gaita's book is very important and needs to be addressed.' **Michael McGee,** *The Philosophical Quarterly*

Raimond Gaita's *Good and Evil* is one of the most important, original and provocative books on the nature of morality to have been published in recent years. It is essential reading for anyone interested in what it means to talk about good and evil. Gaita argues that questions about morality are inseparable from the preciousness of each human being, an issue we can only address if we place the idea of remorse at the centre of moral life. Drawing on an astonishing range of thinkers and writers, including Plato, Wittgenstein, George Orwell and Primo Levi, Gaita also reflects on the place of reason and truth in morality and ultimately how questions about good and evil are connected to the meaning of our lives.

This revised edition of *Good and Evil* includes a substantial new preface and afterword by the author.

GOOD AND EVIL

An Absolute Conception

Second Edition

Raimond Gaita

Routledge
Taylor & Francis Group

LONDON AND NEW YORK

First published 1991
by Macmillan

This new edition first published 2004
by Routledge
2 Park Square, Milton Park, Abingdon, Oxon, OX14 4RN

Simultaneously published in the USA and Canada
by Routledge
270 Madison Ave, New York, NY 10016

Reprinted 2005

Routledge is an imprint of the Taylor and Francis Group

© Raimond Gaita, 1991, this edition 2004

Typeset in Sabon by
Florence Production Ltd, Stoodleigh, Devon
Printed and bound in Great Britain by
MPG Books Ltd, Bodmin

All rights reserved. No part of this book may be reprinted or
reproduced or utilised in any form or by any electronic,
mechanical, or other means, now known or hereafter
invented, including photocopying and recording, or in any
information storage or retrieval system, without permission in
writing from the publishers.

British Library Cataloguing in Publication Data
A catalogue record for this book is available
from the British Library

Library of Congress Cataloging in Publication Data
A catalog record for this title has been requested

ISBN 0–415–33288–5 (hbk)
ISBN 0–415–33289–3 (pbk)

For Martin Winkler,
teacher and friend

Contents

CONTENTS

Preface to the first edition

⟶⟫●⟪⟵

This book began as a PhD thesis under the supervision of R. F. Holland. I owe very much to him as will be evident to anyone who knows his work. I also owe much – probably more than I am any longer able to tell – to many years of critical but sympathetic discussion with Peter Winch and Marina Barabas.

Also, but again in ways that are hard to specify, I owe much to the students at the University of London, especially those at King's College, who, since 1977, suffered my explorations of the themes of this book and who helped me to formulate my thoughts more clearly.

I am grateful to Paul McLaughlin for his comments on the final draft.

Preface to the
second edition

I

To write a preface or an afterword? I decided to do both. The preface
is intended to guide new and previous readers through a conceptual
landscape that may seem, to some degree, foreign to them, and to
remove obstacles to seeing its main features, obstacles I had created.
The afterword develops more forcibly than in the body of the book:
an argument with a radical conclusion.

The book is not altered substantially. Grammatical errors have (I
hope) been corrected, sentences have been shortened, and I have
made other efforts to make my meaning clearer. In service to that
ambition almost every page has been altered.

When the book was first published it proved controversial,
earning high praise and some abuse. Its style and tone were partly
responsible for both. They remain essentially unchanged, though I
would not write now as I did then. Friends of the book convinced
me that short of radical revision, attempts to modify its style and
tone were more likely to deprive the book of its power than make
it more congenial to the people it irritates. I have taken their advice.
My thanks to Bernard Holiday, Christopher Cordner, David Levy
and, most of all, David Saksena.

II

In the Introduction to his fine collection of essays, *Against
Empiricism*,[1] R. F. Holland writes:

A stance has to be taken unless it goes by default, towards the difference between judgements that are of the highest significance for ethics and judgements that are not. In the former case I would say that it is more a matter of registering an experience or marking an encounter, than passing a judgement. I am thinking now of what can be seen in the unprofitable fineness of certain deed or characters – and is pointed to by the unprofitable vileness of others; the difference between the unqualified goodness attested or offended against there and the ordinary run of merits and demerits among people and their works.

Good and Evil 'registers' three 'experiences', 'marks' three 'encounters'. It describes them and reflects upon what strikes me morally and philosophically important about them and attempts to place them conceptually. The 'marking' is, in all three cases, a kind of testimony. In that respect, and others, the book is not morally neutral, but (for good and bad reasons) it is no longer necessary to apologise for that. *Good and Evil* is not, however, a book on practical ethics or a book intended to help the reader answer the question, 'How should one live?' My primary aim is to *understand* those encounters and to place them in traditions of philosophical thought about morality and concern over the meaning of our lives more generally. Even in its most polemical final chapter, my concern is to understand what moral philosophers can be held morally accountable for – what kind of holding to account it is – even in the practice of the discipline. I hope I will not be misunderstood, then, if I say that the book is resolutely and morally passionately an enterprise in meta-ethics. I do not avoid testimony and commitment, but I constantly step back to examine the concepts and assumptions that feature in its descriptions and discussions. *Good and Evil* invites readers to see morality and philosophy from a new perspective; not so much by arguing for this or for that thesis, as by exposing assumptions, showing other possibilities and being sceptical about what we often think *must* be the case.

Of the three encounters, the most important is not the one that I first write about. It appears in Chapter 11 disguised as a response to the compassion Mother Teresa showed to the beggars of Calcutta. Younger readers may not know of her, or they and others who do may have been persuaded by Christopher Hitchens that she was really no saint.[2] Hitchens is wrong, I believe, but I will not argue that here. For me, the most transforming encounter with saintly goodness was not, in fact, seeing Mother Teresa on television and reading her and about her. When I was a young man I worked as an assistant in a psychiatric hospital, in a ward where many patients had been for twenty or more years. There I met a nun who responded without a trace of condescension towards people who were incurably mentally ill and who had been abandoned by friends and relatives, even by their parents. I tell the full story and reflect on it at some length in *A Common Humanity: Thinking about Love and Truth and Justice*,[3] published almost ten years after *Good and Evil*. When I wrote *Good and Evil* I was not prepared to speak so personally.

The wonder of the nun's behaviour has inspired much on my philosophical work because it revealed what a human life could mean. Even people like those patients, who appear to have lost everything that gives sense to our lives, are fully our equals. Yet if I try to explain what it means to say that her love showed me that they were fully our equals ('proved' it to me, indeed for I could not doubt it), I could only say that she responded without a trace of condescension and that the wondrousness of it compelled me to affirm its rightness.

Much of the reflection in this book is about what that can mean. It seeks to understand why 'goodness' (of a kind that invites a capital 'G'), 'love' and 'purity' are words that seem to be indispensable to any attempt to characterise her demeanour, what kind of testimony it compelled and what 'evil' means when it is paired with that kind of goodness. Since *Good and Evil* was first published, philosophers have shown some interest in the concept of evil, but not in the kind of goodness that we so naturally pair with it in our ordinary ways of speaking.

The second 'encounter' is not personal in that way. It came though reading Hannah Arendt's book, *Eichmann in Jerusalem*,[4] in which she records Moshe Landau's inspired intervention at the trial of Adolf Eichmann in 1961, over which he presided. Against those who wished to make a show trial of it, Landau was moved to say that the trial had one and only one purpose – to do justice. From one perspective his point was about the procedures necessary to preserve the integrity of the court. From another (and of course these perspectives do not conflict) he gave voice to one of the sublime features of our system of criminal justice. Justice was owed to the chief architect of the Final Solution, not just for the sake of future legal or political goods, but because it was owed *to him* (as a human being, I am tempted to say), even though there was no doubt about his identity or about his terrible guilt. Only if justice were done for that reason, amongst others, would it be done at all. Only then would the integrity of the court remain intact. That is how I read Landau's remarks.

The third experience is of remorse, which I think of not as a psychological response to wrongdoing, useful to stiffen one's resolve not to offend again, but as a pained, bewildered realisation of what it means (in a sense interdependent with *what it is*) to wrong someone. When it is lucid, remorse, as I characterise it, is an astonished encounter with the reality of the ethical. I describe it variously in the book. In Chapter 4, my example is a Dutchwoman who was involved in a plot to kill Hitler and who ordered three Jews she had been sheltering in her home to leave because the plot would be aborted if they were discovered. Within days of leaving her home all three were murdered. She hated Hitler for many things, she said, but most of all because he made a 'murderess' of her. In *A Common Humanity* I tell the fictitious story of a man who, in a fit of irritation, pushes aside an old beggar who had aggressively demanded money from him. The beggar falls, hits his head on the curb and dies. Though no one would have given a thought to his death were he to have died of natural causes, he haunts the man who killed him, tempting him to kill himself because he can no longer live with himself. After roughly two thousand years of hearing that human beings are sacred, that we are all God's children, we no longer find that remarkable. Step back from that tradition, even a little, and it seems astonishing.

Much the same is true of Landau's intervention. We are perhaps thankful for it, even inspired by it, but not astonished. We have grown accustomed to the idea that justice is owed to every human being irrespective of who they are, what they have done and what attitude they take to what they have done. Some people disagree, of course, but the matter is, at most, controversial for us. Aristotle would have found it absurd and, in a way, he would have been right. I try to reclaim the wondrousness of it for philosophical reflection.

The encounters I mark are dramatic. Holland did not have such occasions in mind when he spoke of 'judgements that are of the highest significance for ethics'. Dramatic though my examples are, I suggest that they all reveal something universal. Or, more accurately perhaps: someone who is claimed by them will take them to reveal something universal in the same way as someone who responds to the parable of the Good Samaritan does. I do not always characterise in the same way what is revealed. Sometimes I say that it is the inalienable preciousness or the infinite preciousness of every human being. (I acknowledge that when 'infinitely' qualifies 'precious' it signals desperation, but no more, I think, than when 'unconditional' qualifies 'respect' or when 'inalienable' qualifies 'dignity'.) Sometimes I speak of seeing the full humanity of someone. At other times I adopt more Kantian idioms and speak of the unconditional respect owed to every human being, or of the inalienable dignity each human being possesses. When I opt for one over the other I rely very much on context to show why. It is clear, I think, why one turns naturally to Kantian idioms when one speaks of what is owed to Eichmann – when one says that even he is owed unconditional respect, for example. It sounds grotesque to say that Eichmann is infinitely precious (though a saint might say just that). But the meanings of these expressions require more attention than I give them. I will say a little more about them in this preface.

The work of saintly love is not always done by religious people. In his wonderful book *If This Is Man*, Primo Levi gives an example. Levi's story is far more dramatic than any of mine, but it will take me to the same destination as my reflections on Mother Teresa in *Good and Evil* and on the nun in *A Common Humanity*. It will also make clear why Kant haunts my thought and why Aristotle is so often a foil to it; it will give some reasons for why I believe that it is a mistake to think that morality has essentially to do with principles of conduct and that philosophical thought about morality is essentially about kinds of practical reasons.

Levi tells of an incident that occurred during his last weeks in Auschwitz. Russian artillery could already be heard in the camp.

After years in the death camp the prospect of liberation seemed only weeks away.

> The night held ugly surprises.
>
> Ladmaker, in the bunk under mine, was a poor wreck of a man. He was (or had been) a Dutch Jew, seventeen years old, tall, thin and gentle. He had been in bed for three months; I have no idea how he had managed to survive the selections. He had had typhus and scarlet fever successively; at the same time a serious cardiac illness had shown itself, while he was smothered with bedsores, so much so that by now he could only lie on his stomach. Despite all this, he had a ferocious appetite. He only spoke Dutch, and none of us could understand him.
>
> Perhaps the cause of it all was the cabbage and turnip soup, of which Ladmaker had wanted two helpings. In the middle of the night he groaned and then threw himself from his bed. He tried to reach the latrine, but was too weak and fell to the ground crying and shouting loudly.
>
> Charles lit the lamp . . . and we were able to ascertain the gravity of the incident. The boy's bed and the floor were filthy. The smell in the small area was rapidly becoming insupportable. We had but a minimum supply of water and neither blankets nor straw mattresses to spare. And the poor wretch, suffering from typhus, formed a terrible source of infection, while he could certainly not be left all night to groan and shiver in the cold in the middle of the filth.
>
> Charles climbed down from his bed and dressed in silence. While I held the lamp, he cut all the dirty patches from the straw mattress and the blankets with a knife. He lifted Ladmaker from the ground with the tenderness of a mother, cleaned him as best as possible with straw taken from the mattress and lifted him into the remade bed in the only position in which the unfortunate fellow could lie. He scraped the floor with a scrap of tin plate, diluted a little chloramine and finally spread disinfectant over everything, including himself.

When moral philosophers discuss an example like this they usually do so to illustrate the concept of a supererogatory act – an act that is beyond the call of duty. It sits at the edge of conceptual territory whose prominent features are notions of obligation, rules, principles, and conditions for the ascription of culpability. Supererogatory acts, the tradition tells us, are the actions of saints and heroes. Those who do them are to be praised, but those who do not should not to be blamed. Because no one can be blamed for doing them, they cannot be obligatory. From that perspective the difference – crucial to the argument of this book – between heroic and saintly deeds does not matter. Also from that perspective – one that finds moral rules and obligation at the centre of its field of moral vision – supererogatory acts teach us nothing important about the nature of morality.

It is, of course, easy to see why what Charles did should be called supererogatory: it *is* supererogatory. But the thought that he did something beyond the call of duty need not be what first strikes one. Instead one might be struck by, or to put it better, one might *wonder* at its *goodness* – the kind that I have mentioned before that might make one reach for a capital 'G'. Such wonder might be informed less by the fact that Charles risked his own life (after ten years in Auschwitz with freedom probably only weeks away) for the sake of a man certain to die within days, than by the fact that he was able to respond 'with the tenderness of a mother'. Then one would be struck, not so much by what he achieved for Ladmaker, nor by the intention which enabled him to achieve it, nor by his motive in so far as that is distinguished from his intention, but by the *spirit* of what he did. For philosophers who argue over whether it is intentions or consequences that really matter morally, the spirit in which someone acts might seem relatively unimportant to an understanding of morality. For others, like me, it can be critical. As much as the behaviour of the nun at the hospital or the behaviour of Mother Teresa, Charles's behaviour showed a goodness to marvel at.

Charles's tenderness would not, of course, have been what it was, let alone have been wondrous, were it not for what he was trying to achieve – that Ladmaker be returned to his bunk as clean and comfortable as possible. That, however, could have been the intention of many different kinds of people and be achieved in many different ways. At one extreme it could have been the intention and achievement of one of the SS officers, not one who was callous, of course, but nonetheless one who never seriously doubted that Ladmaker deserved extermination because he was a Jew. Charles's behaviour is, one might say, at the other extreme.

Goodness, wonder, purity, love – these concepts take one to a different perspective from the one whose conceptual features incline one to be struck most of all by the thought that Charles's behaviour was supererogatory or by the thought that moral reflection is especially concerned with discovering (and perhaps justifying) principles of conduct.

Responding to the claim that morality is a guide to action, Peter Winch pointed out that if it were not for morality, we would have fewer problems for which we need guidance. Were it not for morality, we would most often deliberate only about the best means to our ends. A strange guide, he mused, that first puts obstacles in our way and then suggests ways around them.[5] His point was, in part, that before one has a problem about what morally to do, one must first see one's situation in a moral light. One way of characterising my concern in *Good and Evil* (and in this preface) is to say that I want to show how the world appears to moral reflection about what to do and how to be when it is illuminated by the kind of goodness shown by people like Charles, the nun and Mother Teresa.

In Chapter 11, I say that it was not the superlative development of a natural or moral capacity that enabled Mother Teresa to respond as she did to radically afflicted beggars in Calcutta. I would say the same of Charles and of the nun I encountered at the hospital. True, they were compassionate people, but their compassion was informed by an understanding that it was elicited by people whose preciousness had not been even slightly diminished. Simone Weil says that compassion for the afflicted is 'a more astounding miracle than walking on water, healing the sick or raising the dead'.[6] Elsewhere she says: 'The supernatural virtue of justice consists in behaving exactly as though there were equality when one is the stronger in an unequal relationship. Exactly in every respect, including the slightest details of accent and attitude, for a detail may be enough to place the weaker party in the condition of matter which on this occasion naturally belongs to him, just as the slightest shock causes water which has remained liquid below freezing point to solidify.'[7] Charles's behaviour was the 'miracle' Weil describes. So was the nun's and Mother Teresa's. The reason that Weil calls it a miracle is not because such people are able, very impressively, to resist temptations that threaten to prevent their will from executing a clearly perceived duty. Nor is it because they are able to resist temptations that would obscure clear vision of their duty. At the risk of being misleading, I will say that her point (and mine) is conceptual. It is about the concepts that must be available to us if we are to see things in a certain way, in this case, if we are to see people who are radically afflicted in a way that enables us to respond with a compassion that does not condescend.

Schopenhauer was right to complain that Kant failed to understand the importance of compassion to our understanding of the ethical. Kant was right, however, to think that no extension of compassion or sympathy considered as natural dispositions could take one to an understanding of the distinctive kind of limit another human being should be to our will – a limit that Kant expressed in the Categorical Imperative. There is no need, I argue in this book, to set compassion and moral impossibility or necessity against one another, but the kind of compassion expressed by Charles is conditioned by a particular understanding of what it means to be a human being, suffering as Ladmaker did. I try to characterise that understanding. If I have succeeded, it will be evident why Kant, rather than Schopenhauer or Hume, haunts my thought.

A similar point needs to be made about empathy, which is now such a prized virtue. It was not Charles's capacity for empathy that was wondrous, not at any rate, if that means his capacity to see things and to feel things as Ladmaker did. We are told nothing about how Ladmaker saw things, but it would hardly be surprising if his affliction had made him numb and if years of degradation had made him incapable of any serious conception of his intrinsic worth as a human being, of his 'inalienable dignity', as Kant would put it. To be sure, Charles responded to Ladmaker's condition, but he responded to what it meant for a human being to have fallen into that condition rather than to what it felt like. The wonder of what Charles did is that he responded fully to Ladmaker's degradation, saw fully the depth of it, while affirming Ladmaker's undiminished humanity. I hope, therefore, that it is clear why I emphasise how wondrous it is that Charles could see Ladmaker as he did, rather than what he subjectively felt when he saw him lying on the floor.

Kant would have said that Charles affirmed in Ladmaker a dignity that no human being could lose. If the case I make against them in this book is fair, however, Kantian elaborations, intended to make the affirmation philosophically perspicuous, fail to the point of parody. Alan Donagan said that Kant's famous injunction that one always treat humanity as an end and never merely as a means was Kant's way of rendering, in a way he believed to be more perspicuous to reason, the moral content of the biblical command to love one's neighbour. Donagan formulated it thus: 'always act so that you respect every human being, yourself or another, as a rational creature'.[8] Were someone to ask me whether Kant had succeeded in the ambition that Donagan attributes to him, I would say that he had not. It is a profound question whether Kant was even on the right track, or whether this great philosopher got things quite backwards. Perhaps it is the biblical injunction, stories and parables, that enable us to make sense of the idea that a person is an end in his or herself.

In some of the most moving passages written by a great philosopher, Kant expressed his belief – perhaps one should say his *faith* – that a person broken and embittered by misfortune could act morally in ways quite unaffected by the emaciation of his inner life. His capacity to perform acts that would 'shine like a jewel' would be undiminished. Perhaps such a person could risk his life to make Ladmaker comfortable – could perform supererogatory acts – but he could not do so with the tenderness of a mother.

Nothing, I think, in Kant's account of the will and in his celebration of its capacity to overcome spiritual deadness in a person, could explain the subtle, modulated responsiveness of Charles's demeanour towards Ladmaker. In fact, Charles's vital responsiveness to Ladmaker's need is inconsistent with the spiritual deadness that Kant believed to be no impediment to undiminished moral responsiveness. Yet it is in that tenderness that Charles revealed Ladmaker to be someone precious – a neighbour, to allude to Donagan's account of what Kant was trying to do. For that reason I believe it is more than a cheap shot to point out that it looks like parody rather than philosophical clarification to say that Charles responded to the imperative to treat every human being as a rational creature. Nor will it improve things to say that he responded to Ladmaker as to a fellow citizen in the kingdom of ends. Admittedly, to say that Charles responded to Ladmaker as to a neighbour or as to a fellow human being will also provoke requests for clarification. But if resistance to satirical points of the kind I made just now is any guide, then those expressions look to be of the right kind. They seem to be in the right conceptual territory. I suggest, then, that we do what comes naturally and call the understanding shown in Charles's tenderness a form of love.

III

When we ask what makes a principle a moral principle, a rule a moral rule, an obligation a moral obligation – then I think we should seek at least some part of the answer in the kind of elaboration we give when we express most seriously our sense of what it means to wrong someone. Nowhere is that sense more sober than in lucid remorse. 'My God what have I done? How could I have done it?' Those are the typical accents of remorse. They do not (I argue) express an emotional reaction to what one has done, but a pained, bewildered – or perhaps better, incredulous – realisation of the full meaning of what one has done. But now, if one puts in the mouth of the remorseful person many of the philosophical accounts of what makes an obligation a moral obligation or a principle a moral principle, of the nature of morality and of its authority, we get parody.

'My God what I have done? I have violated the social compact, agreed behind a veil of ignorance.' 'My God what have I done? I have ruined my best chances of flourishing.' 'My God what have I done? I have violated rational nature in another.' 'My God what have I done? I have diminished the stock of happiness.' 'My God what have I done? I have violated my freely chosen principles.' An answer must surely be given to why, at one of the most critical moments of moral sobriety, so many of the official accounts of what it is for something to be of moral concern, the accounts of the connection between obligation and what it means to wrong someone, appear like parodies. It will not help to add to those exclamations, pained responses to the natural harm (physical and psychological) that the wrongdoer has caused. Even if one thinks the parodies to be to some degree unjust, they point unmistakably to the fact that the individual who has been wronged and who haunts the wrongdoer in his remorse has disappeared from sight.

The conception of individuality at work here is not that of a metaphysical particular, nor of a person's individuating characteristics, nor of a striking or charismatic personality. It is the kind of individuality that we express when we say that every human being is unique and irreplaceable. I elaborate it and its importance in Chapter 9 and again in the afterword. In part it is constituted by attachments whose intensity and importance we cannot fathom and which are beyond reason and merit. In so far as we consent to those attachments, they are attachments of and to persons who are required, under pain of superficiality, to distinguish reality from appearances – real love from infatuation, for example. In Chapters 8 and 9 and also in the afterword, I try to explain what lucidity amounts to in this connection and why we are required to try to achieve it. In those sections of the book, I hope readers will find a resolution to what otherwise might seem to be a paradox: namely, that the book is marked, on the one hand, by its strong opposition to foundationalism and, on the other, by its equally strong commitment to a version of the Socratic claim that an unexamined life – a life that does not rise to the requirement to be lucid about its meaning(s) – is unworthy of a human being.

The kind of individuality that I have just sketched is not an objective feature of people in the way their individuating characteristics are. While some of those individuating features may not be objective in the way that difference in height or weight are, they nonetheless give substantial meaning to the claim that we treat people differently because they *are* different from one another. Were we asked to justify that claim, we know what to refer. But if someone were to say that we treat people as unique and irreplaceable because they *are* unique and irreplaceable, though not on account of their individuating features, what would she point to? There seems to be nothing. Yet when parents who are grieving over a dead child say that they cannot yet have another child in the way they might get another pup, they express just this sense of the irreplaceability of their child. And were they asked why they 'cannot' have another to assuage their grief, they would speak of what it is (means) to have and to lose a child in ways that would always refer to the child. Adapting to my purpose a remark of Wittgenstein's, I would say that this kind of individuality is not a something, but it is not a nothing either. It is not a set of natural or metaphysical properties. It is under-determined by what is necessary to it – the other forms of individuality, the responses of people to one another, the unfathomable need that they sometimes have of one another, and more. The history of that need and the forms of response to it have generated and, in turn, been formed by what (following Rush Rhees) I call a language of love.

Rhees was impatient with this kind of talk of individuality. He said 'If one wants to talk of individuality, all right. It means little more than "something that can be loved" '.[9] But he did not take sufficient note of the fact that the language of love is critical as well as celebratory. Central to its critical dimension is the distinction between love and its appearances, a distinction that focuses on whether the lover is sufficiently attentive to the independent reality of the beloved. Reference to their uniqueness and irreplaceability – not just to those who love them, but period – is inseparable from that way of speaking of the independent reality of persons. And as I remarked about Mother Teresa, about the nun in *A Common Humanity*, and now about Charles, to wonder at the nature of their love is not to glory in a superlative achievement, as might be the case when one marvels at a feat of heroism. The wonder directs those who experience it to people who are loved, compelling those who wonder to testify – in astonishment – to a radically transformed perception of them. A religious person might say that the love revealed what it means for a human being to be sacred.

When Rhees said that to talk of individuality, as I have been doing, means little more than to speak of 'something that can be loved', his irritation was, I suspect, directed against the hope that appeal to individuality could rationally ground the love, or other responses. My claim is that love and that kind of individuality are interdependent and that the language of love, historically shaped by and shaping the work of love, yields to us a sense of love's object that makes the love seem right. Rhees after all said, 'something that *can* be loved' (my emphasis). Not anything can be. That is the constitutive role that love plays historically. It also has a revelatory role. Sometimes we see that something is precious only in the light of someone's love for it. Love's capacity to reveal is, in part, a function of the authority of the lover. It also depends on our openness to this kind of authority. That means that we must be open to the language of love and its distinctive critical categories – open to their distinctive grammar. Estrangement from the language of love – perhaps because we are suspicious of it, believing that it should be replaced by a rationally more attractive and tractable language of metaphysics – will prevent us from seeing clearly, perhaps from seeing at all, the distinctive kind of preciousness that human beings can have.

The kind of individuality I have been describing was known to the world before the work of saintly love yielded to us a conception of individuals as infinitely precious. Some of the most moving passages in Homer's *Iliad* depend on it. It was known to Aristotle who, as I said, functions in this book as a kind of test for how a non-reductive humanism looks before our sense of what it means to be a human being is transformed by the works of saintly love. True, this conception of individuality plays no important role in his ethics, but he would not have thought absurd the suggestion that it should.

The love of saints depends on, builds on and transforms that sense of individuality. It deepens the language of love, which nourishes and is nourished by our sense that human beings are irreplaceable and, because of that transformation, it compels some people to affirm that even those who suffer affliction so severe that they have irrecoverably lost everything that gives sense to our lives, and even the most radical evildoers, are fully our fellow human beings. As with the love it transforms, the love of saints plays a constitutive and revelatory role.

In *Good and Evil*, I fail to distinguish adequately individuality as transformed by saintly love from individuality before that transformation. The confusion runs through the chapter on remorse and elsewhere. Much of what I say about remorse – certainly the rhetorical affect of the parodies I offered earlier in this preface and offer also in the book – depend only on the latter conception. Most of what I say in the chapter on individuality and in the afterword, also depends only on it. However, much of what I say about the 'shock' of remorse – that aspect of it that prompts me to say that it 'registers an encounter' – requires a conception of the victim of one's wrongdoing that has been informed by saintly love. Only then, I think, is it intelligible that someone should be tempted to kill himself because he murdered another human being who mattered to no one, not on account of his shame for what his deed revealed about his character, but only because of the deed and what it means to have become a murderer. The same, I think, is true of what I call the 'radical singularity' of the guilty, a singularity that expresses itself in the judgement that it is always a corruption of serious remorse to seek to find consoling fellowship in a community of the guilty. It is not always a corruption of shame to be consoled by the fact that others have done what has shamed one.

The failure to distinguish between a sense of the preciousness of individuals before and after it is transformed by the works of saintly love also spreads serious confusion through my discussion of evil. The book begins with an horrific example taken from Chaim Kaplan's Warsaw diary. Immediately after introducing it, I deny that I did so in order 'to shock or to bully anyone into accepting or rejecting any philosophical positions in ethics'. A student commented that I had succeeded in doing so nonetheless. He was right, or at any rate, his ironic tone concerning my intention was justified. Though I intermittently glimpsed, I never saw clearly, the fact that if a morally serious person is sceptical about whether the concept of evil has an indispensable place amongst our moral concepts, then pointing to horrific examples of it will (rightly) not diminish his or her scepticism. It is not want of moral seriousness or sensitivity that makes such people sceptical. The concept of evil that I elaborate in *Good and Evil* (and also in *A Common Humanity*, more conscious of this point) depends on a sense of the preciousness of human life transformed by the love of saints. If one does not have it (and on my account, one will have it only if one also has a conception of goodness we attribute to saintly deeds) then talk of evil will mark out only what one takes to be especially morally horrible. In that case, given some of the nasty ways people speak of good and evil – the oversimplifying, demonising ways – it is better to resort to the many other ways we have to mark out what is morally horrible.

Because evil, as I understand it, requires a conception of preciousness violated, and because people can do evil for banal reasons, the concept of evil (that I develop) has little or no place in the characterisation of people or their motives. For that reason, people who say that the concept of evil does not help to explain the actions of evildoers are right. Sometimes, however, appeal to the concept is necessary to characterise adequately people's responses – the person whose remorse is informed by a sense that his victim was infinitely precious, or a spectator who responds to wrongdoing in a way informed by that same sense, for example. In *A Common Humanity* I describe the latter kind of case in some detail when I discuss the role that a concept of evil should play in disentangling the many different kinds of moral responses to the Holocaust.

IV

Despite my disavowals, many readers have taken *Good and Evil* to be (implicitly) a religious work, or to require religious commitment if its arguments are to be pressed home. I persist with my disavowals, but I am now more sympathetic to the reasons why people have read it that way. I am also more conscious of the importance of the works of saintly love upon what I say about the preciousness of individuals. The reader will have noticed that am also acutely conscious that 'precious' is a word that sometimes sounds precious. 'Sacred' is so much better. A religious person should have no difficulty in acknowledging that Eichmann was sacred. I am not religious, however, so I cannot use it.

'Sacred' is a word whose elaboration points in two directions – to theological and metaphysical doctrine, and to the language of love. Philosophers, especially bioethicists, have tended to focus on the doctrine. As a result there is little philosophical writing that is inward with the kind of experiences that incline someone to be sympathetic to talk of the sanctity of human life, even if they feel they cannot speak that way themselves. Those experiences are, I think, inseparable from a sense of awe, mystery and beauty that is naturally expressed in the language of love. A philosophical and moral battlefield, where people fight over abortion and euthanasia, is not a good place to develop an ear for its nuances. If one is not to distort the significance of the fact that the language is richly anthropomorphic, one must listen to it with patient sympathy.

We are sacred, some people say, because God loves us, his children. The 'because' indicates love's constitutive role. Religious people also say that the love of saints reveals us to be sacred. Some say that only God's grace makes the love of saints possible. Others say that God loves through His saints. Either way, love plays its revelatory role. Much of this anthropomorphic language elaborates on what it means to be a child of God. 'Child' in 'child of God' is an expression in the language of love. 'We are all God's offspring', doesn't work so well; nor would a religious person who is opposed to abortion speak of the foetus as sacred because it is God's foetus. Such people speak of 'an unborn child', which, I suggest in Chapter 8, is an expression in the language of love. Attempts to extract from this anthropomorphic, often poetic, language a cognitive content whose character is necessarily (*qua* cognitive) separable from poetic form, usually looks banal and seems incapable of inspiring the kind of wonder that is fundamental to religious testimony. Though (for most religious persons) everyone is sacred because God loves all his children, he loves, as parents do, each one of them as an individual. Each of them is called to rise to that fact with the kind of individuating responsiveness that I describe in the afterword. That, at any rate, is the argument of Chapter 13, where I argue that it is essential to serious religious claims that their proponents believe that they deepen our understanding of the world. Their content must, therefore, be available to us in an idiom that gives sense to talk of depth and shallowness. In Chapters 13 and 14 and in the afterword, I try to explain why, and what that idiom is like.

My commitment to what the nun in the hospital revealed is not conditional upon my believing something like she believed. My thought is not that it would be rational to respond without condescension to those patients if it is also true that they were God's children. Nor do I wish to say that the wondrousness of her behaviour gives strong prima-facie grounds for believing in God or for attributing metaphysical properties to the patients. My affirmation is as firm and unreserved as it is metaphysically groundless.

To discuss the works of saintly love with God abstracted from them might seem ridiculous. I did it, though, to meet a point made to me by Stanley Hauerwas. He granted that one could testify to the rightness of the nun's demeanour without thinking the rightness had to be underwritten metaphysically, but he asked whether her behaviour would have been possible were it not for the history of religious practice. That history is a complex mix of doctrine and practice expressed in the language of love – a complex history of the relations between the God of the philosophers and the God of religion. But now, abstract the God of the philosophers from the God of religion. What do we have? Oversimplifying a little, but not I think at the expense of the point, we have God's gratuitous love for his creatures. It now looks as though to say that we are sacred because God loves us provides no reason for believing that the kind of compassion the nun showed and that Charles showed to Ladmaker is rationally intelligible. External to human life and activity the love of God may be, but unless the way it is external provides such a reason, it seems not to do what is needed for someone who believes the rightness of the nun's behaviour is insufficiently accounted for unless there is reference to God or to the metaphysical properties of the patients. Ditto for the rightness of Charles's response to Ladmaker. The religious tradition that speaks of the God of religion rather than the God of the philosophers has often called saintly love absurd. Weil calls it a form of madness. Nothing that can be said about human beings – about their natural or their metaphysical properties – could ground it, in the sense of providing rational foundation for it. It cannot even make it less offensive to reason. How is God's gratuitous love for his creatures different?

V

Inalienably precious, infinitely precious – these are, I have admitted, not always congenial expression. If one cannot speak religiously and if one believes that talk of natural rights, or of citizens in the kingdom of ends, is metaphysically unsustainable and, perhaps, whistling in the dark, would it be better to speak of what is owed to human beings just because they are human beings? If Charles had been asked why he risked his life for Ladmaker, he might have said, 'He's a human being. He cannot be left like that.' When I characterised Charles' demeanour towards Ladmaker I said he responded as though Ladmaker's humanity had not been diminished despite his visible and extreme degradation.

I have admitted that if one wants to say that justice was owed to Eichmann, then it is better to say that it was owed to him as a human being rather than because he was inalienably precious. Clearly, though, there is no neutral elaboration of what it means to be a human being that will render unproblematic the 'because' when one says that Eichmann was owed a just trial because he was a human being, or that one must not torture terrorists with information about 'ticking bombs' because they are human beings. We must be careful, however, about what we make, reflectively, of the absence of such an independent elaboration. One ought not to assume that it would be better to speak of a person, their rights and what is owed to them. That, at any rate, is the burden of the argument in Chapter 10. The argument is, I am afraid, less clear than it should be. It is clearer, I think, in *A Common Humanity*. It is clearer again in *The Philosopher's Dog*.[10] There I develop what I call a naturalism of surfaces – a naturalism defined by the importance it attributes to the living human body and the many forms of its expressiveness in the constitution of the concepts that mark our creatureliness.

Virtue theory – considered as *theory* – construes the virtues as being inseparably tied to a conception of the human good that is enriched by an understanding of how our rationality, our cultural lives and our animality combine. Phillipa Foot tells us in her recent book, *Natural Goodness*, to think of plants and their good when we think about ethics.[11] She took pleasure in being provocative, but she was serious in recommending that we could account for the virtues and why we prized them by extending, in ways suggested by Aristotle, our understanding of what is good for the life of a plant. Such attempts have proven interesting, sometimes ingenious, but often desperate at the crux, in my judgement. There is a better way, I have suggested, to take seriously the concept of a human being over that of a person and to integrate it rightly with nature and culture. Given the sympathy of many virtue theorists for Wittgenstein's later work, it is surprising that they seem not to have seen in Part two of *The Philosophical Investigations* an important alternative to Aristotelianism.

Although I believe that Wittgenstein has pointed to a better way to think of the importance of our humanity to the constitution of some of our most fundamental concepts – and not just our ethical concepts – I do not want to suggest that there is a way of speaking of human beings and their lives which will make the wondrousness of saintly love, tractable (or even less offensive) to reason, or which would justifiably diminish the astonishment at what it reveals. Kant was right to insist that we have obligations to those we do not, and perhaps could not, love. It does not follow that we would find it even intelligible that we have such obligations unless we also found intelligible that someone could love such people. And when we ask ourselves whether we find that intelligible, we must ask ourselves whether a saint could do it. We know the answer.

If someone like Eichmann were the beneficiary of a saint's love, it would be a severe love. It would not count as love unless it were lucid about the evil of his crimes, about the banality of his response to them and about his failure to be remorseful for them. But love it would be. The argument of this book is that it is light cast by such love that enables us to think that people like Eichmann are owed unconditional respect. The same love inspires us to speak of the inalienable dignity of people like Charles. Simone Weil wrote in her diaries: 'If I light an electric torch at night out of doors I don't judge its power by looking at the bulb, but by seeing how many objects it lights up.'[12] Plato's simile of the cave also reminds us that we often do not see the source of what enables us to see things. We often misunderstand what we see, and what enables us to see it. For that reason we often give the wrong names to things.

That realisation drove me to speak of ethical-otherworldliness and to contrast it with humanism which, in this book, I identify with a non-reductive naturalism. Although I outline a sympathetic form of such a naturalism, partly in order to show that it cannot take one far enough, I now regret using the expression 'ethical-otherworldliness'. It sounds either too religious or too theoretically formidable. For the same reason I regret talking of mystery, even though I distinguish between things that are contingently and things that are necessarily mysterious. The latter are not mysterious to us because our epistemic or other cognitive powers are limited. But mystery is a word with much baggage, most of which I prefer not to carry. I should have been content to characterise the wondrousness of saintly love – to mark its conceptual features, to locate it in a sympathetic conceptual space and to leave it at that. Because I went further, some readers may feel that I did so in order to establish a further thesis – that there are deep mysteries for deep people to marvel at.

Throughout this book and in other works I have been critical of the talk of persons as ends in themselves; of the inalienable dignity and their inalienable natural rights when it appears to express foundationalist aspirations. I have been a reluctant critic, however, because wonderful work – in human rights, especially in international law – has been inspired by such ways of speaking. Landau, a German Jew, was educated in the Germanic tradition of jurisprudence, deeply steeped in Kantian ways of speaking. Writing against torture, he insisted that in all circumstances we must respect the 'inalienable dignity' of every human being. In the context he used it and in others in which people often do, the expression 'inalienable dignity' betrays a noble illusion.

Because dignity is essentially tied to appearances it is essentially alienable. The ties that bind it to appearances can be loosened, but they cannot all be cut. We can, and should, develop a generous understanding of the conditions under which dignity is visible. We can learn and, indeed, become astonished at how much dignity survives the degradation of the body, and to some degree, even of the mind, but there are limits. Misfortune can be so severe, criminals can be so unrelentingly cruel, that some people are, as Weil puts it, 'struck one of those blows that leaves a human being writhing on the ground like a half-crushed worm'. That happened to Ladmaker. Then, I believe, only the love of saints can see and reveal the humanity in them. That is why Weil said that compassion for the afflicted is 'a more astounding miracle than walking on water, healing the sick or raising the dead'.

Often I draw attention to the fact that those expressions (especially the Kantian ones) have a power to move and inspire us because of resonances they borrow from more natural (though not thereby less creative) ways of speaking to which they officially condescended. When I wrote *Good and Evil* I was not aware, however, of how often some of those expressions are not only supported by and given power by a language of love, but are sometimes (in some uses) actually part of that language. Then they belong to an ethical conception in which goodness is the focal concept. It is an ethic of renunciation, expressed first by Socrates when he said to his incredulous interlocutors that it is better to suffer evil than to do it and, later in our tradition, deepened by an affirmation that every human being is infinitely precious. In its religious formulation it affirms that every human life is sacred. At other times those expressions move us because they draw power from another ethical conception. They then play a different role and to some degree undermine not only the part they play in the first conception but that conception itself. The defining concepts of that second conception are autonomy, integrity, courage, nobility, honour and flourishing or self-realisation. Sometimes nobility and sometimes honour is its focal concept. It is an ethic of assertion or, at any rate, an ethic for the relatively fortunate.

Both of the ethical conceptions I have just sketched are interdependent with an understanding of what it is to be human being and, therefore, of what kind of compassion it is intelligible rationally to show to a human being. It will be evident that I believe that only the ethic of renunciation can find words to keep fully amongst us those who suffer severe, ineradicable and degrading affliction or of those who have committed the most terrible deeds and whose character seems fully to match them. My point, I wish to stress, is not that a conception of value that has goodness, rather than, say, nobility, as its focus is unable to appreciate the heroic. It is that within that conception what we make of the heroic, the noble, the honourable, the value of autonomy and so on, is transformed by a sense of the inalienable preciousness of each human being. Kantian rhetoric, I now realise better than when I wrote *Good and Evil*, is morally complex. Sometimes it is heroic in a way consistent with the language of love, sometimes in ways that are part of it, and sometimes in ways that undermine it.

VI

At the beginning of this preface I said that some people objected to the tone of this book. Some objected particularly to my claim that even a philosopher, true to the deepest aspects of his or her calling, should fear to think some things, should find some things to be morally unthinkable. Although the tone of Chapter 17 is strongly polemical, my concern was not to say that this or that is unthinkable, but rather to introduce the concept for reflection and to ask what role it had in moral thinking and in philosophical thought about moral thinking. In part, my tone expresses my incredulity that the discipline that prides itself about thinking about thinking has not thought much about *that*. Were I to write about this issue now, my tone would be different (as it is in *A Common Humanity*), but the lament that philosophers yield too unself-critically to a self-congratulatory complacency about their readiness bravely to follow to its morally horrible or nihilistic conclusion any argument they believed to be valid, would be much the same.

Some people found the tone of *Good and Evil* objectionable because they judged it to be arrogant, disdainful, high-minded, and moralistic. I hope they are not right. I will not try to defend myself. Instead, I will press this distinction: one must be clear about whether one objects to being thought shallow or whether one objects to the very idea that talk of shallowness has a serious place in philosophy. Many philosophers speak as though they object on the second count.

For reasons I elaborate throughout the book, but especially in Chapter 15, I believe they are wrong. That they are wrong should be one of the lessons of recent scepticism about ideals of neutrality in ethics. The best reason for the scepticism is not that one inevitably betrays moral commitment even when writing philosophically about ethics. Nor is it that one should honour philosophy's ancient promise to answer the questions of morality. It is that one's subject matter is of a kind whose description and reflective assessment must admit as indispensable, as intrinsic to its content, judgements that this or that is sentimental, or overtaken by pathos, or banal and, perhaps, in ways defined by those concepts, shallow.

None of this, of itself, implies arrogance. Arrogance lies not in the mere application of such concepts, but in their misapplication. Just as there is a tendency to one kind of arrogance amongst those who pride themselves on being tough-minded, hard-headed analytical philosophers, so there is a tendency to a different kind of arrogance amongst those who speak too readily of depth and shallowness. And, it must be admitted, the latter judgements sit uneasily with the kind of neutrality required by philosophy as an academic discipline. It is hard to see how one could sustain fair examining practices if such judgements were made regularly about the work of students. If that is true, and if it is also true that one cannot dispense with such judgement in the full assessment of philosophical problems in ethics, then, as I suggest in Chapters 2 and 17, serious questions follow about the nature of moral philosophy as an academic discipline, at least within a liberal university.

This distinction that I draw in Chapter 14 between sentimentality as a cause of cognitive defect and sentimentality as a form of it is very important, I think. When it is a cause, one can wish (however idly) to be rid of it. More importantly (and this is critical to the nature of the idealised conception of philosophical understanding that I criticise), one can wish oneself to be rid of all that makes one vulnerable to it and yet retain the content of one's thought. But when sentimentality is a form of cognitive defect (a form of the false, as I would now put it) that is not so. Poets, and other writers and artists may wish even more fiercely than scientists to be rid of sentimentality and similar vices, but for a poet to wish to be the kind of creature who is not vulnerable to it, is for his or her to wish to be free of the only idiom in which she can write poetry. To wish to be free of all that makes us vulnerable to cliché, banality, sentimentality and so on in our moral thought – including much of our philosophical thought about morality – is to wish ourselves bereft of ways of elaborating, in the realm of meaning, our full sense of what it means to wrong someone and all that conditions that sense. It is to wish ourselves bereft of the means to elaborate what (in the afterword) M believes distinguishes us from the Vietnamese. That is the deepest reason why understanding in ethics must necessarily be humanly engaged.

I hope now to have assembled the elements of an answer to an objection that must have been forming. Grant, an objector concedes, that, as a matter of fact, when we elaborate what it means to humiliate someone, what it means really to love, to grieve, to be a friend and so on, we often turn to literature. Grant also that no elaboration of what M can readily attribute to the Vietnamese can take us to a full understanding of what it means to wrong someone. Singly or together, however, these points fall considerably short of showing that it is not properly and primarily the discursive work of philosophy, rather than the work of literature and art more generally, first to articulate those things that condition our sense of what it means to wrong someone and, second, to explain how they condition it. Was it not, after all, Plato and Aristotle who (in their different ways) made the point that the distinction between the reality of a virtue and its counterfeits is fundamental to the very idea of virtue? Did they not also offer accounts of what they regarded as genuine virtues, distinguishing them from their counterfeits, explaining why they did so? Was it not Plato, poet and philosopher combined, who warned sternly of the 'ancient quarrel' between poetry and philosophy? And did he not insist that it must be resolved in favour of philosophy?

I cannot hope fully to answer that objection in this preface, but I hope to reduce its force considerably by exposing to clear view two assumptions about the discursive and the cognitive that inform it.

Because literature is imaginative, philosophers have always acknowledged that it can provide much food for the thought of philosophers and scientists, but only when what is nourishing to thought – genuinely cognitive content – can be abstracted from literary style and be brought to judgement before a court of philosophy and science. That is the first assumption. It is informed by a second: that the critical concepts used in literary criticism, or when we try to determine whether we have been sentimentally moved by a real or artistic example, are causes rather than forms of cognitive failure. Abandon the second assumption and the way is clear, I think, to seeing that those critical concepts mark out a distinctive cognitive realm. If one sees that, one will at least be suspicious of the first assumption. How, after all, can one distinguish what is genuinely cognitive from what only appears so? Only, it looks plausible to say, by attention to the critical concepts that tell us what it is to think well and badly in this or that realm of inquiry or reflection.

Moral philosophy, even when pressing its meta-ethical task, its task of understanding this strange phenomenon we call morality and the place it has in our lives, should welcome prose enlivened by the realisation that to think of philosophy as a quest for understanding is not therefore to think of it as ideally free of feeling. Or to put it

(I hope) less ambiguously: it should welcome prose that is informed by the realisation that the constitutive concepts of philosophical thought about ethics – the concepts with which we assess whether we are thinking well or badly – cannot be idealised as concepts which define good and bad thinking for any rational being whatsoever, irrespective of whether they are affective beings and irrespective of whatever lives they lead.

Am I suggesting that the distinction between philosophy and art should be blurred? Yes and no. Philosophy should still be primarily a discursive discipline, distinguished markedly from the writing of novels, poetry and plays. But if the discursive is no longer restricted to the exercise of the kind of thought in which form and content are separable, then, in roughly those parts of philosophy which the Europeans call philosophical anthropology, there will be no marked distinction between the narratives that must to some degree nourish inquiry and philosophical engagement with them.

Acknowledgements
for the first edition

I am obliged to the editors and publishers concerned for permission to use material from the following of my previous publications: 'Integrity', *Proceedings of the Aristotelian Society*, suppl. vol. 15 (1981); 'Better One than Ten', *Philosophical Investigations* 5 (2) (1982); 'Against Empiricism', *Philosophical Investigations* 6 (3) (1983); 'Moral Luck', *Philosophical Quarterly* 33 (132) (1983); 'Virtues, Human Good and the Unity of a Life', *Inquiry* 26 (1984); 'Ethical Individuality', in R. Gaita (ed.), *Value and Understanding: Essays for Peter Winch* (London: Routledge, 1988); 'The Personal in Ethics', in P. Winch and D. Z. Phillips (eds), *Wittgenstein: Attention to Particulars* (London: Macmillan, 1989). I wish also to thank the British Academy for its generous grant.

1

Evil and unconditional respect

The following is a passage from Chaim Kaplan's Warsaw Diary:

> A rabbi in Lodz was forced to spit on a Torah scroll that was in the Holy Ark. In fear of his life he complied and desecrated that which is holy to him and his people. After a short while he had no more saliva, his mouth was dry. To the Nazi's question, why did he stop spitting, the rabbi replied that his mouth was dry. Then the son of the 'superior race' began to spit into the rabbi's mouth and the rabbi continued to spit on the Torah.[1]

I have not quoted this to shock or to bully anyone into accepting or rejecting any philosophical position in ethics – not, for example, to refute the moral sceptic or to bully him into submission or, even, to call him to a kind of sobriety. I have quoted it to appeal to a community wider than one whose sense of philosophical reflection is conditioned by the nature of philosophy as a subject or a discipline (as studied in universities) and for whom examples such as this are a focus for ethical reflection. There is no simple way to identify that community independently of the character of its concern with good and evil. There are those who have been the victims of such evil – Jews and many others, not only at the hands of the Nazis and not only at that time. But there are many others who have neither suffered nor witnessed such evil, yet whose lives and thought have been marked by its presence.

In the face of such evil some people believe that they must assert, and others that they must deny, that even people who have done such deeds are sacred. Few people will say that in full seriousness

1

because only someone who is religious can do it. But there are people who are not religious who want to say what they hope will be a secular equivalent of it and they will hunt for one of the inadequate expressions available to us to do it. They may say that even such people are infinitely precious, or that they are ends in themselves, or they may say, more simply, that even such people are owed unconditional respect, meaning, not that they are deserving of esteem, but that they are owed a kind of respect that is not conditional upon what they have done and that cannot be forfeited. Some will say that even the most terrible evildoers are owed this respect as human beings and that we owe it to them because we are human beings. That amounts to saying they remain our fellow human beings whatever they do. Many find that incomprehensible. They are likely to retort that if someone is to be treated or respected as a human being then they must behave like a human being. That seems to be sober common sense.

In (academic) philosophy examples such as these are often called 'hard cases', by which it is meant that they present serious difficulties for a philosophical thesis and it is implied that philosophical theories are judged according to how they deal with them. Consequentialists often present examples of the increasingly horrific consequences of someone's refusal to do evil to see at what point their opponents will crack. They think of such examples as hard cases that any account must accommodate under pain of inadequacy and they think that they alone can do it comfortably. The concept of a hard case presupposes a certain conception of ethical reflection: that it aspires to be, at best, theorising. Hard cases test theories and, on this conception, provide challenges that may, in principle, be met in thought alone, in abstraction and at a distance from the actual situations they describe.

In *Gorgias*, Polus presents an ever-worsening catalogue of horrors against Socrates who said that it is better to suffer evil than to do it and that it is better for the evildoer to be justly punished than to escape such punishment:

> What do you mean? If a man is arrested for the crime of plotting a dictatorship and racked and castrated and blinded with hot irons and finally, after suffering many other varieties of exquisite torture and seeing his wife and children suffer the

same, is crucified or burnt at the stake, will he be happier than if he gets off, establishes himself as a dictator, and spends the rest of his life in power doing as he chooses, the object of envy and admiration to natives and foreigners alike? Is this what you maintain that it is impossible to prove untrue?[2]

Socrates replies that Polus is trying to frighten him with bogeys. That, from the point of view of someone who sees Polus as legitimately presenting hard cases to test the Socratic claim, will seem to be merely evasive. But we do not know how Socrates would have responded had he actually been confronted with an example such as Polus describes. The difference is relatively unimportant if we think that actual experience of the situation at best supplies reflection with data that might otherwise have been unavailable to it, or a psychological impetus to change our moral principles. Natural though that conception of the cognitive significance of experience may be, it is profoundly mistaken. I shall argue that in Chapter 15, but at this stage I do not want the point of my remark, that even in the presence of such evil as is described by Kaplan some people assert that every human being is owed unconditional respect, to be interpreted in the light of such a conception of the cognitive importance of experience. I am not suggesting that Kaplan has presented us with a hard case that we should use to test certain ethical theories.

Some people who suffered evils similar to the rabbi in Kaplan's report have said that it would be no injustice against those who did such evil if they were to be shot in the street like dogs, for they have forfeited the respect owed by one human being to another. Not anyone would have the authority to assert the contrary against those who have suffered and speak in this way. That is essential to a proper conception of what it is to understand that no human being may be killed in the spirit of ridding the world of vermin. The conditions under which someone would have the right to assert, or even to think, the contrary against them are not easy to specify, but someone could not claim that right just on the ground that he had been sincerely convinced by a philosophical argument.

Someone may be sincerely convinced by philosophical argument that all human beings are unconditionally owed respect yet his sincere profession of it be, as we say, 'mere words', not because his profession of it is undermined by his deeds, but because it is not

3

informed by anything sufficiently weighty in his life to earn the respect accorded to those of whom we say, in such contexts, that they 'have something to say' or that they 'know what they are talking about'. There are empty assertions and denials that human beings are owed unconditional respect and they may be supported by sophisticated and ingenious arguments that give philosophers much to do, but they are not what matters. Those who command our respect, and provide us with a serious sense that there is something to think about when they either assert or deny such claims of absolute value, have arrived at neither their assertion nor their denial by argument. Philosophers often speak as though the subject-matter for philosophical reflection in ethics were statements or sentences or propositions. I believe they are mistaken. The subject-matter for ethical reflection is primarily action and speech which has a certain authority, and when it is speech, it is by those of whom we say that 'they have something to say' because they speak with an authority that derives from the way they have lived their lives.

The authoritative assertion that all human beings are owed unconditional respect is an expression of a sense of absolute value. It is important that it be affirmed against a serious sense of evil of the kind that is described by Kaplan, but that is not merely because we can then be assured that 'unconditional' unequivocally means unconditional, which (we may think) it must if the affirmation is to be an expression of absolute value. To think that would be to think that we could test a claim to absolute value in the same way as we test a generalisation. It appears to assume that it is an idea conceived in less demanding circumstances, or with less than full appreciation of its scope, and that now needs to be tested for its scope. That is a mistake. Respect is owed to those who do such terrible evil as Kaplan describes, and that it is owed even to them is internal to the kind of respect it is in all circumstances. But the claim that it is owed even to them is not the claim that an ethical idea has been taken to its furthest limit and found to be accommodating to cases at the limit. It is the acknowledgement of its profound unnaturalness, of, indeed, its mystery.[3] That acknowledgement is not to anyone who takes a philosophical interest in the matter and is certainly not to someone who presents examples such as Kaplan's in the spirit of canvassing 'intuitions' to test a thesis. It is to someone whose denial

4

has the same kind of authority as has the affirmation that gives the denial its character.

Some people who feel the strain of looking upon the Nazi described by Kaplan as a fellow human being, but who wish to say that he is, nonetheless, owed unconditional respect, are likely to fall back on more abstract concepts to express it. They might say, for example, that he remains a person with certain inalienable rights. The trouble is that the very abstractness that seems to save the claim from being flagrantly unnatural (in a sense similar to the unnaturalness of the injunction that we should love our neighbour), at the same time radically weakens it, and will prompt anyone who is sceptical of its less abstract expressions to question whether there are rights that can under no circumstances be forfeited. He will suspect that it amounts to no more than saying that even someone who does such evil remains a certain kind of limit to our will, while appearing to offer an explanation of why he limits our will in that way. The concept of rights is too thin (in a sense, too mean) to invite us into a deepened understanding of the evildoer and what he did in the light of which we may better understand what kind of limit he remains to our will. To be sure, the concept of a fellow human being does not provide an explanation either. To see someone as a fellow being is to see him as a certain kind of limit to our will rather than to explain (in the sense of providing a basis or a justification) why we should acknowledge such limits on our will. But 'fellow human being' is an expression that invites elaboration of the kind suggested when we say to someone who is doing or contemplating evil, 'Don't you see what you would be doing?', or of the kind with which an evildoer records the pained recognition of the significance of what he did when he says, remorsefully, 'My God, what have I done?' In later chapters I shall argue that the possibility of such elaboration is internal to the kind of seriousness that belongs to the nature of morality and to morality's deepening engagement with other parts of our lives.

A French woman was interviewed in a television programme called *The World at War*. Over a long period, she had witnessed a young Nazi officer sending trainloads of (mainly) children to the death camps. She said that every day since then she had asked herself how it were possible for him to do it. Hers is not a question that invites an answer. It expresses a sense of mystery at that kind of contact with evil, and that sense of mystery is connected with a sense of the reality of evil as something *sui generis*. But that depends on her sense of what he did being informed by concepts that allow for more substantial elaboration than that he violated the inalienable natural rights of the children he sent to be murdered. 'How could he violate their natural rights?' 'How could he fail to see that these children had natural rights?' Such questions cannot express the kind of incredulity *she* expressed and they invite no elaboration that *could* express it. That is one of the reasons why Simone Weil called the concept of rights a mediocre concept:

> If you say to someone who has ears to hear: 'What you are doing to me is not just', you may touch and awaken at its source the spirit of attention and love. But it is not the same with words like 'I have the right . . .' or 'you have no right to . . .' They evoke a latent war and awaken the spirit of contention. To place the notion of rights at the centre of social conflicts is to inhibit any possible impulse of charity on both sides.
>
> Relying almost exclusively on this notion it becomes impossible to keep one's eyes on the real problem. If someone tries to browbeat a farmer to sell his eggs at a moderate price, the farmer can say: 'I have the right to keep my eggs if I don't get a good enough price.' But if a young girl is being forced into a brothel she will not talk about her rights. In such a situation the word would sound ludicrously inadequate.[4]

We have accorded even the most terrible evildoers legal rights, but that should not be taken as a sign that we have found such evil and what is owed to those who do it sufficiently tractable even to make law from our understanding of it. On the contrary, it is a sign that law may express a conception of justice that is sublime. This was well brought out in the trial of Adolf Eichmann in Jerusalem. Hannah Arendt reports that the presiding judge, Justice Landau, said that the trial had only one purpose, which was to do justice.[5] He was moved to say that in protest against those who wished to make a show trial of it and who thought that the only justice that could be done at the trial was to Eichmann's victims. Landau's point was, I think, that if justice were to be done to Eichmann's victims then justice had to be done to Eichmann because it was owed to him. The court could not act against Eichmann in a way that would be expressive of what was owed his victims without such action also being expressive of what was owed to Eichmann as a human being. In those circumstances, that was a just trial. But that is just what so many were not prepared to grant and it was not because they were morally obtuse.

There was no doubt about Eichmann's identity and his guilt. Adherence to strict courtroom procedures was not required to avoid error on either score. For that reason it seemed to many that sticking strictly to courtroom procedures could be justified against the loss of the propaganda benefits of a show trial only on the grounds that failure to do so might turn out to be the thin edge of the wedge – that it might establish a dangerous precedent that would threaten the future integrity of judicial practices. Their thought seemed to be that, unless it was justified by such reasoning, sticking rigorously to courtroom procedures could only be a formality – pedantry indeed – that could not outweigh the benefits of teaching the world a lesson about the Holocaust. How could a mere formality express something so important as the unconditional respect owed to another human being? But of course it seemed a mere formality only to those who thought that courtroom practices are expressions of the respect owed to the accused only when they serve some other end that matters to the accused – the delivery of a truthful verdict, for example.

We may not kill human beings as though we were ridding the world of vermin, even if we kill them just to stop them from doing further evil. We cannot act against others as though they were filth. That is what Judge Landau expressed when he insisted that justice was owed to Eichmann for his sake. It entailed protecting the integrity of the court against the politicians for a variety of reasons, but partly for Eichmann's sake, so that justice could be done to him.

Why may we not act against another human being as though he were filth? Is it because no one is filth? Some people have done the foulest things. If we turn from their deeds to their character we often find it is as foul as their deeds. That should not be surprising. From where else could such deeds have come? The Nazi in the extract from Kaplan's diary seems to be an example. Countless others can be found in the concentration camp literature.

7

Are we sometimes entitled to say that because of the evil someone has done and the evil of his character, he is beyond the reach of a sober remorse? Should we say of Kaplan's Nazi that he is beyond the terrible discovery of himself and what he did? And if he did come to see what he was and what he did, would he have to judge himself to be filth? I would say that he need not, and more strongly, that if his remorse is genuine and uncorrupt and if he is true to what it teaches him, then he cannot. But although I have spoken of the discovery and of the recognition of what he was and what he did and although I will, in later chapters, defend that as a genuine form of understanding, of 'coming to see things as they are', I do not wish to say, flatly, that the reason he cannot, in the light of a genuine remorse, judge that he is filth is because he is not filth. That would suggest that it is *a fact* that he is not filth or that there would be some point in saying, in the emphatic way philosophers are prone to say it, that *it is the case* that he is not filth. I do not wish to say anything like that – not with that kind of (philosophical) emphasis. The claim that no human being is filth and the corollary claims about what may or may not be discovered in a sober remorse are themselves expressions of a sense of absolute value rather than claims that would underwrite such a conception if they were true.

We sometimes say that no human being is all bad. That seems to be false or, perhaps more accurately, there are times when the grammar of the application of concepts like 'part' and 'whole' in the contexts of attributions of good and evil does not allow us to assert or deny it. There are human beings who are so steeped in evil that it seems grotesque even to try to specify what is good in them – as, for example, when people say of people like the Nazi Kaplan describes that they were, nonetheless, good family men. The point here is not that we wish to deny any empirical reports concerning their behaviour to their wives and children. Nor is it that we wish to deny that, ordinarily, behaviour of that kind would justify the judgement that someone was a good father and husband. Nor is it that we wish to say that, in one of the ways with which we are familiar, all was not as it seems, for that presupposes that there are facts not yet on the table that would undermine judgements made in ignorance of them. We should not, therefore, deny that such people had some good in them that showed in their relation to their families, their friends and their neighbours. Rather, we should express our bewilderment about the sense of what we are being asked to understand.

The thought that no human being is all bad may, however, be understood in a way that does not entail grotesque claims about the good parts of radically evil lives. It may simply be the thought that there is no deed or life so evil that it is beyond the reach of a sober remorse and that there is no remorse that requires a person, under pain of self-deception, to acknowledge that it would be best to rid the world of the filth he believes he has discovered himself to be. It is important to remember, however, that there are lives such that if we try to find the good in them from which we could imagine a sober and lucid remorse could grow, we will not find it. And even if we could find it, it would not be necessary to justify the affirmation that no human being may be acted against as though we were ridding the world of vermin. If someone were to say that is mysterious, then rather than deny it, I would emphasise it and warn against the diminution of that sense of mystery by our familiarity with its expression in something that seems as prosaic as law.

There are many people who would not say that we owe every human being unconditional respect, but not because they are under pressure to deny it because of examples such as we have been considering. Within philosophy there are consequentialists who make a virtue out of not saying it. I suspect there are few real consequentialists, that is, people who actually see the world as consequentialist theory would require them to describe it. Life remains richer than consequentialists can officially allow, and if that is not manifest to them in the study or classroom, then the truthful descriptions of people – their characters and actions – in ordinary life will make (perhaps unwitting) non-consequentialists of all but the crudest of them. They are doing their best, however, to ensure that life becomes thin enough for even them to describe adequately.

They may succeed, and there are areas where they are already succeeding for reasons that have to do with their assimilation of the concept of rationality – and more generally, of critical thinking – to the unnaturally high discursive requirements on discussion of public policy in a divided community. As a result, they have convinced many people that there are powerful arguments for killing people whom it would have been thought unthinkable to kill as recently as the 1970s. Life and a thin theory of it might converge at a point closer to the theory than many who call for a sensitive moral psychology, and many who think that consequentialism will always be false to life, would allow.

Philosophers have taken the lead in wondering, and in encouraging their students to wonder, who in our community might be killed or 'helped to die' according to whether or not they are fully paid up persons or according to whether their 'quality of life' is up to scratch. They have often been praised for having the courage to follow their arguments wherever those arguments might take them, and they have followed them to conclusions beyond those that in the seventies were considered to be *reductions to absurdity* of any argument that led to them. Courage is not the quality that first comes to mind to describe the disposition to embrace such conclusions, and despite all the talk of courageous and radical thinking, little consideration has been given to what it is to think courageously, what it is to think the morally unthinkable or, in general, what it is to embrace conclusions that had been deemed, in different ways, to be 'beyond consideration'. In later chapters we shall see how little philosophy, which prides itself on thinking about thinking, has in fact attended to the various critical categories with which we mark our sense of what it is to think well or badly. For the moment we need only notice that the philosophers who urged us to relax the limits on killing other human beings have been part of a shift in the culture at large that predisposed them, and others, to find at least arguable, what previously was judged to be unthinkable. People seem much more ready to judge that certain lives are not fit for a human being than they were, and they are much more ready to appeal to compassion and a certain conception of human dignity to urge the killing of those who suffer terrible afflictions.

2

The scope of academic moral philosophy

Kaplan's diary entry might prompt someone to speak of the reality of evil, though that same person might not wish to contribute to a discussion of what, in the subject, is called 'moral realism'. Philosophical realists argue that moral judgements in general are true or false 'in virtue of the independently existing real world'.[1] They have not been particularly concerned with the reality of evil. I shall argue later that what prompts one to speak of evil in response to the passage I quoted from Kaplan might be inseparable from the sense in which one would speak of its reality. The concept or, perhaps better, ways of speaking of reality are not univocal even within ethics. There are those for whom the concept of evil is eliminable in favour of some more general expression of value, and for whom its use in common speech marks no more than a severe degree of moral condemnation. There are others for whom it is a fundamental and ineliminable category which partners a certain sense of goodness. Hannah Arendt said that the men of the eighteenth century did not understand that there is goodness beyond virtue and evil beyond vice. Those who are concerned with the philosophical issue of moral realism would probably think that she was recommending an addition to what they call our 'ontology'. Even to speak this way, however, is to import a number of philosophical presuppositions that I would rather keep at a distance. I introduced the passage from Kaplan's diaries, wishing to keep my distance from any assumption that 'moral realism' adequately captures what is most serious in talk of the reality of good and evil.

11

I did not offer the passage from Kaplan as an example with which to confront moral scepticism, although I acknowledge, of course, that someone who speaks of the reality of evil will not be morally sceptical and that she will be puzzled and troubled by the fact that our culture is marked by various kinds of moral scepticisms despite the recurrent and highly visible presence of terrible evil on the political and social scene.[2] But precisely for that reason she will not think that quoting such an example would achieve much (certainly not in the subject), and if she knows something about philosophy as a subject, then she will realise that such an example cannot be offered as part of an argument to the conclusion that evil is a reality. She will realise that it can be offered only as an example that naturally prompts a way of speaking whose sense is to be determined. If she is wise she will not wish its sense to be settled too quickly by someone who takes it to be relatively clear, or by someone who thinks she knows relatively early in such discussions what she means when she speaks of the 'ontological' questions in moral philosophy.

Renford Bambrough said that 'We know that this child who is about to undergo what would otherwise be painful surgery should be given an anaesthetic before the operation. Therefore we know at least one moral proposition to be true.'[3] He offered this as an argument *ad hominem* against those who would accept Moore's analogous 'proof' that there is an external world. He thought that by 'parity of reasoning, by an exactly analogous argument, [they could be shown] that we have moral knowledge, that there are some propositions of morals which are *certainly* true and which we *know* to be true'. Bambrough addressed a problem that has been shaped and refined in the subject's history, and someone who is familiar with it develops a philosophical ear for the resonance of the words in italics – so much is conveyed to the philosophically trained ear by that emphatic 'know'. But just as I did not offer Kaplan's extract as a contribution to a discussion of moral 'ontology', so I do not offer it as a contribution to a discussion of moral epistemology.

Stanley Cavell protested against a claim such as Bambrough's that 'mere morality is not designed to evaluate the behaviour of monsters', and he said in this connection that 'morality must allow for its repudiation'.[4] There are a number of issues here of which two are of immediate relevance. First, I have spoken, not of morality, but of evil and a certain sense of its reality. The distinction may be important to someone who thinks, as does Bernard Williams, that morality is a species of the ethical. It may be such a thought that prompts Cavell to speak of the 'limits of morality'. He may mean that we should appreciate the limits of the concept of morality in the exploration of good and evil without suggesting any scepticism concerning the reality of good and evil. I do not know whether he does (I suspect that he does not), but the thought that I have sketched on his behalf is one to which I am sympathetic. Secondly, it may be suggested that we should start in moral philosophy with examples less remote from the experience of ordinary people in ordinary times. But for some people the evil in the quoted passage is not remote, not because they have suffered it or been a direct witness to it, but because its presence determines a large part of their sense of the ethical, of themselves and of their times. Also, as we shall see later, starting from examples which are more immediate and common in our lives can itself distort our sense of the ethical, not because they are common and immediate, but because familiarity may predispose us to a conventional sense of them. They are more likely to present themselves under descriptions which reflect 'the opinion of the many'. Less common examples may free us from this in much the same way as consideration of the past or past thinkers may free us from domination by the present. I have put the point in a way that deliberately echoes Plato: starting with what is immediate and common may be starting in the cave. But there are many ways of starting in the cave and we will not avoid them by fixing on a certain kind of example. In the cave, there is a version of them all.

So many disclaimers and qualifications! But that is partly my point. I wish to offer a starting-point for reflection – philosophical reflection – on absolute value. Not *the* starting-point, not even a starting-point unproblematically within the subject, but a starting-point partly from outside the subject. I do not wish to prejudge the relation between reflection within the subject and reflection outside of it, although I plead for greater philosophical patience for reflection outside and I shall try to undermine the confidence on the part of philosophers that they know what to make of it, that it is for philosophy to delineate all the serious options and that what is said outside of philosophy will, at best, speak for one or another of them.

Philosophers usually begin with a problem as defined within the subject and then invoke what they call our 'pre-reflective' or 'pre-theoretical intuitions' or our 'ordinary moral consciousness' in support of that definition of it and of a favoured solution to it. In many of its forms, this represents a condescending conception of thought before philosophy – basically that it is inarticulate and unreflective. Or so one would surmise from the content of what are said to be our pre-theoretical intuitions. If we effectively distinguish only between, say, philosophical theory and pre-theoretical intuitions, and if our descriptions of those intuitions are tailor-made to suit the terms of a philosophical controversy as that has been conditioned by the subject, then there is virtually no constraint on philosophical insularity. Over two thousand years of reflection that is neither theory nor the expression of intuitions is effectively ignored. Philosophers are then inclined to believe that their theorising is constrained by something external to the subject and they ignore a realm of serious thought and reflection outside of the subject to which philosophical thinking should be answerable. Thus, when I say that I offer the extract from Kaplan's diary as a starting-point outside of the subject, I mean to offer it not under the pretence of intellectual or even philosophical naivety, but rather to guard against its appropriation to a familiar set of concerns which mark what is more or less the current state of play in the subject.

It is common even for philosophers to complain of the thinness of much of moral philosophy (not just modern moral philosophy whose thinness is almost universally deplored). The emergence of 'practical ethics' has encouraged many philosophers, and some people who are not philosophers, to believe that things are getting better. Philosophers now enjoy the benefits of a semi-bureaucratic enhancement of their status to the point where they might set up in private practice as 'ethicists' or hope for an invitation from the prime minister to advise on the ethical aspects of nuclear deterrence. That is, partly, because ours is a culture that no longer distinguishes clearly between wisdom and expertise and we are, therefore, vulnerable to believing that someone with a distinguished chair in 'practical ethics' should have something serious to say on those ethical problems that are of public and political concern. It is also, partly, because people believe that philosophy is the subject pre-eminently suited to the discussion of such matters; that, indeed, it is obliged to do so and that it failed to honour that obligation in its linguistic and analytical phase. We will see, when I discuss these matters in Chapter 17, that such beliefs are sustained by confusion concerning the difference between philosophy as practised by Socrates, for whom it was not and could not have been a subject in the sense in which we speak of it when we speak of students being initiated into a subject, and philosophy as it is for us, in which distinction in moral philosophy is (quite rightly) compatible with foolishness and shallowness. That is why philosophers do not, as a profession, enjoy high esteem amongst that dying breed of non-professional thinkers, for whom there is no generally adequate name, but who are often called 'intellectuals'.

As I have suggested, the reasons for this are complex, and some have to do with the nature of philosophy as an academic practice. However, there is a reason which goes deeper and which will preoccupy us throughout this book. It has to do with the difficulty of understanding quite what we are complaining of when we complain of the thinness of moral philosophy. We may feel that there is a sense in which philosophy must be thin if it is to characterise reality at the deepest level below the appearances. Philosophy is at its highest when it is metaphysics, and metaphysics is not the stuff of novels. So, at any rate, someone might say.

Oscar Wilde said that 'It is only superficial people who do not judge by appearances.' Stuart Hampshire quotes this with approval in his book *Morality and Conflict* and comments that Wilde 'meant by "appearances" surfaces, the direct objects of perception, including styles of expression'.[5] Hampshire's point is that surfaces are not always 'mere' surfaces and that philosophy, for what are sometimes deep reasons, tends to forget this and to judge too quickly that certain things are 'mere' surfaces. The 'surfaces' which Hampshire is concerned to defend against trivialisation are the historically shaped customs, manners, rituals and languages of particular peoples. The difficulty, of course, is to know when surface is 'mere surface'. In philosophy the difficulty is formidable because it is difficult to understand how even to apply such concepts as depth and surface in certain areas. In moral philosophy there has not even been a serious attempt to understand this.

15

If one looks from the outside it makes one dizzy to think what mainstream philosophies have deemed to be mere surface – virtually everything that makes us human! Our bodies are deemed inessential in most philosophies of mind, including most varieties of materialism which are concerned not with the living human form but with matter. In most philosophies of mind and language, the fact that we do not, for example, tinker with one another with screwdrivers when our conversation is not up to the mark is deemed inessential to our understanding of what it is to speak. The fact that it takes time to grow wise is judged accidental to moral understanding, for the dominant conception of the 'cognitive' is of something God might put in our heads 'in a flash', rather as one puts a programme in a machine. From the inside, it all seems unremarkable, but that is partly because we can get used to anything and partly because we do not seriously have to get used to it, for it is 'just philosophy' or, to put it less kindly, 'just talk'. From the outside, the sense in which philosophy deems such things to be mere surface seems to constitute an extremely rarefied and finally irrelevant sense of what is necessary and what is accidental. From the inside it may be seen to be one of the glories of philosophy.

Up to a point, the inside perspective is the right one. It is the one informed by the history of philosophical thought and the subject would be unrecognisable without it. But although this aspect of philosophy is an important part of the history of our culture, it also places philosophy in an uneasy relation to other aspects of the culture, and in a way that is often not a matter for philosophical self-congratulation. F. R. Leavis was, I think, right to be suspicious of philosophy insofar as he saw in it a pressure towards an arrogant philistinism which he connected with its disdain for the particular and the local.[6] He believed that, despite its recent emphasis on language, philosophy had no deep understanding of it because it was not alive to the importance of a language, such as English, being a natural language. Philosophers preferred to call it 'ordinary' language, and the philosophy that was associated with respect for it was (mostly by its opponents) called 'ordinary language' or 'common-sense' philosophy. Both of those names, but especially the latter, suggest superficiality and an incapacity or unpreparedness to go beneath the surface. They were names that encouraged the central

16

tradition in philosophy to rest in its uncritical assumptions about what counts as depth and what as surface.

How much of that is accidental to the subject? That question is complicated by the need to distinguish between philosophy as the practice of a subject or discipline and philosophy as Socrates practised it.

A subject is something of which there may be acknowledged mastery, and the masters of a subject determine what is the state of play in it at a particular time – what has been established, what is controversial, what is at the centre, what is peripheral and so on. This gives substance to the idea of a proper, or even a best, starting-point, or the idea of a best method to settle the problems of a subject. It presupposes (at least in relation to any advanced inquiry) a community which has the authority and the acknowledged competence to determine the agenda, to determine what needs to be taken seriously by anyone who knows their way around the subject, and what could be taken seriously only by someone who is incompetent or, even, a crank. Similar constraints operate upon any substantial conception of theory which would compare itself favourably with scientific theory: the phenomena or data need to be agreed by those whose agreement commands respect because of their acknowledged (and usually certified) mastery of their subject. Only then can we make sense of, for example, the idea of the best of competing theories that explain all the important phenomena.

There is little agreement amongst contemporary moral philosophers about what are the most serious problems in the subject, and so there is little agreement about the most promising way forward. The subject is seriously divided. Is that accidental to the character of the subject or does it reveal something important about its nature?

In her paper 'Modern Moral Philosophy', Elizabeth Anscombe said that anyone who thinks 'in advance' that it may be permissible in certain circumstances to punish judicially a person known to be innocent, shows a corrupt mind.[7] That amounts to saying that anyone who takes consequentialism seriously shows a corrupt mind, and that amounts to a condemnation of most of modern moral philosophy. The subject would hardly be recognisable without its preoccupation with the seemingly endless varieties of consequentialism, and certainly no philosophy student could be considered to

have mastered the subject unless she were prepared to discuss consequentialism as a theory to be taken seriously. How, then, should we
place Anscombe's remark?

Most philosophers would disagree with her – probably 99 per
cent of them. Is she then a kind of philosophical flat-earther? The
question is rhetorical because we have no conception of the
authority with which any of her colleagues could judge her to be so
on that kind of issue. Most philosophers would believe that whether
or not an innocent person may in certain circumstances be judicially
punished is a difficult question, to be settled after we have reason
to be confident of a theory which had been tested on simpler and
less controversial examples. But Anscombe believes that such a question could be controversial only in a corrupt culture and that
consequentialism is unworthy of the place it has occupied in the
subject. Whether or not she is right is, I think, beyond the competence of the masters of the subject to determine. If that is true, then
moral philosophy is problematically a subject, for it is fundamental
to a subject that its masters determine what worthily belongs to it
and what does not.

To be sure, a subject may be in decline, and one of the ways that
might show itself would be if certain issues or theories assumed a
disproportionately large place in it or, in some cases, if they assumed
a place in it at all. But the concept of a subject in decline requires
that it be judged to be so by masters of it properly exercising those
qualities of mind that are internal to the concept of what it is to
master a subject. Possession of those qualities of mind and their
competent exercise distinguish masters from novices or laymen and
masters of a subject from those whose intellectual interests are not
part of a subject. But the qualities of mind for which a student
of philosophy is examined, or for which a teacher is offered a post,
or for which someone might be awarded academic honours, are
not of a kind to enable one who is to the highest degree in possession of them to pronounce, with any authority, whether someone
shows a corrupt mind if she considers, in advance, whether it is
permissible to punish judicially an innocent person. The point will
resurface in different ways at later stages of the book, but for the
moment I wish to point out only this: the problem of finding a style
or a voice in moral philosophy is not simply a consequence of the

problematical relation between moral philosophy and subjects other than philosophy, or even of the problematical relation between moral philosophy and non-philosophical, non-academic thinking outside of philosophy. The difficulty also arises from the fact that moral philosophy has, within itself and to a greater degree than other parts of philosophy, the tension between philosophy as a subject and philosophy as Socrates did it.

Bernard Williams says that the question 'How should one live?' should be the starting-point for moral philosophy. He calls it 'Socrates' question', and although he notes that philosophy was not a subject for Socrates, that Socrates 'just talked with his friends in a plain way', he makes nothing substantial of the contrast between philosophy as Socrates did it and philosophy as we do it.[8] And when he says that Socrates' question should be the starting-point of moral philosophy, he means moral philosophy as a subject.

Williams says that it is important to realise that the ' "should" in the question just means "should" '. He means that although the reasons advanced in favour of an answer may be of a distinctive kind – moral, prudential, aesthetic or ethical – the 'should' favours no distinctive set of reasons. 'No prior advantage is built into the question for one kind of reason over another.'[9] Williams calls the question 'How should one live?' 'a particularly ambitious example of a personal practical question . . . it stands at a distance from any actual occasion of considering what to do. It is a general question – how to live – and it is a timeless question since it invites me to think about my life from no particular point in it.'[10]

The question is not, for most people most of the time, a genuine one. It arises for some people on some occasions. Williams is right to say that it is a question 'which stands at a distance from any particular occasion of considering what to do', if he means that it stands apart from considering some particular course of action. It occurs most naturally when someone is reviewing his life. Has what I devoted my life to been worth it? Does money and success matter so much? Is philosophy worthy of a lifetime's devotion? Such are the natural occasions for that question. It is unclear what someone could be doing asking it, or inviting students and colleagues to ask it, apart from such occasions. It is doubtful whether it was a real question for Socrates as often as he asked it, for it is doubtful whether he ever seriously considered as genuine options the competing answers offered to it by Thrasymachus or Polus or Callicles. But even if he did not regard it as a genuine question for himself, Socrates certainly wished that it should become such a question for his interlocutors. Sometimes it did.

As an example of Socrates' question, Williams refers to a discussion between Socrates and Thrasymachus in *Republic*. There is a better example in *Gorgias* where, in the speech he gives to Callicles, Plato has written one of the most powerful objections to the Socratic life. Socrates argued to Polus that it is better to suffer evil than to do it. Polus resentfully conceded the argument from premises he professed to believe. Callicles had been irritated by Polus' concession and by Socrates' procedure and he was genuinely astonished by what Socrates said. He interjects with the question, 'Tell me Socrates, are you serious or are you joking? For if you are serious and what you say is true, then human life must be turned upside down.'[11] He is primarily astonished because Socrates professes that it is better to suffer evil than to do it and that an evildoer who understood what he had done would seek just punishment, but he is also astonished that Socrates cannot see that his philosophical life is unworthy of any human being who is capable of noble aspirations. This is what he says:

> It is a good thing to engage in philosophy just so far as it is an aid to education, and no disgrace for a youth to study it, but when a man who is now growing older studies it he becomes ridiculous Socrates . . . when I see a youth engaged in it, I admire it and it seems to me to be natural, and I consider such a man ingenious, and the man who does not pursue it I regard as illiberal and one who will never aspire to any fine or noble deed. But when I see an older man studying philosophy and not deserting it, that man, Socrates, is actually asking for a whipping . . . Such a man, even if exceptionally gifted, is doomed to prove less than a man, shunning the city centre and market place, in which the poet said men win distinction. He will spend the rest of his life sunk in a corner and whispering with three or four boys and incapable of any utterance or deed that is free and lofty and brilliant.[12]

Students invariably fail to take Callicles seriously. They smile condescendingly over his speech, confident that they are superior to him
in their understanding of the worth of the Socratic life. They think
that he is a philistine. If, however, we leave aside for a moment his
claim that the study of philosophy is demeaning to an older person,
then what Callicles says in appreciation of the worth of philosophical study is a good statement of the ideals of what we call 'liberal
education'. He does not offer what is usually called an 'extrinsic'
justification for the importance of philosophical study by the young.
He praises it for cultivating certain qualities of mind – an imaginative appreciation of and concern for what is 'fine and noble' – which
is presumably conditional upon an absorption in the subject for its
own sake. He is quite serious in his praise. If we find it hard to
believe that he is serious, it is because we find it hard to reconcile
such praise with his contempt for those who believe that such study
can worthily inspire a lifelong devotion. But therein lies the seriousness of his challenge. Socrates took it seriously. He replies to
Callicles that 'of all inquiries . . . the noblest is that which concerns
the matter with which you have reproached me, namely, what a man
should be and what he should practice and to what extent, both
when old and when young'.[13]

It is almost impossible for us to see Socrates as did Callicles, 'sunk
in a dark corner whispering with three or four boys', because he
shines for us in the light of his historical prestige and because philosophy and academic study more generally enjoy the prestige which
has come with their institutionalisation. If Socrates had had the
opportunity of becoming a philosophical knight and a professor in
a great university, speaking to philosophical conferences around the
world and being an ethical advisor to governments and other great
public institutions, then Callicles might have judged him differently.
But if he did, it would not be because as a matter of fact there
were honours and prestige to be found in academic life. It would
be because he would have come to believe what he did not believe
when he condemned Socrates, namely, that such a life was deserving
of honour.

We think that if ever there was a philosopher deserving of such
honours as the world now bestows on academic and artistic achievement, then it was Socrates. I do not think that Socrates would agree.

The disagreement between him and Callicles is not over whether the philosophical life is deserving of worldly honours, for both agree that it is not. Their disagreement is over the question whether a life intrinsically non-deserving of worldly honours (dramatised by Callicles as a life lived in 'dark corners', not illuminated by worldly fame) could be a life chosen by anyone of noble spirit. It is the essential unworldliness of the Socratic life that is offensive to Callicles' sense of dignity and nobility, as no doubt it was to the many educated Athenians who responded gleefully to Aristophanes' merciless caricature of it in *The Clouds*. Only if human life was 'turned upside down' could an unworldly life be 'deserving of worldly honours'. Socrates agreed, as often did the more complex and ambivalent Plato, which is why their estrangement from the political and public realm ran so deep.

In such a discussion, 'should', as Williams says, simply means 'should'. But the point needs qualification and the most important qualification for Socrates was this: for someone who understands the nature of evil, certain deeds and thoughts are not an option. That is, to be sure, not a strict inference from the belief that someone who knows what evil is cannot do it, but it is reasonable to suppose that Socrates believed it. Socrates apart, however, it can be defended in its own right. There are some things it is evil even to believe, and that good and evil may be an illusion is one of them. The argument for this is developed in Chapter 17, but the point to note here is that it cannot be a requirement on a philosopher to ask a question seriously that is likely to tempt him into what he may judge to be corrupt or evil thoughts. But if we take seriously the question that Williams recommends we ask (routinely as practitioners or teachers of the academic discipline of moral philosophy) of what should be our starting-point in moral philosophy, then that is what might happen. And if we do not ask it seriously, then what does the suggestion that it should be the question at the beginning of moral philosophy amount to?

It is, of course, possible to see a subject in the light of a question which has been, in some sense, fundamental to it while not being a real question for anyone. One could, for example, be inclined to trace its history in the light of such a question. Sceptical questions about the external world or other minds are an example. But that is not what Williams has in mind. He means that the subject of moral philosophy is in grave disorder and that we need an idea of how to sort it out – where to begin to sort it out. He recommends the question 'How should one live?' as the best point from which to begin to put order into the subject. That requires the question to be a real one for the philosopher who asks it. It does not allow one to drive a wedge between oneself as an individual human being and oneself as a philosopher asking a merely 'methodological' question. Socrates insisted that those whom he engaged in discussion speak for themselves, that they say what they seriously believed. He did not want them to report what others had said or what might be argued by someone who thought this or someone who thought that. That insistence is inseparable from the character of his question, 'How should one live?'

That does not fully answer the question whether the undesirable thinness of moral philosophy is internal to its practice as a subject. But it does suggest that it is internal to philosophical reflection on morality that it cannot insulate itself from the kind of reflection which is not recognisably professional and which does not allow for a sharp contrast between experts and laymen, masters and novices. There is, therefore, little reason to believe that the academic practice of moral philosophy has the authority to determine the best style and method of thinking on moral matters, or even what the most serious problems are and how they should be characterised.

3

*Mortal men and
rational beings*

The Kantian tradition in ethics appears to promise the best (philosophical) understanding of the idea that respect is owed unconditionally to every human being. It might appear, indeed, that there is nowhere else in philosophy to seek such understanding. It turns out not to be so, and I will turn to the Socratic–Platonic tradition, but I acknowledge that many would find that strange. Gregory Vlastos believes that neither Socrates nor Plato understands the love of persons for their own sake 'in the uniqueness and integrity of his or her individuality'.[1] Although Vlastos speaks of love rather than of duty, the conception of individuality expressed by Vlastos is one we most naturally associate with Kant, because of the way Kant connects the idea that human beings are a direct, unconditional and unique kind of limit to each other's wills, with the idea that persons are ends in themselves. Even so, the Kantian tradition is quite inadequate on this very point, and we can see why if we consider Alan Donagan's attempt to provide a Kantian reconstruction of what he calls 'traditional morality'. His is amongst the most interesting of contemporary efforts and the most revealing on the point we are interested in.

Donagan is critical of the place given to self-esteem in some recent accounts of ethics. His reason is worth quoting at length.

A clue may be found in one of the finest scenes in which Falstaff appears and in which his creator compels us to see the limits of any conception of value as success. Falstaff has been conscripting troops for the Welsh wars and lining his pockets with bribes for releasing the fit. 'A mad fellow met me on the way,' he remarks, 'and told me, I had unloaded all the Gibbets and prest the dead bodyes.' But when the Prince complains, 'I never did see such pittifull Rascals,' he retorts, 'Tut, tut, good enough to tosse foode for Powder, foode for Powder: they'le fill a Pit, as well as better: tush man, mortall men, mortall men.' That the Prince never makes such a remark shows how different his mode of consciousness is from Falstaff's. He is a man of self-esteem: securely convinced that his plan of life is worth carrying out and confident that he can carry it out; and he accurately registers that Falstaff's scarecrows have no plans and no confidence. Falstaff, while he esteems them no more than the Prince, is yet aware of them as 'mortall men', for whose sake, although he does not say it, the state itself exists. True, he does not let his awareness trouble him much. Yet for all his misdeeds, Falstaff respects other human beings as he respects himself, irrespective of esteem. Respect, in this sense, has no degrees: you either respect someone or you do not; and you respect him for what he is, not for what he does . . .

The theory of traditional morality is inevitably moralistic: and that distracts attention from the fact that its foundation is not moralistic at all. Awareness of that foundation may be found in rascals like Falstaff, but never in precisians who observe the first-order precepts that follow from it, but merely from some secondary reason.[2]

This passage is richly instructive, partly because of its success, but mostly because of its failure. I shall first comment on what is right in what Donagan says and why it is important. He is right to say that Shakespeare 'compels us to see the limits of any conception of value as success'. He is also right to say that 'respect', as he speaks of it, 'has no degrees' and that one respects a person 'for what he is, not for what he does'. Those remarks may seem uncontroversial and not worth making, but when Donagan says that respect is owed for what a person is rather than for what he does, he does not mean for what a person 'morally' is and he makes that clear in his remark about the non-moralistic foundation of 'traditional morality' and also, later, when he speaks of the 'Falstaffian respect for mortal men on which Hebrew–Christian morality rests'.

25

Aristotle would not have found that intelligible. It is a serious question whether his incapacity to do so can easily be extracted from his moral philosophy and it is not clear whether it can be extracted from the modern Aristotelian emphasis on the connection between virtue and human flourishing. Many modern philosophers speak of human flourishing in ways which I suspect Donagan would believe to be at least suggestive of a 'conception of value as success'. (He makes the comments I have quoted in reaction to the Aristotelian dimension of Rawls' moral philosophy.) The question (as I see it – I do not now speak for Donagan) is whether a certain ethical emphasis on flourishing enables us to describe those who are steeped in severe and ineradicable affliction – those who have no prospect of flourishing – as the intelligible objects of the kind of respect shown by Falstaff to 'such pittifull Rascals', or whether it encourages one to see them in a way that makes it inescapable to think, as did Aristotle, that it would be better if they had never been born.[3] Falstaff's pity for 'such pittifull Rascals', understood as pity for his fellow mortals, is an instance of what Donagan calls Respect because it is, at its core, uncondescending. It expresses a sense of a certain kind of inalienable moral equality. The question then is whether an ethics centred on the virtues as a means to flourishing, and which places the kind of weight that Rawls does on self-esteem as a primary human good, has the conceptual resources to reveal a person who has no chance of flourishing and who has no reasonable ground for self-esteem as the intelligible object of such uncondescending pity. In later chapters I will try to show that this is a question of the first importance for ethics.

Now to what I take to be Donagan's failure. He speaks of 'the Falstaffian respect for mortal men on which Hebrew–Christian morality rests'. Earlier he had written:

> In what follows . . . I take the fundamental principle of that part of traditional morality which is independent of any theological presupposition to have been expressed in the scriptural commandment, 'Thou shalt love thy neighbour as thyself', understanding one's neighbour to be any human being, and love to be, not a matter of feeling, but of acting in ways in which human beings as such can choose to act. The philosophical

26

sense of this commandment was correctly expressed by Kant in his formula that one act so that one treats humanity always as an end and never as a means. Since treating a human being, in virtue of its rationality, as an end in itself, is the same as respecting it as a rational creature, Kant's formula of the fundamental principle may be restated in a form more like that of the scriptural commandment that is its original: Act always so that you respect every human being, yourself or another, as being a rational creature.[4]

I have quoted at length so that it is clear what Donagan understands that 'Falstaffian respect for mortal men', on which 'Hebrew–Christian morality rests', amounts to. It is the love of one's neighbour as oneself as expressed in the scriptural commandment, which, Donagan believes, is better expressed in the injunction to respect another human being 'as a rational creature'. Anyone might be forgiven for thinking that hardly seems to be what Falstaff is saying. I will offer a more natural reading of what he says.

'Tush man, mortall men, mortall men.' Falstaff reminds the Prince of his fellowship and equality with 'such pittifull Rascals'. They are his fellow mortals. To speak this way of 'mortals' is to speak of death in an accent of pity, and this accent is both expressive and constitutive of a sense of human fellowship. Donagan says, indeed, that 'Falstaff, while he esteems them no more than the Prince, is yet aware of them as "mortall men"', but he believes that way of describing Falstaff's response to be inferior to a more revealing description of it as being to other rational beings who also die.

Falstaff's awareness of them as mortal men is inextricably connected with his pity. Paraphrasing Wittgenstein, one might say that his pity is a form of his awareness of them as mortal men. Earlier I said that to speak of human beings as mortal is to speak of the fact that we must all die in an accent of pity. That 'we' is not merely enumerative of beings who belong to the same class because of some common characteristic. It is the 'we' that expresses fellowship and is conceptually interdependent with pity in the same sense in which Wittgenstein claimed that our concept of pain and certain natural reactions of pity are interdependent. (See Chapter 10.) Falstaff's remark to the Prince is a reminder of that fellowship ('they'le fill a Pit, as well as better') and it is a reminder that a fellow human being is a certain kind of limit to our will – the kind of limit conveyed by 'respect for him for what he is rather than for what he does'.

Donagan is partly right. It is true that the nature of Falstaff's pity for his fellow men is determined by the fact that they are rational creatures. His pity is not merely for creatures who die, but for human beings who can reflect on their lives and on their mortality and who take different attitudes to what they do and suffer because of such reflection. Were this not so then it would not be the kind of pity which is itself a form of respect. A certain kind of reflectiveness on the part of those whom Falstaff pities is essential to the character of his pity as pity for his fellow human beings. It is internal to the kind of respect owed to them that they are rational beings, but it does not follow, and is not true, that such respect is for their rational nature and is extractable from the pity as a disposition of all rational beings to one another, unconditioned by the concrete form which life takes for them.

'Tush man, rational beings, rational beings.' According to Donagan that is what is morally salient in Falstaff's reminder to the Prince. Why does it sound like a parody? Because it abstracts their rationality as the morally salient focus of his respect. We cannot bring their rationality to the fore in anything like the way required by Donagan and still retain the power of this passage. It has no place in it, not even in parenthesis or *sotto voce*. Donagan ought to find that puzzling. He does not, but it is revealing that when he paraphrases what Falstaff says he seems unable quite to bring himself to speak of Falstaff's respect for rational beings or creatures. He sticks to Falstaff's respect for 'mortall men'. And that obviously raises the question, which concepts do the real work? Donagan says that it is the concept of respect for rational creatures, even though that phrase cannot make its appearance in the Shakespearean passage. Why then can it make its explicit appearance only in philosophy? Why did Jesus not say, 'Act always so that you respect every human being, yourself or another, as being a rational creature'? Is it because this is so deep that only philosophy can reach it?

An answer that naturally comes to mind is that Jesus was not doing philosophy. But my question is not, why did Jesus not write

28

The Groundwork of The Metaphysics of Morals? Respect for
rational nature, its ultimate respectworthiness, is neither for Kant
nor for Donagan something that needs to be brought out by philosophy. The metaphysics and the casuistry rests upon an assumed sense
of the ultimate respectworthiness of rational nature. Thus, although
Donagan says that 'the philosophical sense of this commandment
was correctly expressed by Kant in his formula that one act so that
one treats humanity always as an end and never as a means', he
does not mean that the ultimate respectworthiness of rational nature
requires philosophical elucidation. The indirect proof of this is
that he does not even attempt to do it. There are, to be sure, philosophical pressures to make rational nature the ultimate object of
respect, but that is another matter. It is, to say the least, worthy
of more attention than philosophers give it, that there are philosophical pressures to make something the ultimate object of respect,
even though philosophy cannot (or has not) revealed its ultimate
respectworthiness, and even though its direct claim to be that has
appeared only in philosophy, and, if the Shakespearean passage is
typical, even though it cannot appear without an air of parody
outside of philosophy.

To be fair, it is not quite true that Donagan makes no attempt
to display the respectworthiness of rational nature. He quotes
Augustine saying 'that there is nothing higher in nature' and that
'Reason submits to nothing else as Judge.'[5] But the sense of 'higher'
in which there is nothing higher in nature than Reason is, I think,
the trivial sense that only Reason can judge the outcome of reflection. It amounts to the truism that only thinking can judge the results
of thinking, for there is no such thing as Reason; there is only
thinking well and thinking badly. The various critical categories with
which we mark our sense of what it is to think well or badly are of
a variety that suggests a thinking subject considerably more substantial than is implied by Donagan's definition of Reason as 'a capacity
fixed for all possible worlds to perform acts whose contents belong
to the domain of logic'.[6] Those critical categories leave it open
whether even the relatively narrow sense of critical reflection which
Donagan calls the exercise of Reason will judge something – love,
for example – to be finer than itself. It would, to be sure, need to
be a lucid love, but that is only to acknowledge that Reason (in the

sense of a capacity and a concern for lucidity) will be internal to anything that is ultimately respectworthy.

Augustine is more complicated than Donagan would have one believe. In his *Confessions* he writes:

> And I confess to Thee, O Lord, that I yet know not what time is, and again I confess unto Thee, O Lord, that I know that I speak this in time, and that having long spoken of time, that very 'long' is not long, but by the pause of time. How then know I this, seeing I know not what time is? or is it, perchance, that I know not how to express what I know? Woe is me, that I do not even know what I know not. Behold, O my God, before Thee I lie not; but as I speak, so is my heart. Thou shalt light my candle; Thou, O Lord my God, wilt enlighten my darkness.[7]

We could say truthfully enough that the passage expresses a mind labouring in obedience to the claims of Reason upon it and we could quote it with edifying effect against certain forms of irrationalism. But we could not reveal the power and the beauty of the passage – and hence we could not explain that same edifying effect – without speaking of the love that is manifest so purely in it. We might naturally say that the passage is a fine expression of the discursive capacities of mind which Donagan calls Reason in service to a love of truth. It would be natural and it would not quite be wrong, but it would be misleading in the way suggested by Simone Weil when she said that it is misleading to speak of a love of truth. We should speak instead, she said, of the spirit of truth in love.[8] The passage I have quoted from the *Confessions* is an excellent one to quote in her support, for the spirit of truth in love is exactly what is expressed in it. If we ask 'The love of what?' then no answer could fail to note that, for Augustine, it is the love of God.

Augustine's passage is interesting because the love which it reveals gives the character to the passion for lucidity and to the despair at achieving it which is the passage's manifest content, but that should tempt no one to say that it is an example of the extrinsic concern for truth.[9] Some students used to write *Ad maiorem Dei gloriam* at the head of each page of their exercise books, but it would be an evident misunderstanding to see, in that, the deflection of intellectual endeavour from truth as its intrinsic object. I raise the point here, partly to remedy the impression Donagan encourages us to have of Augustine, and partly to introduce a thought I take up again later – that the non-trivial, the edifying, sense in which it may be plausible that 'Reason is the highest thing in nature' may depend upon an elaboration of thought in service to a certain kind of love. If that is the case it would be better to turn to Plato (at least the Plato of *Symposium*) rather than to Kant for a better understanding of it.

Donagan offers 'Act always so that you respect every human being, yourself or another, as being a rational creature' as a gloss on Kant's injunction that we must never treat other human beings merely as means to our ends but always as ends in themselves. The power the first part of that latter expression has for us cannot be denied, but that does not mean that our ordinary use of it carries the second part of the Kantian thought with it. The Kantian thought is that all action must have an end and that persons are properly ends of action. It moves from the idea that persons are properly an end for practical reason to the injunction that persons are not to be treated merely as means to our ends. The power that the expression has in ordinary speech relies on the movement going the other way. We understand well enough why persons should not be treated merely as means to our ends but our understanding of that does not depend on, or require completion by, the idea that they are ends in themselves. To the contrary, the obscurity of the idea of a person as an end of action is likely to threaten our hold on the idea (if it is an idea) that a person is not to be treated as a means to our ends. As ordinarily used, the injunction that we should not treat anyone merely as a means to our ends is a reminder that persons are (or should be) an absolute limit to our wills of a kind unlike anything else in nature. If someone goes on to say that we should not treat anyone merely as a means to our ends because persons are ends in themselves, then the suspicion naturally arises that he is doing no more than expressing the same thought while appearing to give a justification for it.

Again we have reason to suspect that the concepts that really do the work are those that a Kantian would wish to replace and that what moves us in the Kantian enterprise depends upon the echoes of ways of speaking which the official philosophy condemns as lacking the power to reveal what is really at issue – echoes that remind us, for example, of the various ways of speaking of the love of our neighbour. Donagan takes Jesus' command that we must love our neighbour, the injunction that we must not treat other human beings only as means to our ends but always as ends in themselves, and the injunction to respect rational nature in oneself and another, as formulations that increasingly reveal what is at issue. My parody of Donagan awakens the suspicion that it might be exactly the other way about.[10]

I said earlier that the power of the Shakespearean passage is lost if we substitute the Kantian paraphrase for Falstaff's expressions of pity for his fellow mortals. Have I confused two senses of power: the power to move and the power to explain? Is there reason to think that the philosophical account that clarifies the nature of unconditional respect, or more generally, what it is to be an ethical matter, should have the power to move us in the way poetry does? Or, is it not absurd to expect the language proper to philosophy to be inserted into literary passages as I did in my parody of Donagan's gloss on Falstaff's rebuke to Henry? One may indeed produce a sense of absurdity in that way. Should we not expect the analysis or theory that reveals what is at issue to be extremely abstract and technical and, therefore, expressed in a language which is ill suited for edification?

Rawls says:

> There is no reason to assume that our sense of justice can be adequately characterised by familiar common sense precepts, or derived from the more obvious learning principles. A correct account of moral capacities will certainly involve principles and theoretical constructions which go much beyond the norms and standards cited in everyday life; it may eventually require fairly sophisticated mathematics as well. This is to be expected, since on the contract view the theory of justice is part of the theory of rational choice.[11]

Earlier I remarked on Rawls' comparison of moral with linguistic theory and his suggestion that just as linguistics had developed an extremely abstract and technical theory to deepen our understanding of even relatively banal linguistic capacities, so moral theory could be expected to develop in the same way. Leaving aside that the linguistic analogy could be developed in a direction completely contrary to that taken by Rawls,[12] it is important to note that the construction of a well-formed sentence is a 'capacity' in a sense that invites our understanding of it to deepen through theory of a technical kind. It is a sense of capacity that carries with it a contrast between what is on the surface and what lies below it that is appropriate to scientific theory. But it is plausible that the contrasts between essence and surface, appearance and reality, as they apply in moral philosophy, should invite theorising of a kind whose findings would be expressed in a language so unsuited to the revelation of the kind of seriousness that is peculiar to morality that its substitution for our untheoretical expressions should result in parody.

Any explanation of what Rawls calls our 'moral capacities' must clarify the attunement of moral response to the kind of seriousness that is internal to our sense of good and evil. It is, I think, fair to require that the deliverances of a theory that is intended to reveal (though not necessarily to explain) the character of that seriousness – the kind of seriousness it is – should be substitutable for more common, untheoretical expressions of it in examples such as the Shakespearean passage that Donagan quotes, and in others, such as those in which we find characteristic expressions of remorse. On the face of it, theories that fail to meet this requirement will either be unashamedly reductive or yield parodies of moral seriousness, as the Kantian account is revealed to do when put to this test. Is it silly to say this of a philosopher as great as Kant? I fear it is not. When we turn our attention from the task of developing philosophical accounts of precepts and prohibitions which square more or less with 'traditional morality' or our 'ordinary moral intuitions', and direct it instead to our sense of the terribleness of being an evildoer, then it seems as though a Kantian must say that the terribleness of being an evildoer is something like being a traitor to Reason. That is manifestly a parody of moral seriousness. Remorse often presents itself in the accents of a horrified discovery of the significance of what we did but it is trivialised if we try to express a murderer's horrified realisation in anything like this way: 'My God, what have I done? I have been a traitor to reason. I have violated rational nature in another!' It is not only Kantian accounts that invite such parody: 'My God, what have I done? I have violated my freely chosen and universally prescribed principle that one shouldn't kill people under circumstances such as these!'

Stuart Hampshire says that 'a single criterion morality (classical utilitarianism, for example) deliberately treats our ordinary action descriptions as morally irrelevant except as indicating consequences'. Utilitarianism in particular, he says, 'disregards institutional descriptions, and also descriptions of actions in terms of the motives and the feelings expressed.'[13] He comments:

> If the single criterion in ethics is accepted by someone, that person decides to restrict the peculiar powers of his intelligence and of his imagination; and he decides to set a final limit to the indefinite development of moral intelligence when he prescribes the single criterion to others ... Utilitarian thinking is a kind of moral Esperanto.[14]

The salient point is that the descriptions that are rejected as ultimately irrelevant by utilitarianism are the descriptions through which moral understanding deepens. It is, perhaps, misleading for Hampshire to speak in this connection of 'standard action descriptions', of which 'murder', 'adultery', 'betrayal', 'cowardly', 'noble', 'dishonourable', 'vicious', would be a range of examples. Utilitarians look upon such descriptions as being, at best, pointers to actions whose distinctively moral character is more perspicuously revealed by utilitarian redescription. The important point is not merely that actions thus described have moral significance irrespective of their causal relation to the state of affairs deemed to be the only proper end of moral effort. It is, rather, that our exploration of what it is to be a murderer, a coward, a traitor, and so on, is at its deepest when it is in a natural language resonant with historical and local association. That does not mean that such exploration cannot reveal meaning that is universal. It means only that the universality is of a kind that must find its expression in the natural languages of different peoples. Great plays, poems and novels often have what is appropriately called a universal meaning (or truth), but they are not, thereby, suitable for translation into Esperanto. They are – and my point is that it is not accidental that they are – translated from one natural language into another.

When Raskolnikov repented of his murders he did not merely recognise that he had acted wrongly or that he had done what he ought not to have done. His (intermittent) remorse was a discovery of what it was to be a murderer and of what it was for another to be a fellow human being. The important thing is not to point out with a certain tone and emphasis that he was a murderer. It is that the moral significance of being a murderer is kept alive (for a culture and for individuals) only through a language and art that convey to us its peculiar kind of terribleness. That is why Hampshire is right to dwell on 'epithets usually associated with morally impossible action, on a sense of disgrace, of outrage, of horror, of baseness, of brutality, and, most important, a sense that a barrier, assumed to be firm and almost insurmountable, has been knocked over, and a feeling that if this horrible, or outrageous, or squalid or brutal, action is possible then anything is possible and nothing is forbidden and all restraints are threatened'.[15] The emphasis however ought not to be on the fact that these are natural reactions. Rather it should be on the fact that they are reactions expressed in a natural language whose creative use reveals what it means to be, *in this way*, shocking, outrageous and so on. Such responses of shock and outrage are not merely natural reactions from which reflection may distance itself and to which it may even condescend. They are reactions that provide the basis for the most serious kind of reflection and they condition some concepts from which reflection cannot distance itself without losing its subject matter.

The evil of what he did was revealed to Raskolnikov in his remorse, but his remorse was liable, and at times succumbed, to various forms of corruption. Those corruptions cannot be identified, let alone criticised, within the Spartan critical vocabulary available to utilitarianism. The corruptions of Raskolnikov's remorse were not merely *a result* of his failure to understand properly what he had done, nor were they merely in self-deceiving service to such a failure of understanding. They *were a form* of his failure to understand. Such interdependence of understanding and response is what I want to stress against utilitarianism. It is sometimes conveyed by the word 'sensibility'. Most forms of moral corruption are corruptions of sensibility.

To my mind, the salient point in the passage from Hampshire that I last quoted (although I do not know whether Hampshire would

35

think so) is that the kinds of reactions he cites condition our understanding of what they are reactions to, for they condition the
concepts which are used in the descriptions of the deeds and characters to which we react. To put the point like that shows that more
is at stake than utilitarianism, and more, even, than the failings of
single-criterion moralities. The nature of Raskolnikov's remorse
partnered a certain understanding of evil, which in its turn partnered a certain understanding of what it is for another human being
to be a fellow human being. In the religious language which informs
Dostoevsky's novel, Raskolnikov realised in his remorse that the old
moneylender was sacred. We may not think that is the only or the
best way of putting it, but however we put it, we have to go beyond
forms of utilitarianism and Kantianism if we hope to succeed in
capturing anything remotely like what Raskolnikov understood.

Why did I achieve a parody when I substituted 'rational beings'
for 'mortal men' in the Shakespearean passage? It was because the
Kantian paraphrase so manifestly failed to display the kind of seriousness that is internal to good and evil, virtue and vice, and which,
in this example, would need to display itself in Falstaff's reminder
to the Prince of what he was doing. That, after all, is what Falstaff
is doing. His rebuke to the Prince is at the same time a plea that he
appreciate what he is doing – that he see *the seriousness* of what he
is doing and the *kind of seriousness* it is. Any philosophical account
of morality must display that seriousness, or at least not be at odds
with it in the way that Donagan's theoretical paraphrases of our
ordinary ways of speaking were shown to be. That is part of what
it would be for a theory to have achieved a deepened understanding.

It has been said that moral matters are necessarily serious or that
it is a conceptual truth that they are serious. Sometimes it is said
that they are overridingly serious – necessarily overridingly serious
– which is, at least, to say that someone fails to understand the kind
of seriousness in question unless he judges it to override all other
things that conflict with it. Socrates went further when he said that
if we know what evil is then we cannot do it.[16] Someone who says
that morality is necessarily overridingly serious need not go so far,
but even the weaker claim, which allows for weakness of will and
irresolvable moral conflict, has been vigorously denied, by Stanley
Cavell, for example, who said that 'there [can be] a position whose

excellence we cannot deny taken by persons we are not willing or able to dismiss, but which morally would have to be called wrong. And this has provided a major theme of modern literature; the salvation of the self through the repudiation of morality.'[17] I will discuss that in Chapter 13. The issue it raises now is to what degree should the statement that morality is necessarily serious be qualified by the question 'For whom?'

The claims that moral matters are necessarily serious and that they are overridingly serious have been called 'formal' claims. They have also been called 'logical' or 'grammatical' claims. One way of understanding the idea that something is a formal claim about morality is to see it as a claim about *the nature* of morality, a claim that would be contrasted with a concern about what (morally) to do. It is sometimes expressed as a contrast between what is formal and what is substantial, but a claim about the nature of morality might itself be a substantial claim insofar as it is a moral claim, or insofar as it is inexpungeable by a claim from within a particular moral conception. When Socrates said that it is better to suffer evil than to do it and that the evildoer is necessarily 'miserable and pitiable',[18] he expressed a very substantial claim, one that was the expression of a particular moral conception and one that would, as Callicles observed, 'turn human life upside down'[19] for anyone who accepted it. But it was also offered as a claim about *the nature* of evil, for Socrates was saying that someone did not understand what evil is unless he understood that an evildoer is 'miserable and pitiable'. That is, admittedly, a controversial reading of Socrates, but it is an intelligible one and, therefore, sufficient to secure the point. Clearly it would be implausible to say that the Socratic claim as I have characterised it is a logical or grammatical claim, or that it is a claim to be settled by looking at the meaning of certain moral words.

To say that matters of good and evil, virtue and vice, are necessarily serious would be to say that someone who says, 'But that *is merely* evil', does not understand what it is for something to be of moral concern. (Suppose someone were to say that the fact that an act is evil is an insufficiently weighty consideration to counterbalance the pleasure it would give him to do it.) Some philosophers have been content to relativise the idea of seriousness to particular persons. They say that something is of moral concern for some person if it satisfies certain formal criteria (in the case of Hare, prescriptivity and universalisability)[20] and if it overrides other matters for him. One reason for thinking that is mistaken is this. Someone must not only take seriously what he claims to be of moral concern to him; his taking it seriously must be capable of being taken seriously by others. That will not be achieved merely by the fact that it overrides other things in his life, because that could be grotesque or banal. Rush Rhees used the expression, though not quite in this connection, that 'it must go deep with him'.[21] That reveals what is at issue, more perspicuously, because there are limits to what *can go* deep which are set by what *can be* deep.

I do not wish to say that a morality cannot be shallow or that it cannot reflect a cheap understanding of life, but I am claiming that such judgements upon it cannot be dismissed as irrelevant to its claim to be a morality. A morality must claim (though we may judge that it fails) to deepen rather than cheapen our understanding of what we care for. That fact argues for a deeper integration of morality into a concern for the meaning of our lives than is usually acknowledged by philosophy. I will develop that point in later chapters.[22] For the present, I want to point out that it places certain restrictions on the content of anything properly called a morality. We cannot say that anything may be of moral concern for us and still claim that it deepens the relevant area of concern. Nor can we say that it is irrelevant whether morality deepens or cheapens our understanding of our lives without making it unintelligible what morality's claim on us might be. Suppose someone who acknowledged that his sexual morality cheapened our understanding of the meaning sexuality has in human life, but who then said that did not matter because morality is one thing, the meaning of things another. Or, someone who said 'I know it is sentimental and irredeemably banal, but there it is; it is my morality.' The requirement that morality must at least intelligibly claim to deepen rather than cheapen our understanding of human life entails that it must offer a deepened perspective on the good and ill we suffer. That promises a different perspective on the connection between morality and those goods and ills than does the common idea that morality is an instrument whose purpose is to secure those goods and enable us to escape those ills as much as is possible. Morality, I am suggesting, supervenes upon and deepens our sense of the facts of human life and human nature, which the varieties of naturalism take to be important.

If someone says that something is a moral matter for him, then this is a claim on our serious regard, a fact that we sometimes express when we say that we must respect conscientious objection. The usual context is one in which someone explains why he must or cannot do something. When a person says that, for him, such and such is a moral matter, or more commonly that it is, for him, 'a matter of principle' or 'conscience', then we may not say that that is a fact of no importance – no more than we may say it to someone who pointed out that a proposal would put his health or even his life at risk. In the moral case we do not have to agree with his actual judgement nor even agree that *it is* a moral matter, but if he is to claim our serious attention, as he intends and expects because he has told us that it is for him a moral matter, then he cannot at the same time flagrantly undermine that possibility by saying something which, with the best will in the world, we cannot take seriously. The notion of seriousness is, therefore, not to be replaced or explained by what might appear to be the less obscure notion of 'overriding-ness', given a behavioural elucidation relative to each person. That something is, for a particular person, an overriding, prescriptive and universalised 'principle' is not, of itself, the slightest reason for taking it seriously.

I said earlier that the assertion that morality is necessarily serious invites the challenge: for whom? I have argued that we must say more than that it is so for the person who professes it, but anything stronger must await further discussion. Whether, and to what extent, someone can claim to be 'outside of morality' in the sense of being indifferent to its demands and yet claim to understand it, depends upon whether, and in what way, one can understand it impersonally. I shall argue later (Chapter 15) that the personal character of moral understanding requires a kind of engagement which is incompatible with someone saying he understands what it is to be a murderer, a coward, a traitor and so on, and that he understands the way it matters to some people, but that it matters not at all to him.

There are three things I would now draw attention to. They are important to my argument and will be developed in further chapters, but it is important to note them now to prevent certain

MORTAL MEN AND RATIONAL BEINGS

misunderstandings of what I have been saying. The first is that the integration of morality with concerns about the meaning of life is agnostic on the question of whether there is a radical dualism between morality (or perhaps a certain conception of good and evil) and other forms of value, or whether, as Williams suggests, that sense of dualism is a consequence of the distortion of the ethical by the spurious concept of the moral (he calls it 'the morality system').[23] The second is that the connection between what we can treat as a moral claim and what can go deep with us shows that what makes something of moral concern cannot be revealed to us only by deliberative or imperatival modalities like 'ought', 'must', 'cannot' and so on. Rather, it is also (perhaps primarily) revealed by descriptions of action and character that reveal what is serious, what is deep, what is shallow, what is sentimental and what is truthful and so on. Descriptions of action and character are not moral descriptions only by virtue of their connection with deliberative or imperatival modalities, whatever the purely formal feature of those modalities. Yet that, if I understand them, is what is claimed by certain philosophers in agreement with Hare. They seem to believe that the morally pertinent dimension or 'element' in a judgement (that an action is base, for example) is the implicit judgement that the action ought not to be done, when that 'ought' satisfies certain formal requirements. The logically proper object of remorse, for them, is the judgement that such and such was done, when (morally) it ought not to have been done. If, however, what it is for something to be a moral matter is an inexpungeable part of the meaning of our actions and (more generally) our lives, then it is implausible to deny that the descriptions with which we express our sense of that are, at least, conceptually interdependent with their modal implications. Another way of putting that last point is this (taking remorse as an example): the object of remorse is not an action under the characterisation, 'I ought not to have done it.' Rather, it is an action under a description that discloses what one did in a more substantial way (the kind of description that would be forthcoming in an elaboration of 'My God. Don't you realise what you did?'). Descriptions of actions and character through which we explore our sense of what we have done and what we are, of what is fine and what is tawdry, of what is shallow and what is deep, of what is noble and what is

40

base, and so on, are not merely descriptions of convenience on to which we project a more formal sense, focused on imperatives, of what it is for something to be of moral concern. It was on this point that the success of my parody of Donagan's Kantian reconstruction of Falstaff's rebuke to the Prince depended.

The third thing I would draw attention to in order to prevent misunderstanding of what I have said is that judgements like 'This cheapens our understanding of sexuality', or 'That is sentimental', or 'That is banal', or 'That does the dirt on life' are genuinely *judgements*, and that they are fundamental to morality and also to philosophical thinking about morality. If someone were to remark, as D. H. Lawrence did of a certain way of thinking about sexuality, that 'it does the dirt on life',[24] but then went on to say that that did not matter because it was a moral way of thinking, then unless he was being ironic or unless the sense of what he said was dependent upon a sophisticated contrast between morality and, say, the ethical, his remark would be a clear sign that he did not understand what it is for something to be a moral matter. Therefore, when judgements like those above are expressed, judgements about conceptions of the nature of morality, they cannot be dismissed as conceptually irrelevant, emotive reactions. They are a proper, indeed essential, part of critical philosophical thought. I acknowledge, however, that their acceptance *as judgements* depends upon a richer conception of critical thinking and of the relation between thought and feeling than is presently available in the mainstream philosophical tradition.[25]

Philosophical thinking about morality should clarify how a particular account of it can deepen our thinking, and it must show that the account allows, to the reflective but non-philosophical person, the possibility of an ever-deepening understanding of the nature of moral significance, an understanding that is at least continuous, and must certainly not be at odds, with the philosophical account.

An objection may still be pressed, however, in something like the following way. The discontinuity between the results of ordinary reflection and philosophical reflection which I have been trying to expose and upon which I played to achieve my parody against Donagan, is precisely what Kant had in mind when he said:

> Everything that is empirical is, as a contribution to the principle
> of morality, not only unsuitable for the purpose, but is even

highly injurious to the purity of morals; for in morals the proper worth of an absolutely good will, a worth elevated above all price, lies precisely in this – that the principle of action is free from all influence by contingent grounds, the only kind that experience can supply. Against the slack, or indeed ignoble, attitude which seeks for the moral principle among empirical motives and laws we cannot give warning too strongly or too often; for human reason in its weariness is fain to rest upon this pillow and in a dream of sweet illusions (which lead it to embrace a cloud in mistake for Juno) to foist into the place of morality some misbegotten mongrel patched up from limbs of very varied ancestry and looking like anything you please, only not like virtue, to him who has once beheld her in her true shape.[26]

That he had a point can be seen when we notice that it seems that no amount of lyrical improvisation on the love of our neighbour or on a sense of human fellowship, on our common mortality or on compassion, etc., will take us to the idea of an unconditional respect for all persons, for reasons which are obvious and which Kant pointed out. The point can be put generally and with as little controversial metaphysical commitment as possible, by saying that reflection which is in the same idiom as the things which have the power to move us will, just because of its dependence on feeling and the local resonances of a natural language, be unfit to reveal the generality, stringency and constancy required of moral response.

To understand both the objection and what might be said in response to it, we need to look more closely at the kind of seriousness which I have claimed is internal to our sense of good and evil.

4

―――――――――

Remorse and its lessons

In Chapter 1 I referred to a television series called *The World at War*. A Dutch woman was interviewed in an episode on the Nazi concentration camps. She had given shelter to three Jews fleeing the Nazis, but after some days she asked them to leave because she was involved in a plot to assassinate Hitler and judged that it would be at risk if she were caught sheltering Jews. Within days of leaving her house the three were murdered in a concentration camp. She said Hitler had made a murderess of her, that she hated him for many things but most of all for that.

I shall not quarrel with her judgement of what she had done – that it made a murderess of her – although I understand why many would. Any argument over her response would need to judge the significance of the differences between what she did and those deeds that inform our sense of the seriousness of murder. In one clear sense she was not a murderess. No court would judge her to be that. Indeed, she did nothing that would bring her before a court. Perhaps more significantly, no one could seriously say to her, nor even of her, that she was, morally speaking, a murderess. Not even the relatives of the three who were murdered by the Nazis could say that. How, then, can I say that I do not quarrel with her judgement?

She did not, I believe, judge herself as she did in ignorance of what I have acknowledged. Nonetheless, her sense of the seriousness of what she did is captured in her judgement on herself. The Jews were hunted by those who would murder them in the spirit of ridding the world of vermin. They needed shelter but she refused it.

43

Many others did the same. But as I said, the significance of these and other things remains to be judged.

In judging their significance we should not give undue weight to the fact that she is not to be blamed for what she did. People can do morally terrible things yet not be blameable for them, or not, at any rate, in a way commensurate with their terribleness. In *that* sense they are not *accountable* for what they did. No one can point a finger and hold them to account. They cannot be *accused*. It would be wrong to infer that they are not morally responsible for what they did, meaning, that they should not feel remorse for what they did and that our relation to them cannot be conditioned by a moral description of what they did. Those who believe this often appeal to a sharp contrast between the psychological and the moral. With that contrast in mind they say that they understand why the Dutchwoman should feel terrible, that it is natural, perhaps even morally good that she feels terrible, but she should not feel remorse for what she did because it is irrational to feel remorse for an act for which one cannot (rationally) be blamed.[1]

'Blame' is a word with many connotations and it is sometimes used in a general way to mean no more than 'to hold responsible'. The chorus held Oedipus responsible for his unintentional deeds for which he showed remorse. It did so through the quality of its pity for him, for the evildoer he had unwittingly become. To hold someone responsible in this sense means to hold them, to fix them, in a lucid response to the significance of what they did. It means that the moral significance of what they did must not be evaded, neither by them nor by us, but it does not, thereby, mean that we find fault with them, that we can accuse them, or that we find them culpable. Those are all specific and different human acts (different kinds of holding responsible) and are therefore liable to moral appraisal and criticism even when the person to whom they are a response is uncontroversially a wrongdoer. They are species of the genus 'to hold responsible', but there is no act which is merely that.

The tendency to connect moral responsibility too tightly to culpability has led to a moralistic distortion in much contemporary discussion of moral responsibility. Those who, in certain circumstances, rightly refuse to blame someone, occasionally fall into a sentimental social and psychological determinism in order to justify what they take to be the logical corollary of their refusal to blame, namely, the refusal to apply moral descriptions. Those who rightly react to the sentimentality and to the suspect determinism often fall into an unpleasant moralism that is supported by an implausible voluntarism in order to justify their sense that moral descriptions are appropriate. The idea that a person who judges that someone has done evil (logically) must blame him in a sense which conflicts with pitying him appears to be, at least partly, a rationalisation of our apparently natural, but unsavoury disposition to point fingers at one another disguised as moral theory or conceptual analysis. It leads to an unnecessary sense of conflict between pity and moral judgement and is responsible for the unedifying tone of much of the contemporary discussion of the relation between crime and social circumstances.

A serious conception of responsibility need not be connected so tightly with conditions of culpability. We can say that *a person is morally responsible for what may claim her and us in one of the many forms of serious and lucid moral response*. It is common and natural to think that a critical assessment of such a response requires a critical assessment of its object, independently of the response itself. (How else are we to assess whether responses are appropriate or rational?) However, *what* can claim us in serious moral response need not, at all levels, be establishable independently of what is revealed to us by authentic and authoritative response.

Ways of responding, like intuitions, are not self-authenticating if that means that they are beyond critical scrutiny. But it does not follow that we have, *at all levels*, independent critical access to their objects. A deeper exploration of this is the task of later chapters, but it is important even here to note and to describe, more accurately than philosophers generally do, how contrary to the appearances such a thought is. One way of responding is often judged in the light of another, and what needs more accurate description is the critical grammar that determines our sense of the authority with which one thing shows up another as being, perhaps, sentimental or self-indulgent. The quality of the Dutchwoman's response teaches me what its proper object can be, and so what a serious relation to it can be. That is why I call it authoritative. She was not sentimental or morbid or self-dramatising. Of course, I can only make

45

such judgements because of what can be said of the kind of thing she did independently of the character of her response to it. But I came to see the moral significance of what she did in the light of her response – a response that is naturally characterised as remorse.

When Kant said that even in the presence of Jesus he would need to step back and turn inwards to listen to the deliverance of Reason, he was partly right and partly wrong.[2] He was right insofar as he wished to stress that the acknowledgment of Jesus could not be a blind response, but he was wrong to think that insofar as we responded because we were moved, then to that extent we responded blindly. He was right insofar as he thought that lucidity required one to be obedient to the critical grammar of *thought* (Reason), but he was wrong to believe that that critical grammar is conditioned by an a priori conception of what it is to think well and what it is to think badly which necessarily excluded feeling as something extraneous to it. Aristotle was closer to the truth when he said that if we want to know what justice is then we should turn to the example of the just man – but we must have eyes to see.[3] For Aristotle, *the education of feeling and character was an epistemic condition of right judgement on what could only be disclosed in authoritative example*. It is common to read Plato as being closer to Kant on this matter, as saying that all examples need to be judged according to a standard independently of them and which is revealed to Reason purified of feeling. Yet it is possible to read him as having said first what I have attributed to Aristotle, with the addition (whose importance we will appreciate in later chapters) that ethical understanding is possible only in the light of the form of the Good.

I want to concentrate on something else the Dutchwoman said. She said she hated Hitler for many things but most of all for making a murderess of her. From one perspective – an external perspective on the terrible evil and suffering of that time – her reaction may seem inappropriate to the relative insignificance of what she had done. Surely (it might be said) she had better reasons to hate Hitler than any that connected him with what she did. Indeed, someone might say that in the face of all the evil and suffering of that time, it was indecent of her to place her own guilty suffering as being so important. In reply she might say that there is a sense in which she does not *place* her suffering at all, that, if anything, it placed her.

To make clear what I mean by that, I shall (to begin with) consider two critically sympathetic responses to her sense of the weight of her guilt.

First, someone who appreciated that our reaction to evil done is different from our reaction to evil suffered and who realised that her guilty suffering in recognition of what she had become plays a different role in her life from her suffering over the loss of her own family, might suggest that she gain a perspective on her guilt by placing it in relation to the many mass murderers of the time. That would be appropriate, however, only if she failed to distinguish in an important way between what she did and what they did. The fact that she said that she hated Hitler most because he had made a murderess of her, together with the facts mentioned earlier, is no reason to think that she did. She might be thankful that her guilt is not greater than it is, but that leaves her guilt and her suffering recognition of it exactly as it was.

Secondly, someone might note that her guilt is necessarily personal and that it is natural to what is both personal and painful that it is not overwhelmed by knowledge of the suffering of others. A spectator's horror at the suffering of another person is easily over- whelmed when she sees the sufferings of countless others, to the point where she is likely to lose any sense of their individuality. Her own suffering is not like that. No matter how many die and suffer around her, her own severe pain will not leave her to merge into an indeterminate sense of horror. Our sufferings, provided they are severe enough, stick with us.

Remorse, too, sticks with us, although corrupt forms of it merge readily enough into a sense of common guilt, where all are guilty and so none is. But it sticks with us in a way radically different from other forms of suffering. Someone who is true to her remorse will always reject, as inappropriate, consolation that is based on her recognition of the guilt of others. Any other kind of suffering (except perhaps the kind Simone Weil called 'affliction'[4]) may be consoled when we see it in the light of the suffering of others.

Isak Dinesen said that all 'sorrows can be borne if you put them into a story or tell a story about them'.[5] That is not true of the sufferings of the guilty, if they are true to their recognition of them- selves as guilty. Although we may all suffer in recognition of what we have become in becoming evildoers, we cannot look on this as part of our common lot or our common condition in the way that we do when we accept our mortality or our vulnerability to misfortune. The capacity to say 'we' – we mortals, we who have suffered together – not merely enumeratively but in fellowship, consoles. 'We of this family', 'we of this nation', 'we who have been left behind' when said at a funeral, are examples of the 'we' of fellowship. It is always possible for the consoling 'we' of fellowship to revert to the merely enumerative 'we', and with severe suffering there is characteristically an oscillation between the two. It is sometimes said that we are always alone in our grief and when we die, to protest that there is something illusory in a sense of fellowship in such instances. Whatever truth there may be in that, it is not that there is never genuine and uncorrupt consolation to be found in the capacity to speak in fellowship with those who grieve as we do and with all who must die as we must. But there can be only corrupt consolation in the knowledge that others are guilty as we are.

The Dutchwoman spoke personally, but not as she would had she said, 'I hate Hitler most because he murdered my family.' The 'I' that answers in remorse to the recognition of guilt is not the 'I' that naturally and properly partners the 'we' of fellowship. Those who, in remorse, suffer in guilty recognition of what they have become are radically singular, and for that reason remorse is a kind of dying to the world.

'World' is a difficult word, especially in philosophy. I mean by it here what we mean when we say the world has become lost to those who are self-absorbed, as may happen to someone who is self-absorbed in the fear of her impending death. We mean that she cannot speak out of a sense of fellowship that is conditioned by unselfcentred and sympathetic responsiveness to others. The 'world' in this sense is a common world, and its kind of commonness is marked by the 'we' of fellowship. The radically and continuously self-absorbed lose, but are not thereby lost to, the common world. Only an enumerative use of 'we' may come out of self-absorption of this kind.

Remorse, because it is a kind of dying to the world, can be mistaken for self-absorption and its kind of dying to the world. But remorse is not self-absorption. It is, amongst other things, a form of

48

the recognition of the reality of others – those we have wronged. Corrupt forms of remorse *are* a form of self-absorption. Then the 'I' of self-absorption becomes a false semblance of the radically singular 'I' who is discovered in genuine remorse. I call genuine remorse a kind of dying to the world because it is the discovery of a dimension of ourselves that cannot enter into common and consoling fellowship with others. That is why I said the Dutchwoman did not *place* her guilt. It could not be placed by any story we might tell of our common sufferings. Nor could she be asked to gain a perspective on it by comparing it with what others had done and suffered.

When we hear of the sufferings of others, when we become alive to the reality of others in their suffering, we often say that it enabled us to place our own suffering in proper perspective. That is partly because our self-absorption competed with the recognition of the reality of others, and therefore with the recognition of the perspective within which we can place our own pain. Remorse, however, does not compete with the recognition of reality. On the contrary, it is a form of the recognition of reality. Therefore, when the Dutchwoman said that she hated Hitler most for making a murderess of her, she was not, despite the comparative expression, vulnerable to the rebuke that her moral sense of that period would be more edifying if she hated Hitler most for the millions of human beings he murdered. That rebuke would have point only if she cared too little for what others had suffered, as would be the case if her remorse were a form of self-absorption, for it is a mark of the self-absorbed that they care too little for others. But she cannot be accused of moral self-indulgence, of caring too little for the suffering of others, merely because she said that she hated Hitler most for making a murderess of her.

Guilt and remorse (which I take at least often to be the suffering recognition and acknowledgement of one's guilt) as I have been speaking of them are not psychological phenomena. The notion of the psychological is obscure, but I take it to refer to facts about our common and individual natures. Fear, anger and jealousy are examples of psychological phenomena, as are neurotic or corrupt guilt feelings. They can be compared and discussed, and this comparison and discussion is not only an expression of common human fellowship, but a condition of it. Its consoling power is the basis of psychotherapy. If moral psychology is the study of the relevance to the nature of morality of facts of our common human nature as they might enter a sense of human fellowship, then guilt and remorse, as I have characterised them, are beyond its scope.

What I have said about the consoling comparability of psychological phenomena is also true of many moral phenomena. It is true of the virtues and vices because their character is conditioned and limited by an empirical understanding of human possibilities. It may be a proper rebuke against moral haughtiness and *hubris* to remind someone who judges their failings of character too harshly that she is only human, meaning that she should gain a perspective on her failings by remembering she is not alone in such failings. Aristotle rightly noted that there are sufferings beyond any human capacity to endure and he thereby set an empirically conditioned limit to accusations of cowardice. If even Achilles could tremble in fear, if even the bravest of heroes could be broken by fear, then that may be proper consolation to others in a similar situation. Similar things could be said in relation to the other virtues because of the relation of virtue to character. Our virtues and vices reveal what kind of human beings we are, and therefore judgements in their name are necessarily relative, under pain of *hubris*, to what is humanly possible.

It is different with guilt. It should be no consolation if what we did was also done by the best of people. That is not pride because remorse does not focus on what kind of person we are. Its focus is on what we have become only because we have become wrongdoers. I would say of guilt what Brian O'Shaughnessy said of action: 'It is like a leak from another realm or world into this world – we stand within and without nature.'[6] It is therefore not inaccurate or fanciful to say that the guilty, in recognition of what they have become, have a sense of being placed elsewhere: *placed*, because of their concentrated radical singularity under judgement; *elsewhere*, because their suffering can find no relief in a humbling acknowledgement of their humanity.

Reflection on remorse might prompt someone to speak of the 'special authority' or the 'special dignity' of the ethical. It might prompt someone to speak of the ethical as something *sui generis*, and even of it as something otherworldly, irreducible to a humanist understanding of it.

I hope that I have shown how misconceived is the modern tendency to be suspicious of remorse. (It might be thought to be more accurate to say that the suspicion is of guilt and feelings of guilt, but I am – oversimplifying a little – treating guilt feeling as remorse which is itself the pained recognition of the significance of our guilt, guilt being the *condition* of one who is a wrongdoer.) In one of the most fundamental ways possible the modern hostility to guilt and guilt feelings threatens a proper understanding of good and evil, and a proper sense of our humanity and of the independent reality of others.

The reasons for the hostility to remorse are various, ranging from a reductive functionalism about value, that focuses on the superficial thought that guilt serves no purpose (why should it?), to the most high-minded of them, which scorns remorse as a form of self-indulgence at the expense of a proper concern for the victim of our wrongdoing. There are, to be sure, almost infinitely many corruptions of remorse, and some may be, as Iris Murdoch says, the subtlest and most seductive of moral corruptions, but they are corruptions.[7] Remorse as I have described it is an awakened sense of the reality of another. It is time for me to begin to explain what I mean by that. It will take some chapters to do it.

It is strange, and sometimes it is mysterious, that other people can affect us as deeply as they do. Our sense of the reality of other people is connected with their power to affect us in ways we cannot fathom, as that is revealed in the fact that our lives seem empty when we lose those we love or, in a different way, in the destructive nature of certain dependencies. Although we often cannot fathom this power, we accept it as part of human life: if we are plunged into grief or despair because of it, we may hope that time will heal our suffering and that life will reassert itself in us. It is not so with guilt. Time, working alone, is denied the right to heal guilty suffering, if the suffering is lucid. What may heal it is as strange as the suffering itself – repentance, atonement, forgiveness, punishment. We are so familiar with this that we have lost a sense of its mystery.

We are perfectly familiar with the fact that a person might commit suicide because she became a murderer, even if she murdered a total stranger whose death would otherwise mean nothing to her and who was, if measured according to those qualities which are relevant to

51

self-esteem, utterly worthless. We might condemn suicide like that as confused and as the expression of a corrupt rather than a lucid remorse, but we find it perfectly intelligible. The fact that we do is part of our conception of the gravity of murder and of what another human being may mean to us. Any account of the seriousness of murder that does not give prominence to the way the murderer becomes haunted by his victim will be inadequate to the way remorse is an awakening to the terribleness of what was done. We have already seen, in Chapter 3, that many moral theories are inadequate in exactly that way. They would say that the murderer discovers in her remorse how terrible it is to become someone who broke a certain principle or rule. The absurdity of that cannot be ameliorated unless the concrete individual who was murdered assumes the kind of prominence I tried to convey by saying that a murderer is, in her remorse, haunted by her victim. But the accounts which I have criticised look upon that as extraneous to the murderer's understanding of the moral significance of what she did. The contrary point I wish to make is that a certain sense of her victim's individuality is internal to a murderer's understanding of the moral significance of what she did, and that it is part of what it is to be aware of the reality of another human being.

The power of human beings to affect one another in ways they cannot fathom is partly constitutive of that sense of individuality which we express when we say that human beings are unique and irreplaceable. A deeper exploration of this will be the task of Chapter 9. For the present it is important to note that our need of certain other human beings is partly constitutive of a certain sense of their preciousness and of their reality, but it is also, in some of its forms, destructive of it. That is why the need human beings have for one another has been a target for a familiar kind of moralism which fails to recognise that our sense of the independent reality of another human being, the acknowledgement of which is said (by the moralist) to be threatened by need of that human being, is itself conditioned by the terrible effect that the loss of a human being may have on us. Something similar is true of remorse. Remorse is a recognition of the reality of another through the shock of wronging her, just as grief is a recognition of the reality of another through the shock of losing her. Both are liable to egocentric corruptions. Our

52

dependencies, even at their best, tread a fine line between awakening a sense of the reality of another and submerging that sense in one of the many forms of egocentric absorption. Exactly the same is true of remorse. But the egocentricity is not merely a feature of the corruption, it is its central feature. Love must sometimes find its expression in grief, and our sense of the reality of other human beings must sometimes find its expression in remorse.

There are two common, natural and related misunderstandings of remorse which are often thought to follow from the fact that the importance the victim assumes to the one who has wronged him, and who acknowledges that wrong in remorse, depends entirely on the wrongdoer's sense that she has wronged her victim. The first is that remorse teaches us nothing about the nature of our sense of what it is to wrong another because it is conceptually recessive in relation to it. The second is that the recognition that we have wronged someone is best revealed in reparation, and that is where we should locate a proper sense of the seriousness of what we did. Reparation rather than remorse is expressive of what it is to take another seriously. These misconceptions underlie the modern objection to remorse as a form of self-indulgence.

I shall take the second point first. Remorse and reparation are not exclusive of each other, and without a serious concern with reparation, where it is possible, remorse would be corrupt. Reparation for what, though? The obvious answer is that it is for the wrong we have done. But how should we understand that?

Bernard Williams discusses an example in which a lorry driver, through no fault of his own, runs over and kills a child.[8] He points out that the driver will feel quite differently from a spectator, even if the spectator was in the cabin with him. His regret will be of a different kind – the kind for which it matters that *he* did it. Williams calls this 'agent-regret' and brings out the difference between regret *simpliciter* and agent-regret by suggesting that if the lorry driver's sense that he owed something to the child's parents could be satisfied by an insurance payout, then his regret would not be agent-regret. The point is not so much that there are some sufferings that cannot be relieved by money. It is that some regrets are directed not only to what we did or to its effects, but also at the fact that *we* did it. Williams speaks of agent-regret rather than remorse, partly because he thinks that remorse can rationally be directed only on to voluntary actions, and partly because his discussion is an expression of a long-standing suspicion of morality which goes through many phases and which I will discuss again later. But Williams' excellent point about the insurance money brings out that reparation is not directed only at the natural effects of what we did. The point which emerges from my discussion of the Dutchwoman (though it is not Williams' and does not follow from his) is that when remorse is appropriate, reparation is a response to a sense of what we did and what our victims suffered, both of which are *sui generis*.

The point has often been made, particularly in discussions of consequentialism, that ethical concern is not merely with the effects of *what* we did but also with the fact that *we* did it.[9] Of course, we can no more do philosophy by italics than we can by shouting it, but an important distinction has been invoked and needs to be clarified. Part of what is intended is that human beings with normal projects and interests cannot see themselves as replaceable units in a system of cause and effects, and that morality cannot require this of them. It is, therefore, wrong to say that we should concern ourselves with *what* we did rather than with the fact that *we* did it, partly because, in some cases, that *we* did it is internal to the character of *what we did* and, as we shall see, to what the victim suffered. Consequentialists have not merely an inadequate sense of evil done: they have an inadequate sense of evil suffered.

To say emphatically that certain philosophers have an inadequate sense of evil *done* is not to say that they have an inadequate sense of agency, not anyhow if that suggests that they require an improved, but morally neutral, philosophy of action. It is the expression of an ethical perspective on action and of an ethically conditioned sense of individuality. Williams' example was not, of course, an example of evil done. Indeed, it was part of his point that the interesting contrast is not between remorse and regret but between regret and agent-regret. That is part of his attack on a Kantian kind of dualism between morality and everything else. Or, perhaps more accurately, on a sense of dualism, which he thinks is most clearly represented in Kant, between what he (Kant) takes morality to be and everything else. Williams would say, I think, that in ethical contexts the emphatic sense of 'done' has been assimilated to the contrast between remorse and regret, whereas it is, in fact, conditioned by the contrast between regret and agent-regret. Up to a point he is right, but the relatively bare notion of agent-regret is clearly inadequate to the kind of remorse I have been describing. Moreover, there is good reason to believe that remorse is not rationally dependent on a sense of culpability. Remorse is not, as Williams takes it to be, rationally appropriate only for voluntary actions, and the contrast between the personal and the impersonal that is implied by remorse is different from that implied by the distinction between regret and agent-regret. The 'I' that is acknowledged in a serious response of agent-regret is not the radically singular 'I' that is discovered in remorse.

The other and more direct objection to what I have been arguing was that remorse is a reaction to an independently intelligible conception of wrongdoing and is a psychological state structured by it. The main reason for this claim is that (leaving neurotic cases aside) we cannot feel remorse unless we judge that we did wrong. That is true, but it does not entail that remorse and our sense of wrongdoing cannot be conceptually interdependent. Wittgenstein said that pity was a form of the conviction that another was in pain. He meant, I think, that our natural dispositions to pity are one of the determinants of our concept of pain.[10] Whatever is to be said for that, it would be naive to think that we could show it to be wrong simply by pointing out that we pity someone *because* we see that she is in pain.

We can see the point more clearly if we consider an example discussed by Peter Singer. He asks whether there is a moral difference between 'going over to India and shooting a few peasants' and failing to give money to Oxfam.[11] He knows that most people think there is a serious difference but he wonders whether they should. After some discussion of the moral difference between acts and omissions, he concludes that the judgement that it would be *murder* (or something morally the same as murder) not to send money to Oxfam is too harsh, but he then goes on to say: 'an ethic which put saving all one possibly can on the same footing as not killing would be an ethic for saints or heroes [but this should] not lead us to assume that the alternative must be an ethic which makes it obligatory not to kill but puts us under no obligation to save anyone. There are positions in between these extremes.'[12] He says that after ruing the fact that it is quite difficult to avoid killing people (by acts of omission). I therefore take him as at least seriously inviting us to consider that a saint may properly judge himself to be a murderer (multiple murderer, indeed) merely because he forgot to send his monthly subscription to Oxfam.

A person who says that he knows what evil he has done by 'going over to India and shooting a few peasants', yet who shows no grievous remorse, is someone who understands neither what he is saying nor what he did. A person who says that *he is as one who did this* because he failed to give money to Oxfam, but who showed no grievous remorse, does not understand what he is saying either. But if he should feel such remorse as does someone who had murdered people, then he would need to do more than philosophise about acts and omissions to convince us he was not insane. In the absence of an appropriate, morally intelligible, possibility of remorse, the expression 'morally the same as', in 'failing to give money to Oxfam is morally the same as "shooting a few peasants"', idles. But that, I think, is not an entirely philosophical judgement. It is the judgement of one who speaks out of a certain conception of moral value which philosophy cannot underwrite as the 'right' conception, and in the light of which what Singer says is not so much false as it is frivolous – which is not to say that national or personal omissions in relation to those who are starving cannot be seen in a morally serious light. On the contrary, it is because they can that I say what Singer says is frivolous.

I am not arguing that if we do not feel remorse for some action then that action (or omission) cannot properly be said to be evil. It is perfectly proper to say that an action is evil although none of us feels, or would feel, remorse for doing it. Singer wishes to say that an action may be morally wrong even though our capacity to recognise it outstrips our morally reactive emotional capacities to keep in step with that recognition. He will say that it is principally a matter for psychology to explain why that is so, and he will say that it is because of the true deliverances of 'cognition' or 'reason' that we progress morally, rather than because of our sluggish and conservative affective life. He will say that recognition of the truth can outrun our capacity to cope with that recognition, and that philosophers, especially, should not encourage the idea that an emotional reaction to a judgement or practice may discredit an *argument* for it.

I would deny none of this *understood in a certain way*. It is, after all, no more than the edifying rhetoric of a familiar kind of philosophical self-congratulation. My argument was not that since we do not feel remorse we need not or ought not to feel it, but rather, that if we find the claim that we ought to, or that we might, morally unintelligible in connection with a kind of action, then we cannot find intelligible the claim that such an action was evil. That is not to deny that our sense of which actions are an intelligible object of remorse might change (as it did with some who justified slavery) and that an action might, indeed, be evil though we did not find it an intelligible object of remorse. *However, that our sense of what is a morally intelligible object of remorse can change is not a reason for saying that what we judge to be evil can, and in some cases 'rationally' should, outrun it.* Yet that is what is often suggested, and it is made to seem more plausible by contrasting our 'pre-reflective intuitions' with the deliverances of reason. I have not been speaking of our 'intuitions', and the 'claims of Reason' cannot outrun what we find intelligible.

Singer would not be very interested in remorse. No consequentialists are, and I am not now suggesting that they should be. He is concerned with what he (mis)takes to be Reason's deliverances on what we ought (morally) to do, and I do not now wish to say that he should not be. I am concerned only to argue that a certain conception of remorse is internal, partly grammatically constitutive of a certain conception of what it is for something to be morally right or wrong and what it is for a concern to be a moral concern. For consequentialists, remorse, although perhaps psychologically ineliminable and so consequentially significant, is conceptually, at best, peripheral to a right understanding of the nature of morality, which is, for them, essentially given by our manifold consequential relations to species of natural evil. By way of contrast, when Socrates said it was better to suffer evil than to do it and that the evildoer was necessarily 'miserable and pitiable', he was urging an understanding of the nature of good and evil for which a recognition of the kind of harm an evildoer had done himself, only and necessarily because he was an evildoer, was conceptually necessary. I take the harm to be what is revealed to the pained recognition that is remorse. Socrates would not judge consequentialism to be a misunderstanding of good and evil or a mistaken theorising of it: he would judge it to be no understanding of good and evil at all.

Suppose that we go to Singer's room to find him about to hang himself from the rafters. We ask him why he is doing this and he says that he cannot live with the multiple murderer he became when he failed to renew his bank order to Oxfam. We would not conclude that he was a saint whereas poor Fred, who hanged himself only last week after 'going off to India and shooting a few peasants', was morally rather ordinary. The example is absurd, and that is my point. We do not believe that someone could kill himself because he judged himself to be a murderer because he failed to renew his banker's order to Oxfam, no matter what philosophical beliefs we credit him with, unless we judge him to be unhinged. And to say that a person could believe something only if he were unhinged is one way of finding it unintelligible that we ought to believe it under pain of irrationality.

The point does not depend upon the different beliefs we may have about suicide. We may believe that suicide on account of moral despair is always wicked or irrational or both, or we may believe that it is seldom either. My point merely depends upon it being part of our conception of the seriousness of murder that we find it intelligible that a murderer might commit suicide because of his grief at what he had become. If it is always wicked or irrational, then these are corruptions of something that is fundamental to our sense of the evil of murder and is, in its way, a false semblance of a serious and lucid response to it.

If we judge someone to be unhinged then we cannot think of him as being seriously remorseful. Remorse requires a sober collectedness, or perhaps, more accurately, it aspires to it as a perfection belonging to its nature. A person who is unhinged cannot be responsive to the demands of remorse, and someone who cannot be responsive to its demands cannot be in remorse, for to be in remorse is to be in disciplined obedience to its requirements. That is one way of understanding the idea that the mad cannot know what they do: they lack the kind of inner unity to be responsive to the claims of morality. Moral understanding requires a kind of integration (a kind of integrity) of a moral subject who is more substantial than merely a rational agent.

Moral understanding requires that those who would claim to have it should be serious respondents to morality's demands. Someone who cannot be responsive to morality's demands is one for whom morality has no reality. The 'reality' of moral value is inseparable from the reality of it as a claim on us, and serious responsiveness to that claim is internal to the recognition of its reality. (That is the element of truth in 'non-cognitivism', particularly emotivism.) To understand, for example, what we are contemplating if we are contemplating murder, we must understand what it is to be a murderer, which is to understand rightly in what way it matters. I discuss this more fully when I turn to more detailed exploration of Socrates' claim that it is better to suffer evil than to do it and of its relation to his claim that we cannot do evil knowingly. For the present, it is sufficient to say that the inner disintegration characteristic of madness makes impossible the serious responsiveness to the claims of morality that is internal to the recognition of their reality. That is one reason for not calling remorse a mere feeling, or a mere attitude. Remorse is, amongst other things, a disciplined remembrance of the moral significance of what we did. It must be disciplined if it is to avoid self-deceiving re-descriptions and the corruptions peculiar to remorse itself – self-abasement, morbidity, and many others. Kierkegaard called remorse an 'emissary of the eternal' in which 'everything is called by its own name.'[13] To describe remorse as a feeling or attitude to the fact that we did what we (morally) ought not to have done, harnessed to a resolve not to do it again, is seriously to underdescribe it.

The point against Singer can be evaded only by denying the connection I have been exploring between remorse and moral seriousness. But if I am right in my *reductio ad absurdum* of Singer's conclusion, we can deny that connection only at the expense of the point of his argument. Singer traded on a certain sense of moral seriousness when he said that there is, at least, a case to be made for believing that failing to give money to Oxfam is morally the same as killing people. The point of his argument is to reveal the act and the omission to be the same in important respects relative to an unstated but accepted sense of the seriousness of murder. There would have been no point in securing the similarity only by altering our sense of the seriousness of murder. But if he did intend radically to alter our sense of what it is to be a murderer, what reason would anyone have to agree with him? If the idea of what it is to be a murderer that Singer appeals to in his example is not the one with which we are familiar, or continuous with the one with which we are familiar, then the point of his argument is lost. But the idea that someone could seriously understand herself to be a murderer, yet not suffer grievously in remorse, is not one with which we are familiar. Nor should we find edifying the idea that we would be morally more clear-sighted if we became familiar with it.

Singer would say that all that is required for serious, or at any rate sincere, remorse is that someone should believe that she did what morally she ought not to have done. My argument has been that the absurdity of the suggestion that failing to send money to Oxfam might be morally the same as 'going to India and shooting a few peasants' reveals two things. First, how superficial Singer's conception is of what it is for something to be morally the same as something else. Secondly, how thin his conception is of what it is for someone to *believe* that she did what (morally) she ought not to have done. The point is not merely epistemic. I am not saying that we can tell what is evil and what is not by considering whether we feel remorse for what we do. The slave owners of the American South did not find it intelligible that they should feel remorse for raping a negro slave girl – not, at any rate, of the kind they would if they raped a white woman. (That is just the kind of example Singer uses in support of a conception of critical moral thinking whose superficiality I hope to reveal in Chapter 9.) My discussion of Singer's thought experiment is intended to show that we cannot say that something is morally wrong unless it is an intelligible object of remorse. Further, that something is not an intelligible object of remorse for us merely because an argument has compelled us sincerely to assent to a conclusion that it is morally wrong. Our understanding of remorse is not conceptually recessive in relation to an independently intelligible conception of moral wrongdoing. The two are, at least, equal partners.

I acknowledge, however, that my argument depends upon a certain understanding of remorse as expressive of the seriousness that is inseparable from a certain sense of morality. According to that understanding – whose grammar I have been trying to display – we could not show what it was for something to be a moral matter without showing how it would appear in the light of a serious remorse. I do not think that philosophy can show that any proper understanding of morality must be like that. When I say that *we* would not find this or that intelligible or when I appeal to certain *reductios*, I am not making assertions about our common understanding, but rather, I am inviting agreement with my interpretation of a common, but by no means universal, understanding of morality. My argument is that remorse is a central and inexpungeable determinant of what it is for something to be a moral matter, and therefore of the sense of expressions like 'morally wrong', 'morally ought', 'morally terrible' and 'morally the same as'. Singer clearly does not think that. Nor, officially, do most philosophers. Consequentialists certainly do not. They would treat my conclusion as an illusion that arises from confusing the psychological with the moral. Sometimes, they would say, this confusion runs so deep that it shows itself in the 'grammar' of certain conceptions of morality. I have (they would continue) described only the conceptual shadows cast by the psychology of remorse as it has been structured by certain confused beliefs, and I have mistaken this for philosophy. I have no simple and quick response to this. This book is my response.

The philosophy of what I have been arguing is, I believe, to be found in Plato.[14] Socrates said that it is better to suffer evil than to do it. He said that the worst evil that a person could suffer was to be an evildoer, that an evildoer is miserable and pitiable just because he is an evildoer. He said that to Polus, who was incredulous. Implicit in his incredulity was the assumption that he knew what evil is and that it was a further question whether someone caught up in it is harmed by it. He thought he knew what evil is and he then looked around for the harm. Polus is not the only one to have been incredulous at what Socrates said. Here is Aurel Kolnai:

> When Plato argues that 'to suffer wrong is better than to inflict it' and that 'the just man is happy' – he was not the first and by no means the last dealer in such edifying stock-in-trade – I feel impressed with the mass of intellectual distortion, *bel esprit*

ungenuineness and cheap preaching packed into a concise aphoristic form. In the plain natural sense in which it is better to win than to lose battle, or better to be the rider than the horse, or an eater of beef than a beast of prey, it is patently better to inflict wrong (that one gets away with it is presumed) than to suffer it; and in an equally plain moral sense, he who does not inflict wrong is a better man than he who does.[15]

That last sentiment excluded, Kolnai says what Polus said, and in much the same tone.

Philosophers who think that Socrates is concerned to give a 'rational justification' for being virtuous understand him to be providing a motive for being virtuous when he says that an evildoer harms himself. His has been described as an ethics of 'self-interest'. The tyrant Archelaus drowned his brother by throwing him into a well. Those who say that Socrates argued for an ethics of self-interest presumably mean that Socrates would say to Archelaus that he should not throw his brother into the well because he (Archelaus) will be harmed more than his brother.

It is true that Socrates would say that if Archelaus knew the evil he did then he could not have done it. It is also true that Socrates would say that unless we know the harm we do ourself when we do evil, we do not know what evil is. Does that entail that if we understand what Socrates intended, we are given a reason not to do evil? Polus understood Socrates as meaning that, which is why he looked around for the kind of harm the evildoer suffers and wondered what it might be compared with, wondered what place it had in a catalogue of horrors.

Consider what Socrates said in the light of the Dutchwoman's remorse, or what amounts to the same thing, consider her remorse, in a Socratic light, as the understanding of what it is to do evil and what becomes of us when we do it. Socratically, remorse is a recognition of the reality of evil. More, it is a recognition of the reality of evil for which it is necessary to understand the harm evildoers do themselves. That means that although remorse is not the only way we recognise the reality of evil, neither is it a contingent route to its recognition.

Pity for the evildoer is another form of the recognition of evil. Socrates says, I think, that if we do not pity an evildoer, then we do not know what evil is – that indignation in the face of evil is a failure to understand what we are confronted with. That means we would have misunderstood Socratic pity for the evildoer if we asked: But what of the hard-hearted – those who would acknowledge the harm evildoers do themselves but who say that it is no more than they deserve? That is more difficult to understand. I do not mean that it is difficult to understand that we might pity an evildoer. We might sorrow over a friend for just that reason, and parents often do so over their children. That is not necessarily because of other things our friends or children suffer, nor is it because of the more manifest suffering of remorse. They might suffer no further consequences, nor the pain of remorse (in which case, those who care for them might sorrow more deeply). What is difficult to understand is the claim that if we fully understand the evil someone does (to us or others), then we will (necessarily) pity them – that if we do not, then we will show that we do not really understand what we claim to understand.[16]

We may pity an evildoer just because he is an evildoer. That enables us to understand that the evildoer is 'miserable and pitiable', independently of anything else which may happen to him. Evildoers cannot pity themselves while understanding what they did and what they have become because they did it. If they did then remorse would be a kind of self-pity; yet that is what I have argued remorse cannot be if it is true to its nature. To put the point Socratically: self-pity excludes the proper recognition of the harm the evildoer has done himself. The kind of harm Polus was looking for, and commentators like Dodds and Irwin with him, is not of a kind to exclude self-pity as incompatible with a proper recognition of the kind of harm it is. For the present, I will put the point this way: the terrible recognition of what we have become is a necessary condition of the recognition of the evil we have done. But it is not sufficient, and the questions that have been asked about the kind of self-concern it is and whether it could provide a motive for not doing evil are to be answered by attending to why it is insufficient. We are back to our earlier worry – that it is insufficient because it is not properly concerned with the victim. What kind of concern should that be?

5

Evil done and evil suffered

Philosophers often discuss an example in which a person is presented with a dilemma. If he kills one innocent person, ten others will be saved. If he does not, they will all be killed. The example usually comes up when consequentialism is at issue. Consequentialists present such examples as 'hard cases', usually with the complacent assurance that they can deal with them, meaning that their theory provides them with a clear answer to the question, 'What should be done?' They think that is a virtue.

Those who think that it is clear that one should be killed to save ten (they are not always consequentialists) often accuse those who deny it – or even those who are uncertain – of indulging an illegitimate self-concern, of being too precious to 'dirty their hands', of being preciously concerned with their integrity, or of preferring that others should suffer evil than that they should do it. The accusation – that those who insist that we cannot do evil though good may come of it are preciously concerned with their integrity – is sometimes justified. R. F. Holland put the right perspective on the matter when he asked, rhetorically, whether in such a situation a saint would be concerned with his integrity. He brings out the relative mediocrity of the concept.[1] The deeper issue is that those who think it obvious that one should be shot to save ten have no serious sense of evil – neither of evil done nor of evil suffered.

How should we characterise the evil of murder? Here is one sort of answer. That on which the ethical gets its grip when someone is murdered is the fact, the overridingly important fact, that he is dead. After all, what is so bad about being murdered if it is not,

64

essentially, that we are dead when we did not want to be? Is not the difference of moral seriousness between theft and murder the difference between the results of these actions: death in the one case and the loss of property in the other? The evil suffered by someone who is murdered is the evil of an unwanted death. The evil suffered when someone is murdered is the same as the evil suffered in a fatal car accident; the dead are all equally dead, however they came to be that way. Nature brings evil through necessity and chance, but intentional human actions fall under neither of those headings, which is why we take a special attitude towards evil done, that is, evil when it is the effect of the voluntary causality of a human agent. A distinctive, but derivative and reducible, language of good and evil attaches to these special causes of death. Put more generally: actions are evil by proxy when they result in evil states of affairs. There are many *bona fide* forms of evil, but moral evil is not one of them.[2]

The central idea in this way of conceiving evil done is of action as power – power to alter, control and arrange. We have power for good and evil because we engage causally with natural goods and ills, with what makes us suffer and with what makes us glad. The ethical is a species of the practical and, as such, is purposive: its purpose is to make life better for ourselves and others. G. J. Warnock said as much when he said that the 'object' of ethics is to 'ameliorate the human condition'. Were it not for ethical commitment, Warnock believes, our condition would be worse than it already is.[3] According to this picture, the ethical not only roots itself in, but is in all of its uncon-fused varieties reducible to these facts of, the human condition: we are creatures who can suffer and who can be happy, and we are creatures capable of intelligently directing and controlling the causal power inherent in action. The point was well put by Polus in *Gorgias*:

> There are many arts ... among mankind experimentally devised by experience, for experience guides our life along the path of art, inexperience along the path of chance. And in each of these different arts men partake in different ways, the best men following the best arts.[4]

He believes that the exercise of practical reason is mostly concerned with, and conditioned in its character by, an attempt to limit our vulnerability to chance, the brute necessity of natural and social forces and the power of other agents. The exercise of practical intelligence is the intelligent control of the causal power we have as agents to limit our vulnerability to suffering.

The conception I have just outlined is almost hypnotic with common sense, which is why some treat the refusal to shoot the one to 'save' the ten with incomprehension and sometimes even with derision. Is it not clear, they ask, that once someone is in such an awful situation the aim of moral thinking is to 'ameliorate' it, and is that not done by having one corpse rather than ten? What can someone who refuses to shoot be thinking of? The fault must lie in something 'inner', for the structure of action is basically this: person–act–effect. Ethically, acts collapse into the voluntary causation of certain effects, so what is left but the self? They must be distracted by the enchanting but morally irrelevant complexity of their subjectivity, for what is not moral preoccupation with effects must be mistaken moral preoccupation with the self and its 'integrity'. Other things being equal, it is clearly a better state of affairs that there be one dead rather than ten, so how can it be evil to bring about a state of affairs that all compassionate persons would regard as better?

It is a characteristic feature of discussions of such examples that the dilemma is presented from the point of view of the one who might do the killing. That seems perfectly natural, for is it not his problem? However, he is not the only one in the situation who has a problem. Everyone is caught up in the evil of it. The one who might be shot and the ten who might be saved must ask themselves what they hope for, and hopes, like actions, may be good or evil. Even so, someone might object that although the others are in that way implicated, they have a problem only because, and only to the extent that, the one who has been asked to do the shooting has a problem. In which case, do not all the problems collapse into 'What should he do?', which is best asked impersonally as 'What should someone in such a situation do?'

I do not want to ask 'What should be done?' The situation that I will characterise is too empty of detail to allow such a question to be asked sensibly. I will focus on what might be said by one person involved – one of the ten. I do not claim that anything like what he says *must* be said. Only, that what he says complicates the description of what are the morally salient features of the situation.[5] Bernard Williams says of a similar example that 'the men against the wall are obviously begging him to accept' the 'invitation' to kill the one.[6] Why obviously?

We could imagine a more extended dialogue than I will present. We could give a voice to the one who might be shot or, rather, we could give him many voices. I see no reason to think that these voices must converge on the question, 'What should he (who has been asked to do the killing) do?' Even the person in my example who says, 'Not for my sake', is not, thereby, committed to the judgement that he *ought* not to be shot. To be sure, only the one who might do the killing has something to *deliberate* about, for only he is called upon to act. The thoughts of the others are thoughts about their relation to what he might do. It does not follow that their thoughts must be thoughts about what they ought to do.

The one who is selected to be shot might plead to be shot. It does not follow that he believes (or should believe) that the person to whom he addresses his plea *ought* to shoot him, and that is not because his plea is not a 'moral' plea. Even if he knows that the one to whom he is pleading believes that he (morally) cannot kill him, still, in pleading as he does, he need not think that the other ought to reconsider. He pleads because he must, and he need have no thoughts about what the one to whom he addresses his plea must or ought to do. He *hopes* that the other will respond to his plea, and that is different from thinking that the other ought to respond to it or that he ought to shoot him anyway.

The executioner may shoot the one in the hope that ten others will survive, and he might do it because he thinks that he *must* do it. It does not follow that in order for this to be a sense of *moral* necessitation he must think that anyone in a similar situation must do the same. And if he thinks he must do it, he may still think it evil – which is not to say that he must think it the *lesser* evil and that he is rationally compelled to choose it.

In the following, one of the ten who might be saved by the shooting of an innocent person calls that shooting evil. I do not think it follows that he must say (or, *pace* Richard Hare, at least *think*) that therefore it must not or ought not be done. Do I intend his speech as an argument that the killing would be evil? Only in this manner and to this degree: it is meant to foreclose one way of talking about the killing and its relation to the ten. That is, although of course the killing is terrible it is 'the right thing to do', and therefore not evil. If he kills one to save ten, even because he believes that 'he must', the fact that he believes 'he must' does not mean that he should not plead for the forgiveness of the one he kills and those related to him and also for the forgiveness of those he 'saves'. In later chapters we will have occasion to examine, in more detail, the philosophical assumptions that make such commonplace points problematic. We will have occasion to note the modal diversity of moral response.[7]

One is to be shot to 'save' ten. One of the ten speaks as follows to the person contemplating murder:

> If he dies, then I will live, because he died, and because there are nine others with me. Each of the nine others will be able to say the same. Yet when he is dead, will I be able to console myself by saying that he died only one-tenth for me? Though you think that you must kill him not for me or for any of the others taken individually but for all of us taken together, when he is dead each of us must accept the fact that insofar as he was murdered for our sake, he died for each of us singly and undividedly. Each of us, in his singularity, is implicated in the evil of his murder.
>
> There are ten of us but we do not make 'a ten'. None of us can say 'A little for me but mostly for the others'. Someone cannot die, a little for one and a little for another, and someone cannot share his guilt, like a loaf of bread, a little for one and a little for another. Though each of us is one of the ten whom you wish to save, no one of us in this evil situation can (morally) become one-tenth of something. We cannot be taken together as 'something of ten units', and be placed on the scales against his singularity. If there were not nine others, if there were only he and I, and I were to say 'Let him die, I am as ten' then anybody could see that I was being ridiculous. Yet that is how it is, even now.
>
> If ten people, each alone, came to a raging stream, each would know that if he were to cross it alone he would be swept

away. Together they may link arms, and each person's strength and stability would be increased. The strength and weight of the ten would be added to each. Strength can be added to strength, weight to weight and volume to volume, but we cannot link arms now and say that each must give of his moral weight to the others so that we might all survive. It is a mistake to think that a person has moral weight that can be added to by another so that, in that way, each as part of many becomes weightier than one alone.

A person can make a gift of his life to another. Suppose someone had received such a gift, and suppose him to be grateful, but suppose also that he discovers that the one who had sacrificed himself did so not only for him, but also for another. Would he become churlish and complain that his gift had diminished in value, that he now had only half of what he had before? Could he say that, previously, his gratitude had been excessive? As it is with this person's relation to the good of the other's gift, so it is with each of us in relation to the evil of this person's murder: the relation is unaffected by the presence of others. If you must count, then let it be like this: one, one, one . . ., and when there is no more 'one' to be said, content yourself with that and resist the temptation to say 'And they total ten whereas there is only one over there.'

The one to whom I have given this speaking part sees the other who might be killed as being killed for his sake, although not only for his sake. It is this relation of 'being for the sake of' that makes problematic the weighing and balancing metaphors which are so important for the one to whom the speech is addressed. This can, perhaps, be brought out in the following way. Suppose each of those in a group of ten said in unison, 'Alone, my physical weight is no more than yours, but as one of ten I will tip the scales against you.' There is nothing odd about that. But if each of a group of ten were to say, in unison, 'Let him not die for my sake but for the sake of the others', then we end up with something odd, because the recommendation of each is undermined by the fact that they recommend it together. Who would 'the others' be? It might seem as though that could be avoided if they said 'Not for my sake alone . . . etc.' in which case the reply could be, 'That is how it will be, not for any of you individually but for all of you taken together.' But it was against just such a response that the speech I composed was directed. For each of the ten, the understanding of what it is for the killing to be for his sake is such as to render morally irrelevant the fact that from the point of view of the one who might do the killing, it is for the sake of them taken together.

The dilemma of the one who might do the killing cannot present itself to him as 'Should there be one dead or ten dead', because, as it stands, that fails to mention anything that he might do. Yet, I think the answer presents itself to him like that – it is better that there be one dead than ten. And that shows something about the way in which he conceives his actions. That answer to his question presents itself from a certain perspective on agency – agency under the perspective of 'arranging'. The question is 'What is the best arrangement here?' and the answer is 'The best arrangement is that there should be as few dead as possible.' His sense of responsibility hinges on whether, at the end of it all, he has arranged things well or badly, and the only criterion for whether his deed of arranging is good or bad is whether the arrangement is good or bad. For him, seeing the matter in this way, the moral character of an action is very simple and is completely determined by the character of a state of affairs. That is why consequentialists move with such ease from the judgement that it is better that *there be* one dead than ten, to the judgement that it is better *to kill* one person, though he is innocent, to save ten others. Their reply to the ten would be, 'Each of you says that he is prepared to die. But when it is finished it is I who must count the corpses. How can I avoid the conclusion that it is better that there be only one?'

His dilemma is about what to *do*, and as soon as he sees that in the light of the consideration that it would be better that there be one dead than ten dead, as soon as he begins to suspect that his dilemma about what to do would, or at least should, be resolved, completely and without remainder, by his judgement about what arrangement would be the best, then his sense of what he might be doing becomes simplified, and his dilemma loses much of its dreadfulness. Then talk of 'squeamishness' comes naturally. The kind of dreadfulness that killing a human being is seen to have when its moral dimensions are exhausted by the judgement that it is better that there be one dead than ten is such that the incapacity to do the deed is, indeed, squeamishness. It is the same *kind* of incapacity people suffer when they cannot drown kittens or kill their own meat, even though they have no moral objections to doing so. But as Williams has pointed out, to describe the refusal to kill an innocent person in such a situation as squeamishness is not to point to a morally relevant but hitherto neglected aspect of the situation: it is already to see the situation in the morally flat light of consequentialist theory.[8]

It might seem a cheap argument to suggest that consequentialists consider the incapacity to kill a human being as of the same kind as the incapacity to kill an animal. I do not think that it is, for when we begin to disregard the ways in which the people for the sake of whom we do evil are morally implicated in what we do, then we begin to look at them from the standpoint of the Royal Society for the Prevention of Cruelty to Animals. We begin to look at them only as creatures who should be spared further natural suffering, which is not to see them as human beings who can suffer the moral harm of being implicated in the evil being done for their sakes. That was chillingly illustrated in the lives of certain revolutionaries who were driven by what Arendt called 'the passion of compassion'.[9] Che Guevara, for example, said that if they were to succeed in their task, he and his guerrillas must transform themselves into 'cold, calculating, brutal killing machines'.[10] From the beginning to the end he was obedient to a certain kind of compassion, and from the beginning to the end that compassion demanded that he change the world for the better. But that same compassion disguised the profound disrespect expressed in the way he looked upon those for whom he did evil and concealed it from him. That he did evil is a judgement that he would pass on himself, which is not to say that he would have done otherwise if he had to choose again. Socrates would say that the compassion was counterfeit, not because it was 'insincere' but because it was sustained by a failure properly to understand the ethically conditioned nature of its object – a human being – and the ethically conditioned character of what a human being may suffer. We tend to pride ourselves both on our historically unparalleled respect for persons and on our compassion. We should not be so naive about the ways in which our sense of these may come into conflict.[11]

71

If someone believes that our capacity for action is, above all, the capacity intelligently to control the changes we can effect in the world, then his model for the ethical will be an administrative one. It has been pointed out many times that consequentialism has a certain theory of action from which all else follows. It is important to notice, however, that the nature of the relation between the ethical and what might be assigned to the philosophy of mind or to philosophical anthropology, is reciprocal. The person in our example thinks of himself as having been placed in a situation where it is said to him, 'the outcome is in your hands'. In that case, although his first thought will be for the person he has been directed to kill, he cannot think about that person without thinking about the others. And so the problem seems inescapably to present to him as one of numbers, as one in which he is to exercise the administrative power he has. Quite naturally, he begins to count corpses.

It is different with the others. Insofar as they do their thinking from their own situation, their perception will be unaffected by any idea of the administrative. Their problem is not whether at the end of the day there will be one dead or ten dead – that is not within their power. It is, as I have tried to show, whether they may justifiably hope for and inwardly consent to the killing of another for themselves. Their gaze does not go to and fro, from one to ten and back again. It stays fixed on the action to be performed. Although each knows that the perspective of the doer of the deed is necessarily different from his own because of his necessarily different relation to the ten, although each knows that the doer of the deed can make little of his 'radical singularity' and that for the doer of the deed his singularity is the countable singularity of a corpse, the perspective of the doer of the deed cannot be his. When it is finished, each faces something different.

My example shows that the most important philosophical question concerning such examples is not, 'What ought to be done?' The most important question is how to characterise the situation and to capture the evil in it. Consequentialists take the evil out of it. It is often remarked that they have no sense of evil *done*. I have tried to bring out that they have no sense of evil *suffered*, beyond the varieties of natural harm suffered. Their sense that it is an evil situation is, basically, that it is a situation in which certain kinds of natural harm will be caused by human agents with certain kinds of motives. Thus, whatever they may secure against those who oppose them by increasing the number of victims, it is not what they intend. They intend thereby to reveal that theirs was all along the right characterisation of what is ethically at stake. They appear to think that if, under the pressure of an ever-worsening catalogue of horrors, one agrees with consequentialists about what to do, then one has revealed that one was a closet consequentialist. Often they help the process along by calling consideration of the consequences of what we do or refuse to do *'consequentialist'* considerations, implying that they have a monopoly on taking consequences seriously. It is all of a piece with the fact that they call such examples 'hard cases', as though it were a virtue to have a theory which provided a decision procedure to settle even the most grisly of them. But it is mere prejudice to believe that it is an obvious virtue of a philosophical account of ethics to characterise our sense of the ethical in such a way as to yield to a decision procedure for what to do in any conceivable situation.

6

Naturalism

Good and evil are *sui generis*. That is part of what I have been attempting to argue since Chapter 4. It might be objected that this is inconsistent with my claim in Chapter 2 that Falstaff's compassion for other human beings as his fellow mortals is internal to the character of his unconditional respect for them. It may have seemed then that I committed myself to a naturalistic conception of the kind of seriousness that I said is internal to morality and which the Kantian account is unable to capture. But an implication of my argument in the previous chapter is that compassion cannot be the basis for ethics because the contrast between real and counterfeit compassion is itself ethically conditioned. To explore this more fully, I want to consider something that Bernard Williams says:

> He [the amoralist who cares for some people] gives us, I think, almost enough. For he has the notion of doing something for somebody, because that person needs something. He operates with this notion in fact only when he is inclined: but it is not itself the notion of his being so inclined. Even if he helps these people because he wants to, or because he likes them, and for no other reason (not that, so far as these particular actions are concerned, he needs to improve on those excellent reasons), what he wants to do is *to help them in their need*, and the thought he has when he likes someone and acts in this way is 'they need help', not the thought 'I like them and they need help'. This is a vital point: this man is capable of thinking in terms of others' interests, and his failure to be a moral agent

74

lies (partly) in the fact that he is only intermittently and capriciously disposed to do so. But there is no bottomless gulf between this state and the basic dispositions of morality. To get him to consider [the situation of those he is not inclined to help] seems rather an extension of his imagination and his understanding than a discontinuous step onto something quite different, the 'moral plane'.[1]

The distinction Williams draws between helping only those whom we like when we feel like it and helping those 'who need help who are not people who at the moment [we] happen to want to help or like'[2] depends (if the second is to be continuous with morality) upon our having a certain kind of concern for others as independent beings. The question, therefore, is whether that involves something on a 'different plane' from the spread and persistence of the kind of desire to help that is capricious and limited in its scope. To answer that question we need an understanding of what it is to see another human being as an independent being or as an 'end in himself' or, as we sometimes put it more simply, as a human being. My argument thus far has been that to see another as a human being is to see her in a moral light which conditions the character of our dispositions to her. If that is so then we cannot reasonably hope to get to 'morality' by extending pre-moralised dispositions, or dispositions whose character is not conditioned by morality. Earlier, I said that the contrast between real and bogus compassion is an ethically conditioned contrast. I meant, first, that compassion is a concept that requires the distinction between genuine and counterfeit forms of it, and secondly, that the application of that distinction (our sense of what it is *really* to care for another) depends upon a sense of others that is ethically conditioned and involves the idea that they are the kind of limit to our will that we express when we say that they are owed unconditional respect. That would be involved in any deepened understanding of what it is to care for them.

When Williams says that morality is not being on another plane from the desire to help others because they need help, he has, at least partly, in mind the idea of morality as defined by a certain sense of duty or obligation which contrasts with compassion or the relatively ordinary desire to help someone. Much fun has been made of the Kantian contrast between helping someone because we believe that we ought to and helping someone because of a compassionate response to their needs. There is, however, another contrast, which is between someone who helps because she thinks that she ought to, and someone who, in response to the question why she helped, simply replies that she saw nothing else to do, or, more simply, that she had to do it. We should be less inclined to contrast this last example with compassionate action (motivation), although a sense of moral necessity is expressed clearly enough. On the contrary, rather than thinking that such a person was motivated by something other than compassion or by something in addition to compassion, we might think her compassion to be especially pure, perfected by a proper understanding of its object – the reality of a suffering human being. Instead of contrasting compassion and a sense of moral necessity, we might judge that only a compassion conditioned by such a sense is properly responsive to the reality of a human being's suffering – where the emphasis is not just on suffering but on the fact that it is the suffering-of-a-human-being. Another way of putting the point would be to say that the character of a proper response to human suffering is conditioned by the ethically conditioned individuality which is internal to our sense of a human being as something more than a member of the species *Homo sapiens*, and to our sense of another as a distinctive limit to our will. It may, therefore, be true that the best reason for helping someone who needs help is simply that we see that she needs help, but our sense of what helping her for that reason amounts to will be distorted if we think the distinction between acting out of a sense of duty and acting out of a desire exhausts our (moral) thoughts about it.

The idea that good and evil are *sui generis* has taken many forms. In most of them it has focused on good and evil *done*. It is important to see that it applies also to good and evil suffered. In *Gorgias* Socrates says that a criminal may welcome her just punishment, for 'he who is punished justly suffers what is good'.[3] In the same spirit, Simone Weil says:

> The just man must be thanked for being just, because justice is so beautiful a thing, in the same way as we thank God because of his great glory. Any other gratitude is servile and even animal.

76

The only difference between the man who witnesses an act of justice and the man who receives a material advantage from it is that in such circumstances the beauty of justice is only a spectacle for the first, while for the second it is the object of a contact and even a kind of nourishment.[4]

If we are treated justly then we receive not merely certain natural benefits or goods, but also just treatment *as a distinct and irreducible object of gratitude*. And a person who is the victim of injustice suffers not merely a determinate form of natural harm, such as the wounds inflicted by torture, but also the injustice of it, which is a separate and irreducible cause of his torment. If the victim is murdered then he suffers not only the evil of death, but also the evil of having been murdered. We sometimes say that death came mercifully to those whose suffering has become unbearable, but we do not say that of the murdered dead, even if they were racked with pain and their bodies were rotting with disease. The murdered dead must be acknowledged to be victims of an evil that is not reducible to the fact that they have been unjustifiably killed. Sometimes we express it in the idea that the murdered dead cannot rest until they are avenged or until their murderers are punished.

If the unhappy dead are nothing but the dust in which they lie,
And blood not paid for blood,
There is no faith, no piety in any man.[5]

The victim enters the remorse of the one who wronged her (irreducibly) as one who was wronged. If she was betrayed, for example, then that is an irreducible dimension of the evil she suffers, whether or not she suffers any of the natural harms which are normally consequent upon betrayal. If the one who betrayed her is to see that her victim suffered the evil of betrayal, she must find it intelligible that her victim is the kind of being who can suffer that kind of evil. We will see in Chapter 9 that human beings have sometimes found it unintelligible that certain other human beings could suffer the kind of evil that determines the character of the kind of remorse I characterised in Chapter 4. We will also see that their finding it unintelligible is connected with their finding it unintelligible that those human beings are individuals in the sense in which we mean it when we speak of human beings as irreplaceable. Slave owners did not find it intelligible that they could wrong their slaves in that way because they could not find it intelligible that their slaves could suffer that kind of evil.

Remorse as the recognition of the reality of evil – evil done and evil suffered – is the recognition of evil as *sui generis*. It is fundamental amongst the ethical determinations of human individuality. The pain of remorse cannot provide a motive for an ethics of self-interest as that is usually conceived, because the self that discovers itself in remorse and the self that seeks only its reductively conceived interests are incommensurable. The explanatory power of an appeal to self-interest requires that the self which seeks the satisfaction of its interests understands itself under the descriptions that specify their 'enlightened' satisfaction. Archelaus, whom Polus presents as a counter-example to Socrates' claim that evildoers are 'miserable and pitiable', could not understand himself, his motives and his desires under Socratic redescription.[6] If he so came to understand the evil he did, Socratically, he would not learn something which could provide him with a motive, relative to the interests and desires of the man Polus described. A child has a better understanding of the fears and hopes of old age than Archelaus, Polus or Callicles have of how they would be if they understood themselves Socratically. They would have to understand that the harm they do themselves as evildoers cannot be separated as a motive from the acknowledgement of another as an absolute limit to their wills. The religious expression of the thought is that the shock of the recognition in remorse of what one has become is the shock of the acknowledgement of the sacred in ourselves and in our victims.

The point is fundamental to understanding the Dutchwoman. Her reaction is to her part in the evil done to the three she asked to leave her home. It is a reaction to the evil she was caught up in, just as the speech I gave to one of the ten is in response to the evil he is caught up in. In both cases it is essential to see that the evil suffered by those who are murdered is not simply the natural evil of an unwanted death. The distinctive character of evil – the character that prompts one to call it *sui generis* – does not merely remain with the deed or with the character of the evildoer. It spreads beyond the evildoer to the victim. The belief that the Dutchwoman overreacted is, at least in part, a consequence of a failure to see that that belief depends on a naturalistic reduction of the evil suffered by those she evicted from her home to the evil of their death, and a reduction of her remorse to a natural psychological reaction to her part in the causal story that ended in those deaths.

Attention to remorse may help one to appreciate the inadequacies of reductive naturalism. We shall see that it also exposes the inadequacies of a non-reductive naturalism, and that is a far more important lesson, but it must wait until Chapter 12. We may prepare for it by looking more closely at both forms of naturalism.

The attempt to explain the nature of morality as a system of regulative rules, the character and content of which are determined by their instrumental role in enabling us to secure certain fundamental human goods and to avoid certain fundamental human ills – ills that can be described independently of any moral conception – is an example of reductive naturalism. It is an attempt with many variations (some crude and some subtle), but its guiding idea seems to many people to be natural and obvious. Different kinds of reductive naturalism fall under that general description – certain kinds of contractual theories and certain functional accounts of the virtues, for example. Reductive naturalists claim that an understanding of the nature of morality is available to anyone with reasonable intelligence and with knowledge of the relevant facts of human nature. It does not follow that they must claim that someone who understands the nature of morality has thereby reason to be moral. Some claim this and some do not. Some say that an understanding of the nature of morality gives anyone who is rational reason to be moral. Others say that it gives reason to be moral only to those who are rational and who have relatively normal desires. Others again say that it gives reason to be moral only to those who have certain desires whose absence makes no one abnormal.[7]

Reductive naturalism has sometimes been criticised on the grounds that 'morality does not admit of external justification'. The trouble with that way of putting an important point is that the argument is about what is and what is not external to morality and, as we have just noted, a reductive naturalist need not try to justify morality if that means offering reasons which should be compelling for all who are normal and rational. Nonetheless, the impetus to reductive naturalism often betrays (especially amongst philosophers) a desire to display the relation between moral rules and dispositions on the one hand, and certain goods and evils on the other. Appreciation of that relation (they believe) will give all who have normal desires and dispositions reason to be moral under pain of irrationality. This offers, as an ideal, a morality or a 'code of living' which is rationally reconstructed from the mess of our present moral 'intuitions' in the light of the best and most complete social, psychological and biological theories of human nature. It assumes that morality is derivable from a source in such a way that someone who fails to appreciate the source and morality's derivation from it can (without begging any moral questions) be judged to be lacking the relevant powers of appreciation. Were this not so, the proposed reconstruction would lack the authority to be called 'rational' or 'informed', and would therefore lack the authority to adjudicate between seriously competing conceptions of what it is for something to be of moral concern.

Non-reductive naturalists believe that we cannot explain or display the nature of morality by appeal to what can be described independently of it. Thus, for example, they will point out that what a person will count as good and harmful is to a significant degree dependent upon his understanding of morality. Or, they will point out that the way we express our appreciation and condemnation of the virtues and vices is not reducible to a functional or instrumental construal of them. The general criticism could be put like this. An account of morality is not adequate merely because it prohibits the right things, permits the right things and shows why we praise this and condemn that; it has also to do justice to the character of our appreciation, condemnation, abhorrence and so on. To put the point cryptically: morality cannot be explained by reference to purpose because morality is the judge of all our purposes.[8] There is no end such that someone who refuses to take the only available means to it may be convicted of failing to understand the very nature of morality. Furthermore, most motives and dispositions which might plausibly be offered as displaying the nature of morality require a contrast between their genuine and counterfeit forms, which is itself ethically conditioned.

The two most common forms of reductive naturalism have been consequentialism and more recently certain instrumental accounts of the virtues. No one is a consequentialist only because she has been convinced by consequentialist theory. The world has to appear in a certain way before consequentialism can even begin to present itself as a likely candidate for its reflective clarification. To the extent that consequentialism is a theory, it is a theory about what consequentialists can take morally seriously. The fatal defect in consequentialism is not that it cannot (if it cannot) generate the right prohibitions, nor (a more recent emphasis) that it cannot relax the 'counter-intuitive' consequences that seem to follow from its (mis)construal of the impersonal character of moral thought and deliberation. It is, as we have noted in earlier chapters, that it ignores, sometimes arrogantly and sometimes merely neglectfully, the multiple determinants of our sense of what our actions morally amount to. Consequentialists, because of their one-dimensional restrictions on what is 'strictly speaking' morally perspicuous in descriptions of action and character, would make most of our appreciative moral vocabulary redundant. In the light of that, their pronouncements on what is permissible and what is not are philo-sophically peripheral to anyone who is not already very close to them – to anyone, indeed, who does not have that pre-philosophical sense of what can and cannot be taken morally seriously, that makes plausible the idea that some form of consequentialism may turn out to be right. I would intend what I have already said about remorse to go some way towards showing that. In later chapters I will speak of our relation to the past, of a certain understanding of the unity of a person's life, that consequentialism can make no sense of.

Elizabeth Anscombe wrote a very influential paper in which she argued that much of the talk of 'obligation' and of a moral sense of 'ought' idled in the absence of a religiously underwritten moral law that gave those notions sense.[9] She suggested that a secular moral philosophy should turn from its barren preoccupation with such modalities to a more substantial and fertile concern with the virtues and their relation to human flourishing. She suggested that we might learn from Aristotle. Many philosophers have taken her advice. Contemporary moral philosophy is marked by an

81

Aristotelian revival, not only amongst scholars, but also amongst moral philosophers generally, some of whom actually write as Aristotelians or as neo-Aristotelians. The same cannot be said for Plato: Greek scholars do not really take him seriously (few of them write as living Platonists or neo-Platonists) and he is generally looked upon as a muddled pre-Aristotelian. There are one or two exceptions. Iris Murdoch and R. F. Holland, for example, write about Plato without condescension; they write, if not actually as Platonists, then as philosophers in whom Platonic ideas are alive, and find new forms of expression.[10] But they are outside the mainstream of the subject and they have not influenced the scholars.

Peter Geach said that we need the virtues 'as bees need their stings'.[11] It should not be controversial that human beings need at least some of the virtues. We need, for example, courage. But as Geach forcefully says himself, we need it, amongst other reasons, so that we will not be led into evil through cowardice. It may be granted that any normal human being needs courage, whatever her projects and hopes may be, if she is not to go merely *wishfully* through life, if she is not to be deflected from *whatever* projects she may have because of her cowardice. She will also need temperance and some degree of truthfulness. These are important facts about human life. But it is also true and equally important that there are dimensions to our appreciation of the virtues which are not reducible to that kind of functional construal of them. To take just Aristotle as an example. He praised certain forms of courage as noble and certain forms of intemperance as swinish. Our sense of the value of courage, even if it is necessarily conditioned by the fact that we need it, is not reducible to the fact that we need it, whatever we say we need it for. Courage is something we value, if not in ways independent of its instrumental relations, then in ways not reducible to them either. The same may be said of the other virtues. The important question is not whether we need them to achieve ends which can be described without reference to them (for we do). The important question is how far our acknowledgement of our need of them will take us in understanding their nature.

Philosophers who have been sympathetic to teleological construals of morality along Aristotelian lines have usually argued several things. First, that Aristotle was right to see an intimate connection between the notions of a good person, of that person's good and of the good for human beings. Secondly, that the connection is of a teleological kind that will display the rationality of moral judgements and practices when they are seen in this light. The accounts have mostly been reductive, focusing on the virtues as means to independently identifiable goods. The subtlest attempt has been by Alasdair MacIntyre who hopes to argue for a non-reductive teleology of the virtues which is canonically legitimated and, at certain points, discursively underwritten as a requirement for any sound account of the self and of action.[12] But just because of these foundationalist aspirations, his account often turns out to be reductive after all. To take just one example. He gives the 'making and sustaining of family life' as an example of what he calls (technically) a 'practice'.[13] Speaking of the virtues in Homeric society he says: 'My household's fidelity is the basic guarantee of its unity. So in women, who constitute the crucial relationships within the household, fidelity is a key virtue.'[14]

Fidelity is needed for the unity of the household. But why? There are two sorts of answer. The first appeals to the natural consequences of infidelity – jealousy, most obviously – which would be destructive of the household. It is the sort of answer that invites questions such as: 'How natural are these destructive passions?' and 'Might they not be overcome?' It invites empirical study of other cultures in an effort to determine how natural certain feelings and dispositions are to human beings. The second answer depends upon one seeing fidelity as an ideal in whose light our sense of sexuality, and the requirements we think are internal to it, is transformed. These requirements, which are thought to be internal to sexuality and to offer a deepened perspective on it, will depend upon considerations relevant to the first answer, but they are not reducible to them – just as marriage is conditioned by certain natural dispositions, but is not reducible to them because they are transformed under the couple's understanding and responses to a vow. A marriage understood in the light of such a conception of a requirement to fidelity can only jokingly be described as a 'cooperative human activity through which goods internal to that form of activity are realised in the course of trying to achieve those standards of excellence which are appropriate to, and partially definitive of, that form of activity, with the result that human powers to achieve excellence ... are systematically extended'.[15]

The first answer to why infidelity should be a threat to the household gives clear point to the teleological emphasis – to the idea that fidelity is prized as a virtue because of its functional role. What about the second answer? Infidelity, understood in that way, may also lead to the break up of a household but it does not provide the same point for a teleological emphasis, because although certain functional notions may be internal to it, the conception of fidelity expressed in it is not reducible to them. The modal expressions of such requirements to fidelity as are expressed in the second conception are characteristically non-teleological. Couples are not faithful in that way *for* anything, and the pain which infidelity causes and which may drive them to separate cannot be characterised independently of a sense of betrayal whose character is conditioned by those requirements. The fact that the functional considerations which are relevant to the first answer are necessary to an adequate account of the conception of fidelity expressed in the second, even though it is not reducible to them, should alert us to why it is misleading to say that, according to the second conception, fidelity is valued *for its own sake*, or for its *intrinsic value*. MacIntyre says (and he is by no means alone in thinking this sort of thing) that, 'when teleology, whether Aristotelian or Christian, is abandoned, there is always a tendency to substitute for it some version of Stoicism. The virtues are now not to be practised for the sake of some good other, or more than, the practice of the virtues itself.'[16] But that, I hope, is exactly what my discussion reveals to be a misunderstanding, one which, I suspect, tempts people into reductivism. One could put my point about the conception of fidelity expressed in the second answer this way. *It is not valued for its own sake; it is valued in a way that is not reducible to its inexpungeable teleological dimensions.*

A connection between morality and human needs, as they are understood independently of any conception of morality, seems necessary if morality is to be serious. Many people believe that the connection must be instrumental – that morality must serve our needs. That thought might be expressed in the slogan that morality is made for human beings rather than human beings for morality. It is a natural thought which invites (although it does not require) the further thought that morality has been distorted into an oppressive institution which is partly sustained by the belief that morality is *sui generis*. From a philosophical perspective, morality conceived as *sui generis* might appear to someone who thinks this way to be a gratuitous interloper into human affairs. From a sociological or psychological perspective the idea that it is *sui generis* may be seen as a rationalisation in aid of those who have a stake in the oppressive character of the institution. Someone who is inclined to such a view will say that we may at least free our minds of such mystification if we remember that morality should be our servant.

Artefacts are made for us rather than we for artefacts, but that should not prompt a reductive conception of craftsmanship and of our appreciation of its products, even though we are sometimes the victims of our own products. A variant of reductivism has recently been inspired by the thought that morality may be compared to a craft, and the idea has been expressed in the reductive account of the virtues I have already outlined. But reflection on craftsmanship should teach an anti-reductive lesson.

Many crafts have a constitutive instrumental or teleological grammar – those that are concerned with the construction of functional artefacts. If a cabinet-maker makes a table, then it had better stand up and meet all the other functional requirements for a table. But if only functional criteria determine his sense of whether he has built a table well or badly, then he is not a craftsman in the sense in which we speak when we praise furniture as 'craftsman-made' meaning that it has been given a certain kind of attention. We distinguish between someone who is merely skilled, even if superbly skilled, and someone who is a craftsman. A cabinet-maker who is also a craftsman will, generally, be horrified at the suggestion that he use screws to secure joints even if the objection to using them has little functional relevance, and within limits, even if it is counter-functional. He will think of it as a kind of violation of his materials, for if he is a craftsman he will care for the wood in ways that are not reducible to its functional properties, although his concern cannot be entirely independent of functional considerations either. The concerns, the modes of appreciation, which are internal to craftsmanship will count for nothing if the table collapses.

85

It makes sense for a craftsman to say that an entire age has lost the understanding of what it is to make furniture, meaning not that furniture-makers do not possess the relevant skills, but that the difference between a skilled carpenter and a craftsman does not matter to them or to their customers. But that would make no sense if the criteria for what it is to make furniture well were purely functional. It makes no sense to say that an entire age has lost an understanding of what it is to be a dustman (although it makes sense to say that an entire age has lost an understanding of why it matters to do even such humble jobs well). Craftsmen, like all whose self-understanding is conditioned by their having a *vocation*, are engaged in a limitless process of self-exploration through an exploration of what they do. What they are and what they do come together in the concept, 'what it is to be an X' (a craftsman, a nurse or a teacher, for example). Certain forms of the question 'What is it to be an X?' depend upon a kind of contrast between appearance and reality that allows for the idea of an understanding which may deepen without limit. Not all concepts are like that and not all concepts that invite a contrast between appearance and reality are like that. Concepts whose constitutive grammar is purely functional (the concept of a dustman, for example) are relatively transparent, and even though some are very complex, their complexity is finite and of a sort that enables us to expect that opinion on what it is to be such an X will converge amongst competent inquirers. The concept of what it is to be a craftsman is not like that, nor are moral concepts, which is perhaps why Aurel Kolnai said that 'a feature of resistant opacity actually belongs to the essence of moral emphasis'.[17] I discuss the matter again in Chapter 15.

Philosophers have sometimes sought to understand the virtues by analogy with crafts, but they have thought of crafts merely as skills. Terence Irwin says that Socrates thought that virtue was a craft, but he means that Socrates thought it was a skill, that Socrates believed that the virtues were means to an independently characterisable end – *eudaimonia*.[18] Aristotle has also been understood in this way. Later I shall argue that neither Socrates nor Aristotle thought this. In terms of the contrasts that I have been drawing, the idea that virtue is a skill is a reductive-naturalist idea, whereas the idea that virtue is, or might be, clarified by analogy with a craft is not.

The analogy with crafts, properly understood, would suggest that virtue is irreducible to purpose, while at the same time implying a necessary relation to it. That I think is a more plausible understanding of virtue – one that brings with it a better understanding of practical wisdom than does the analogy with skills. Wisdom, as distinct from expertise, requires our understanding to deepen in ways which it makes no sense to require of someone who need only discover what the function of something is. It suggests a better understanding of the importance of the past and of tradition, and, therefore, a much more plausible understanding of moral education.[19] But I will not focus on these now. My main point is to suggest that an analogy with crafts may reveal that morality may be necessarily and instrumentally related to human needs without being wholly explicable by reference to them.

Not all the crafts are functional, and not all of those that are functional relate to human need. Nonetheless some do, and they have a robustness that is internal to their dignity. What is related to human need is never trivial, even though some of it does not bear too much talking about. The Xenophonic Socrates may be vulgar, but he is not vulgar only because he sees dignity in what is related to necessity. Some things lose their beauty if they are functionally deficient and become, instead, ridiculous. A beautifully crafted table that will not stand up properly is an example. An aesthetic dimension marks much of our appreciative sense of the virtues, but that does not mean that it overlays the moral as an element that is extractable and relatively frivolous by comparison with the aspects of the virtues that are functionally related to human need. The thought that if morality has a dimension which is *sui generis*, then it is a relatively frivolous aesthetic dimension or, at least, a personal, supererogatory dimension, is another reason why some people are inclined to reductive accounts of morality, even if they allow for a non-reductive account of something they believe to be less serious than morality – ideals, for example.

There is a contrast between the aesthetic and the moral, but it is not absolute. Aristotelian virtue has an ineradicably aesthetic dimension. Aristotle believed that a good human life was lived in the enjoyment of the deserved esteem of one's peers. He believed that to be not merely one of life's goods, but its chief good. That is evident if we read him unprejudiced by a conception of morality that is deeply influenced by Christianity. The distance between his understanding of the virtues, which he believed to be constitutive of a well-lived and 'happy' human life, and ours is well brought out in his remarks on friendship. He considers whether it is the highest expression of friendship to lay down one's life for a friend and rejects it in favour of the thought that it is finer to allow our friends to lay down their lives for us, for in such a case we get only life, whereas they get a shining and glorious deed.[20] The unashamed enjoyment of our noble deeds and, if we are lucky, of a life blessed with many such deeds, is alien to that part of ourselves which is influenced by a Christian understanding, not of nobility, but of Goodness – that is, the kind of Goodness that invites a capital 'G'. It is a part of ourselves that finds fine expression in the story of St Jerome who, called to an appointment with Jesus, made himself late by stopping to help a stranger free his cart from the mud in which it had sunk. The point, of course, is that that was his appointment with Jesus. Goodness, as we understand it, cannot be achieved by pursuing it directly. The surest way to ensure that our deeds are not good is to do them for the sake of being or doing good. That observation is commonplace, but it is not, as seems often to be thought, adequately captured in the injunction that a virtuous deed must be done for its own sake or in the claim that virtue is its own reward.

Aristotle said that virtuous deeds must be done for their own sake, but for him that meant they must be done out of love for their fineness, which he further specified as their nobility. His point was not that it is permissible to exploit the needs of others as opportunities for noble action, but rather, that the pleasurable appreciation of the nobility of our deeds, even in their performance, is no obstacle to their virtue but is, indeed, internal to that complex motive which he called 'doing them for their own sake'. The propriety of this kind of complex motivation is acknowledged in Christian-influenced morality only in the case of evildoing, when we must refrain from harming someone, not only on the account of the harm they will suffer, but also on account of its evil, which is something suffered in addition (though differently) by both the evildoer and his victim. Someone who is murdered suffers not only the natural evil of death but also the evil of having been murdered, and the murderer suffers the evil of becoming an evildoer. Both good and evil are, according to this conception, *sui generis*, but they are not symmetrical. We must refrain from harming someone because of an appreciation of the evil we do them, but we cannot help someone because of an appreciation of the goodness our deed will display.[21]

According to the conception of virtue and its place in human life which I have claimed is Aristotle's, it is of the essence of virtue that it appear (be manifest) to those who are worthy to judge and honour it. That does not mean that we may act for the appearance rather than the reality of the virtue. Rather its *reality as a virtue* whose exercise is partly constitutive of a good human life lies (in critical part) in the fact that it illuminates that life as one deserving of public honour. It is not a base conception of virtue. It expresses the uncoy enjoyment of an uncorrupted worldliness in which the public expression of the esteem of our peers and our enjoyment of it are not only permissible, but to be pursued as constitutive of the good life.

I remarked earlier on the difference between an Aristotelian conception of what it is to do a virtuous deed for its own sake and the conception familiar to us from (at least) Christianity, according to which a virtuous deed must be done for its own sake but in a way that excludes the actor's delight in its virtue. We can see the character of this difference more clearly, and we will better understand the complex relation between the moral and the aesthetic, if we remember that, for Aristotle, an appreciation of the fineness of a virtuous deed is, at its highest, connected with its nobility, and if we note Ackrill's perceptive observation that 'beauty' would not be the right word to capture the aesthetic dimension of fine Aristotelian deeds.[22] We have, however, a conception of morality according to which goodness rather than nobility is the most important concept, and we connect this, quite naturally, with beauty. Simone Weil has rightly said that we are often struck by the beauty of saintly deeds.[23] That is partly because of their purity, which is of a kind that is interdependent with the concept of Goodness.

Virtue and Goodness are connected in complex ways with necessity. If that connection becomes broken or too attenuated, then the aesthetic dimension of our appreciative vocabulary threatens to lapse into the 'merely aesthetic', into a kind of 'practical' aestheticism. Courage, for example, ceases to be seen as a virtue if exercised in what are believed to be frivolous or, at least, unnecessary exploits. For some, mountaineering is an example. The concept of goodness is closely tied to need, to being responsive to the needs of others. Simone Weil went so far as to say that all obligation is tied to need. That is to link two notions of necessity – moral necessity and the necessity of need. Whether or not one wishes to go so far, it seems to me she is clearly right in thinking that moral necessity is (conceptually) tied (not always directly) to what is inescapably serious in life. Hence the importance of the fact that we *need* the virtues. Not everything that is properly called morally serious is illuminatingly described as a need, not even as a need of the soul. But something which was indifferent to substantially identified human needs would not be called a morality. Human needs are not merely contingently amongst the many objects of moral response. Morality deepens our sense of them.

I do not wish to say that teleological construals of the relation between the seriousness of virtue or morality and human needs are either complete in their expression of the many dimensions of this relation, or adequate to the deepest of them. Simone Weil, for example, thought the relation between moral necessity ('I cannot' or 'I must' do such and such) and the necessity of need to which moral necessity is responsive is corrupted by teleological construal. I have tried to suggest what might be fruitful in the analogy between virtue and certain crafts. Of course, virtue is not a craft, for many reasons which Plato, amongst others, revealed. I have merely tried to show that the analogy has point.

To say that morality is *sui generis* is not to say anything mysterious, not, at any rate, if we mean that it is irreducible to modes of teleological relation (purpose, function, means, etc.) to things characterised independently of morality. Given the place of fear in human life, it is not hard to see why certain instances of courage should be thought noble rather than merely useful. In some sense it must be true that we will understand morality by *placing* it in a proper understanding of the human condition and of human nature. But it is not true that we can make rational sense of morality only if that placing is causal or teleological and with reductive and foundationalist aspirations.

These points are relatively simple and obvious, and they seem to me to be quite decisive against reductivist accounts in ethics. Why then do such accounts persist? Why is there a more pervasive tendency towards reductivism in ethics than elsewhere?

There is no one answer to that question. The impulse to reductivism has more than one source. One that should not be underestimated is the sheer incapacity to acknowledge something new unless as an explanatorily reducible variant of the old, which, of course, is precisely not to acknowledge something new. Hannah Arendt has shown how often this occurs in politics.[24] It can be connected, as Plato often pointed out, with the self-congratulatory thought that we have 'seen through things'. Thrasymachus is like this. So is Polus. Plato depicted them as stuck at the second stage of the ascent from his famous cave. They are the ones who, freed from the chains that constrained them to look in only one direction at the shadow play on the cave wall, realised that the shadows were caused by a puppeteer who danced his puppets in front of a great fire. So delighted were they with this discovery and the pleasures of their condescension, that they went no further in an exploration of what was 'reality' and what was 'mere appearance'. The 'shadows' represented, amongst other things, ethically untransformed desires and dispositions, and Plato's point was that only a limited account could be given *even of them* in the absence of an appreciation of the ethical as something *sui generis*. Nietzsche comes to mind. His brilliant account of the pathologies of what he called a 'slave morality' can only be appreciated for what it is, namely an account of the pathologies of certain Christian virtues, if we recognise what he did not – that corruptions of, for example, remorse, are indeed *corruptions* of it.[25]

A suspicion of morality that invites a reductive characterisation of it may be banal or it may be serious. Thrasymachus represents the banal version. The serious version focuses on the unsavoury moralism we have already noted in Chapter 4 and which has seemed, to some, to be so much a part of morality that they have actually claimed it to be part of the concept of morality. Certain ways of connecting morality and praise and blame are forms of the corruption we have already noted. The idea that moral judgements must be universalised is another.

We must distinguish two aspects of the claim that moral judgements must be universalised. One is right and trivial. The other is wrong and can be offensive. It is right but trivial to say that if a

91

person judges that an action by a certain kind of person in a certain kind of situation would be cowardly, courageous, squalid or wicked, then he must judge the same for any other person of the same kind who is in relevantly the same situation. That is merely the requirement that we be consistent in our judgements. But it may be wrong and offensive to say that if a person judges in a particular situation that he ought to do such and such, then he is committed to judging that anyone relevantly like him in a relevantly similar situation ought to do the same. It may be offensive because it tells us that we ought, sometimes, to be presumptuous, for it is sometimes presumptuous even to *think* that another person ought to do something, even though we are quite sure what we ought to do if we were in their situation. Richard Hare, who claimed that it was merely a logical point, a point, indeed, about the meaning of moral words, that we were required to universalise our judgements about what we (morally) ought to do, said that, although it might be offensive to tell someone that he ought to do such and such, it is not offensive to *think* it.[26] But thinking something may be a concrete act against someone just as saying something may be. In that respect, thinking that everyone ought in certain circumstances to do such and such is quite unlike thinking that because one believes p to be true, one must think that anyone who believes not p is mistaken. As Hampshire once put it, there is a weak normative implication in forming a belief. That is merely a logical feature of belief. To express one's acknowledgement of it is not arrogant.[27] And clearly, a person's mere expression of the implications of the fact that she believes something – that others ought also to believe it – does not invite moral judgement.

Part of the problem is an expression of the tendency to think that a moral judgement just *is* a judgement that something ought or ought not to be done. If a person sees a situation in a moral light then she must see a relevantly similar situation in a moral light, indeed in the same moral light under pain of inconsistency. And if to see a situation in a moral light is to see it as one in which a person ought/ ought not to do something, then we must think that a similar person in a similar situation ought/ought not to do the same thing. Did I not concede as much earlier? Indeed, did I not say that it was trivially true?

It is true that if we judge that we would be doing evil in certain circumstances, then we must judge that anyone like ourselves in relevantly similar circumstances would also be doing evil. But it does not follow that we must judge that he ought not to do it. If someone judges that a person is contemplating doing something evil it does not follow that he must judge that that person ought not to do it. It is true that if we judge that someone is contemplating evil then we cannot be indifferent to it. That is part of Hare's point. It is part of the point that moral judgements are essentially practical. Hare (like many others) takes the essential practical element of moral judgements to be an imperative which is naturally, and best, expressed in a judgement about what ought to be done. But all that is required to satisfy the conceptual point (if it is one) that moral judgements are essentially practical is that someone who makes a moral judgement must not be indifferent to what she judges. Moral judgements must claim the person who makes them in serious moral response, *but the modal expression of those responses may be diverse.* And I would say they must be diverse because they are different and concrete acts in relation to those who are judged. If I say that what you are proposing is wicked, then I claim you and am claimed myself, in serious response to that judgement. What that response is, however, will depend on the circumstances. I might say that you ought not to do it, or I might think that presumptuous. I might *think* that you ought not to do it, but not feel that I can say that you ought not. Or, I might judge that in this situation, even to think it is presumptuous. I might fervently *hope* that you will not do it, and that would be a moral hope because of its object, and because I judge that to be all that is morally possible between us on this matter on this occasion. The modalities in which we express our judgements on, or of, what others have done or would be doing are themselves the expression of our moral relations to them, and as such they are judged according to the circumstances.

There are situations in which the modal implications of our judgements are conditional upon people recognising what they do not yet recognise. Those situations are of at least two kinds: ones in which the person is within epistemic reach of the modal claim, and ones in which she is not. If we are speaking to a friend who is morally serious, but who, for some reason does not acknowledge the moral descriptions under which her action falls, then it is not idle to say that she ought to acknowledge the descriptions and the modal claims internal to them. To say of Hitler, however, that he ought not to have murdered the Jews and others strikes me as fatuous. He is, and was at the time, beyond the epistemic reach of such a remark. It therefore idles in much the same way that thoughts or statements that a person ought to do something idle if that person lacks the relevant interests or desires. But it is not fatuous to say that Hitler did evil.

What are the modal implications of the judgement that Hitler did evil? At the time they might have found expression in the realisation that he had to be stopped. If they did, then they would also find expression in the realisation that he could not be stopped as though he were not fully a human being. If someone judged at the time that Hitler should be killed if possible, then he must also judge that even Hitler (morally) could not be shot in the spirit of ridding the world of vermin. And so on. There may also be the implication that Hitler could only understand himself under that last judgement, and that if he understood himself under it, then he could not continue in what he did. I do not say that anyone must make those judgements if she judges that Hitler and his deeds were evil. I offer them as examples which satisfy the requirement that a moral judgement which is seriously made cannot be one to which the person who makes it is indifferent. But nothing I have said commits me to saying that Hitler ought not to have done what he did. Even less would it commit me to saying, when he was alive, that he ought not to do the evil he did.

There are other and deeper objections to the idea that moral judgements must be universalised, and I shall discuss them in later chapters. My concern here is to display the moral objections to it – to reveal why the focus on 'ought' as the only appropriate modal expression of moral response can lead, even if unwittingly, to the identification of morality with moralism. It is unfortunate that a philosophical thesis about the nature of morality, a thesis which mistakenly but sincerely claimed to be only a logical thesis, should have coincided with the unpleasant predilection we human beings have to tell others what they ought to do. We should, therefore, not be surprised if it played its part in making people suspicious of morality and in tempting them into reductive accounts of it, based, in part, on the realisation that what passed as moral seriousness, and what philosophy endorsed as belonging to the essence of moral seriousness, was in fact the rationalisation of an unpleasant part of our nature.

7

Modalities

It seems mere common sense to believe that the reason we ought not to do something brutish or cruel or wicked is *because* it is cruel, brutish, wicked, etc., and that the character of that 'ought' is given by its connection with the concepts of wickedness, cruelty, etc. In other words, it seems mere common sense to believe that moral modalities are given their character by those descriptions that reveal the moral character of an action. If there is a need to assert what seems to be merely common sense it is because some philosophers have said that for something to be wicked or brutish or treacherous and so on, just *is* for it to be something that (morally) ought not to be done.

There are a number of issues here. We shall see that the belief I described as mere common sense is problematical – that the 'because' in we ought not to do it 'because it is cruel, brutish, wicked, etc.' is problematical, even though there is point in asserting it against those who say that for something to be cruel or brutish just is for it to be something that ought not to be done. That (second) view of what it is for something to be a moral matter encourages philosophers to think that philosophical thinking is a matter of extracting, clarifying and ordering *principles* from the confusion of ordinary practice.

The idea that morality is captured in principles which state what we ought to do, and that that 'ought' is of a special kind, is classically captured in Kant's distinction between hypothetical and categorical imperatives.[1] It is a distinction that has been much criticised, but a number of issues are often run together which need to be distinguished.[2] There is a question about the role of reason, of whether someone who fails to acknowledge that moral requirements are binding upon him is thereby irrational. There is a question about the role of knowledge or understanding, of whether a person who fails to acknowledge that moral requirements are binding upon him and fails to acknowledge the moral character of his deeds lacks knowledge or understanding of what he does. There is a question about agency, of whether every intentional action must have a pre-existing and independently identifiable desire as part of its cause. There is a question of whether it is idle to say of someone who says that he cares not a fig for morality that, even so, there are things he morally ought to do. There is a question about how thin the moral subject can be in order for it to be able to understand what it is for something to be a moral requirement. There is the question whether morality is *sui generis*. All these questions arise when one thinks about the contrast between hypothetical and categorical imperatives, but they are distinguishable and seem to allow for different combinations of answers.

We might say, for example, that those who do evil do not *understand* what they do, without thinking that they are, thereby, *irrational*. We might say that understanding is sufficient for action and thus deny that all intentional actions require some desire which is part of their cause, but not think that kind of understanding is available to a creature without desires. (We might think that certain natural affective dispositions of human beings are internal to what it is for something to be a moral matter and perhaps, also, in the individual case, to its understanding.) We might think that morality is *sui generis*, but also that moral action is motivated by desire transformed by an understanding of its *sui generis* character. (Plato seemed to think this.) We might agree that it is idle to say that a person ought to act according to moral requirements even though he cares not a fig for them, but not think that is because (in some non-trivial sense) the claim that he ought to fails to engage with his desires or interests. We might accept that morality is *sui generis* without thinking that the moral modalities (ought, must, cannot, etc.) are *sui generis*. We might acknowledge that an action was motivated by feeling while denying the Humean account of this. (We might, for example, say that an action which was motivated solely by the recognition that a person needed help was an act of pity of an especially pure kind, and find point in distinguishing it from an act motivated by a sense of duty and any other self-consciously moral motive.) And there are other possibilities.

The questions that concern me in this chapter are whether the modal expressions that express the result of moral deliberation are different in moral contexts than in others, and what the connection is between them and those descriptions that inform our sense of the moral character of what we did and which allow for an elaboration of the kind I said was unavailable to Kantians and consequentialists. The difficulty is that such elaborations – the kind that are forthcoming in a deepened sense of what we did as that may appear to us in remorse, for example – seem to tilt in a naturalistic direction. In Chapter 3 I argued that the concept of a fellow mortal allowed for an elaboration which revealed the seriousness of what was at stake in Falstaff's rebuke to the Prince in a way that Donagan's Kantian paraphrase did not. But that raises the question of how such descriptions may be elaborated in ways which deepen our understanding of the kind of seriousness internal to morality, while being, at the same time, elaborations of our sense of morality as something *sui generis*. They appear, more naturally, to invite deepening by a naturalistic moral psychology.

One way of expressing, in a more general way, what lies behind the contrast between categorical and hypothetical imperatives is to say that human beings are a limit to one another's wills as nothing else in nature is. That seems to focus on modalities operative on the will – 'ought', of course, but also other expressions of necessity and impossibility. Philosophers have only recently been interested in modalities of necessity and impossibility as they occur in moral contexts because they had previously thought them to be merely colloquial, loose and misleading expressions of judgements about what (morally) *ought* to be done. The situation has recently reversed somewhat. Philosophers have argued that the emphasis on 'ought' is misleading, and Bernard Williams has suggested that the notion of the categorical imperative is a distortion of certain forms of practical necessity – those that 'go all the way down' (by which he means those which are conditioned by desires and dispositions which are constitutive of our sense of who we are).[3]

I have already reported Williams as saying that if a person cares for some others, if he occasionally helps others because they need help, then even if he does so only when he is so inclined, the movement from where he is to a serious moral concern for others, is not 'a discontinuous step onto something quite different, the "moral plane"'. There are many different issues here. One is whether he must move to a different understanding of what he does and fails to do, and, with that and through it, to a different understanding of what a human being is. If so, is the acquisition of that movement on to 'something quite different, the "moral plane"'? I have suggested that yes is the answer to both questions. I argued, in effect, that if he wants to help another, then he must, if his concern is to be a moral concern, see the other as, amongst other things, an intelligible object of his remorse.

The primary question is not whether he must move from *wanting* to help to judging that he *ought* to help, but how he must see the person he wants to help. The question of whether, on the one hand, he must move to thinking that he ought to help or whether, on the other, his desires must be transformed by a content irreducible to his previous contents is a question of secondary importance. For a slave owner, for example, it is not a matter of him 'extending his sympathies', nor of him coming to see that there are things he ought or ought not to do, but of him *seeing his slaves as the intelligible objects of certain kinds of sympathies*. It is therefore not necessary that the movement from where an amoralist is to where he would be if he showed serious moral concern for others requires that his motivations appear to him in a distinctive and self-conscious moral idiom. He need not move from wanting to help others to seeing that he *morally ought* to help others. But there is a closely related question I did not discuss, which is whether the modalities operative on his will (if he says, for example, that there was nothing else he could do) must, nonetheless, be *sui generis* if what he does in helping another is expressive of his moral understanding.

I said earlier that philosophers have recently been interested in the modalities of necessity and impossibility as they occur in moral contexts – in 'must' and 'cannot', for example. It is easy to see why they have traditionally been suspicious of such expressions. First, it seems plainly false, in those situations where a person says that he (morally) must or cannot do something, that that action is literally necessary or impossible for him. Secondly, because what is impossible for me may be possible for you, such expressions seem to personalise morality in illegitimate ways.

Expressions of moral possibility and impossibility *do* most naturally take a primarily personal rather than impersonal form. That is because of the irreducibly personal character of moral deliberation, and also because of the personal character of the kind of thinking which is directed towards a deepened moral understanding of those descriptions of action and character whose grammar is interdependent with the grammar of moral deliberation. In this chapter I will argue the first point. I argue the second in Chapter 14.

Consider this quotation from Thomas Nagel, in which he expresses, almost to perfection, a common and mistaken view about the nature of moral deliberation.

> The ordinary process of deliberation, aimed at finding out what I have reason to do, assumes that the question has an answer. And in difficult cases especially, deliberation is often accompanied by the belief that I might not *arrive* at that answer. I do not assume that the correct answer is just whatever will result or has resulted from the consistent application of deliberative methods – even assuming perfect information about the facts. In deliberation we are trying to arrive at conclusions that are correct in virtue of something *independent* of our arriving at them. If we arrive at a conclusion, we believe that it would have been correct even if we *hadn't* arrived at it. And we can also acknowledge that we might be wrong, since the process of reasoning doesn't guarantee the result. So the pursuit of an objective account of practical reason has its basis in the realist claims of ordinary practical reasoning.[4]

The instructive thing about this passage is that Nagel does not realise that he has achieved nothing in it. He does not see that his persistent italicisation suggests his conclusion only because it begs it, and he does not see it because the philosophical tradition has established a certain tone for reading those words, when they are italicised in such a context (one might call it the tone of *prima facie* realism). It is not surprising, therefore, that they seem to Nagel to offer 'phenomenological' support to his conclusion. If we read the passage without philosophical prejudice, then what he succeeds in saying is unremarkable, apart from when he says that we do 'not assume that the correct answer is just whatever will result or has resulted from the consistent application of deliberative methods', for although there is an unexceptional reading of this (the fact that I have been careful in coming to an answer is not what we mean in calling it a correct answer), it is clear that Nagel has in mind a version of philosophical 'anti-realism'. Very likely it is what he and others have called 'Wittgensteinian Idealism'.

An innocent reading of the passage no more suggests anti-realism than it does realism. Both are philosophical theories of the significance of things that no one would deny – that I may admit that you were right and that I was wrong, or that my arriving at a conclusion, however carefully, is not what makes it right. But if someone expresses that last truism as does Nagel – 'In deliberation we are trying to arrive at conclusions that are correct in virtue of something *independent* of our arriving at them' – then he is not registering the 'claims of ordinary practical reasoning', but is instead inviting his reader into a metaphysical reading of 'we are trying to arrive at conclusions that are correct in virtue of something independent of our arriving at them', which has been encouraged by his italicisation of 'independent' and by the metaphysical reflex that the phrase 'in virtue of' usually triggers in such contexts. Rush Rhees protested against this kind of distortion when he said, 'Of course there are *discussions* on moral questions. And I may say, I wish to God I could see what I ought to do – or "I wish I knew whether the decision I have taken was right". But this does not mean that in some sense the answer is already settled (as in the case of a crime committed) and that my difficulty is to *find* it.'[5]

Nagel writes of deliberation in general. He seems to believe that the sense in which 'I might not arrive at (an) answer' is the same whether I am deliberating about which is the safest route off the mountain or whether I am wondering if I can leave my injured companion on the mountain to fend for himself. He thinks that moral deliberation is simply deliberation with a moral subject-matter, that its being *moral* deliberation is external to its character as deliberation. The 'difficulty' of which he speaks is then (as Rhees

101

says it must be for someone who thinks this way) the difficulty of tracking down the right answer, of finding it. Or, more precisely, that is what Nagel believes to be the 'cognitive' dimension of the difficulty. Presumably he will acknowledge that the fact that it is a moral difficulty will add a dramatic psychological dimension to it, as does the likelihood of dying if one takes the wrong route off the mountain. Nagel holds constant the notions of a problem, of a deliberative difficulty, of a correct solution, across a general conception of practical reasoning. He assumes that their application in moral deliberation leaves their 'cognitive' grammar unaffected. He is not unusual in this respect.

If I deliberate about which is the safest route off the mountain, then I think about which route someone (like myself) should take in these circumstances. According to Nagel, if I deliberate about whether to leave my companion to fend for himself, then I think about what one (like myself) should do in these circumstances. In both cases I enter my thought, in the first instance as a datum (someone with such and such characteristics), and in the second instance (logically) trivially as the one who must act when thought has delivered its result. I say 'logically trivially' because although Nagel would acknowledge that it is emotionally significant to me that I am on the mountain and must act, rather than in my study plotting routes on a map, and that it is I, rather than someone else, who must find his way off the mountain, that does not affect his sense of the logical character of deliberative reasoning. For a 'logician' of practical reasoning, the fact that it is a particular individual who must act is irrelevant. Practical reasoning, insofar as it is *reasoning*, is essentially impersonal. In contemporary philosophy this is most transparently at work in decision theory which depends upon the idea of a perfectly rational agent in whom practical reason works without error.

When one first looks at it, it seems as though such an account must be right, for when I deliberate I am concerned that my action be of a *kind* appropriate to my situation and to my aims. Personal facts about myself are often relevant to determining the kind of situation I am in and the kind of action that would count as a solution, but these facts too are facts of a certain kind. To deliberate, then, is to think about what kind of action I, being a kind of agent, should perform in this kind of circumstance; because, as was said earlier, deliberation is about which action is appropriate to the problem. It is difficult to see how we can make sense of the concept of an *appropriate* action unless we link it to kinds of agents in kinds of situations. This conception of practical reasoning is common to both 'cognitivist' and 'non-cognitivist' accounts of ethics. For a non-cognitivist, my 'freely chosen principles' are a fact determining the kind of agent I am.

Compelling though this conception may be, it is seriously mistaken, at least in its application to ethics. If I am deliberating about which is the best route off the mountain and I fail to arrive at an answer, I can pass the problem over to my partner. It is only accidentally my problem. If I am deliberating about what morally to do, then I cannot pass my problem over to anyone else. It is non-accidentally and inescapably mine. I may seek and act upon moral advice, and I may say that I received the 'right' or 'true' advice, but seeking advice on a moral problem is quite different from seeking advice on what are normally called 'practical problems'. If I seek your advice on which is the best route off the mountain, then the nature of what I do in asking for it, and what you do in giving it, is conditioned by the fact that I may hand the problem over to you completely (perhaps you are better at it, or perhaps I have lost my nerve), by the fact that I may consult manuals and by other such familiar facts. But if I must make a moral decision by Monday, I cannot come to you on Friday evening, plead that I have little time over the weekend to think about it, and ask you, a rational and informed agent and a professor of ethics to boot, to try to have a solution, or at least a range of options, no later than first thing on Monday morning.

Such differences are not external features of moral problems on the one hand, and practical problems on the other. They condition what we mean by a problem, by a solution, and thus by *thinking*, in the one case and in the other. The fact that there can be no manual of morals, no theory of its practice which plays the same role as does mountaineering theory to mountaineering practice, no quiz shows or no whizz kids of moral dilemmas and no Nobel Laureates in Morality, is intrinsic to our understanding of what it is to have a moral problem and what it is to think about it. We often express this by saying that moral problems are personal.

What I have said so far is no more than a reminder of things that make up our common wisdom about morality. The personal character of remorse after the deed (as I described it in Chapter 4) and the personal character of the problem before the deed are internal to our sense of the seriousness of morality. We cannot give an account of the *kind* of seriousness it has without reference to its personal character, which means that we cannot account for the *kind of difficulty* we find in moral deliberation without reference to its personal character.

Nonetheless, it is understandable that Nagel should have thought that he was characterising how moral deliberation naturally appears to the person who is deliberating – that he was giving a kind of phenomenology of deliberation. And it is easy to see why reflection seems to endorse the deliverances of such a phenomenology if we recall the remark I made earlier – that we cannot pass on our moral problems to someone else for a crack at their solution. It is puzzling that it should be so, for at least two reasons. First, because what cannot be done seems so close to what can be done when we seek moral advice. Secondly, because if we invoke the personal nature of moral judgement and decision as a gesture towards explaining it, then we seem to invoke it at the wrong point, *before* the decision. It is easy to see that if I must make a decision then I must make it, but it is hard to see why I cannot delegate the preparatory thinking for it. I can check it and I am not bound to accept it, just as with my accountant's review of my tax options. And it can be agreed that there is a sense in which everyone must do their own thinking, whether it be about mathematics or about morality, for as Simone Weil remarked, a collective cannot as much as add together two and two: only an individual mind can do that.[6]

The perplexity arises because we treat the difficulty of seeing what (morally) to do as a difficulty for thought which is no different in kind for the person whose problem it is than for a class of moral philosophy students rehearsing an exercise in 'practical ethics'. And that is because of a general conception of what thinking is and the way it is impersonal. Thinking, according to this conception, has to do with propositions, their truth-value and their logical bearing upon one another, and these can be assessed by anyone with the requisite capacities of mind, none of which makes necessary reference to the individual who has them. Hence it is felt that if we are to understand the way morality is personal, then we must locate its personal character somewhere other than in thought. That gives rise to the widespread but curious belief that if a person faces a moral dilemma, where no considerations seem to speak more for one course of action rather than another, then he must either introduce some extra-moral consideration ('utility' is often mentioned) if he is to settle the matter in thought, or abandon thought which has *ex hypothesi* exhausted itself, and act gratuitously. That shows a misunderstanding of what makes a moral consideration a *consideration*, which is a misunderstanding of what it means for it to 'bear' on, be relevant to, its conclusion.

Peter Winch disputed the claim, advanced by Sidgwick and agreed to by most philosophers, that 'if I judge any action to be right for myself, I implicitly judge it to be right for any other person whose nature and circumstances do not differ from my own in certain important respects', and he did so by considering the dilemma of Captain Vere in Melville's *Billy Budd*.[7] After he distinguished his position from a Protagorean relativism of which he suspected he would be accused, Winch says:

> I am holding that if A says 'X is the right thing for me to do' and if B, in a situation not relevantly different, says 'X is the wrong thing for me to do', it can be that both are correct ... But this certainly does not mean that if A believes that X is the right thing for him to do, then X is *made* the right thing for A to do by the mere fact that he thinks it is.
>
> One way of expressing what is puzzling about the class of expressions we are examining is to say they seem to span the gulf between propositions and decisions. And we feel inclined to ask, how *can* a gulf like that be spanned? A man in a situation like Vere's has to decide between two courses of action; but he is not merely concerned to *do* something, but also to *find out* what is the right thing for him to do. The difficulty is to give an account of what the expression 'find out' can mean here. What I have suggested is that the deciding what to do is, in a situation like this, itself a sort of finding out what to do; whereas I think that a writer like Sidgwick would have to say that the decision is one thing and the finding-out quite another.

It is because I think that deciding is an integral part of what we call 'finding out what I ought to do' that I have emphasised the position of the agent in all this.[8]

It may seem that Winch is merely arguing the following. Finding out what morally I ought to do (in a situation such as Vere's) is personal because decision is internal to what finding out is in such a situation and decisions are necessarily personal ('it makes sense to say that a man has decided what he will do, not that he has decided what somebody else will do').[9]

I do not think that Winch is arguing so simply, but, even if he is, he gives reason to think that it cannot be so simple, and that the necessarily personal character of decision cannot take us to the heart of the matter. For he goes on to say:

If, as I have argued, deciding what one ought to do is not a matter of finding out what anyone ought to do in such circumstances; and if, as I have also suggested, there is a genuine sense in which it does involve the notion of 'finding something out', what account am I to give of the latter? It seems to me that what one finds out is something about oneself, rather than anything one can speak of as holding universally . . . Thus Vere . . . [is led to] an understanding of what is and is not morally possible for himself in these circumstances. But these are moral modalities. If he were asked to give an account of what the possibility or impossibility consisted in, he could only rehearse the moral arguments which led him to his decision.[10]

We have already noted that expressions of moral possibility and impossibility are (logically) primarily personal, but that is not because of the necessarily personal nature of decision. I am not denying that decision is internal to what we call 'finding out' in such situations, but I am emphasising, as does Winch, the distinctive character of *moral* decisions. The personal character of expressions of moral necessity, and of moral reflection more generally, is not merely the necessarily personal character of decision as such. Nonetheless Winch is right to think that the deepest objection to the universalisability thesis will expose the mistaken conception of the impersonal character of moral deliberation which underlies it. He expresses this insight when he says that in moral deliberation deciding is internal to finding out. He is also right in thinking that to be fundamental to the characterisation of moral modalities.[11]

It may be objected against me that I have too easily secured the contrast between moral deliberation and some other forms of deliberation by distorting the nature of practical reasoning about non-moral matters to the point where it is accidentally practical. There is some truth in that objection. The conception I have sketched of the wrong kind of impersonality in practical thinking, and which I contrasted with moral thinking, does fail to reveal why practical reasoning is practical in a sense that implies more than that it is about practice and contingently applied in practice. It is about thinking about what we should do and then applying the results of such thinking to practice, as though it were grammatically irrelevant *to the kind of thinking it is* that actually one must act. A sense of the inadequacy of such a conception may lie behind the sympathetic exploration of Aristotle's claim that the conclusion of a practical syllogism is an action rather than a proposition. If the conclusion were merely a proposition, then it, and the thinking towards it, would be the same between ourselves who must sometimes act and beings who did not act, but who merely contemplated our lives and amused themselves by thinking what one would do in such and such circumstances if one happened to be an agent.

That cannot be the right understanding of practical thinking of any kind, but it leaves my basic point untouched. An account of that kind of practical reasoning which I contrasted with moral thinking and which revealed itself to be essentially practical, that is, thinking *essentially called forth in practice* rather than merely about practice and contingently applied in practice, would still need to distinguish when it is essentially personal, in ways that I have indicated, from when it is not. It would still need to distinguish when a problem is essentially mine and when it is only accidentally mine.

Bernard Williams argues that expressions of impossibility in practical deliberation are what they purport to be – genuine expressions of impossibility. The 'word "cannot" of practical necessity', he says, 'introduces a certain kind of incapacity'.[12] He argues that if a person says that he cannot do such and such, but does it and does it intentionally, then it is not true that he could not do it. 'Cannot' is, in this respect, importantly different from 'ought not to', for if a person says that he ought not to do such and such, then it may remain true that he ought not to do it even if he does it. In any event, he need not retract his judgement that he ought not to have done it. Williams suggests that the tendency to regard physical incapacity as 'literally' incapacity is due to the fact that if a person physically cannot do something, then he cannot do it unintentionally either. He also says that 'the point which is implicit in this way of expressing these structures of thought is that there is nothing special about *moral* necessity, in any of the narrower senses of that expression, which relates specially to such things as obligation; though there may be a broader sense – an ultimately broad sense, relating to character and action – in which all really serious examples of such necessities are moral necessities'.[13]

It seems, at first, obviously true that if someone says that he cannot do such and such, but then does it intentionally, then he must retract the claim that he could not do it, or at least admit that he had not voiced a genuine impossibility. That is certainly sometimes true, and it may be true when moral impossibility is properly called an incapacity; but not all moral impossibility is an incapacity, and when it is not, if a person does what he said that he could not do, then he need not admit that it was, after all, something he could do.

Williams points out that 'A cannot physically do X' does not entail that 'A would fail to do X' if he tried, 'since in many cases there is not anything that counts as trying'. He goes on to say that 'The most that follows from "A cannot do X" is that either it is true that if he were to try to do X he would fail or it is impossible that he should try to do X, and that disjunction follows equally in the case of the incapacities (physical incapacities and incapacities relating to character) which are under discussion here.'[14] That is true, but there are interesting differences in the ways that it is impossible to do something. It is impossible that a person should try to run a mile in five seconds. It would be nonsensical to suggest that anyone should try. But if anyone had said to Luther when he said, 'Here I stand, I can do no other', that he should, nonetheless, give it a go, then that would be nonsensical in quite a different way. Within the class of incapacities to do with character, moral instances are distinguished from the rest as paradigmatically, if not exclusively, those that rebuff, as nonsensical in the second way, any suggestion to try. If we wish that a person would do what he says he (morally) cannot do, then we do not urge him to try, but rather, to see the situation differently. Whereas if he says that morally it is possible for him, but psychologically it is not, then it *makes sense* to say that he should try, even though it might not be the most sensible thing to say and even though trying may be only indirectly in his power – by means of a strategy or a therapeutic technique, for example.

If we wish someone to see his situation differently when he says that there is something he (morally) cannot do, then often we urge him to give a deliberative voice to what he has 'ruled out' as 'impossible' to do. But as Winch points out, we cannot describe how he sees his situation independently from what he finds possible or impossible to do.[15] That is what he means when he speaks, in the passage I have already quoted, of the interdependence (in such contexts) of decision and discovery. That is not to deny that two people may speak of being in the same moral situation and that one may say that he must act in such and such a way while the other says it is impossible for him to act in that way. To say that they are in the same situation is only to say that there is no relevant difference in their characterisations of what is relevant to their deliberations. Winch says in his discussion of Vere's decision to execute Billy Budd that he (Winch) could not act as Vere did against an innocent person. In a sense, therefore, he saw the situation differently from Vere. He weighed Budd's innocence differently than Vere did. But, and this is Winch's point, we cannot characterise how Winch weighed it differently from Vere except by saying that he found it impossible to hang a 'man innocent before God' and that Vere did not.[16] There is no difference in their descriptions of the character of that innocence and of its importance to their judgements, no difference, that is, which explains why Vere acted one way and Winch thought it impossible for himself to act that way. But given my previous discussion of the irreducibly personal character of moral deliberation this should no longer be surprising or puzzling, or a sign of irrationalism.

Williams is too literal-minded, I think, in trying to reveal why expressions of moral necessity should be taken seriously. Part of the trouble is with his idea that an expression of moral impossibility is the expression of an *incapacity*, and that is connected with his inattentiveness to the way the character of moral necessity is conditioned by the grammar of what it is to have a moral problem – in what sense it is a *problem*. He fails to do justice to the difficulties in the concept of moral necessity – difficulties which are expressed in the fact that it is natural to say of someone who says that (morally) he cannot do something that in a sense he can and in a sense he cannot. Williams wants to say, flatly, that cannot just means cannot and that therefore if someone does what he said he could not do then it shows that he could do it. He treats the problem as though it were merely a problem in the philosophy of action. When Luther said that he could not do otherwise, it seems obvious that there is a sense in which he could have done. But Williams wants psychically to nail him to the floor. We can see his mistake more clearly if we note the different ways these expressions may be used in the second or third person. There is a sense of 'You can't' and 'He can't' which must be retracted if the person spoken of, or to, does what was said he could not do. There is another sense (an expression of shock perhaps) in which, if he does, then there is no need to retract. In the latter cases, we feel no pressure to say that since he did what we said he could not do, then either we misjudged what he was capable of, or we should have said that he ought not to do it.

If expressions of moral impossibility were merely the expressions of an incapacity, then the first-person singular expression of them would not have the kind of priority it has. But Luther would not have expressed himself more precisely if he had said, 'Here one stands, one ought (can, must) do no other.' There are, as we have just noted, second- and third-personal forms of the expression of moral necessity, but when they are used in such a way that they need not be retracted if the person does what we said he could not do, they are quite different from second- and third-personal expressions of psychological or physical impossibility, where the claim is based upon a knowledge of the kind of individual we are speaking of or to. Then the first personal case is not primary. There are moral cases where if someone does what we believed he could not do we realise that we did not know him as we thought we did. But there are other cases where this is not so and, as we noted earlier, they are not cases where we feel we used the wrong modal expression.

Williams notes that if a person says that he cannot do something and if what he says is true, then it cannot be an *option* for him. That is true, but it is not true that if someone intentionally does what he said he morally could not do, then he must admit that it was, after all, an option for him.

There are two different senses in which something is not a moral option for us. The first is that it can have no speaking voice for us in a piece of practical reasoning. It is allowed no deliberative voice. The second is that if we do it we will not be able to live with ourselves, or the evil of what we did so pollutes whatever we may have gained by doing it, that it destroys any intelligible purpose for which we did it.

Some considerations are permitted no speaking voice in a piece of practical reasoning, period, whereas others are permitted a speaking voice for some people but not for others. If someone considers stealing a pullover from a shop because he likes it, then he cannot offer the fact that he likes it as even an extremely weak justification for stealing it. Such considerations are, as John McDowell put it, silenced rather than outweighed.[17] In the example I have just given, the consideration that he will not have the pullover he likes if he does not steal it is a consideration that is silenced for anyone who understands what stealing is. It is deliberatively silenced, period. There are, however, considerations which are silenced for some people but not for others. For some people, but not for others, the fact that they cannot continue in their career is not a consideration which should have even a weak, speaking part in deliberation over whether to have an abortion.

The fact that something should have no speaking part in moral deliberation does not ensure that it does not. Nor, of course, does the fact that we judge that something should be *deliberatively* silenced ensure that it will be *motivationally* silenced.[18] But these two failures are different. If we allow a speaking voice to what we had judged should have no such voice, then that will be because we rightly judge that we are mistaken, or because we are deceiving ourselves, or because our minds have become corrupted. If we act on considerations we judge to have no proper place in deliberation, then we are abnormally weak-willed, or in despair, or (if it is intelligible) acting wrongly for its own sake. I discuss these cases again in Chapters 13 and 17.

Situations in which a person seriously judges that he could not live with himself if he did a certain thing are rare. Rarer still are situations in which such a judgement turns out to be true. They are, I think, of two kinds. One is when the deed is radically evil. The other is when, although it is not radically evil, a person's guilt destroys, as Williams puts it, 'the projects with which he identifies himself'. Williams' Gauguin might have been such an example. It is the second kind of example I have been considering. The first will not allow someone to think that, though he could not live with himself having done the deed, someone else similarly placed might, without being judged to have acted wrongly.

Williams says that 'there can come a point at which it is quite unreasonable for a man to give up, in the name of the impartial good ordering of the world of moral agents, something which is a condition of his having any interest in being around in the world at all'.[19] Put that way, I would agree. However, I think that Williams wants to say that there comes a point at which any morality properly aware of what conditions it must acknowledge the limits of its claims. I agree this far: it is not for anyone to moralise to such a person. But Williams simplifies matters here. What had the power to give sense in such a person's life might no longer have the power to do so once it is immersed in his guilt. Perhaps Williams would think such a guilt pathological unless it were for a deed that was radically evil. I see no reason for believing that. But he would be right in thinking that is hardly a 'victory' for morality. Also, if the person we have been speaking of does not do what he judges to be evil, he might, none-theless, have been right in judging that he renounced what gave sense to his life. Often that will not be a victory for morality either. Williams is right on this too: neither Kantians nor utilitarians have provided an understanding of how morality can save such a person from despair. That is partly because they construe the costs of moral-ity on the model of pain rather than despair. They think it is merely a matter of nobly enduring our pain for the sake of a moral demand. They say nothing about the light that morality might throw on our sufferings if they threaten to make us despair of anything being good or even making sense. There comes a point at which an appeal to dignity, to nobility or to courage seems shallow. For Kant, the man, there was prayer. But for the philosopher?

112

It should be clear that when I speak of guilt I do not mean to speak of it as a psychological phenomenon. As a psychological phenomenon guilt is assuageable. I intended to refer to an evildoer's understanding of what he had become in doing what he did, to how that enters his sense of why he did it and to how it affects his relation to whatever he may have achieved by it.[20] What that understanding is and what the possibilities and impossibilities are for him will be conditioned by a conception of value which can have no discursive guarantee of its rightness, or even, in some cases, of its intelligibility. Someone whose sense of morality leaves him on some occasions with only different entries into despair might think that his sense of morality had reached the limits of intelligibility. That does not, however, mean that he must think that his understanding of morality had found its *reductio ad absurdum*.

An onlooker might be inclined to say that, surely, there is something he can do, that there are no *real impossibilities* here. That is partly right. If someone says that he cannot do what he judges morality requires him to because he would need to renounce what gives sense to his life, then he might be right and he might be wrong. There is always, at least for some time, the hope that life might reassert itself in him. It almost always does. He cannot, however, hope that life will reassert itself against his guilt, for that is a hope he can justifiably have only if he believes his guilt is pathological. If he believes that, then he will not say that he cannot do it, or if he does, it will not be a moral 'cannot'. It might of course be pathological or morbid even if he does not think it so; if, for example, he thought that the hope that life would reassert itself was a kind of treachery to the moral. But it is not pathological only because he cannot have such a hope. What he believes to be impossible is that what had previously given sense to his life should both present itself under the description that determines his guilt and remains a source of strength to him. That, as we noticed in Chapter 4, is the sort of thing that prompts some philosophers to speak of the special authority of the moral and of its being *sui generis*. The way Williams speaks of character, and of incapacities conditioned by it, is too undifferentiated to engage with what prompts this way of speaking.

8

Meaning

Suppose that someone is driving behind an open lorry. She sees that it is carrying animals, perhaps to market. They are cruelly cramped in small cages, evidently thirsty and in pain. She pities them and is angry that they should be treated so. Then she sees a child in one of the cages. She no longer even notices the animals. She may never forget it. Some nights she may wake screaming.

That is the sort of thing that makes us speak of *human beings* and *animals* in the sense that suggests a radical difference in kind between *us* and *them*. The fact that we speak this way has prompted some philosophers to speak of human beings and *other* animals as though to remind us that we, too, are animals. But it is absurd to suggest (if it is seriously suggested) that we ever forgot it – that we ever forgot, indeed, that we are mammals. We have sometimes exaggerated the differences between us and certain animals with respect to those properties and capacities which figure prominently in the lists which philosophers contrive of what are the necessary and sufficient conditions for being a person. But, as Cora Diamond pointed out, the fact that we may discover that *differences* between us and animals with respect to such properties and capacities are not as great as we had thought does not diminish our sense of the *difference* (in kind) between human beings and animals, between *us* and *them*.[1] It would make no difference to the example with which I started this discussion if Washoe the clever chimpanzee were in a cage next to the child.

Those who are critical of the radical distinction in kind between human beings and animals which is implied in the way we generally speak, and which is implied in the kind of reaction I described above, are so because they assume such distinctions to be rationally justified only if there are relevant differences in capacities and properties such as the capacity to feel pain, or intelligence – capacities and properties, that is, which are empirically or empirically-cum-conceptually demonstrable. That is perfectly natural, for some people believe (often rightly) that differences in the way we treat or respond to things must be justified by relevant differences in those things. They also believe that we should not cite the fact that someone is a member of the species *Homo sapiens* to justify treating her differently from a jelly fish, except insofar as that is shorthand for referring to various capacities characteristically possessed by a member of the species *Homo sapiens* which are relevantly different from those characteristically possessed by jelly fish. They like to draw an analogy with racism and sexism, saying that it is no more relevant to cite the fact that someone is a human being in order to justify treating her differently from jelly fish than it is to cite the fact that someone is black or a woman: to do so is to be speciesist.[2]

From one point of view this looks to be the plainest common sense. The trouble is that it is naive to assume that anyone ever seriously thought that it was relevant merely to appeal to the fact that we belonged to the biological species *Homo sapiens*. (We shall see why in Chapter 9.) And, as we shall see, it is equally naive to think that the kinds of properties which interest philosophers when they ask what is a person, and which we often share to some degree with higher animals, play the kind of role in our treatment of one another which is assumed by those who argue that differences in treatment must be justified by relevantly different properties of those kinds. That philosophical perspective from which we are encouraged to reassess our sense of how we might justifiably treat animals distorts (and indeed cheapens) our understanding of human life. We may oppose it for that reason, without disagreeing in our judgements about how to treat animals with those who argue that it is speciesist to treat animals differently from human beings unless those animals possess relevantly different properties.

Someone who believes that the concept of 'speciesism' sheds light on the way we treat animals will not be moved by my example, even though it is partly offered as a *reductio ad absurdum* of the use to which that concept is put. She will acknowledge that we are very likely to react as I described, but she will say that is because of our deeply ingrained speciesist assumptions. She will remind us that not all human beings will react as the one in my example did. If the child were black and the person driving behind a slave owner, it might well have been different, just as it may have been if the child were Jewish and the person driving behind a Nazi.

The lives of animals have no meaning, or they have meaning in only an attenuated sense. I mean that as a grammatical remark – partly on the idea of an animal (as when we speak of human beings and animals) and partly on the idea of meaning. It is what lies behind the contrast between animals and human beings, as it is expressed when we speak of *us* and *them* and as it is expressed in the response I described in my example of the child in the cage. The sense of 'meaning' to which I am appealing is sometimes expressed in the contrast between a concern for the meaning of our lives as opposed to a pursuit of happiness. It is also connected with certain ways of speaking about the soul. The difference between human beings and animals is sometimes expressed by saying that only human beings have souls. There is a way of speaking of the soul which suggests that it is a speculative matter whether there are souls, and if there are, which beings have them. There are other ways of speaking of the soul, in which it is a conceptual truth that human beings have souls but animals do not. It might seem that the latter way of speaking of the soul cannot be interesting – that the interesting concept of the soul is the one that makes it a speculative, metaphysical question whether human beings and other beings have souls.[3]

It is important to remember how we speak of the soul when we are not speculating about it – when we speak, for example, of soul-destroying work, or when we learn that the ancient Greeks said that a man loses half his soul the day he becomes a slave. Neither of these ways of speaking depends on a metaphysical assumption that human beings have souls which may be destroyed or divided. But these are not trivial ways of speaking.

Only something living can have a soul. That is the beginning of my 'conceptual geography' of the non-speculative conception of the soul. 'Life' is a word with many meanings. There is a sense in which it excludes plants. That sense is conveyed when we speak of 'a life',

116

as when we exclaim 'What a life!' There is, of course, a sense of
'life' which includes plants. It is the sense which suggests that our
understanding of the nature of life and of what is living may be
deepened by scientific inquiry. The sense of 'life' as it is conveyed
in the exclamation 'What a life!' excludes plants, and does not invite
the thought that our understanding of life must be deepened by the
'life sciences'. It makes no sense to say of a plant kept in conditions
in which it could not flourish, 'What a life!' It makes sense to say
it of some animals and not others – dogs, for example, but not fleas.
It is connected with the fact that dogs may be given names, but it
can only be a joke to name fleas.

When we say that only human beings have souls and we do not
intend it as a disputable metaphysical proposition, the concept of a
soul is a spiritual concept and spiritual concepts apply only to what
may have an inner life in the sense we mean when we say that some
people have a deep or rich inner life, whereas others have a shallow
inner life. Only human beings (of the beings we know) have an inner
life. That is because only human beings can reflect on what happens
to them, and take an attitude to what happens to them because of
such reflection. An animal can suffer, but it cannot curse the day it
was born. An animal can be afraid, but it cannot be ashamed of its
fear and despise itself. An animal can be happy, but it cannot be
joyous. An animal cannot give of its substance to certain pursuits
and be admonished for doing so. One could go on almost indefinitely. The problems of life's meaning cannot arise for an animal.
Only a being for whom life can be problematic can have a spiritual
life, and therefore have a soul.

It may be clearer now why I say that the lives of animals have
no meaning. I do not mean that they are of no moral consequence,
nor do I mean that it makes no sense to speak of the dignity of
certain forms of animal life and living. I do not believe that my
remarks have any bearing on any serious discussion of how we ought
to treat animals. It is compatible with vegetarianism and with its
denial. But points I have made are important to understanding how
we should describe what we do to, and with, animals – to why, for
example, we cannot *murder* them. Animals that are killed do not
haunt those who kill them in remorse, because animals lack the individuality that is internal to our sense of human preciousness and

which is, therefore, internal to our sense of what it is to wrong another. Animals emerge from their species character in only an attenuated way. Some animals, partly because of what they empirically are and partly because of their relationship with us which is underdetermined by how they empirically are, emerge (to a limited degree) as individuals from their species character. Some animals are given names and enter our lives in ways that bequeath them an attenuated form of the kind of individuality we acknowledge in human beings when we say they are irreplaceable.

Our sense of the irreplaceability of human beings is conditioned by many things, but an aspect of it which is connected with our present concerns is that, as Hannah Arendt said, *who* people are, the distinctive individuals they are, is often revealed in a story of their life.[4] A biography is a story of a life that tries to reveal its meaning, and that is connected with the way it reveals the individuality of its subject. It would be absurd to write the biography of an animal, except anthropomorphically as is done in children's stories. That is because an animal does not have the kind of individuality which it is the object of a biography to reveal, and its life has no meaning which it is the object of a biography to disclose. The reason why an animal's life has no meaning is not because it has no purpose. (Indeed it is more natural to speak of the purpose of an animal's life than it is to speak of the purpose of human life, which should alert one to the fact that the question of the meaning of life is by no means the same as the question of the purpose of life.) An animal's life does not have meaning because an animal cannot live its life deeply or shallowly, lucidly or opaquely, honestly or dishonestly, worthily or unworthily.

I remarked in Chapter 4 that although our responses and reactions are not self-authenticating, the interdependence between some of them and what they are responses to places limits on the degree we can step back from our responses in order to judge whether they are rationally appropriate to their objects. The point emerges in various parts of this book and is developed in Chapters 9 and 10, but it will be helpful at this stage to explore the relation between certain facts of our nature, certain kinds of response and certain cultural determinants through which our sense of the meaning of those facts and responses is deepened.

Women sometimes love their unborn children. Some people wonder whether that is sentimental because they wonder whether what a woman carries when she is pregnant is an appropriate object of love. They will say that to describe it as I have, as her love for her 'unborn child', is to beg a lot of questions. They will say that we must first, as objectively as possible, understand what the 'status' of the foetus is, so that we may determine whether it is properly called a child and also to determine whether it is an appropriate object of love.[5]

Rush Rhees said that there can be no love without the language of love.[6] That means that there cannot be love without certain ways of talking about what we love, without argument about what it is appropriate or even intelligible to love, about whether something is worthy of our love and whether what we feel really is love, and so on. The language of love is exploratory and critical as well as celebratory. With respect to this example, it is important that what she loves is 'of her own flesh and blood'. But that description is problematic in the same way as is the description 'her child'. Its being 'of her own flesh and blood' is not a pre-scientific way of speaking. It is not a way of speaking that is clarified or rendered more precise by, for example, genetic theory. It is not a way of speaking that gestures towards the biological causation of motherly feeling. There is no harm in speaking of biology in this connection, so long as one does not mean by 'biology' that which is most deeply understood by the science of biology. Its being 'of her own flesh and blood' is an expression that plays an important role in our understanding of her love, *but it is an expression in the language of love* rather than one that pre-scientifically gestures towards something underpinning that language. It could be an expression that disappeared without replacement in a scientifically sophisticated community. It would disappear in a community in which all babies were 'conceived' in test tubes and developed outside of their mother's womb.

It is important that the child grows in its mother's body, that her body changes with its growth, and that these changes can appear to us as beautiful, for this provides a focus for love's tenderness without which there could be no love. A foetus growing in a glass jar on her mantelpiece, with many of its 'morally relevant empirical properties' in plain view, could not be an object of her love, for her love could

119

find no tender expression (which is not to say that a serious concern for it could find no expression). Or, perhaps more accurately, it could not if that were a general practice in a community. The pleasure of a woman with child at the changes in her body is the opposite of narcissism. It is the expression of her love for her child, and the possibility of such expression is a condition of that love. Her pleasure may also be a wonder at what she partakes of. The object of her wonder has a generality that is, sometimes, expressed by saying that she is in wondering awe at the miracle of life. But her sense that she partakes of something miraculous is conditioned by her love of the living child within her. The 'facts of life', the 'biological' facts relevant to her love and to her wonder, are all available independently of the development of scientific theory and knowledge. Our sense of them and of the way they define her creatureliness – her animality – is not deepened by biological science.

Suppose someone were to point to a foetus growing in a glass jar and to ask, rhetorically, how could it be called a child? His rhetorical tone would be partly justified, but mostly not. He would be right to suggest that we could not, or that we would at least find it very difficult,[7] but he would be wrong in what he thought that showed. Those for whom it is natural to speak of a pregnant woman as 'big with child' do not mean that she had been caused to grow big by something they *believed* or *conjectured* to be a growing child, but which turns out to be the same kind of thing as is growing in the jar. 'Big with child' (in this way of speaking) does not mean: caused to grow big by something that belongs to the natural kind *Homo sapiens* and which might, or might not, have the relevant properties to be grouped along with paradigmatic exemplars of the word 'child'. If we ask what, in that case, she is big *with*, then it would not be wrong to say that she was big with child. But the sense of that is given by the use of the expression as a whole ('big with child') and by the kind of place it has, because of its echoes and resonances, in certain ways of speaking in a certain culture. The phrase 'with child' is not detachable from 'big with child' in the way it would need to be for someone who says that it is an arguable matter whether she is big with (a) *child*. By way of contrast we may say that we discovered in the case of a woman with a hysterical 'pregnancy' that she was big only with wind.

120

Suppose, now, someone who was struck by a particular woman's love for her unborn child – struck by the realisation of what that love could be. She had seen many women joyful in their pregnancy but this seemed to her to be different, although she gave little thought to it. Now she finds herself pregnant, but resentfully. She considers an abortion but hesitates in recollection of the other woman's love. After some reflection, she thinks she cannot have an abortion; that it has become impossible for her. She says, 'I came to see what I would be doing if I had an abortion.' She might have said, 'I came to feel differently about having an abortion.' What if a philosopher said that the latter was the more exact expression of what had happened – that the former could be misleading in its apparent 'cognitive' implications?

She still feels resentful. No doubt she wishes she did not, but not because it would be 'nicer' to feel different, in the spirit of an advertisement on the London Underground: 'If you're pregnant and like it – fine. If not phone . . .'. She wishes she were not resentful because she judges her resentment to be a failing in the same way as she might if she felt it towards a born child. She judges herself in the light of the love she remembers. For her it is the kind of love that makes abortion impossible. We might want to add that it makes it morally, not psychologically, impossible for her. There would be some point in that relative to common ways of drawing a distinction between the psychological and the moral. On the other hand, this is the sort of example that exposes the limits and unclarity of such a distinction.

We cannot understand how abortion came to be impossible for her except by seeing how she understood what she would be doing, and that involves seeing how she would describe what she is carrying, what she would rid herself of if she had an abortion. I do not think that we can understand her finding it morally impossible to kill a *foetus* (consider the impossibility of her saying '*my* foetus' in the tone in which she may say '*my* child') except insofar as that is implicitly redescribed. That is why it is not wrong, or inexact, for her to say, 'I came to see what I would be doing' rather than 'I came to take a different attitude to what I would be doing.' I am not saying that the former is the right way of putting it. Rather I am denying common philosophical construals of the character of the contrast.[8]

In recollection of the love she witnessed, she came to realise what she would be doing. Should we say, if we are to speak 'strictly', that she came to *realise what kind of thing she would cause to die*? I do not think so, for that way of speaking suggests that we can have a 'morally relevant' redescription of the foetus (it is a thing of the morally relevant kind 'K', say, 'child') independently of our active relation to it. What else could be its point?

'I see now what I would be doing. I would be causing the death of my child.' That would be an elaboration tilting in the wrong philosophical direction. It suggests that we should make the same sense of what she does, whether she kills what naturally grows in her womb or whether she kills what typically grows in a jar on her mantelpiece; for insofar as it focuses on the effect of her action on a thing of a certain natural kind, then it is the same natural kind whether it is in her womb or in a jar. Many philosophers would say that is exactly as it should be. They would say that killing a foetus in a glass jar is the same as killing it in the womb – that if one is the killing of a child then so is the other, if 'killing a child' means 'killing something of an independently determinable natural kind'. My argument has been against that understanding of the matter. If in the light of the other woman's love she were to say, 'I would be killing my child', then she speaks in the language of that kind of love, even though she feels no love but feels, instead, resentful. The language of love is not simply expressive of feeling as the emotivists and those who opposed them in the name of 'cognitivism' understood it. That is part of the point of saying that there is no love without the language of love.

Love is conditioned by its object, but love also yields its object. That is part of what I have wanted to bring out through this example. Wiggins asked, do we desire things because they are good or do we think them good because we desire them? Both, he answered, and went on to say that the answer is not compromised by the fact that the 'because' is different in the one case from the other.[9] I would say the same of this example. We love what is precious to us, and things are precious to us because we love them. The contrast between inventing or making and discovering cannot be applied in any simple way here.

One woman's love discloses its object as precious to another because of its *authority*. It would not have that authority were it not for the kind of person she is. Another woman's love might have seemed, and been, sentimental, or it might merely have lacked the power of revelation. She had to be of a certain character and her love had to have a kind of purity. That would not be possible if her culture did not make it possible for her, and if she had not responded with a disciplined purity to the conversational intimations of that culture. I mean, if she did not make the language available to her in her culture living and resonant with the authority of her disciplined enactment of it in speech and in action.

What we call a 'living culture', or that in a culture which is 'living', I would describe as that which has the power to invite us into conversation. Sometimes that power is indirect in its influence, as when we can speak in certain ways only on stage, or in church, or ceremonially, but when this nonetheless constrains how we speak in our everyday lives and enters that speech, indirectly, through quotation or through discussion and reflection of what is said on stage, in church or ceremonially. What we say ceremonially (unless it has become 'mere' ceremony), what we say seriously in prayer or what moves us on stage, has its echoes in what we say more ordinarily and makes certain other ways of speaking possible or impossible for us.

I said earlier that there is no love without love's demands and that they are revealed through the grammar of love's language. Cats do not love their kittens. But I would not distinguish, as did Kant, between 'pathological' love and the love he preferred to call respect.[10] He did not call it 'pathological' because he thought it sick, but because he thought it was something suffered, or at any rate that it was not conditioned by a principle of activity responsive to moral modalities. I have tried to bring out how a woman's love for what she carried in her pregnancy was of something precious and marked it as that for a witness to her love. The other was a witness, not merely in that she was a spectator to it, but as one whose trust was claimed by the authority with which the love she witnessed revealed its object under the descriptions that made it intelligible as the love of something precious. I have tried to bring out that those descriptions have to be made living and authoritatively resonant through the integrity of a disciplined but creative engagement with them. I have called that engagement 'conversational' because such descriptions must 'speak' to us before they can invite us into such engagement. They speak to us because they resonate with the authority of past speech. If that engagement lapses, then after a time, so does the authoritative resonance. 'Sacred' has become such a word for us. It no longer has the power to stop us saying things such as, if life is sacred then we ought to maximise its instances, even if that means killing the innocent.

The problem often is to see how much is accessible to us beyond its mere acknowledgement. Even if the value we acknowledge is of the highest kind, even if we think that finding a place for it in our lives would immeasurably deepen them, we may nonetheless be unable to find a place for it in our living speech. Why that should be so is one of the deepest problems in the epistemology of value, but it is so and marks one of the fundamental differences between judgements of value and our ordinary paradigms of true and false beliefs, in which a truth acknowledged is a truth possessed. That is a truism in aesthetics. We must find our own style in architecture, painting, poetry and music. Moral and spiritual value is closer in its epistemology to art than to science. When we turn to 'past values', it is not because we have reassessed them in the way we might a scientific hypothesis which we had thought discredited, nor because we have found that our ways do not 'work' (although there can be something of that in it). It is because (though not only because) some aspect of the past speaks to us again and enters a new conversation.

I have tried to reveal the interdependence between certain ways of speaking, certain physical facts of our nature, and certain pre-linguistic reactions that mark our condition as human beings; and not only as human beings but as a certain kind of animal. I said that cats do not love their kittens, but I would not deny that mother cats and human mothers have something important in common. We sometimes call it 'a maternal instinct'. However, I do not think that a scientific inquiry into the nature of that 'instinct' will throw light on what I said about a woman's love for her unborn child. When we speak in this connection of a maternal instinct we are not committing ourselves to a theory of the biological causation of a certain kind of response or disposition. We speak this way to mark our creatureliness; to mark, for example, what we have in common with the cat and her kittens. That means that we mark that it is in our common creaturely natures to act in a certain way, but nothing, I think, much more definite than that.

If someone now says that we act in ways like other animals because of certain causes that science investigates, then that is partly true, but it does not matter, not to our understanding of our creatureliness or to the way that enters our understanding of ourselves. It matters no more than a scientific understanding of the causes of death matters to our understanding of the way in which death marks our creatureliness and our common mortality with all living things. It matters no more than that its being 'of her own flesh and blood' may mark nothing more definite than that her child grew in her body, was made out of it and was shaped by it, and by its father's entry into it.[11] That is not to deny the importance of scientific knowledge, but only to place it. Ironically, misplacing it is liable to threaten our understanding of our creatureliness and of the way it enters our understanding of ourselves as human beings. That, however, is a topic too large and too complex to engage here. My point is to emphasise the way a non-scientific, though not thereby an essentially pre-scientific, appreciation of our animality engages with the cultural in a mutual determination of the meaning of what it is to be humanly pregnant, and, more generally, of what it is for something to be an intelligible object of love. The deeper exploration of how that sense of animality enters into a proper understanding of ourselves is not, for the most part, to be achieved by science.

She loves her unborn child as she does because, barring misfortune, it will grow into an adult human being. That does not mean that she cannot love it as she does even if she knows that it will not – if misfortune has already struck. To speak of misfortune is to speak of chance in the accent of pity. It is true that we cannot properly describe what she carries when she knows that it will not develop into a normal human being without describing it as of a kind that normally grows into healthy adulthood. But if someone now asks whether the fact that this child will not grow into normal adulthood determines what it now *is*, then I think the answer is that there is no neutral determination of what is evoked by that emphatic 'is'; which is to say that there is no neutral determination of the significance of that fact for how she can speak of what she carries, and so for what her love can be.

125

There are those who say that if her child will not develop beyond the psychological and intellectual capacities of certain animals, then it is morally on the same level as those animals. The animals, however, are not as they are through *misfortune*. To speak of the child as a victim of misfortune is to keep him amongst us, as Falstaff kept those 'pitiful rascals' amongst us when he reminded the Prince that they were 'mortall men'. We depend on love and pity to show us how. It is the same with all our relations to the afflicted.

She could not love her unborn child as she does unless it were something that, barring misfortune, would grow into an adult human being. Many philosophers focus on a normal adult human being as a paradigm for moral response, and then, from there, try to assess what else is a fit object for moral response. That presupposes that we could respond to adults as we do independently of how we respond to children and unborn children, for it presupposes that our responses to adults are conditioned only by the properties and capacities they possess when we respond as we do – that it is contingent to our sense of what we respond to that it has grown into an adult human being. Parents do not respond to their children that way. They respond to them as to those whose life-story begins with their conception, and there is a limit to the kind of discontinuity in the description of its subject that such a story can bear. If they could properly be drowned at birth then they cannot be sacred in adulthood, or even of 'infinite worth'.

I said earlier that the lives of animals do not have meaning or that, if they do, then they have it in only an attenuated sense. Some people say that human life has no meaning either – offering that as a courageous intellectual discovery, of courageously seeing through our propensity to seek false consolation in the idea that our lives have meaning. They usually mean that meaning is projection on to 'things as they are', and that things as they are are intrinsically meaningless. They are confused, I think, in a way that can be revealed by asking what it would be for life to be intrinsically meaningful. Or, by asking upon *what* meaning is projected. Then, as Wiggins has pointed out, they look to be committed either to a concept of things as they are, upon which no attitudes could intelligibly be projected, or to a more homely conception of 'things as they really are', but which thereby threatens the contrast between things as they

126

are and as they appear to us when we project meaning upon them.[12] But I am not here concerned to argue the case against those who say that talk of the meaning of human life is confused and probably cowardly as well. Given the obscurity of the concept of how things 'intrinsically' or 'really' are, or how the world 'really' is independently of our projections upon it, the onus is clearly on them to make their case. I am here concerned with the grammar of a certain way of speaking of the meaning of a human life.

Human beings can live as though their lives had no meaning in the sense in which I am concerned with it, and in a way that is independent of any metaphysical denial of meaning. They can do it in two ways.

The first becomes apparent if we recall that a person may suffer the harm of betrayal, although no natural consequences of betrayal followed and although she knew nothing of it. Suppose, for example, that her closest friend had betrayed her to the secret police but the person to whom she had been betrayed was immediately killed and so nothing came of the betrayal. Even so, she was betrayed, and someone who knew it might pity her just for that reason. If it makes sense to pity her, then it makes sense to speak of the harm she suffered. Socrates makes the point in *Gorgias*, and although, as is often the case, he gets to it by way of a bad argument, it is an important point. It connects with his claim that no one does wrong knowingly, for he wishes to say, at least, that a coward (for example) flees, not as he thinks to safety, or not only to safety, but also into cowardice. That, Socrates believes, is something he would not do if he understood what it was to be a coward. Some people regard the claim that a coward flees into cowardice, or that a person betrayed suffers betrayal, as trivially true and of no moral consequence. There are others who think it is of fundamental importance. Those who think it matters naturally speak of the *meaning* of the deed. That is preferable to speaking of its intrinsic properties, because it avoids unnecessarily contentious metaphysical commitment and because it connects better with the idea of a deepened understanding of what we do. It is naturally expressed as a deepened understanding of the meaning or of the significance of what we do.

There is another way people may not be concerned with the meaning of their lives. Whether or not we are concerned with it in

127

this way, indeed whether or not we can make sense of such a concern, will have a profound impact on our conception of ethics. It involves a certain conception of the unity of a person's life.

It is natural to think of a human life as a movement between birth and death; that we should judge a life as fortunate or unfortunate according to whether or not certain characteristically human goods are attained and whether certain characteristically human evils are avoided. It is a conception of human life as essentially a space of opportunities between birth and death. The opportunities are provided by luck, foresight and initiative and they secure goods that human beings naturally desire and whose radical absence drives them to despair and to judge that their lives are not worth living. Morality is then seen as in service to the achievement of such goods, or as placing limits on the methods of achieving them, or, more plausibly, as a combination of both. It is seen as *essentially occasional*, that is to say, as something whose nature it is to intrude only on certain occasions in a life. The image is of linear movement: the past recedes into a realm of secondary concern; the present and the future are what primarily matter, and the past matters only insofar as it is prudentially (or sentimentally) relevant to the present and the future.

It is, as I said, natural to think that way, but there is another way, which is to see the past as not reducible to a prudential concern for the present or the future. We may betray our past or make a mockery of it. One of the reasons Socrates gave for not fleeing from prison was that to do so would betray his past.[13] Judgements like that reveal a concern for the past which is not merely prudential, which is not only a concern to learn from it for the sake of the future. Someone who takes such judgements seriously sees her life as having a distinctive kind of unity, or as aspiring to such unity. It is quite different from the unity given to a life by singleness of purpose. A person may singlemindedly pursue a particular project throughout her life without caring for her past, except insofar as being mindful of its lessons helps her in the future pursuit of her projects. The difference between those who care for the past in ways not reducible to a prudential concern for the future, and those who do not, constitutes a fundamental ethical and spiritual divide.

The first of the ways of being concerned with meaning does not entail the second, but someone who finds the first intelligible will not have difficulty in finding the second intelligible. Both are found in Plato and Aristotle. Both are different from the sense in which someone finds no meaning in her life when she is depressed.

Aristotle said that the wicked could not be happy.[14] He did not say that they were *unlikely* to be happy, which is the most that a moral philosophy in service of a reductive teleology of the virtues could realistically hope to say. Those who have hoped to argue for an intimate connection between a person's good and his being good under the inspiration of Aristotle, and by way of a reductive teleology of the virtues, have either missed the categorical tone of his denial that the wicked could be happy, or they have acknowledged it and whistled vigorously in the dark. Furthermore, a reductive teleology of the virtues inspired by an independently characterisable conception of human flourishing cannot account for the *demeanour* in the face of misfortune which Aristotle evidently admired when he spoke of those who 'bear with resignation many great misfortunes ... through nobility and greatness of soul'.[15] He did not prize this *for* anything – not because, for example, it might enable us to cope with misfortune so that we could be in the running for more flourishing in the future. What Aristotle said makes sense only in the light of a concern for the meaning of a life.

It is often argued that Aristotle's conception of the relation between virtue and the human good is mediated by a biological conception of human *ergon*. MacIntyre, for example, speaks of Aristotle's 'metaphysical biology'.[16] It is, of course, not difficult to see why commentators should speak this way. But Aristotle is, I think, more complicated.

Eudaimonia is often translated as 'happiness', but recently many moral philosophers have suggested that we could understand better what Aristotle was concerned to say by understanding it as meaning 'flourishing'. So, instead of saying that the virtues were means to happiness, it has been suggested that they should be understood as means to human flourishing. There are obvious difficulties with translating *eudaimonia* as 'happiness', but it would be worse to take it as meaning 'flourishing', or to take its sense as best revealed by that concept. Aristotle took seriously the question whether *eudaimonia* should seriously be affected by what happened after a person's death, although he finally judged that it was not. We can still call someone unhappy if his body has been thrown to the dogs, even if it sounds a little archaic. We understand why Antigone pitied her dead brother. To say that he is not flourishing is, at best, a black joke. Similarly, 'Call no man flourishing until he is dead' does not sound too well either, yet it is Solon's saying, that we should call no man happy until he is dead, that introduces Aristotle's relatively lengthy and decidedly uneasy reflection on whether the misfortunes suffered by someone who is dead could deprive him of *eudaimonia*.[17] And there is no doubt that Aristotle would have readily understood Socrates' claim that he would betray his past if he fled from prison, but such a betrayal and its implications for a judgement of Socrates' life could not be expressed in the thought that if he fled from prison he would cease to flourish (even though, no doubt, that would also be true).

Aristotle did not speak directly of a concern for the past which was not at least an indirect concern for the future, but there is every reason to think that what he meant by a 'complete life' included such a concern. He said that *eudaimonia* was to be predicated only of a complete life.[18] Some take that to mean that a person should not be counted happy too early, because we cannot know what might happen later – that we should not count our chickens before they are hatched. That thought is essentially future-directed. There is another way of understanding it which is as saying that the meaning of a life cannot be grasped except as a unity in which the significance of the past is disclosed. That is consistent with Aristotle's concern for what happens to a person after she is dead, for unless she is thought to survive her death, what happens after it can only bear on the completeness of her life if we are concerned with its meaning. Aristotle was in no doubt that the dead could suffer misfortune. He was uneasy whether that misfortune could affect *eudaimonia*. But if the sense of *eudaimonia* is conditioned, as many say it is, by a biological or quasi-biological conception of our *ergon* (often translated 'function'), then he might have been expected to make short work of the idea. For if he thought the '*ergon* argument' was a quasi-biological argument, then he could be expected to say that no argument from a human being's biological *ergon* to their happiness can be affected by what happens after death. And, of course, no argument from their biological *ergon* to their happiness can be affected by their relation to their past unless we are concerned only with its bearing on the future.

We have already noted the importance for ethics of the fact that 'life' is not a word with a univocal sense. If a doctor asks for a person's life history, then that is one thing. If someone is asked to write her biography, that is another. A person's biography does not necessarily end after she is dead. Nor does it begin when she is born. A biography is concerned with the meaning of a life, and will include whatever bears on that meaning.

What if we tried to construe the '*ergon* argument' according to the idea that a human life has unity given by its meaning? It would look something like this. Human beings are distinguished from animals by the fact that their life has meaning. That distinguishes them more radically from animals than reference to their capacities and properties does. Our *ergon* (taken now as our task, our work, or as McDowell suggests, 'what it is the business of man to do'[19]) is to be understood according to the claims that meaning makes upon us. Responsiveness to those claims is the responsive recognition of our *ergon*. *Eudaimonia* is predicated of a complete life (a unity conditioned by meaning) which has been faithful (true) to the distinctive character of our *ergon*.

If it is distinctive of human beings to lead a life which has meaning that bestows on that life a distinctive unity, then it is perfectly intelligible that the recognition of that should claim us in fidelity to it. Anything more specific will depend upon what kind of meaning we think it has. There can be argument, as Aristotle acknowledges, about what constitutes *eudaimonia*, although the hedonistic life will not be a serious candidate because it lacks any concern with meaning and therefore with what is distinctively human. The hedonist does not care whether her life has coherence and unity. She has no concern for the past except insofar as she might learn from it for the present and the future. The argument does not offer an external justification of morality or virtue. There is no serious reason to think that Aristotle was concerned to provide that. The only reason for thinking it is a reductive construal of the *ergon* argument which has recently been helped along by the biological connotations of 'flourishing'. It is not, I think, a good reason. But, as with Plato, I would renounce the exegetical argument. Call my argument 'Aristotelian' or 'neo-Aristotelian'.

MacIntyre has argued for a reconstructed Aristotelianism along lines similar to my argument. He introduces the idea of 'the narrative unity of a human life' to replace what he calls 'Aristotle's metaphysical biology', in an argument which hopes to get from virtue to happiness.[20] MacIntyre seems to think that the idea of life as a narrative unity, disclosing its subject, can be demonstrated to be a requirement for any philosophy of action and persons. He says that actions would not be intelligible except as embedded in a narrative and that the concept of action requires the concept of intelligible action. Furthermore, he claims that a 'narrative concept of selfhood' is required for a coherent account of a person being the same person through time. He thinks that understanding human life as having the unity of 'a narrative quest' will enable us to decide rationally which of incompatible goods to pursue and how to order goods so that we know what is deserving of the highest praise and what is not. He thinks it will enable us to understand better the virtue of integrity or 'constancy', which he thinks to be the same as 'singleness of purpose' and which (he thinks) cannot be specified without reference to a whole human life.[21]

These are ambitious claims for something he thinks can be demonstrated to be a requirement for any philosophy of mind and action. He asks, 'In what does the unity of an individual life consist?' and he answers, 'Its unity is the unity of a narrative embodied in a single life. To ask, "What is good for me?" is to ask how best I might live out that unity and bring it to completion. To ask, "What is good for man?" is to ask what all answers to the former question must have in common.'[22]

MacIntyre fails to notice something fundamental. He has two conceptions of what it would be for something to have a narrative unity and mistakes them for one. They are, on the one hand, the conception of the narrative unity of action and self as that might be required for any philosophy of mind and action; and on the other hand, the conception of a life as having the unity given in a story which reveals its meaning. The gap between a hedonist singlemindedly pursuing pleasure, with only a future-directed concern for her past, and Socrates, faithful to his past, cannot be spanned by a morally neutral philosophy of mind and action. The hedonistic life has a kind of unity – the kind given by constancy of purpose.

132

However, there is no need to speak here of a narrative unity, no more than we need speak of the narrative unity of an animal's life. We do not display a life as having a narrative unity merely by telling what occurred and was done in that life. The unity is inseparable from a concern with its meaning. There is no discursive route from a morally neutral philosophy of mind and action to showing that a person must be concerned with what meaning her life has, or even whether it has meaning. She might be concerned only to pursue and secure certain goods. Furthermore, if we are concerned with the unity of a life as given by a certain conception of its meaning, that conception is not discursively underwritten against other conceptions of its meaning.

MacIntyre ignores the interpretive incompleteness of all meditation on stories, partly because he overplays his argument against those who would say that a life itself intimates, or invites, no particular narrative genre.[23] He rightly attacks the idea that significance can be made of something that has no significance. But from the idea that a narrative form is not merely a projection on to intrinsically insignificant content, it does not follow, and I think it is not true, that a narrated tragedy, for example, merely follows the contours of an intrinsically tragic life, and that an account of that life in a genre other than the tragic must distort it.

MacIntyre says that man 'becomes through his history a teller of stories that aspire to truth'.[24] He also says that the narrative quest is a quest for 'increasing self-knowledge and knowledge of the good'. But now the problem arises that, since a story can continue after a person is dead, a person cannot understand herself as disclosed in such a story. MacIntyre says that agents are always authors, but he does not attend to the fact that they can be authors of their life-story only while they are alive.

What significance may agents as authors attach to the fact that their story will go on after they are dead? One answer might be that they should attach no significance to it. They might say, with Aristotle, that what happens after a person is dead cannot affect what is fundamental to her understanding of herself and her life. But that cannot be a judgement entailed by the idea of a narrative unity of a human life. Nothing in the idea of the narrative unity of a human life entails the primacy of the first-person narrative. On the contrary, it is more natural to think of the narrative self as essentially elusive to the person whose story it is, for no one is in a privileged position to disclose her life's meaning in a story. How much, and in what way, such first- and third-person asymmetries matter will depend upon differing conceptions of value. The idea that life has a narrative unity cannot ground, or be part of what grounds, a particular conception of value. There is nothing unintelligible in the idea that the self which is constituted in meaning should be essentially elusive to the person whose self it is. I would think the narrative self is such a self, although my argument does not depend on it being so. It depends only on it being true of some narrative selves. If someone thinks that who we are is essentially disclosed in a story that does not lapse into insignificance when we die, then she will acknowledge a narrative quest for self-knowledge to be impossible. She will believe that the narrative self is essentially beyond her authorship, and she will believe that to be an important part of self-knowledge. If we reject such a conception, then it will not be because it is based on a mistake in the philosophy of mind and action. It will be because we do not grant such power to what happens after death to alter the significance of what was done before it. That is the expression of *a moral conception of fortune* and its relation to what should matter most to us, of the relation between fortune and what we sometimes call our 'innermost selves'. The 'innermost self', however, the self which is most important to know, is not an empirically or *a priori* demonstrable entity. It is the child of a particular conception of value and has no home outside of it. It is conceived and nourished by categories of meaning which deny power to fortune to affect what we believe should matter most to us.[25]

There are those who would think it absurd to say that self-knowledge could be a hostage to fortune. Such a person would deny that a person lacks self-knowledge if she does not know that her dearest friend betrayed her, or if she does not know that she is an adopted child. Yet, when people learn such things, they often feel that their past has become lost to them and they must understand themselves anew through a newly understood past. Betrayal and serious deceit may poison the past through which we had understood ourselves. Betrayed friends know much about their feelings and dispositions towards their friends, independently of knowing that they are betrayed, but I see no reason to say that only that kind of knowledge is knowledge of who they are.

A person who does not understand his motives and feelings does not understand herself in one way. A person who does not know that she has been betrayed does not know herself in another. I do not deny the difference. The significance of the difference is not, I think, determined by a neutral philosophy of the self. To say that there is something in us that is not touched by fortune is to say more than that there are descriptions of what we feel and do that stand, whatever further descriptions fortune may force upon us. It is to attach a value to that, and often a supreme value.

I said earlier that an ethics centred on the notion of flourishing is essentially future-directed. A conception of value that is essentially future-directed cannot speak of fidelity to our life as a whole, for that must include the past. I suggested that we might construe Aristotle's 'ergon argument' as saying that it was distinctive to human beings that they could be claimed in fidelity to their lives, and so to themselves, as constituted under certain categories of meaning. I argued, against MacIntyre, that this was not a demonstrable requirement for any sound philosophy of mind and action.

What are the consequences of my arguments? First, we should no longer see the ethical as something essentially occasional – as merely relevant to those occasions, however few or many, when we must make ethical decisions. That does not mean that the ethical is temporally dominant, that it is everything, or that there are no other goods which may conflict with it and which are partly constitutive of it. It means that the ethical is constitutive of what it is to be a human being and what it means to lead a human life. It gives renewed force to the idea that certain pursuits, or lives, are 'fitting' or worthy for a human being. It also gives sense to the concept of destiny, that is, to the idea that we must discover what, in our circumstances, must be our way of being true to the task of living a properly human life. It opens a different perspective on suicide, on other lives and what is good in them.

These are grammatical points which open the way to seeing sense where one had not before. But there are two senses of 'sense' here – the minimal one according to which we no longer find something unintelligible or irrational, and another which implies more of a commitment. The gap is important. The kind of reflection characteristic of philosophy can take us to the first but not to the second.

Suppose someone who thinks that the dead are the irreducible objects of our love for them, our obligations to them and our actions towards them. She means that if we pity a dead person, then if we are asked how we should understand this, we should say that we pity him, the dead person, Smith. There is no shortage of people, including philosophers, who will say that this is 'strictly speaking' unintelligible unless you believe that Smith has in some way survived his death. They will say that unless Smith has survived his death, then if he is dead he is no more, and so cannot be the object of a lucid pity.

The person who pities Smith does not (or should not) deny that Smith is no more. She does not say: 'Ah but he is. He is the object of my pity, of my love and obligations. He is the one for whose sake I act when I fight to rehabilitate his name.' She says all these things, but not that they amount to a denial that Smith is no more. She rejects the metaphysical emphasis in the assertion that Smith is no more. 'Smith is no more' means no more than (adds nothing to) Smith is dead.

What could justify the metaphysical emphasis? The psychological redescriptions of what we feel and what we do, which someone who would speak with that emphasis would offer, does not, for these redescriptions are recessive in relation to it. I mean that she says things like, 'Smith exists only in your memory', under the pressure of the metaphysical emphasis. Nor will anything that merely amounts to saying that Smith is dead justify it. Sometimes such things appear to, but that is because they are said with the same emphasis. 'But Smith *feels* nothing, he is *upset* by nothing; the dead are *dead*', for example.

Could there be a philosophical argument about the nature of personal identity which showed that the metaphysical emphasis is warranted? I think not, for the person who pities Smith does not think that Smith has identity in the way that he had when living. The person who pities Smith could say, 'There is a sense in which Smith does exist, and that sense is given by the grammatical possibility that these kinds of relations to Smith have him as their irreducible object.' But that would be to concede too much to the metaphysical emphasis, or at least it would be if it were thought to be an answer to the demand that Smith be shown to exist. The demand was that Smith be shown to exist in a sense that exhibits the 'rationality' of saying that it is Smith, the dead man, that one pities. That demand is not satisfied by saying that Smith exists in the sense that he is the irreducible object of the pity (and other things). But then, it cannot be satisfied, for the only thing that would satisfy it is that Smith be alive or that he be a ghost.

I think that the reductivist can be made to see that his charge of irrationality or of residual superstition will not stick. I do not claim to have said enough to show that, but my argument here is not against the reductivist. It is an argument *ad hominem* against the non-reductive naturalist. Suppose then that reductivists drop the metaphysical emphasis and concede that it is not irrational or residually superstitious to pity the dead or even to say that we can act *for their sake*. Does that mean that they will now pity the dead and act for their sake? I think not, at least not only because of that concession. They do not even have to take it seriously in the sense of seeing this as of any significance in human life. It need not enter their thoughts about anything they believe to be significant in human life. They could be like someone who was shown that there could (rationally) be a moral concern for the past which was not just a species of concern for the future, but who nonetheless thought it irrelevant to anything she could take seriously.

Suppose now someone who does take it seriously, not only in that she acts and feels in relation to the dead in ways I have described, but also in that this enters in a fundamental way into her sense of what human life is. Suppose also that she sorrows deeply and bitterly because of something she failed to do before a friend died. Her sorrow is bitter because she is haunted by the thought, 'If only . . . but now it is, forever, too late.' Someone might say to her that, without in any way intending to belittle her pain and sorrow, there is a sense in which it is not too late, for her bitter sorrow is itself a form of reconciliation with the dead. He might try to explain this by saying that her sorrow is a significant part of the story of her dead friend's life – a story that discloses its meaning. Is that irrational? No more, I think, than erecting a gravestone *for the sake of* the dead. Consolation may be found in the same spirit, with the same sense of its meaning and with the same understanding of what kind of meaning it is. Even so, the person who sorrows might think this is going too far, not because it is irrational but because it offers false consolation. If she thinks that, it will be because her pain will not allow her to move beyond her friend's death on this matter. That will give a certain emphasis to her saying, 'It is of no use to him now; he is dead.' It is not a metaphysical emphasis. The one who said that it is not too late need not think he offered false and sentimental consolation. He may still believe it to be lucid consolation based on the realisation of what is possible in relation to the dead. The first person might come to see things as the second does or it might go the other way, but there is no purely discursive route between them.

Reductivists tend to think this is all the grammatical shadow play of the psychological. The truth in what they think is that the dead are not the metaphysical objects of our affections, our obligations or our actions. They will think that if the dead are not the empirical or the metaphysical objects of our affections and deeds, then they 'are' not, except in our thoughts. I have already suggested that it would be misleading to suggest that such a person has too restrictive an 'ontology', for that suggests that we need an 'ontology' of the dead, and that could only be a joke. It is true that someone who comes to see that it is not irrational to feel for and act in relation to the dead has, in one way, come to understand something. Someone for whom such understanding clears obstacles to it becoming something significant in her life, and to her sense of it, will think of herself as understanding something too, but it is a different mode of understanding – not because it is a queer 'cognitive' vehicle to a strange destination, but because its grammar is different. It is a grammar which, for example, draws a different contrast between the personal and the impersonal than does the grammar of the first kind of understanding. That is, in part, because it draws a different contrast between feeling and thought, between how one feels and 'how things are'. Those contrasts are neither univocal nor absolute.[26]

We would not speak of the dead as we do if it were not for the place they have in our feelings and our lives – that our lives are empty for a time, for example. It does not follow that the way we

138

speak is 'strictly speaking' in consequence of an unreflective response to a psychological shadow play. Furthermore, we would not for long continue to speak as we do if we acknowledged only that that way of speaking is not irrational. It does not merely grow out of our feelings and our behaviour towards the living. Rather, these – our sense of the dead and our sense of ourselves – are entwined in a reciprocating determination of meaning. Our attitude to the dead is, for example, connected with our sense of the irreplaceability of persons. Even if we think that it is not irrational to speak as we do of the dead and of our relations to them, unless that way of speaking illuminates and is illuminated by other dimensions of our lives, we will not take it seriously. If we do not take it seriously then we will feel no pressure to speak that way, and therefore no need to accommodate that way of speaking into a moral understanding of ourselves and into an understanding of the nature of morality.

The 'illumination' of which I have just been speaking is not the illumination of neutral data by a theory for which there are discursively establishable criteria of adequacy. I am thinking of the kind of understanding a person claims when she says that she has come to see the importance of the past in ways not reducible to a concern for the future – if she says, for example, that one has obligations to the past. With regard to the concept of taking something ethically seriously, I would put my point like this. Speech can only deepen our understanding of what has been spoken of in certain ways before. That is why certain words are 'called forth' in authoritative response. Some things can lose their power to call forth words in this way – when, for example, the ways in which they have been spoken become dead to us.

I have repeatedly invoked the notion of 'taking something seriously', and in characterising it I have invoked a dialogical metaphor. Rather than saying that we see a (moral) situation I would prefer to say that we let it speak to us and are claimed in response. Of course that, too, is a metaphor and should not run away with us. Iris Murdoch said that there are two dominating metaphors in moral philosophy – the metaphor of vision and the metaphor of movement.[27] I do not think that is true if it means that these must dominate, although I think that it is historically accurate enough. Murdoch says that, 'Words do not themselves contain wisdom.

Words said to particular individuals at particular times may occasion wisdom.'[28] She connects wisdom with attention and that with vision. I would connect it with what is spoken, as she does in the passage I have just quoted. We live in a world bathed in speech. A 'moral situation' presents under what has been said of it, and trying to find what we will say of it, trying to describe it and trying to understand our situation and what we ought to do, is a dialogical enactment.

Am I just saying in an obscure way that moral situations necessarily present under some description(s)? In that case, perhaps the metaphor of 'reading' would be a corrective to that of vision. I wish to say more than that. I would argue that the epistemic grammar of moral descriptions involves what I have been calling 'authoritative disclosure', as I tried to instance it in the example of the woman whose love for her unborn child had the authority to reveal to another what it would be to have an abortion. This is at least in harmony with an important empirical truth. Our thought is thought in a tradition and is shaped by those we respect and admire. We learn by being moved and we learn, or try to learn, when we may trust what moves us and ourselves in being moved. To be sure, that is (or ought to be) critical respect and admiration, but that does not mean that we seek a transcendental vantage from which to assess all that we are disposed to believe when we are moved. If there is no such vantage point from which we can 'see the world as from no place within it', and if all moral thought is not a reductive elaboration on what is indisputable, then our thought is inescapably, dialogically, in the midst. There is no other place from which we can have anything to say or anything to learn about the kind of meaning of actions and lives that I have elaborated in this chapter.

9

※

Individuality

Human beings limit one another's wills as does nothing else in nature. That is a recognisably Kantian thought. It is also Socratic. When Polus boasts of the power he believes oratory gives him over others, Socrates tells him that he has forgotten his geometry, meaning, I think, that he (Polus) has forgotten that there are limits other than those of physical and psychological force.[1]

Kant did not recognise this in Plato, partly because he misunderstood the emphasis on *eudaimonia*, and partly because neither Plato nor Socrates saw any need to express their sense of the *sui generis* character of the harm suffered by an evildoer, and by his victim, in ways that introduced a special motive that contrasted with desire. They were wiser than Kant on this matter (and had fewer traps to fall into), because Kant's contrast between action motivated by duty and action motivated by inclination (the way he drew that contrast and the importance it had for him) distorted his sense of the way human beings uniquely limit one another's wills. It also distorts the sense in which a victim of evil is more than a victim of whatever natural harm is internal to the evil done to him. Kant distorted both of the things he was most anxious to draw attention to.

We may acknowledge that the harm of which Socrates spoke could not provide a motive for resisting evil (thus conceding something important to Kant), while acknowledging his fundamental insight that an understanding of the nature of ethical seriousness depends upon a sense of the way evildoing affects an evildoer. I have been trying to do both. The reductivist who looks in the Socratic account for a justifying reason why we should avoid evil and the non-reductivist who deplores what he believes to be its reductivist implications – both assume that Socrates was, in a quite ordinary sense, providing reasons for behaviour. Kant failed to understand the degree and extent to which moral response was conditioned by what belonged to what he called inclination. But it would be unjust to single him out because of this. It has been misunderstood quite generally even by those who (like Williams) would think they had not misunderstood it and who would, indeed, criticise Kant for having done so.

Kant was deeply impressed by the fact that a person could be hardened by misfortune to the point of being unresponsive to the suffering of others in any way which could be described as a form of pity, yet still be able to rise to the requirements of morality, including those requirements which belong to the virtue of charity. There is truth in that, but we cannot extract it unless we record a number of important qualifications.

First, morality requires of such people an attitude towards their hardheartedness; they must judge it to be a moral failing. Secondly, there are some things they cannot do if they are hardhearted; they cannot show tenderness and so they cannot be, for example, a proper father or mother, or a proper husband or wife. Thirdly, they are likely to fall into a banality of spirit that makes them unable to be a proper respondent to what claims them in moral response. Kant failed to see this because of his single-minded focus on the moral 'ought' as a unique and irreducible modality. He failed to understand moral understanding, and therefore what we have to be in order to speak and act morally. Protracted sorrow, and certainly bitterness, under-mine moral response because they undermine what nourishes it, which is not a purely rational will but a vital and nuanced capacity to attend to the different voices and tones of what claims us. Much moral failing is not a failure to do something that falls under a rule or a principle: it is failure to rise to what we are called to become – someone who is authentically present in speech and deed.

Suppose a student comes to see his teacher. The student is good but rather wild. He has a certain disdain for the academic practice of his subject. There are often relatively routine ways of dealing with that: he is muddled and presumptuous and so there are relatively obvious things to be said. But underlying his muddle and presumption is an intellectual and spiritual seriousness. In relation to this, too, there are many relatively ordinary things to be said. But now when he comes to his teacher's room his teacher sees that this is no ordinary occasion. He knows that he is called upon to show the dignity of the subject through his relation to it. No doubt he has already, to some degree, done so, for otherwise the student would not have come to his room, but he cannot merely tell him what his thoughts are on the subject. He does not and cannot have a clear idea of what to do. If he thought he did and acted accordingly, if he thought that in such a situation one ought to do such and such, then he would fail to do what he is now called upon to do. That is not how his past must enter what he says and does.

He is not required to think something new. Perhaps he will say what he has said before, but he must bring to his speech, he must make living in his speech and demeanour, the integrity of his relation to his subject. He knows this and he also knows that there is no technique for doing it, although there might be a technique for appearing to do it – for creating an effect. If he created an effect, he would be failing his student, whatever his student thinks. If he does not fail him, he will not, thereby, know what to do next time. There is nothing determinate he can try to do: he cannot try to find a description of an action of a certain kind appropriate to the kind of situation he is in and then try to do something which would satisfy such a description. That is what is implied in the thought, 'one ought to do such and such in situations of this kind', and in common accounts of practical reasoning. However, there is no sufficiently determinate description of the kind of situation he is in. There is no general description of what it is to disclose in one's speech and demeanour what a serious relation to a subject can be. If he knew beforehand that the student was coming and what would be required of him, he could not, to any significant degree, prepare himself for it. That does not mean that what he says and does comes from nowhere. On the contrary, it is nourished by his past, what it has made him and what he has made it through his fidelity to it, but his past does not enter as something that has provided data and principles which he hopes will be adequate for the future. He might be too tired to rise to what he is called to be, yet act 'impeccably' through an effort of will. We often fail others in this way.

143

The Kantian picture of a rational will badly misconstrues the nature of moral and spiritual energy and what conditions it, and this misconstrual is encouraged by focusing on the notion of 'obligation'. That is why I have spoken of moral *response*, and sometimes, to emphasise its active nature and the nuanced interaction between past and present, of moral *responsiveness*. When I say that the Kantian picture of the unconditioned rational will reflects a misunderstanding of the nature of moral and spiritual energy, I do not mean merely that it is lacking an adequate motivational psychology. As previously, I want to stress the connection between the reality of the moral and its being made manifest in authoritative speech and disclosure.

The person who so evidently moves Kant, someone who has been embittered and broken by misfortune but whose capacity to respond to the requirements of the moral law is not thereby diminished, is not a person who suffers remorse as I have described it. If he is a murderer, then that his victim is dead does not matter except insofar as he must be dead if the other is to be a murderer. That is a manifestly inadequate conception of the seriousness of murder – that the fact that someone is dead matters only because it brings our action under the moral law.

Is that a caricature of Kant's view? I think it is not. It is a consequence of his position that a murderer may understand the seriousness of what he has done, though he cares not at all for the fact that his victim is dead. Something like that must be true for Kant, because although someone is not murdered unless he is dead, the Kantian division between inclination and duty excludes sorrow for his death as internal to the moral response to his murder. His death is internal only to the description of the deed as one which falls under the moral law. A murderer's moral response to his victim is determined solely by his sense that his victim suffered a violation of the respect owed to all rational beings. That he suffered the natural harm of being killed is presumably relevant only to pre-moralised inclination – natural pity perhaps. We have already seen that the moral significance of murder is disclosed, for Kant, in a terminology that is proudly indifferent to anything that is conditioned by the fact that we are human beings in addition to being rational agents. That is clearly revealed in the fact that for Kant our

144

capacity for moral response is in no way diminished by the fact that natural human feeling is completely extinguished in us. The distinction between inclination and duty undermines the right kind of internality between the evil of, say, murder as *sui generis* and the natural importance of death in human life. That is why the particular person's death appears unimportant against something more general – that we have violated rational nature in another.

It is not hard to see why Kant should think this. For one thing, our sense of the evil we have done ought not to be dependent on the victim actually engaging our sympathies. He may be a complete stranger to whose fate we may be quite indifferent. Or he may be so evil that we cannot feel anything for him although he was brutally murdered in an act of vengeance. Or he may have welcomed death because he suffered so terribly. None of that, however, alters the evil of his murder and that he suffered the evil of it as a distinct harm irreducible to the natural harms he suffered. We can see why the responses which are engaged by suffering and death as natural evils, and which are dependent on the victim mattering to us in some natural way, should be judged to be irrelevant to the evil of murder. But it does not follow from what we may grant in this connection, that the absence of such responses may not have been seen as moral failings and, more importantly, it does not follow that they are not, in general, *fundamental to our sense of what is an intelligible object of moral response.*

We saw what went wrong when Donagan tried to give a Kantian exposition of 'traditional morality' and achieved, instead, a parody. He tried to show how the precepts of traditional morality will become perspicuous to understanding when their Kantian essence is extracted from the descriptions that are conditioned by our humanity – those descriptions through which we explore what we do and what we are and in the light of which we naturally believe that we may understand ourselves morally. It has been said that the contingencies that mark our humanity provide the moral law with its content relative to us, but not with its form. It would be closer to the truth to say that our humanity provides the moral law with an occasion for its exercise, or to say, as did Stanley Cavell, that our humanity is merely a host to the exercise of pure practical reason.[2]

The Kantian scheme undermines the internality of feeling and moral response even when the nature of that response and its object are *sui generis*. Kant often appealed to the idea that duty was owing and possible when feeling had died, and that it was *required* whereas feeling could not be. His famous remark that Jesus' command that we should love our neighbour could not be taken literally because love cannot be commanded has often been quoted. It is certainly true that we must respect those we cannot love, but it does not follow *that we could think of someone as an intelligible object of respect unless we also saw him as the intelligible object of someone's love*. It is compatible with the acknowledgement (which the Kantian point exploits) that we must respect those we cannot love, that we can only see someone as the intelligible object of respect in the light of someone's love.

The Kantian thought is that inclination takes as its objects something unconditioned by moral description, and that thought is partnered by the suspicion that inclination is inherently egocentric. Kant has been unjustly accused of thinking that anything he included under his extended sense of the concept of inclination – desire, for example – was inherently selfish.[3] But there are ways of being egocentric without being selfish, and we can see the importance of this for Kant if we reflect on the way he was troubled by the vulnerability of inclination to various contingencies. His worry was not merely that our inclinations to pity, for, example, were vulnerable to misfortune and so might disappear (that charity would be unreliable if we depended on charitable inclinations). His worry was that, in at least some cases, the fact that an inclination disappeared revealed its egocentric character.

Suppose someone who is passionately in love. He would die for his beloved. But when he ceases to be passionately in love he forgets her and has little interest in whether she is alive or dead. It is common enough. His love need not have been selfish – he was prepared to die for her and, *ex hypothesi*, that was dependent on nothing that would normally be called an ulterior motive. Yet his concern for her was dependent upon his feelings in a way that reveals that *she* did not figure sufficiently, or in the right way, in what provided the energy for his deeds, and that his preparedness to die for her was therefore egocentric even though it was quite unselfish.

The point can be put more generally. Amongst what Kant called inclinations are some that we need to be true to. Love is like that. It has its demands to which we must rise. Kant failed either to see this or to realise its importance. But he was right to think that if the disappearance of an inclination revealed something about its character, then it retained that character even if it should, contingently, continue forever. What is important is not its mere continuation but its transformation, because its possessor has acknowledged certain requirements. That is what Williams misses when he says of the amoralist that 'to get him to consider [the situation of those he is not inclined to help] seems rather an extension of his imagination and understanding than a discontinuous step onto something quite different, the "moral plane"'. He fails to see that being true to the requirements which are internal to certain desires, if they are not to be egocentric, is part of what it is to be struck by the independence of another human being, of what it is to be struck by his reality.

One way of seeing Kant's distinction between duty and inclination in the light of what I have been saying would be to see him as thinking that whatever requirements might be internal to certain inclinations (whatever requirements are internal to love, for example) are not of the kind that can take us to morality. Only when we recognise others as moral limits to our will are our deeds sufficiently informed by *them* (those others) for us to escape the suspicion that our inclinations are egocentric, and that is where Kant is right against some of his critics.

We may see the nature of my objection to him more clearly, if we remember how much I have emphasised the connection between our sense of the reality of other human beings and what we suffer because of them. Kant could not allow that, or at any rate he could not allow its relevance to morality, because of the kind of connection he saw between moral good and the will. In Chapter 4 I emphasised how strange the suffering of remorse is, and how it brings together both a sense of the significance of the evil we did and a sense of the reality of our victim.

I suspect that Kant and many other philosophers of seemingly different viewpoints find it strange too. They prefer to say that it is not the particular person who is wronged who is so important. It is the principle. Or, it is rational nature. They will say almost anything so long as the particular person drops out and becomes merely an instance of something else that carries the moral weight. They will say that it cannot be him, John Smith, because it would be exactly the same if it were someone else in the same circumstances. Is that not already given in my example of a murderer who neither knew nor cared about his victim? His victim might have been anyone?

It is true that his victim might have been anyone, and that if it had been someone else and the circumstances were the same, then his moral response would have been the same. However, in remorse he is not haunted by everyman. He is not haunted by his principles. He is not haunted by the moral law. He is not haunted by the fact that he did what he ought not to have done (why should that drive anyone to despair?). He is haunted by the particular human being he murdered.

Should I not say that what is morally terrible is that he killed *a human being* and that, of course, he will be haunted by the *particular* human being he killed? If that is to counter what I have been saying, then it must imply that being haunted by this particular human being is extraneous to his, and to our, moral understanding of what he did. Otherwise, to say that what is morally terrible is that he killed a human being is only to say what is obviously true and has been acknowledged – it would have been the same if he had killed a different human being. But what is so terrible for him is not that he killed a representative of humanity. The universality I acknowledge when I say that it would have been the same if he killed anyone else in relevantly similar circumstances will not yield an understanding of the moral significance of what he did (not to him and not to a theorist), to which the individuality of his victim is extraneous and of only psychological interest. Nonetheless, it is true that he feels as he does because he has murdered a human being. But now there is no emphasis on the indefinite article. It means that he would not have felt this way if he had killed a cat.

Evidently what is needed is an understanding of the matter that reveals both why he would feel the same were it any other human being in relevantly similar circumstances, and why the particular human being he murdered is not devalued into a mere instance of something more general which is supposed to provide the ethical (non-psychological) dimension of remorse. An analogy, perhaps, would be someone grieving over a lost child. She grieves as she does because it is her child, and would grieve so over any other of her children, but her grief focuses, irreducibly and indivisibly, upon this particular child. If it were not so, her grief would be as suspect as a remorse that had a representative of humanity, or a moral principle, as its focus. She loves her child because it is her child and as she loves her other children because they are her children, but in order to do that she must love them in their particularity.

A murderer's remorse is as it is because he murdered a human being, but in order for him to understand *that*, his victim must remain with him in his distinctively human individuality, for that is what it is to *be* a human being in any sense that makes the murder of a human being an immediately intelligible object of remorse. That individuality is obviously not detachable from the concrete, historical human being. If he murders John Smith, then John Smith does not become a mere instance of a unique mode of human individuality. It would therefore be ambiguous and misleading to say that it does not matter that it was John Smith he murdered. He murdered John Smith, and the individual, historical, murdered John Smith is the focus of his remorse. But it would have been the same had he murdered John Brown or Betty Jones.

When Hare says that moral judgements are expressed in terms none of which are irreducibly singular, he means that situations enter moral judgements irreducibly as *kinds* of situations, and that if John Smith is being judged then it is not only to John Smith that the judgement applies.[4] There is some truth in this, but we have already had occasion to see that it is not so simple, and we will again. For the present we should note that Hare ignores the significance to the nature of the moral, that John Smith has a name and not a number. Hare thinks of human individuality, as do many philosophers, as exhausted in numerical and qualitative distinctness.

I have said that we often record our sense that there is a mode of human individuality different from that. We sometimes express it simply by saying that human beings are irreplaceable in the way that nothing else is. We sometimes express it more desperately – I mean, conceptually more desperately. Earlier I quoted Vlastos saying of Plato that he had no understanding of 'the love of persons, worthy of love for their own sake ... in the uniqueness and integrity of his or her own individuality'. Hannah Arendt said that we cannot bring out *who* someone is in description, for description is always of *what* someone is.[5] Neither of these ways of focusing on that mode of individuality to which I am also alluding is satisfactory. Yet with Vlastos, it is the phrase 'the integrity of his or her own individuality' that is important; and with Arendt, what is important is the thought that there is a form of human presence that is not wholly explicable in terms of the impact of a person's individuating features. My claim is that this individuality is internal to our sense of what it is to wrong someone.

It is not to be confused with the emphasis on partiality which has preoccupied philosophers arguing against the kind of impersonality required by both consequentialists and Kantians. Or, rather, its relation to partiality is complex. When I emphasised how strange it is that a murderer should be haunted by an anonymous tramp whom he murdered, I did not mean to suggest that his remorse would be more intelligible if he felt it for murdering a friend. If it were, it would not be that *kind* of remorse, and that is partly what is captured in the claim that his remorse is for the fact that he murdered a human being. There will be dimensions to his guilty suffering if he murders his friend that will be absent if he murders an anonymous tramp. However, the deep terribleness of either murder lies in the fact that he murdered a human being. But, as I have already argued, that does not mean that his friend stands in as a representative of humanity. It means that the nature of what he suffers in remorse because he murdered his friend is conditioned by the fact that he should suffer it if he murdered an anonymous tramp. And that is to say that it is fundamental to his understanding of friendship that *it be bound by moral constraints which are what they are precisely because the evil of murdering a friend is the evil of murdering another human being.* But the dialectic is such that, in order to be seen as a fellow human being, someone must be seen as one who could be someone's friend. That is a condition of his being within the conceptual reach of his murderer's sober remorse.

When I say that in order to be seen as a fellow human being the anonymous tramp must be seen as someone who could be someone's friend, I mean that he must be seen as someone who is subject to the demands which are internal to friendship, as someone of whom it is intelligible to require that he rise to those demands, no matter how often he actually fails to do so. That is compatible with him being such a nasty fellow that nobody could befriend him, for it is to see his nastiness from the critical standpoint of what is required for friendship. He is not like a bad-tempered dog. The general point is this. For the tramp to be within the conceptual reach of his murderer's remorse he must be seen to be 'one of us', a fellow in a realm of meanings which condition the way we may matter to one another. But now I would say that friendship is, in turn, conditioned by what is disclosed in remorse. A friend is one who can be wronged, and remorse teaches us what it is to wrong another. I would put the point more generally like this. The nature of remorse is underdetermined by what is internal to it, by what is necessary for someone to be within its conceptual reach. It discloses the fundamental determinant of our understanding of what it is to be a human being. It is fundamental because it radically transforms what conditions it. What it is to be a friend, what it is to be a husband, what it is to be a lover, what it is to be a respondent to another's call to seriousness – these are transformed under the shock of what a human being is disclosed to be in serious remorse.

Against consequentialists and Kantians alike, Bernard Williams argued that the moral subject is irreducibly a person with a particular character – one who has 'projects and categorical desires with which that person is identified'.[6] That might seem obvious, were it not that for both consequentialists and Kantians the moral subject is considerably less than that – something less liable to being conditioned by what is accidental (being born in a particular time and place, for example) and which is, from their perspective, parochial.

Williams says that 'differences of character give substance to the idea that individuals are not inter-substitutable'.[7] That may be misleading, because the fact that individuals are not inter-substitutable is not so much an *idea* as it is a feature of our relationships with one another and of our sense of ourselves. A physical object that has, as we say, 'sentimental value' for us is not inter-substitutable with a like object, but it would be misleading to say that that is because we have an *idea* of it as something irreplaceable. Not anything can be of sentimental value to us, and the kinds of things that can

151

be are marked out by the place they have and can have in human life. A lover can treasure a flower but not a piece of cow dung.

It is more complex when we speak of the irreplaceability of persons. We are tempted to say that we treat persons as irreplaceable because they *are* (intrinsically) irreplaceable. I called it a temptation to say that. More accurately, the temptation is to a certain philosophical construal of it. Many human beings – slaves for example – have been treated as replaceable because they have been seen as replaceable in the sense in which we would wish to deny that human beings are replaceable. (There are other, legitimate ways in which a slave may be seen by his master as replaceable or irreplaceable – because of his unsurpassed strength for example – but which are not relevant to the sense of human uniqueness which I am exploring.) All people are, for some purposes, treated as replaceable, just as all people are sometimes treated as means to other people's ends. But just as no person is to be treated, on any occasion, only as a means to an end, so no person is to be treated, on any occasion, only as someone who is replaceable. He must be treated on every occasion in ways which reflect that his individuality conditions the way he limits our will. There have been human beings who have not been treated this way.

When persons are treated as replaceable in the way we think they are not – that is, when they are denied the special kind of individuality we think fundamental to them as persons – it is not because they are not seen as having characters 'in the sense of having projects and categorical desires with which [they are] identified'.[8] The slave owner is perfectly aware that his slaves have characters in that sense. It is because their desires and projects are denied a certain content – the content that conditions our sense that persons are irreplaceable. If the slaves wish to bury their dead as a mark of respect, for example, then the slave owner cannot think that to be the same kind of desire he has when he wishes to bury his dead. The burial service is for him (in his case) expressive of, and (as a practice in his community) part of what conditions, his sense of the dead person's irreplaceability. To take another example. If a slave killed himself because he could no longer bear his affliction, his owner could not think of the slave's suicide in the same way as he can think of the suicide of a friend who also killed himself in despair. In the case of the friend, thoughts about the terribleness of suicide, perhaps of a Christian kind, make sense to the slave owner, but it is not so with the slave. The slave is seen as 'putting himself out of his misery', and that is more or less the end of it. The difference has to do with the different ways in which the two lives are thought to have meaning, with what despair of that meaning can be, and so with what suicide may mean. These differences bring with them different conceptions of human individuality. We put animals 'out of their misery' because their lives have no meaning, or if they do, only in an attenuated sense. Whatever we think about euthanasia, we may not do it in the spirit of putting a person out of his misery. It may not be done in a spirit conveyed by the connotations that expression has for us – without being radically demeaning.

Williams is right to say that 'differences of character give substance to the idea that individuals are not inter-substitutable', if he means that differences of character are a condition of that idea having substance. He is right, too, in thinking that our sense of the irreplaceability of persons has not been given to us only by morality, but rather arises out of certain human relationships, in particular certain partial relationships, which are as much the source of morality as they are its object.[9] However, the bare notions of projects and desires (categorical and otherwise) cannot do the work Williams wishes of them. We must not only see that someone has 'projects and categorical desires with which that person is identified'. We must be able to take those desires and projects, and so him, seriously. That is a condition of his having the kind of individuality we mark by speaking of his irreplaceability.

The same applies to what is said by many philosophers concerning our obligation to treat interests equally. We cannot, by appeal to an abstract principle, treat someone else's interests seriously if we find it unintelligible that they deserve to be taken seriously, or that they have the same meaning as do the interests of some others. The slave, in my previous example, has an interest in seeing that his friend is properly buried, but if his master finds it unintelligible that his suffering could have the depth which makes it appropriate to speak of despair, then he will find it unintelligible that a funeral service for a black slave could be expressive of what it is for a white person. The idea that we ought to treat interests equally appears to be part of an account of what it is to take others seriously. In a sense it is, but as it is usually put, it fails to look into its starting-point. Like the Kantian point about persons as ends in themselves, it depends on something which it distorts.

It is of the first importance in ethics that we should understand what conditions our sense of the kind of human individuality Kantians hope to express when they say that persons are ends in themselves, and for how long this can survive philosophical misconstrual and, indeed, hostility. Williams thinks it is conditioned by our partial attachments and by the way our projects and desires give sense to our lives. It is also conditioned, as Cora Diamond pointed out, by our attitude to the dead, by our naming rather than numbering our children and, as I have emphasised, by more explicitly moral conceptions – of guilt for example, as something that cannot be shared in the way other forms of suffering may be. Such things make our partial attachments what they are. Most of them are not just things we do because it is in our nature as a species to do them. Their role in our lives has to do with the sense they make for us, and that is never underwritten or guaranteed by appeal to certain facts of our nature. The sense we have of human individuality is one in which our partial attachments and more explicit moral conceptions are interdependent.

The sense we have of persons as irreplaceable is connected with our sense of their preciousness. Both are vulnerable to philosophical and moralistic devaluing of what conditions them. Williams quotes a passage from D. A. Richards' *A Theory of Reasons for Actions*, in which Richards says that we ought not to love or show personal affection to others 'on the basis of arbitrary physical characteristics alone, but rather on the basis of traits of personality and character related to acting on moral principles'.[10] Williams justifiably calls this 'righteous absurdity', and goes on to say, 'It is of course true that loving someone involves some relations of the kind that morality requires or imports more generally, but it does not follow from that that one cannot have them in the particular case unless one has them generally in the way that the moral person does.'[11]

Williams mislocates the place where we should look for generality. It is not so much in the lover's relations to others, but in how he has to see his beloved in order for her to be an intelligible object of his love. She is an intelligible object of his love only if he sees her as subject to the requirements of love, the claims which are internal to our sense of what counts as real love and what merely appears as love. Notoriously the claims of love (certainly those of erotic love) are not the same as those of morality. But they are not wholly other than those of morality either. To love someone is to be unable, while loving them, to tolerate the thought that one day we might be entirely indifferent to what should happen to them. Exactly that happens often enough, but it is condemned as much by love as it is by morality. That is a thought that lovers will be inclined to entertain about *this* person rather than persons in general, but it carries implications for persons in general, for it is a thought about the beloved as someone who may be *wronged*, which is not something she can be only as someone's beloved. That is partly what makes her an intelligible object for his love, and that notion has generality built into it.

We do not usually love people for their moral qualities, nor should we try to, and indeed we have one ideal of love for which that would be an unambiguous failing – the unconditional (but not unconditioned) love of parents for their children. An important reason why we should not, is that if we try to make love something reasonable or rational, then we threaten our hold on the manifestly non-reasonable 'belief' that human beings are precious. If we followed Richards' advice we would place any number of human beings beyond love, even beyond their parents' love. That is hardly an edifying thought.

I have said that our sense of the reality and of the preciousness of other human beings is partly, but importantly, tied to the fact that they have a power to affect us in ways we cannot fathom. There is nothing reasonable in the fact that another person's absence can make our lives seem empty. Richards is no doubt uneasy with that power and would prefer to limit it to those who merit it. The trouble is that no one merits it. It is because it is not a matter of merit that we are struck and bewildered by this dramatic manifestation of individuality. If such attachments are to be love, however, we must at some level consent to them. Otherwise they are a form of enslavement. As Plato recognised, that means bringing them under certain conceptions of goodness – conceptions of goodness sufficiently in harmony with moral goodness to enable them to be celebrated

155

without that seeming like a black mass. That means, at the very least, that love cannot be steeped in evil as a condition of its existence and fulfilment.

The power of other human beings to affect us in ways I have often drawn attention to is not primitive. We must first take them seriously, and to do that we must find it intelligible to ascribe certain kinds of thoughts and feeling to them. I alluded to this when I discussed the slave owner's relation to his slaves. I shall try to make the point clearer by commenting on a discussion by Cavell of what he calls 'soul blindness'. He wants to understand what people might mean when they speak of seeing a human being as a human being, and he considers the claim that a slave owner does not see slaves as human beings. He replies:

> What he really believes is not that slaves are not human beings, but that some human beings are slaves ... When he rapes a slave or takes her as a concubine, he does not feel that he has, by that fact itself, embraced sodomy ... he does not go to great lengths either to convert his horses to Christianity or to prevent their getting wind of it. Everything in his relation to his slaves shows that he treats them as more or less human – his humiliations of them, his disappointments, his jealousies, his fears, his punishments, his attachments.[12]

He then imagines a slave owner saying 'they are not human beings' and asks what he could mean. He concludes:

> He means, and can mean, nothing definite. This is a definite frame of mind. He means, indefinitely, that they are not *purely* human. He means, indefinitely, that there are *kinds* of humans ... He means, indefinitely, that slaves are different ... It could be said that what he denies is that the slave is 'other', i.e. other to his one.[13]

Take that last sentence: 'He denies ... that the slave is "other", i.e. other to his one.' Cavell means, I think, that the slave owner denies that the slave has his kind (the slave owner's kind) of individuality – the kind of individuality that shows itself in our revulsion in being numbered rather than called by name and that gives human beings the power to haunt those who have wronged them, in remorse. If

156

the slave owner could be haunted by the slave girl he raped, then her days as a slave would be numbered. That does not mean that he would not rape her, but it would then be as he would rape a white woman. The difference is that the evil he did her would now be within the intelligible reach of his remorse. It was, I think, the mark of the racially based slavery of the Southern States of America (when slave owners were unselfconscious and felt little need to invent rationalisations which focused on the empirical properties of their slaves) that whatever a slave owner did to his slaves was not within the conceptual reach of his remorse.

One way of characterising remorse in its difference from some other moral reactions is to say that it is possible only over what has the power to haunt us. That power is a certain kind of individuality. It is, I think, what Cavell means by speaking of someone as 'other to my one'. He means, other to my *one*. That is not obscurantism. I have already given sense to it in Chapter 4 when I discussed the one/ten example and when I discussed the remorse of the Dutch-woman. The individuality, the power to be other to his one, the power to be present to him, that the slave owner fails to acknowledge in the slave girl he rapes, conditions and is conditioned by his finding it intelligible that certain moral descriptions should apply to her – the kind that mark our sense of what it is to be a fully human being when we mean more than a fine member of the species *Homo sapiens*.

If we accept Cavell's invitation to see the slave girl as converted to Christianity, then we may also imagine her married. In the eyes of the slave owner, her conversion and marriage must be in inverted commas, for in his eyes she ('they') must lack that form of inward-ness necessary for a Christian understanding of them (the kind of capacity for a deepened understanding which I discuss in Chapter 14). Were he to grant her that capacity, then that would of itself be a form of her humanity becoming manifest to him, of his seeing her as 'another perspective on the world' (in the sense in which we use that expression to remind ourselves, and others, of the reality of another human being). It would be internal to his sense that she may explore her sexuality with any depth, which is, itself, internal to his sense of it *having* any depth, and which alone gives sense to the idea that rape is a form of violation. For a Christian, Christianity offers a deepened understanding of sexuality, in the light of which it is transformed. But that is dependent upon one having the depth to receive it, and that is not a brute fact about the species. It has little to do with the kind of intelligence for which he may have bought his slave girl to do the household accounts. As far as that kind of intelligence goes, his slave girl may be more intelligent than his wife and daughter and he may know it. But if he granted her the capacity for a deepened understanding of sexuality, which he would have to if he seriously believed that she had been married as a Christian, then she would be 'other to his one'.

He can rape someone who is married, yet she can be beyond the reach of his remorse only if he sees her merely as 'married'. He rapes her as he does, that is, as a slave girl, because her sexuality is outside the (conceptual) space of the kind of pity whose character is determined by its taking a suffering human being as its object.[14] However he pities her, it is not as someone of whom he finds it intelligible to believe that suffering could go deep. If he pities her, it cannot be as one who may be grievously wronged, as one whose sexuality has been violated, because his sense of what he can do in raping her is limited by his sense of what her sexuality can mean for her. (His slave-owning neighbour may think him cruel, but he may think that he is also cruel to his dogs.) It is true, as Cavell says, that when he rapes her he does not, thereby, think that he has committed sodomy. It is in some ways worse. She appears to him as sufficiently unlike an animal for him not to feel disgusted, but sufficiently like one for her sexuality to have no meaning.

It is tempting to say that he treats her like an animal or as something half-way between animal and human life – as though he believes that suffering could mean little more to her than what it does to an animal, but believes also that she has certain capacities and properties which animals do not have. Or, to put it another way, it is tempting to say that he treats her as an animal of an extraordinary kind – one that can speak, do the accounts and so on. That would be misleading and Cavell is right to point it out. His responses to her are as to something of a different kind from animals. That is why Cavell says that the slave owner can mean only something indefinite when he says that she is not human or not fully human. But Cavell seems to assume that 'human' as we mean it in this context is a relatively determinate classificatory term. The slave owner may not know quite what to say if he is asked why 'they' are not human beings, but he most definitely means that 'they are not one of us'. When we use the expression 'human being' in this way, we have, and could have, no determinate sense of its extension and, after a certain point, we can have no sense in advance (no sense informed by theory) of what will count as a human being. That contrasts with the expression 'Homo sapiens', whose extension is determinate and determined by scientific theory.

The slave owner does not fail to see the kinds of things I have been referring to because he fails to see her as a human being. To fail to understand (know) such things *is* what it is for him to fail to see her as a human being in the only sense that is relevant, that is, as something more than *Homo sapiens*. If he saw her as married (without the inverted commas), then (I do not mean only then) he would have to take her sexuality humanly seriously and, therefore, be threatened by the realisation of the evil he did to her. That realisation is remorse. Cavell is wrong to say that 'everything in his relations to his slaves shows that he treats them as more or less human', and that his sense of their difference is 'indefinite'. The slave owner treats his slaves as many philosophers would have us treat human beings – as members of a species with certain empirically discoverable and morally relevant capacities.

There are many moral descriptions, *definite* moral descriptions, of what his slaves are, of what they do and suffer, that the slave owner must withhold. Why does he withhold them? To take the example of the raped slave girl again. Perhaps he cannot see human sexuality as fully present in a black body, no more than he can see fully human sorrow in a black face, not just because it is black, but because these features cannot express it for him. Perhaps his sense of her sexuality is that 'they screw like monkeys'. He certainly thinks that 'it cannot be for them what it is for us' – nothing amongst 'them' really counts as betrayal for nothing really counts as being faithful. Perhaps he cannot hear dignity in their speech or in their music. Cavell's slave owner and his friends thought of themselves as Christians. They thought of their slaves as 'Christians'. He and his friends could think of themselves as Christians only because they could think of themselves as serious respondents to the question,

'What is it to be a Christian?' That is not a capacity of the same kind as the capacity to speak, to remember, to think or to be self-conscious, and its acknowledgement in another is not of the same kind as the acknowledgement of such capacities.

Did his slaves not discuss what becoming Christians meant to them? Did he not overhear them? He probably did, but what do we assume he heard and what, in this context, is it *to be able to hear*? Did he hear the inwardness that informs authoritative and authentic speech? He knew they could be clever. He knew they could speak in imitation of their masters. He knew they could speak the lines of the Bible. But if he could not hear the affliction in their music, how could he hear Christian inwardness in their prayers? Yet, clearly he could not hear the affliction in their music, for if he did, then he would see his actions under descriptions that would bring them into the conceptual space of a serious remorse.

I said that the slave owner *could* not have heard the affliction in their music. Should I not, at most, say that he *did* not? I would not, because that does not capture the distance between him and his slaves, between his slaves and those he would not dream of making slaves, even though he might treat them unjustly. If he rapes a white girl and is deaf to her agony, then I do not know how he has to change if he is to hear her and be seized by horror at what he does, but it is importantly different from how he must change if he is to see the evil he did to the slave girl he raped. It is connected with the fact that in relation to the white girl he keeps remorse at bay only through self-deception, through self-deceiving descriptions of her and, therefore, of what he did. If he must deceive himself about the slave girl, then she has reason to hope that her days as a slave will soon be at an end. Perhaps he will then invent empirically relevant differences between negroes and whites. Perhaps he will say that negroes are less intelligent, or that they have a different evolutionary history. Perhaps a pseudo-science will emerge. The time will then have come to ask him to demonstrate what the differences are between whites and negroes and what relevance they have.

The racist taunt, 'Would you want your daughter to marry one?', is instructive. If it revolts you that someone whom you think seriously capable of love should be physically tender to certain peoples, then talk of respecting them as persons begins to idle. It does not revolt the slave owner that someone whom he thinks seriously capable of love should love and be physically tender to a white woman he rapes. What can be a proper object of tenderness can be violated – it is part of what gives sense to the idea that it can be violated. When I speak of someone whom the slave owner thinks to be seriously capable of love, I mean that he sees her as subject to love's claims even if she does not rise to them. We can only love those that others could love too. That is part of what I meant when I said that we can only love those whom we see as intelligible objects of our love. We cannot, unilaterally, make something intelligible.

The slave girl is not an intelligible object of her master's love. That means that, in his eyes, she is not an intelligible object for anyone's love. He does not think, 'We cannot love them but they can love each other', for he speaks as he does of 'us' and 'them' because he denies that kind of meaning to their feelings, responses, actions and lives. If he thought the slave girl could be loved by her husband, then he would know her as one who could return that love in wifely response. Then when he rapes her he would know that he rapes a wife. But that is what he does not know. If she were to become pregnant he could not see what she carries in pregnancy as something precious. Nor can he think that she can understand it as something precious, even if she says that it is, and even if she kills herself in her grief when he forces her to abort it because he needs her to work.

Something is precious only in a world of meaning in which the slaves are denied fellowship. That is why they are 'them'. That is why the slave girl's love for her husband and for her unborn child has no power of revelation for the slave owner. The slave owner knows that his slaves have interests, desires, feelings, hopes for the future, memories of the past. He ascribes to his slaves those capacities and properties philosophers list when they try to determine what the necessary and sufficient conditions are for being a 'person'. The reason they are slaves is not because he thinks that they lack them, but because he denies them a certain content.

Previously I reported Rush Rhees as saying that there cannot be love without the language of love. That is because without the language of love there could not be the claims of love and there is no love without love's claims. No doubt, there must be more than, and much that has to be before, the language of love. Rhees would be the first to point it out. There must be bodies with which we feel at home and through which love's tenderness can find expression. More primitively, there must be faces. We could not love what did not have a face – which was of a *kind* that had no face or which (a machine for example) had a face only accidentally. (I do not mean that we cannot love a human being who has no face because of some terrible injury.) The slave girl had a face, but it was not one her master could find in the poetry which informed the language of love which taught him what love was through its celebration. Peter Singer said that you do not have to like black people in order to acknowledge their rights.[15] There is a sense in which that is true, but it is often said, and he said it, in a way that hides a terrible falsehood.

There is no point in telling the slave owner that his slaves are, after all, human beings (or fully paid up persons), and there is no point in challenging him to *demonstrate* that his slaves are different from him and other whites in some 'morally relevant' respect. Their differences and their difference seem apparent to him. He cannot demonstrate them. But neither can it be *demonstrated*, not to him or to anyone else, that they are not as he sees them. It could not be demonstrated that someone whose face appeared as is caricatured in the *Black and White Minstrel Show* could not play Othello, that someone with such a face could not mean the words he was given to speak, because someone with such a face could not suffer as Othello did and speak Othello's words with power and authority. The reason why he cannot play Othello is not because he cannot utter those sentences and it is not because he cannot utter those sentences in ways such that, were we merely to hear them (perhaps over the radio), they would move us deeply. It is because it is impossible for us to take them seriously when they come from a face like that. We cannot find it intelligible that suffering could go deep in someone like that. For the slave owner, the slaves' humanity is epistemically impotent. But the kinds of properties that philosophers generally believe to be morally relevant are fully visible to him.

How does it become otherwise? Certainly not through philosophy, nor through science – no more than philosophy or science could teach us to see dignity in faces that all look alike to us. It would be like trying to *prove* that you could cast a *Black and White Minstrel* face to play Othello. When we do come to see dignity in a face, or human sexuality in a body, or hear human sorrow in a song, or slip into conversation when previously there had been only instructing or commanding, then human individuality and a human moral subject become manifest together, one as the condition of the other.

The slave owner was evilly mistaken about his slaves, but not as he would be if he started inventing empirically relevant differences between them and those he would not dream of holding as slaves. That his slave girl was a Christian and not merely a 'Christian', or that she was a proper respondent to love's claims, or that her body could invite, and worthily receive, a tender caress, or that her affliction could lacerate her soul – these are not things he could learn from books, whether they were scientific or philosophical, nor could he learn them by looking and listening more attentively in the sense in which that might yield more detailed empirical information. If he came to see his slaves like this, then we would say that he sees them as human beings and we would be right to say that he had 'come to see things as they are', but the grammar of that should not be misunderstood. What he must learn has to do not with facts and the consistent application of principles, but with meaning – with the meaning that the lives of his slaves can have, with what they can understand, feel and do and, therefore, with what they can be.

10

'An attitude towards a soul'

I have often spoken of our sense of the *reality* of another human being, and I have connected it with the fact that we may be affected by others in ways we cannot fathom and in ways against which we cannot acceptably protect ourselves. This emphasis on the interdependence of object and response is recognisably Wittgensteinian, although it has also been important to philosophers coming from other directions. David Wiggins asked whether we desire something because we think it is good or whether we think that something is good because we desire it. He answered that both are true, and that this is not equivocation or in other ways compromised because the 'because' is different in both cases.[1] I would say (I am not sure whether Wiggins would) that we would not have the concept of something's being good were it not for the (general) fact that we desire things, but in any individual case the object of desire presents itself as good. In the one case the 'because' is relative to an individual and in the other it is relative to general human responses, natural or conventional. That is a constitutive interdependence. There is a third, epistemic, dimension. Actions have the power of revelation; a certain kind of love, for example, might reveal its object to us. But that supervenes on the other two and, as I emphasised, is culturally dependent. That *kind* of cultural dependence did not figure at all prominently in *Philosophical Investigations*. It is controversial whether it is implicit in it. Rush Rhees argues that it is, and that it is basic to Wittgenstein's sense of what language is,[2] but it is certainly not to the fore, and when Wittgenstein speaks of human beings in the *Investigations* he seems, as Cavell says, to be thinking of them in ways shaped by a certain response to scepticism:[3] 'What gives us *so much as the idea* that living beings, things, can feel?';[4] 'My attitude towards him is an attitude towards a soul. I am not of the *opinion* that he has a Soul.'[5] Those remarks have deep ethical implications, but they are not made in direct response to ethical questions. If we took the route to be direct, we would lose sight of Wittgenstein's radicalism. Indeed, it might be thought that my discussions of slavery and pregnancy are Wittgensteinian in a way that denies him his radicalism, because they suggest that traditional epistemology and philosophy of mind are adequate for the ascription of those kinds of capacities and properties that figure in the lists that philosophers compose when they try to determine what are the necessary and sufficient conditions for being a person.

Wittgenstein's radicalism consists in denying the adequacy of the traditional picture even at that level – at the level, for example, of the ascription of sensations. We might then wonder how the two levels are to be combined, because the point I was making seemed to depend upon the adequacy of the traditional picture for the ascription of sensation. The difficulty might be put this way. It may seem as though I was saying that the traditional picture is perfectly adequate to the epistemic and general grammar of the concept *Homo sapiens* (taking that to include mental properties) because the properties in question are empirically-cum-discursively attributable, but that it is not adequate for the concept of a human being insofar as that means something more than *Homo sapiens*. It may seem, indeed, that my criticism of other philosophers was essentially the criticism that the concept of a human being, insofar as it differed from the concept *Homo sapiens*, is merely the concept of *Homo sapiens* plus something which is epistemically continuous with the knowledge of *Homo sapiens* or a projection on to it (the latter being a 'non-cognitivist' account of the moral connotations of some of our ways of speaking of human beings).

I do not think that I am committed to such a view, although I elaborated it because it would be understandable if someone were to think that I am. But it is time to make finer distinctions. I hope to place what I have said in a more detailed discussion of what may be learnt from the *Investigations*. I do not intend the following discussion to underpin what I have said in previous chapters, especially

165

in Chapter 9. What I said there must stand independently of the controversial account of Wittgenstein that follows. My aim is to make
what I said clearer by placing it and by making finer distinctions.

Let us recall the traditional picture as it applies to slavery. It is
this. The slave owner did not know or believe that his slaves had
certain morally relevant properties or capacities, or he knew that
they did, but failed to apply his principles consistently, or his perception of the non-natural moral properties they had in common with
his fellow whites was clouded because he had powerful interests in
not seeing things as they are. The salient thought is that if he sees
that his slaves have the same properties and capacities as his fellow
whites do, then he should treat them as he does his fellow whites.
Because this account focuses on the matching of principles and properties, it will range over any entity that has such capacities and
properties. It does not matter whether it is black or white. It does
not matter whether it is a human being or some other creature. It
does not even matter whether it is a living being (if a machine can
be said to have them then our principles must regulate our conduct
appropriately to such machines). All that matters is whether it is
an entity that has properties and capacities relevant to one's moral
principles.

From one perspective this looks to be no more than a truism. We
must show things to *be* (relevantly) different if we are to justify
treating them differently. No one would flatly deny this. The slave
owner treated his slaves differently from those he would not dream
of making slaves because he saw his slaves as different from them
in morally salient ways. It is, however, not a truism that this should
be expressed in the way I have just sketched. I hope already to have
gone some way to showing that.

The philosophical account I sketched above yields, I believe, a
naive account of racially based slavery and of racism more generally,
but it is an account virtually forced on philosophers by their limited
sense of the elements out of which a philosophical account can be
built. This limited sense of what may go into an adequate philosophical account is conditioned by two assumptions. First, there is
an assumption about what it is to be in cognitive possession of
whatever may be morally salient in our responses to one another.
Secondly, there is an assumption about what belongs to the surface

in any such account and what lies deeper and is the essence of the matter. That second assumption has already come up on a number of occasions in my discussion. It first appeared in my discussion of Donagan – the language in which Falstaff expresses his unconditional respect for other human beings is thought to belong to the surface while the Kantian reconstruction is thought to go deep and to express what is essential. With respect to the present range of examples, the philosopher's sense of what belongs to the surface is even more breathtaking – our human bodies, their characteristic inflexions and demeanours and the conventions of their expressiveness. The deepest of Wittgenstein's lessons against philosophical theorising lies in his different sense of what, even for philosophy, belongs to the surface and what is essential. It is a lesson against a false sense of depth and against a false sense of penetrating the appearances.

The slave owner sees his slaves as different from those whom he would never dream of enslaving. It does not follow that his relation to those he would not dream of enslaving rests upon his belief that they possess the kinds of capacities and properties philosophers list when they try to answer the question, 'What makes an entity a person?', together with his possession of certain moral principles. Or, if not this, that he sees in them certain irreducibly moral properties. *A fortiori*, it does not follow that the way he treats his slaves, or the fact that he has slaves, shows either that he does not believe they have those properties or that he fails, for whatever reason, to apply his principles consistently. Nor does it follow that the difference in his relations to his fellow whites and to his slaves is to be accounted for by the success or failure of a cognitive capacity whose proper exercise yields the kind of knowledge that is logically independent of the fact that it is primarily *of* human beings *by* human beings. That does not mean that his understanding of what is morally important cannot extend beyond human beings, but if it does (as it does to a degree with animals and as it might with other creatures) then it extends non-accidentally *from here*, that is from amongst our human selves, from a humanly circumscribed sense of epistemic location.

Wittgenstein said that 'only of a living human being and what resembles (behaves like) a living human being can one say: it has sensations; it sees; is blind; is deaf; is conscious or unconscious'.[6]

He did not mean, merely, that human beings were, for us, a paradigm – that human thought and feeling constituted an epistemic bench mark – for our knowledge of what may feel and think and so on. He meant, I think, that the forms of our interaction conditioned the general and epistemic grammar of the way we speak of 'the mental', in such a way as to place severe restrictions on anything that could seriously be meant by a 'non-anthropocentric' conception of how things 'objectively are'. But I have put the point in a language which threatens to obscure the radical nature of his point. It is not that our humanity places certain things beyond our epistemic reach. Rather that it places certain limits on what we can conceive as being beyond that reach (that, for example, there was something which is what it is – subjectively – like to be a bat), of what we could conceive as being the possible objects of knowledge of an ideally epistemic being. To say that it is a requirement of objectivity that we step back to the point where we see human beings *as merely amongst* the many possible entities that can think, feel, etc., and that a human perspective is only one (limited) epistemic vantage point inferior to 'the point of view of the universe', is a classical philosophical instance of sawing away the branch on which one is sitting. The further we move (in the hope of seeing the world 'as from no place within it') from what we judge to be merely accidental and local, the more attenuated becomes our sense of the concepts with which we describe what is within our epistemic reach and also *of what it is for something to be within our (or an ideally rational being's) epistemic reach*. It means that our understanding of what it could be for other creatures to think, feel, speak, etc., is inexpungeably anthropocentric. Not, however, in the bad sense of that term which suggests a failure to see things as they are. Wiggins puts it well: 'Criticism often involves finding the right distance from the point of view of a direct participant; and there is no limit that can in advance be set upon that right distance, except that it must not reach into incomprehension.'[7]

Applied to what philosophers call the ascription of mental predicates, one might put the point like this: to think that our sense of another human being is of an entity to which we have truly ascribed certain mental capacities and properties – on the basis of the proper (though limited) workings of the kind of epistemic capacity I

168

sketched above – is to think of another human being as an object (a mind-cum-body object) with a subjective dimension only unto itself. That is why Nagel thinks that subjectivity or consciousness provides a special problem for the ideal of objectivity which he expresses as 'seeing the world as from no place within it.'[8]

The first thing to notice about this picture is its epistemological passivity. According to it, we are in the world as spectators 'cognising' certain properties of certain entities. We classify entities as belonging to different kinds according to their different properties by means of the operation of a cognitive capacity which is (conceptually) independent of action and effect. It could be a capacity operative in beings of radically different physical kinds from us and, indeed, in beings who had no will (or at least who could not act in the world) and who had no feelings. More strongly, action and affect are external to the grammar of the objects of the exercise of such a capacity. To be an object of properly cognitive possession is to be an object of a kind to be appropriated by a capacity that is logically independent of will and affect. Our cognitive appropriation of the world is as spectators who, as it happens, are also beings who act and who feel. The point is not merely that knowledge is a state that is motivationally inert. It is that its proper objects are of a kind to which any rational being may be indifferent. This picture is consistent with the acknowledgement that thinking or perceiving are activities.

The picture, as I have painted it, is very general and there have been many objections to it at that general level. They may be expressed in the slogan that we cannot prize the world apart from our concerns and interests – that we cannot make sense of the world as available to that kind of cognitive appropriation. That is to say that we cannot make sense of that kind of cognitive appropriation and of a conception of the world – of things 'as they really are' – as the proper object of such appropriation. At a general level that is one of Wittgenstein's lessons and, at a general level, it was put most forcibly amongst contemporary philosophers by Stuart Hampshire in *Thought and Action*.[9] The decomposition of this picture is, for good or for ill, part of contemporary philosophy and it has been part of a new attack on non-cognitivism in ethics.[10]

It is a moot point how much non-cognitivism depended upon such a picture, but it certainly depended upon a conception of the cognitive such that it was essential to something's being a proper object of knowledge or belief that it could be known or believed without that further affecting our non-cognitive dispositions. It was part of the conception of the cognitive that informed non-cognitivism in ethics that whatever was cognitively appropriated was, of its nature, something to which we could be indifferent. We can think that without also thinking that the world can be prized apart from our concerns and interests. Artefacts illustrate the point. We can know that there is a chair in the room and be indifferent to it. One strand amongst contemporary reactions to non-cognitivism has been to argue the following. In some cases, if we understand or know something, then we are disposed to act in certain ways or to feel in certain ways quite independently of that understanding engaging with independently characterisable and pre-existing desires, in the way conceived by Hume when he said that Reason by itself moves nothing.[11] Its thrust has been self-consciously anti-Humean and is a much stronger claim than that the world cannot be prised apart from our concerns and interests.[12]

In its most general form, the stronger claim is congenial to what I have been saying in previous chapters, but it is uncongenial in the form it has characteristically taken. Those philosophers who have argued it have been impressed with the application to ethics of a visual analogy in ways which strike me as obstructive of a better understanding of the nature of moral understanding. They have been inclined to speak of the perception of moral properties in ways alien to the drift of my argument, which has focused on a dialogical analogy.[13]

One reason why I invoked the dialogical analogy is to emphasise the right kind of *intersubjectivity* that is internal to (even if it is not sufficient for) any sense of moral objectivity. And it is in this connection that I would speak again of our sense of the reality of another person. For according to the forms of cognitivism that are influenced by the visual analogy, we speak as we do of human beings as distinct from *Homo sapiens* because human beings are *Homo sapiens* plus moral properties. Such cognitivists differ from non-cognitivists only in that non-cognitivists believe that the moral resonances of the way we speak of human beings are projections, whereas cognitivists believe they are resonances responsive to objective moral properties.

(We will ignore the minor complications of Kantian forms of objec-
tivism – I have discussed them sufficiently to make it clear why they
would present only minor complications to the point I am now
making.) But now one might ask from what perspective does that
seem a *small* difference?

In the previous chapter I made use of Cavell's phrase 'other to
my one' to explore the kind of reality characteristic of a human
being. The question that naturally arises is whether it sheds light on
our concern to understand the unique kind of limit each human
being is to the will of another, or whether it is just another way of
speaking of that limit. We can sharpen that question by noticing
differences in the way Cavell speaks of another human being as
'other' – differences which correspond, on the one hand, to the
difference between the way in which my discussion in the previous
chapter was recognisably Wittgensteinian and, on the other, to
Wittgenstein's concerns in the *Investigations*.

Cavell writes: 'Ought not there [to] . . . be an objection to the
argument from analogy concerning its narcissism? Call the argument
autological: it yields at best a mind too like mine. It leaves out the
otherness of the other.'[14] What Cavell tries to capture, or evoke, by
the expression 'the otherness of the other' is a kind of dynamic interaction which is not a consequence, but the condition, of what some
philosophers call 'the ascription of mental predicates', or 'the attribution of mental properties or capacities' – not a consequence, but
a condition, of what we call intersubjectivity. The point might be
put this way: we need a proper account of objectivity based upon
a proper account of the 'otherness of the other' or, as Wiggins puts
it, of the '*alterity*, the otherness of the subjectivity of others'.[15]

The classical problem of other minds is to determine whether
there are more things of a particular kind than one. At one level it
is merely a kind of taxonomical problem: can I (the sceptical inquirer
into what can be justifiably included in a book on what can be
known) know whether these things (bodies) are also another kind
of thing (minds or minds-cum-bodies or persons)? I can if I can
know that this thing, which moves around in certain ways, has a
certain physical shape, etc., also thinks and feels. The difficulty
seems to be that whether or not it can think or feel is beyond my
epistemic reach. But whether I believe, as does the sceptic, that this

is irredeemably beyond my epistemic reach, or whether I believe that it is, albeit inferentially, within my epistemic reach, or whether I believe that it is directly within my epistemic reach through intuition or some other mode of 'direct access', the sense of epistemic capacity, its proper objects and its achievement, is basically the same. Whether I get it inferentially or whether I get it directly, I get what philosophers tend to call 'propositional knowledge' – that there are other things of a particular kind in the world. Contemporary philosophy, which is not much troubled by scepticism, thinks of other minds in the same way, except that its problem is not whether there are other minds but where else they might be. Do dolphins think? Do machines think? Does a brain in a vat think?

What can be wrong with this? What could knowledge that there are other people be if not knowledge *that* there are other people? The idea that propositional knowledge of the physical properties of a person and propositional knowledge of their mental properties are both knowledge of them as a kind of *object* – that it is insufficiently attentive to the 'otherness of others' – seems to have only rhetorical force, sustained by ignoring the difference in kind between mental and physical predicates.

No one will deny there is a difference in kind (logic, grammar) between mental and physical predicates. However, the question is whether our sense of the difference in kind adequately marks our sense of the difference between human beings and trees as objects of knowledge while it is tied to the idea that we know that something is a human being if it has certain properties, just as we know that something is a tree if it has certain properties. Sounds are different in kind from sights, and both are different in kind from thought, but are they different in kind *qua* facts, or *qua* objects of propositional knowledge? The question is: How are we to mark our sense of the difference in kind between mental and physical predicates in such a way as to get right our sense of the difference between our knowledge that there are other human beings and our knowledge that there are trees? I am suggesting that we get it wrong if we think of our knowledge that there are other human beings, and our knowledge that they think and feel, as propositional knowledge composed of concepts of a certain logical character (the character that makes them different in kind from concepts of physical objects).

172

Perhaps my question, whether our sense of the difference in kind between mental and physical predicates is sufficient to account for our sense of the difference between our knowledge that there are human beings and our knowledge that there are trees, is too obscure, or too vague, to be answered. Any answer will depend upon what counts as a difference in kind sufficient to mark our sense that other human beings are differently *present* to us than are trees, chairs, etc. If we wish to say that treating our knowledge of other people as propositional knowledge alongside the knowledge that there are trees, etc., gets wrong our sense both of the knowledge of other people and of their reality (despite the acknowledgement that there are profound differences in kind, even amongst forms of propositional knowledge), then more needs to be said about why it gets it wrong. More needs to be said about why that loses the 'otherness of the other'.

Peter Winch is concerned with the same problem in his paper entitled 'Eine Einstellung zur Seele'. He quotes this passage from Simone Weil:

> The human beings around us exert just by their presence a power which belongs uniquely to themselves to stop, to diminish or modify each movement which our bodies design. A person who crosses our path does not turn aside our steps in the same manner as a street sign, no one stands up, or moves about, or sits down again in quite the same fashion when he is alone in a room as when he has a visitor.[16]

Winch was discussing the passage from Wittgenstein which I have already quoted. ('My attitude towards him is an attitude towards a soul [*eine Einstellung zur Seele*]. I am not of the *opinion* that he has a soul.') He argues that having 'an attitude towards a soul' is not consequent upon the ascription of particular states of thought to people, but rather a condition of it. What Cavell means by 'the otherness of others' is expressed by Simone Weil when she says that 'the human beings around us exert just by their presence a power which belongs uniquely to them'. That is what is missed by speaking of human beings or persons as entities with certain properties and capacities assessed for their relevance to certain rules or principles of conduct or to our interests and desires, in the same way as the recognition of the properties or capacities of anything else in nature.

The quotation from Weil is an excellent example of an attitude towards a soul in the sense in which Wittgenstein speaks of it, and it is also an excellent example of another human being as 'other' to oneself in the sense in which Cavell speaks of it in my most recent quotation of him. But it is also clear that someone may be, in this sense, 'other' to a slave owner. We have no reason to assume that the slave owner 'stands up, or moves about, or sits down in quite the same fashion when he is alone in a room' as when his slave is in the room, although Weil was at times inclined to say just that. Immediately before the passage quoted by Winch she says:

> It is not for want of sensibility that Achilles had, by a sudden gesture, pushed the old man glued against his knees to the ground. Priam's words, evoking his old father, had moved him to tears. Quite simply he had found himself to be as free in his attitudes, in his movements, as if in place of a suppliant an inert object were there touching his knees.[17]

And immediately afterwards she says:

> But this indefinable influence of the human presence is not exer-cised by those men whom a movement of impatience could deprive of their lives even before a thought had had the time to condemn them. Before these men others behave as if they were not there.[18]

She speaks in the same tone of those who passed by the man tended by the Good Samaritan.[19] But the slave owner need not treat the slave girl he rapes that way. Is there a connection between points such as I have just been making and the points I made in the previous chapter? It seems unlikely if we limit what we can learn from what Wittgenstein said about an 'attitude towards a soul' to the concerns that dominate the *Investigations*.

Before we look more closely at Wittgenstein, it will be profitable to ask what Weil meant by that 'indefinable influence of the human presence' which she said was 'not exercised by those men whom a movement of impatience could deprive of their lives'. An answer suggests itself if we attend to an account quite different from hers and which links with my previous discussion of propositional knowledge. It goes like this: If during a storm I see that my path is blocked by a fallen tree, then I may be dismayed and even frightened. If I see that my path is blocked by an enemy soldier, then, too, I may be dismayed and frightened. In both cases I 'cognise' that there is something before me which has certain properties and I react with dismay and fear because of that realisation and what it means in these circumstances – briefly, that I am endangered in certain ways. In both cases I deliberate about what to do on the basis of my assessment of my situation. What I conclude will be dependant upon my assessment of the objective features of my situation, which include my affective reactions to it and my capacities to deal with it.

The sense in which an enemy soldier is an object for my epistemological grasp (this account continues) is no different from the way in which the fallen tree is. The sense in which he is epistemically present to me is no different from the way in which the tree is. What is to be known about the tree and the enemy soldier is logically independent of my affective reactions. Of course a human being is a thing of a different kind from a tree, but a tree is also a thing of a different kind from a boulder. All three are different in kind because of their properties. They are not, therefore, *real* in different ways, nor are they epistemically present in different ways. I may react differently to them, but that is because of my beliefs or knowledge about their properties. It is a property of the enemy soldier that he has an intention to stop me. I may guess that he is as frightened as I am. This knowledge will affect any strategy I may devise to get past him, but it bears on my strategy in the same way as does my assessment of the size of the tree. It is true that my moral principles may limit the strategies I may devise to get past the soldier, but that, too, makes no difference to the sense in which he is epistemically or 'ontologically' present to me. We do sometimes speak of human beings being present to one in ways quite different from anything else in nature, but that is a misleading way of speaking of the way our epistemic grasp of their properties affects us or the way our actions in relation to that knowledge may be limited by our principles. Thus (this account acknowledges), what Simone Weil says is half true. We *do* tend to react differently to human beings than to other things, including other kinds of animal. The reasons for this are various and are not hard to find, although their detailed

175

elaboration may belong to one or other of the sciences – biology, of course, but probably psychology too.

Such an account as I have sketched in the last two paragraphs, and which contrasts with what Weil says, seems natural. It seems to accommodate whatever is right in the thought that human beings are present to one another in a distinctive way and to ward off what is obscurantist in it. What, then, can be wrong with it?

When Wittgenstein said that we might say that pity was 'a *form* of conviction that someone else is in pain'[20] (my italics) he evidently meant to contrast that with the idea that pity is a response consequent upon something more properly called 'a form of conviction' or 'belief' or 'knowledge'. It is natural (not only to philosophers) to think that pity is an 'affective' state or disposition which is to be contrasted with, and which is dependent upon, a 'cognitive state' such as believing or knowing that someone is in pain. (After all, the fact that someone is in pain cannot move us to pity him unless we believe that he is in pain.) We conceive of this cognitive state as being the result of the exercise of a capacity which yields an appropriate cognitive object, and we think of this capacity and its exercise as logically, though not causally, independent of the affective dispositions of any particular person. (The causal interchange goes both ways: the deliverances of this capacity affect us and our affections affect its working, not only in giving it direction but also in providing it with energy.) It is Wittgenstein's lesson that in the case of what we call 'knowing' or 'believing' that another is in pain, this capacity and its deliverances (propositional knowledge) are fictions. Knowledge that another person is in pain is not an achievement that can be characterised independently of certain affective dispositions.

One reason why this seems preposterous is that we can know that someone is in (severe) pain and yet be utterly indifferent. The possibility of indifference in the face of such knowledge is, as we have noted, the motive for many non-cognitivist accounts of ethics, which are built on the assumption that mere knowledge is essentially something we can be indifferent to.

Much knowledge is like that, even when the concepts involved in it are themselves conditioned by certain characteristic actions and reactions. The concept of a chair, for example, is conditioned not only by our interests, but also by certain physical dispositions ('It is part of the grammar of the word "chair" that *this* is what we call "to sit on a chair"'[21]). However, we can know that there is a chair in the room and yet be entirely indifferent to it. Our indifference will call for comment only if something else connected with our interests and desires is known about us. This corresponds to the Humean picture. But Wittgenstein did not mean that the knowledge that there is a chair in the room triggered a disposition to sit. And the reason why Wittgenstein said that pity was a form of conviction was not merely because reactions of a certain kind are internal to the concept of pain. We do not capture what is at stake here by putting it in that general form. What he meant is not captured by thinking of it merely as a further instance of his general polemic against a passive, spectator's conception of concept formation.

Indifference in the face of another's severe pain does, of itself, call for comment. This proves nothing, but it is an important counter to the Humean picture which suggests that when two people both know that a third person is in pain, and one comes to his aid whereas the other does not, then it is the action of the first which calls for (philosophical) comment. It then seems that we must give the person who helps something in addition to his knowledge, presumably because he has moved and 'everything is moved by pushing and pulling'.[22] Our actual practice, however, tends to go the other way. We add something to the person who does not help. We say for example that he is hard-hearted, or that he believes that charity encourages such people in their indolent ways, and so on. The Humean picture misplaces the onus by shifting our focus away from such things to a static world in which everything is still. So we begin to wonder how anything moves.

There is indifference and there is indifference. If you tell me that Leeds is roughly two hundred miles from London, then I may ask, 'What is that to me?' That is one kind of indifference. You may remind me that I plan to travel to Leeds next week, and that is one way of engaging my concern. But if you tell me that someone is in pain and I ask, 'What is that to me?', then that is a different kind of indifference. We call it callousness. That suggests the possibility that pity is not merely a psychological state with which knowledge must engage in order to overcome the essential indifference which is thought to be internal to mere knowledge. *It suggests that pity is normative for the descriptions of the forms of our indifference to the suffering of others.*

It is usually said that the reason indifference to another person's pain calls for comment is either because it is unusual or because we tend to pass unfavourable moral judgement upon such indifference. To take the last point first – that in calling the indifference callousness, for example, we are passing unfavourable moral comment on it. *How then should we describe the indifference upon which we pass that judgement and which is supposedly internal to knowledge as such?* We could say that someone saw another in severe pain and continued what he was doing without, as we say, 'batting an eyelid'. And suppose he says that he clearly saw that the other person was in severe pain, but it meant nothing to him? Does he express the pure fact of his indifference unadulterated by moral judgement? He expresses his callousness.

It seems to need no explanation why we pity someone in pain when we do. Pity is a response to something essential to pain. But if we ask to what it is a response, then we say something trivial like it is a response to the painfulness of pain, or to the hurtfulness of pain, or to the fact that pain may be terrible. If we ask which pains are terrible, it is tempting to reply that they are the very painful ones. That is one reason why philosophers prefer to speak of the essential phenomenological qualities of pain, or of the subjective qualities of pain, or the *qualia* of pain. It sounds less trivial. But it amounts to the same thing. What, in this connection, are the phenomenological qualities of pain if not its painfulness? It adds up to little more than saying that pain is painful and there are degrees of it. And it goes with this thought to say that pain *qua* pain, considered only as painful, the pain itself, the phenomenological quality of pain, can be the same in a dog or a human being, and indeed in a fly or an earthworm.

Wittgenstein was suspicious of such a thought, not because of his supposed verificationist tendencies, nor because he confused the epistemic inaccessibility of a fly's pain with the metaphysical possibility of it being in pain. He did not think it is clear what is being said. The reason he was suspicious is because the question of whether or not an earthworm is in pain involves a conception of pain such that, if it were epistemically accessible, it would be a piece of propositional knowledge. We think in the case of flies or worms that either they are or are not in pain and that we may never know. The kind of knowledge we have in mind here is propositional knowledge.

If it is intelligible to ask whether a fly is in pain when someone plucks off its wings, then it should be intelligible to wonder whether it is in agony. But our problem is not that we do not know whether a particular fly is in agony or whether flies are ever in agony. Our problem, I think, is that we do not know *what to make of the idea* that a fly might be in agony. What if someone were to say, 'Of course we do: *qua* an "entity" or a "being" in pain and considered only as the bearer of a sensation, a fly in agony would feel more or less as we do when we are in agony and we know what that is like by imaginatively extracting the *qualia* of our agonising sensations from other aspects of our (complex) subjectivity.' That, I think, is not an answer to the doubt but simply the expression of incredulity that such a doubt should have arisen at all. How, after all, *do* we feel when we are in agony? The only answer can be: like we feel when we are in agony and do we not know from our own case what that is like? The trouble, here, is that we treat all the differences between us and flies as being physical conditions necessary for the capacity to feel pain, or as epistemic clues or signs that something is in pain, or as things in addition to pain (memory, anticipation, etc.) which may complicate even its phenomenological qualities.

The idea that we might make sense of the possibility that a fly is in agony is perhaps encouraged by the idea that we can pity a fly when someone plucks off its wings. However, if someone says that he has no idea of what it would be for a fly to be in pain or agony, then he need not deny that it is cruel to pluck off its wings. It is, after all, a kind of benchmark of cruelty: 'I suppose you were the kind of little boy who plucked the wings off flies.' Our sense of its cruelty does not depend upon the conjecture or the belief that the fly is in pain, just as our reluctance to turn on the tap to wash the spider down the plughole need not be due to a sense of 'what it is (subjectively) to be' a spider washed down a plughole. (If we wished to teach children not to wash spiders down plugholes we should be careful with remarks such as, 'How would you feel if you were washed down the plughole?') It is the wanton mutilation of a living thing that justifies our claim that it is cruel to pluck the

179

wings off a fly or to wash a spider down the plughole. In this case pity is not a form of the conviction that the fly is in pain.

Walter Bonnatti climbed the north-west face of the Dru solo. As he made his preparations at the bottom of the face, reflecting that he was probably a fool to embark on such a project, he noticed a butterfly swept up the face by the updraught. He pitied the butterfly and reflected, without a trace of sentimentality, that he and the butterfly would probably both perish in the ice higher up the face.[23] Bonnatti need not have assumed that the butterfly would have sensations as it froze to death. His pity was engaged by a sense that he and the butterfly would share a common fate.[24]

If it is intelligible that a fly should be in agony, then it is intelligible that someone should believe that a particular fly is in agony – the one that is having its wings plucked off, for example. But what could show that he believed it? Could he be traumatised by it? If he were sensitive, would he be? The kind of effect the sight of a human being in agony might have upon a person is unintelligible in the case of a fly. If someone woke in the night screaming saying that he was haunted by the agony of the fly (or a moth caught in the flame of a candle), we would not know what to make of him. That is not because we believe that he cannot be certain that the fly is in agony. In pointing this out I am not drawing attention to the effects of our beliefs, or to an epistemic clue that might justify our beliefs. In Chapter 4, when I appealed to the example of someone who claimed he was killing himself because he had forgotten to send money to Oxfam, I am trying to expose what it is intelligible and what it is not intelligible to claim to believe.

When Wittgenstein asks, 'What gives me *so much as the idea* that living beings, things, can feel?', he is not asking for an epistemological clue as to why he should think that other members of the species *Homo sapiens* are likely to have sensations, whereas stones are not – that they behave like him, for example. The reason is not because behaviour cannot take us to certainty. On the contrary, *if they behave like us*, if for example they *wince* or *smile*, then no doubt arises whether they are sentient beings. When we stand on their toes and they wince, we may be uncertain whether they wince in pain or embarrassment, but we do not doubt that they are capable of such feelings. But if their behaviour is not of a kind that rules doubt out of consideration, if it is described as mere colourless movements, then it is no longer clear why it should even provide a clue. In other words, if we describe behaviour as we normally do, then the sceptical question cannot arise. If we do not, if we describe it in a way that is not already saturated with the mental (as a groan or a smile, for example), then it can no longer provide a clue. It can provide no reason for even mooting an argument from analogy. Wittgenstein's answer to the question, 'What *gives me so much as the idea* that living beings can feel?', is that nothing gives me so much as the idea, for it is not a matter of my having an *idea*. Hence, 'My attitude towards him is an attitude towards a soul. I am not of the *opinion* that he has a soul.' If we take it as an idea, then we will always give the wrong kind of answer to the question, 'What gives one so much as the idea that living beings feel?', and the wrong reason to explain why we do not speculate about the mental life of stones. This clearly says more than that the epistemology of the second- and third-person ascription of mental states is different from the epistemology of physical predicates. After all, the sceptic is going to say that, whether he abandons his scepticism or not. Indeed, he would never have been a sceptic were that not so.

In the absence of an attitude towards a soul, behaviour proves nothing, just as the fly's wriggling proves nothing if the question arises whether it feels pain.[25] With such an attitude, behaviour cannot prove anything that the sceptic is interested in having proved, for the need has lapsed. When Wittgenstein said that only of a living human being and what behaves like a human being can one say that it feels and thinks and so on, we are inclined to ask the question, 'What counts (in this connection) as behaving like a human being?' I think he would answer that it must be something that counts as *expressive* behaviour (moans, cries, etc.) in the sense in which flashing neon lights wired to a person's 'pain centres', which flashed whenever he was in pain, would not. If it were seriously in question whether something behaves expressively, then we would not think of it as behaving like a human being. But if it is not in question, then a creature's behaviour cannot be the basis for conjecturing whether it is sentient or has mental states. When all its behaviour is such as to raise a question, then there is a gap between us and it which no speculation can bridge. That is not because there is an answer we cannot find.

It is because too much of what gives sense to the concepts with which the question is posed has been taken away.

It is part of the idea that 'an attitude towards a soul' is a condition of the ascription of mental predicates that we do not ascribe pain to a creature on the basis of its behaviour and then say that this creature is at least in that respect a conscious being. Rather, 'an attitude towards a soul' is *the condition of the behaviour being appreciated as the behaviour of a conscious being*. The point is that behaviour is not what is usually thought of as an epistemic route, direct or indirect, inferential or criterial, to something's being 'another mind'. Behaviour is an epistemic route (it is the basis upon which I know) that you are now, in these circumstances, in pain. But that is different. I *know* that another is in pain, but I do not *know* that he is another mind. And I *know* that he winced, but I do not *know* that wincing is expressive of something mental, or of a state of consciousness.

However, it is not as though an attitude towards a soul is something separable from, something more general than, for example, reacting with pity to someone's groaning. It is not an attitude which is (partly) constitutive of a general concept such as 'conscious being', such that, having acquired possession of it, we can then apply more specific terms. We bind someone's wounds, but look into his face. That is an attitude towards a soul. We do not look into his face to acquire (or retain) the general category 'conscious being' which serves as a general basis for the specific attribution of pain. We move neither from pain to conscious being, nor from conscious being to pain. That will look surprising only to someone who is seeking a route between one or the other of a kind travelled between propositions.

Wittgenstein is not, therefore, offering an alternative epistemology. To put it that way would underplay the radical nature of his critique of epistemology – a critique which claims that 'I know that there are other humans beings' as a pseudo-epistemological proposition. That is why we should not think of 'an attitude towards a soul' as a peculiar epistemological route to the consciousness of another. But that is not because Wittgenstein denied that there is anything for the route to get to. It is not because he denied there is such a thing as consciousness (which is why it is so misleading to call him a behaviourist). Far from denying what we might call the mystery of another's subjectivity, he can be read as defending it against its trivialisation by the traditional epistemological picture – the one that informs scepticism while it attempts to refute it. There is, indeed, more than behaviour in certain circumstances. There is all that we call 'the inner life' or 'the life of the soul', but that is trivialised if we think of it as consisting of states which are the appropriate objects of the kind of cognitive appropriation as it is conceived in the traditional picture. (And not only because it may invite us into the wrong construal of the sense in which an inner life is 'inner'.) If we think of the 'inner life' as consisting of mental states which are fitting objects of propositional knowledge, then it does not matter whether we also think of those states as causes of behaviour or as standing in some other relation to behaviour.

It is sometimes said that each person is a perspective on the world. It is meant not as a truism, but as a reminder of a certain mystery in another's subjectivity. It is mistaken to think that Wittgenstein thought there was no mystery. The mystery tends to get expressed (Nagel is an example) in terms of the inaccessibility of another person's consciousness to the objective grasp of another. Wittgenstein agrees that another's subjectivity – that he is another view on the world – is not within our epistemic grasp. But he was not, I think, saying, that because the metaphysical distortion of that mystery is couched in a mistaken epistemology, the sense of mystery is itself an illusion engendered by such a metaphysic.

Our sense of the reality of another human being is partly conditioned by the thought that he is another perspective on the world; which is why the remark is never offered as a truism. It is offered as a reminder of the kind of reality we are speaking of when we speak of the reality of another human being or person – a reminder that he is not merely a being with these thoughts and those hopes, etc. It is not a remark to be placed alongside such observations, nor is it a summation of him. It is a way of placing him, a way of reminding ourselves of what we are acknowledging when we acknowledge that he has such thoughts and such hopes. That is why Simone Weil was able to say that if we remembered that another human being is a perspective on the world as we are ourselves, then we could not treat him unjustly.[26] I am not saying she was right (in fact, I will presently argue that she was wrong), but I want to draw attention to the naturalness of this expression in that context. But it could not do the work it does, it would not have that naturalness, if it were merely the metaphysical point that there is something in another person's perspective on the world which is inaccessible to others. That introduces not mystery, but, at best, irresolvable perplexity.

There *is* something mysterious about human beings that invites (I do not say we ought to accept the invitation) characterisation in terms of the relative contingency of our bodily being and the relative necessity of our personal being. I am thinking of, for example, the mystery of the birth of a child or the mystery of death. It is natural for parents to think that the children they have they, in some sense, necessarily have. As we learn more about genetics we realise, at one level, how utterly accidental it is that our children should have been those children. I say 'at one level', because at another level it seems quite incomprehensible. Something similar is true of death. When a person dies it often seems to those who loved him quite incomprehensible. No amount of logical elaboration on the natural decay of the body eases this incomprehension. Nor does metaphysical speculation on an immaterial soul.

When people say that to have a child is to be intensely aware of the mystery of bringing life into the world, they do not mean 'life' as it would be of interest to a biologist. They mean, I think, 'life' in the sense in which we speak of it when we speak of a creature 'having a life', and it is natural to think of life, spoken of in that way, to be connected with subjectivity, but not subjectivity in a sense as meagre as is conveyed by the notion of a sensate creature. It is connected with what can be a point of view on the world, and in the case of human beings that is connected with the kind of individuality I spoke of in the previous chapter. Only then does it make sense to say, as Simone Weil does, that if we realised that another human being is a point of view on the world just as we are ourselves, then we could not treat him or her unjustly.

I believe that some of what we try to express when we say that another human being is a perspective on the world is expressed by Wittgenstein when he says that our attitude towards another human being is an attitude towards a soul, and it is more finely expressed when he reminds us that 'if someone has a pain in his hand, then the hand does not say so (unless it writes it) and one does not comfort the hand, but the sufferer: one looks into his face'.[27] Looking into his face is the expression of sympathy. It is a way of saying that we understand how it is with him; *what it is to be* one who suffers as he does (with the resonance which Nagel wants for that expression, but cannot get with bats).[28] The gesture would be idle in the absence of a serious conception of how it is for him, of how his world is coloured by his suffering. But Wittgenstein's point here is that that kind of reaction (why call it mere behaviour?) is part of what conditions our understanding of the concept 'the-world-as-it-appears-to-him'. That is why it can function as the kind of reminder it does.

It is not merely a fact about pain, a causal property of it, that it can poison our world. It is part of our concept of pain, part of what makes the requisite connection between pain and suffering. It is not pointless to ask what it is about pain that makes it the appropriate object of pity. One wants to say that it is intrinsic to pain that it hurts, and that it can hurt terribly. But that says no more than that pain can admit of degrees. The idea that it is merely a causal property of pain that it can poison a life suggests that we have an idea of the terribleness of pain, the sense in which pain is suffering, independently of its place in the life of a creature of a particular kind (as we do with the concept of heat, for example), and in the case of human beings, independently of its capacity to destroy a life. The picture is the one we encountered before – pain has a certain *qualia*, call it its painfulness, or its hurtfulness, and this *qualia* (which we all know from our own case) admits of degrees which may rise and fall in isolation from anything else. It has led philosophers to imagine a world with so many units of pain in it and another world with so many other units of pain. They acknowledge, to be sure, that pain has causal properties which can make our sufferings worse. It can make us curse the day we were born, and that distinguishes human beings from animals. But *qua* pain, it can be the same in a human being and any other sensate creature. And here the thought must be that language is inadequate to describe the *qualia* of pain because we can say only trivial things like 'it is painful' or 'it hurts'. But everyone knows from his own case what it is – it is what makes you groan when you groan in pain, for example.

It is not so easy, however, to extract the intrinsic *qualia* of pain from its effects as this picture would have us imagine – to extract it as an independently intelligible object of our pity. For any *x*, if *x* is in pain then it is an intelligible object of our pity – that is the thought, and its point is to suggest that all we need for pity to be appropriate is the pain. But that thought seems unclear. Take pain out of a life, its tendency to mutilate a life, and it is no longer clear that we have an object of pity. That at any rate is the question Wittgenstein raised in the passage I have been quoting: 'How am I filled with pity *for this man*? How does it come out what the object of my pity is?'[29]

When we pity a creature in pain we do not pity an 'entity' in pain of such and such severity. Our pity takes a more substantial object. When it is for a human being it is irreducibly for a human being. I do not mean merely that if we pity a human being, then it is that human being we pity, and if we pity a dog then it is that dog. I mean that when we pity a human being in pain then we pity him, irreducibly, as a human being, whereas if we pity a dog, then we pity it not as a dog but as an animal of a certain kind, which would include cats and horses, though not worms. When we pity a human being, our pity for him is not different from our pity for a dog, because a human being suffers other things in addition to his pain. It is different because of *the meaning* pain can have in a human life and because of what a human life can mean. An animal in severe pain is 'put out of its misery'. Even when, as was reported of an Argentinian soldier who fell into a fire in the Falklands, a human being is killed so that he will be spared further suffering, he is not killed in the same spirit as we would shoot a horse. It is not that we feel differently about it, that we find it more difficult, or that we feel more sorrow. That is not what is most significant. What is most significant is the descriptions, the categories of meaning, under which we understand our reluctance and our sorrow and what we are doing. The Argentinian soldier was not eaten afterwards. That fact, and many others of the same kind, determine what the shooting was.[30]

How far can this take us in understanding the slave owner's relation to his slaves or the Samaritan's response to the man in the ditch? Only some of the way. Take first the Samaritan. His behaviour is quite different from the behaviour described by Simone Weil when she says that 'no one stands up, or moves about, or sits down in quite the same fashion when he is alone in the room as when he has a visitor'. What she says is a good example of that kind of attitude to a soul which is relevant to the question, 'What gives us so much as the idea that another living thing thinks and feels?' But the Samaritan's behaviour is not an instance of the kind of primitive reaction which is a condition for the ascription of mental predicates. It goes well beyond that: it is offered as an example of what it is to love our neighbour.[31] When the lawyer asks, 'Who is my neighbour?', it would not do to give an example merely of someone who turned away our steps in a way that an inanimate object does not. *He* is not the one who is a neighbour to the one who fell amongst thieves. Simone Weil does tend to speak of those who walked past as though they did so in the way they would if there were merely an inert thing in the ditch. Perhaps they did, but if they did, it would seriously underdescribe the Samaritan's response simply to contrast it with that, to say that he responded as to a soul, or as to a fellow human being, in the sense in which that is conveyed by the quotation from her essay on the *Iliad*. Somewhere in her notebooks she says that if a person comes across another in the desert who is dying of thirst, and if he has water in his canteen, and if he has enough for himself, then he will give the other person water. She describes this as 'automatic'. It could be another example of a primitive reaction, or of the kind of attitude with which Wittgenstein is concerned in the *Investigations*. But such a person could be a slave owner and the one to whom he gives water could be his slave, yet there be no inconsistency. If the slave owner gives his slave water there need be nothing in this act to suggest that he should, in consistency, release his slaves. There is nothing wrong with describing this as a reaction to a fellow human being, as, indeed, the kind of action that is constitutive of our sense of a fellow human being. But that is not the sense in which the Samaritan's actions were as to a fellow human being. The sense in which the Samaritan's actions revealed the other to him as neighbour is connected with the concept of love. And that is something that emerges only in a culture which can distinguish genuine from corrupt forms of it. That does not mean that we cannot describe the Samaritan's actions as 'automatic'. He acted without reflection, but his actions were in response not merely to the suffering of another human being, but to what it *means* for that human being to suffer as he does.

Wittgenstein's thoughts in the *Investigations*, applied more or less directly, are also of limited help in understanding the slave owner. When he rapes the slave girl he does not respond to her struggling as though it were like the undergrowth against which he struggles when he cuts his way through the swamp. He does not respond to her struggles simply as an obstacle to be overcome if he is to realise his purpose (Weil tends to speak like this). He need not be blind and unresponsive to the suffering in her eyes and in her screams. He may try to shut his eyes, or silence her screams. He may even be ashamed of not relenting in the face of what he hears and sees.[32] He does not treat her as someone who would turn aside his steps only in a way that a lamp post would, or as someone whose presence in the room would go unnoticed, or as someone who would not be welcomed as a fellow human being if he were marooned on a desert island. All this comes out in the fact that he may later recriminate himself for his lack of pity, but that does not mean that she is then an intelligible object for the kind of remorse he would feel if he felt it for raping a white woman. It does not mean that he could find it intelligible that he violated something precious. He may have felt much the same when he beat his dog. The way he fails to treat her as an unconditional limit to his will, to treat her as a human being, is not captured by the kinds of remarks made by Wittgenstein in the *Investigations*. They put one on the right road, and what one sees further along the road is of the same general form – the interdependence of concept and response – but much else of a cultural kind needs to be added.

11

Goodness

Much of my discussion has been about remorse and about evil. That might seem an unduly negative focus for a discussion of absolute value. Philosophers have sometimes discussed the relation between the negative and the positive emphasis in morality. They have noted, for example, how basic prohibitions are to morality, and when people think of absolute value they often think of universal prohibitions, or of actions which are not permitted whatever the consequences. If I have contributed to such a discussion then I will have done so inadvertently, for I have not had it in mind. I have emphasised remorse because it is fundamental to an understanding of the ethical determination of what we are. What it can mean to do evil to another is basic to our understanding of others and of ourselves.

I have argued that remorse is internal to the deepest of the ways we speak of the 'reality' of evil. If that is so, then evil cannot be an independent focus of fascination. The idea that evil could be clear-sightedly desired for its own sake and that its enactment could be clear-sightedly celebrated is based upon a confused conception of the nature of its reality. Thus, although I focused on evil and on a certain sense of its reality, and although I emphasised what an appreciation of its reality teaches us, it is at least consistent with this emphasis (even if it is not required by it) that evil can be understood only in the light of goodness. I shall yield to the temptation to express it Platonically and say that evil can be understood only in the light of 'the Good'. Is there reason to speak that way? If there is, then it can only be if we also speak of evil and of its irreducibility to forms of 'bad'. Most people are resistant to speaking that way because it strikes them as simple-minded and, often, dangerous. But some speak of Good and Evil and others of Good and evil. Kolnai speaks of the 'thematic primacy of Evil' and the 'ontological primacy of Good'.[1] These matters are much discussed amongst theologians.

I do not wish to speak of an 'ontology' of good and evil, just as I do not wish to speak of an ontology of the dead. If someone were to say that I should stop prevaricating or indulging a bogus sense of subtlety and to declare whether I believe evil to be a reality or whether I do not, then I would say that the challenge cannot be met in the spirit in which it is issued, I would say it for the same kind of reason I gave for rejecting the question whether or not the dead existed. There cannot be an independent metaphysical inquiry into the 'reality' of good and evil which would underwrite or undermine the most serious of our ways of speaking. I would say: now you may see why someone should speak of the reality of evil, and now you may see why the same person might say that Good is the only reality. We are likely to misunderstand what a person who speaks that way means if we try to press him into acknowledging that he is contradicting himself. It would be better, at least in ethics, to banish the word 'ontology'.

Apart from thinking that speaking of Good and evil betrays a melodramatic moral sensibility, someone might think that the capitalised 'G' records only the sense that moral good is good *sui generis*. Kolnai seems to think that. He argues that we record our sense of the irreducibility of evil to bad by the special word 'evil' (he notes that this is so in other languages also), but that we do not have a special word for a *sui generis* moral good because of the kind of unity between all things that are good.[2] I do not know whether those (few) who would speak of 'Good' rather than 'good' speak that way because of the influence of Plato, even if they have not heard of him. Plato spoke of the Form or the Idea of Good as eternal, indestructible, separately existing and not of this world: that is to say considerably more than that moral good is good *sui generis*.[3]

After he had been condemned to death, Socrates addressed these words to the jury: 'You too, gentlemen of the jury, must look forward to death with confidence and fix your minds on this one truth – that nothing can harm a good man either in life or after death.'[4] That is seldom discussed by Platonic scholars and it is generally

190

assumed to be irrelevant to understanding whatever may be philosophically substantial in both Socrates and Plato. I said earlier that,
while I renounce any exegetical argument, I could not but refer to
Plato and to Socrates, since much of what I have to say has been
shaped by thinking about them. Let me therefore offer, without further apology, a reading of what Socrates may have meant and of
Plato's relation to it.

Socrates did not mean that a person who lived virtuously could not
suffer terribly. And when he speaks of the good man who cannot be
harmed he may not be thinking, primarily, of the deeds of such a
person or of their character. His attention may be on the attitude that
it is possible to take to the kinds of misfortunes that threaten despair.
In *Symposium* he seems to be saying that if a person sees his life in
the light of a certain kind of love then nothing need cause him to
despair.[5] He spoke out of his own life and out of the only love that
filled it – his 'one love', philosophy. That is, I think, what astonished
Plato. It astonished Aristotle too, who was moved to say, in effect,
that only someone who was irresponsibly determined to argue for
a thesis at all costs could say such a thing.[6] And although Aristotle's
discussion of the relation between fortune and *eudaimonia* is at times
uneasy (in a way that was aptly parodied by Hardie when he said that
Aristotle thought that a good man could be happy on a rack if he were
a very good man and if the rack were not so good[7]), Aristotle believed
that it was obvious that there may come a time in any person's life
when his sufferings are so great and so prolonged that it would have
been better for him never to have been born.[8]

If Aristotle had been a reductive naturalist who believed that the
virtues were a means to an independently intelligible conception of
human flourishing, then his reaction to Socrates would not have
been interesting. But he was not, and so the gap between him and
Socrates is of a kind to reveal something important about both
of them. Aristotle agreed with Socrates that what counted as harm
was, often, ethically conditioned, and he agreed also, that if a person
sees his misfortunes in a certain ethical light, then even though they
may be many and severe, they need not diminish that person's
gratitude for a life which he is still able to see as 'complete and
lacking in nothing'. But he insisted that this was true *only up to a
point*, and judging by his tone in both the *Nicomachean* and the

Eudemian Ethics, he scorned Socrates' denial of such a limit as cheap high-mindedness.

Aristotle's reaction to Socrates is the most serious in the history of philosophy. I call it a 'reaction' to Socrates rather than a 'Criticism' of him because Aristotle offers no argument. He only asks a number of rhetorical questions and relies on his own discussion of the relation between virtue and *eudaimonia* to show up Socrates (and in this he has been remarkably successful, for almost all commentators think that Aristotle extracted what was worthwhile from Socrates' extremism). It is not a failing that he offered no argument, because nothing would count as an argument against Socrates. That is not because Socrates had a watertight argument in defence of what he said: it is because what he said is beyond the reach of argument either directly to defend or to oppose.

It is clear that Socrates' profession that a good man cannot be harmed depends upon the point that what counts as harm may depend upon an ethical perspective in the light of which not even death need count as a harm. Argument can reveal this if there is need for it, and those (very few) who have defended Socrates have developed this point. It does not, however, take us beyond Aristotle, who understood it well enough and who, indeed, made it central to his own ethics. He said that great and protracted misfortune can 'crush and maim' happiness but that 'even in these [circumstances] nobility shines through, when a man bears with resignation many great misfortunes, not through insensibility to pain, but through nobility and greatness of soul'.[9] But, as I have said, Aristotle thought that an ethically conditioned perspective on our own or another's misfortune could take us only so far, and he believed that there were some lives which were steeped in such appalling and ineradicable affliction that it was a requirement of a sober humanity to acknowledge that they were irredeemably ruined. To refuse to do so was a high-minded indecency, which cheapened everything that human beings hold precious. Or so I hear his tone. His reaction to Socrates was similar to Orwell's reaction to Gandhi when Orwell said that we had to choose between being a saint and being a human being.[10] Almost everyone will agree with Aristotle, but what I have said on his behalf is not an argument, and I do not know what would count as an argument in its support.

When Socrates said that a good man cannot be harmed, he did not add, *sotto voce*, 'with a bit of luck'. That, I believe, is what astonished Plato, and the deepest impulse in his ethical philosophy is to vindicate Socrates – the historical Socrates – against the kind of reaction which Aristotle expressed so powerfully. Aristotle went to the limits of any accommodation which humanism or a non-reductive naturalism can make to the point that what a person counts as harm depends upon his ethical perspective.

I raised the question in Chapter 3 whether an Aristotelian emphasis on the relation between virtue and flourishing – of the kind favoured by many contemporary philosophers, anxious for what they take to be a richer and more congenial ethic than is offered by the Kantian tradition – had the conceptual resources to reveal someone who has no prospect of flourishing as an intelligible object of anything but a condescending pity. It will, I hope, now be clear why I raised the question and why I focus on Aristotle. Understood non-reductively and refined by a developed psychological theory, he represents the main hope for the non-reductive and urbane humanism to which much contemporary ethical writing aspires. I must try to explain more clearly why I think that.

The central question is whether we can see those who have no share in what gives our lives sense as our moral equals. In practice we mostly do not. Simone Weil has often and forcibly pointed out how many and subtle are the forms of our condescension:

> The supernatural virtue of justice consists of behaving exactly as though there were equality when one is the stronger in an unequal relationship. Exactly, in every respect, including the slightest details of accent and attitude, for a detail may be enough to place the weaker party in the condition of matter which on this occasion naturally belongs to him, just as the slightest shock causes water which has remained liquid below freezing point to solidify.[11]

Often it is worse:

> Men have the same carnal nature as animals. If a hen is hurt, the others rush up and peck it ... Our senses attach to affliction all the contempt, all the revulsion, all the hatred which our reason attaches to crime. Except for those whose soul is

193

inhabited by Christ, everybody despises the afflicted to some extent, although practically no-one is conscious of it.[12]

At another place she says:

> As for those who have been struck the kind of blow which leaves the victim writhing on the ground like a half-crushed worm, they have no words to describe what is happening to them . . . compassion for the afflicted is an impossibility. When it is really found, it is a more astounding miracle than walking on water, healing the sick, or even raising the dead.[13]

Is what Weil points to merely a psychological phenomenon, one of practical moral importance but of no importance to reflections on the nature of morality or of good and evil? Some might protest that we do not believe that the afflicted should be despised, that we do not even believe that they may be condescended to, even if we often cannot help doing it. They may say that affliction cannot deprive a person of what makes him/her a proper object for undiminished moral response; that the fact that we cannot help ourselves condescending to the afflicted in countless subtle ways does not count against that. But then the question is, why is there such a terrible discrepancy between what we believe and how we act? If we believe that those in apparently ineradicable affliction are of infinite worth, or that they are infinitely precious, why do we act as though we do not believe it?

If someone is in deep despair, then nothing matters that is not merely physical or brutishly sensate. If he is betrayed, then that does not matter to him unless it has physical consequences, because his life, which is empty of meaning, cannot receive what has meaning. To look on a life as one in which it is unintelligible that there should be meaning is to see it as empty of what is distinctively human. It is worse than merely to see it as empty of goods and opportunities. It is to see it as empty of all that can matter, morally and spiritually. We tend to see the lives of at least some of the afflicted like that – as lives in which we find it unintelligible that anything, except of the most primitive kind, could matter. If we find it unintelligible that anything could matter to someone living such a life, then we cannot think that any evil done to him, or by him, can go deep with him. We noticed, in Chapter 9, the connection between seeing someone as an absolute limit to our will and the possibility that things could go deep with him, and we saw how that functioned in our sense of the division between 'us' and 'them'. The implication of that argument is that we should not try to overcome the unjust uses of the distinction between 'us' and 'them' by trying to find an Archimedian point. Rather, we should include 'them' amongst 'us'. That was done with slaves because their masters found it intelligible that they were, after all, capable of a depth of feeling and thought. But where can we find the depth in a life irredeemably deprived of meaning? There is something importantly true in saying that we do not believe that the afflicted should be despised, or even condescended to. But the question is whether we understand ourselves in 'believing' it.

Aristotle's sense of the absurdity of what Socrates said does not rest on anything that might, in any straightforward way, be characterised as empirical understanding of what is possible or impossible for human beings. It is quite different, for example, from his judgement that there is physical suffering beyond human strength to endure. The necessity expressed in that judgement is based upon an empirical knowledge of human life. The necessity internal to the judgement that it is absurd to say of a human life lived in protracted and ineradicable affliction that it is a life for which it is, nonetheless, possible to be thankful is of a different sort, for it is connected with the sense of the expression 'a good human life' – with what we could possibly *mean* by it. The thought that it *must* be possible for misfortune to ruin irredeemably a person's life, however virtuous he may be, is not an empirical thought and neither is its denial. That is why Aristotle said that only someone who is prepared to argue for a thesis at all costs could say that a good man could not be harmed. He knew that this is not the kind of claim that Socrates could support, by reports of what he had seen or what he had heard from travellers. We can go abroad and discover that there are many braver even than Achilles, but we cannot go abroad and discover a good man who could not be harmed. The necessity that is internal to the expression of a sense of absurdity when that sense is informed by an empirical understanding of human nature is defeasible in the standard way – by counter-examples. The sense of necessity which is internal to the judgement that there are lives such that it would be better for those who suffer them if they had never been born is not in the same way defeasible by counter-examples.

I have emphasised that Aristotle understood that what a person counts as harm depends on his understanding of value, and that he believed that a certain understanding of virtue and nobility enables us to consent to even great misfortune without bitterness. He understood too, I think, that we could look upon our life with a gratitude that was not, in any straightforward sense, conditional upon the weighing of the good and ill in it. He speaks of the gratitude we owe unconditionally to our parents for the life they have given us, and if, as I suggested, the 'complete life' of which he says *eudaimonia* must be predicated is a life seen as a whole in the light of a certain understanding of its meaning, then he is able to say that someone can express an attitude to his life which is not an assessment of how things turned out for him.

That may seem absurd for two reasons. First, how can a judgement on our life fail to be a weighing of the good and ill in it? Secondly, it suggests that a life could be, as Aristotle put it, 'complete and lacking in nothing' in a sense which turns aside the judgement that, since it had been a life filled with pain, it would have been a better life if there had been less pain. These are natural thoughts, but, of course, they apply to any life, not only to lives in which there has been much suffering. Once we think of lives as measured on a scale between the lives of those of whom we think it had been better if they had never been born and the lives of those whom we think blessed with every fortune, then there is no life that might not have had a little more of some natural human good. That should make us pause, I think.

Norman Malcolm reports that when Wittgenstein was on his deathbed he asked his housekeeper to 'tell them [his friends] that it has been a wonderful life'.[14] Wittgenstein was not expressing an assessment of his life. He was not making a *considered* or *judicious* remark. He was not expressing a *judgement*. He could not appropriately be asked to reconsider and perhaps to qualify what he had said. It belongs to the grammar of what he said (although of course not of the sentence that he spoke) that it deflects any invitation to him to reconsider it and for us to assess it. We misunderstand what he said if we think it could have engaged with the question whether he really wanted to say that it was *wonderful*. Someone who understood what Wittgenstein meant could not suggest that although he said that his life had been wonderful, it had not really been *wonderful* although it had been, on the whole, quite good.

Malcolm says he found it deeply moving that Wittgenstein should say this in the face of the evident misery that had marked much of his life, but he did not suggest that knowledge of that misery might provide a reason to challenge the strict veracity of what Wittgenstein said. There is a sense (perhaps it is the primary sense) in which the remark that one had had a wonderful life *would* be an assessment. Someone could then invite the person who had made it to reconsider, and a spectator could assess it for its accuracy – could assess, for example, whether it was an exaggeration. But it is noteworthy that although Malcolm confesses himself puzzled in the face of Wittgenstein's remark because of the pain in much of his (Wittgenstein's) life, he does not so much as hint that Wittgenstein might have been exaggerating. If Malcolm had done so, he would not have been moved in the way that he was. That is why I said that Wittgenstein was not passing a judgement on his life, and that his was not a considered or a judicious remark (which does not, of course, mean that it was thoughtless). He expressed gratitude for his life considered as a certain kind of whole, as having the kind of unity I tried to characterise in Chapter 8. But his gratitude was not to fortune, in the usual sense, for then it would have been conditional upon an assessment of how fortune had dealt with him.

I have discussed this example, in the first instance, as one which reveals that it is possible to take an attitude to one's life which is not indefinitely revisable according to where one stands on the line between irreversible affliction and blessedness. It reveals what, at first sight or in the abstract, seems paradoxical, namely: that we cannot *flatly* say of any life, not even a life in which there had been much suffering, that it could have been better if it had been blessed with more fortune. A human life can be seen under the aspect of that kind of unity that gives it a kind of completion, and indeed a kind of perfection, that resists any such appraisal. Perhaps that is what Aristotle meant when he said a happy life was 'complete and lacking in nothing'.

Wittgenstein said in his 'Lecture on Ethics' that a feeling of 'being absolutely safe' was an 'experience' he would cite as an expression of absolute value.[15] Aristotle would have thought that absurd for the same reason he thought it absurd to say that a good man could not be harmed. It is natural to think that Socrates and Wittgenstein expressed the same attitude, and that Wittgenstein expressed it again when he was dying. But if that is true, then it shows that the relatively formal point that we may look upon our life and express gratitude for it in a way that is not conditional upon an assessment of it can take us no closer to understanding the attitude that I have suggested is common to Wittgenstein and Socrates, than does the formal thought that we may consent to our sufferings in the light of an ethical perspective on them. (Indeed, there is reason to say that they are different aspects of the same thought.) That means that even though we may see in Wittgenstein's remark on his deathbed the same sense of absolute value that he expressed many years before, the relatively formal point which I have been making (namely, that it was not an assessment of his life) will take us no closer to the idea of absolute value than will the formal idea that we may take an ethical perspective on our sufferings. It will take us no closer than Aristotle was to Socrates.

When Wittgenstein said that he felt absolutely safe, he said that he was speaking personally, but he did not mean that he was merely expressing his personal opinion. He meant that what he said (in certain circumstances the forms of words might, and perhaps would have to, be different) can be said only in the first-person singular. We cannot say that others are absolutely safe. However, that does not mean that someone who is able to say it believes that it has no application to others. Someone who says it would not say of another, whatever his circumstances, that it is impossible that he should say it. But each person must find his own words to express gratitude for the gift that has been his life. The refusal to deny that anyone might say it is the right response to Aristotle's taunt when he asked who, but someone arguing for a thesis, could say that Priam was happy.

We are now in a position to detect some confusion and misunderstanding in Aristotle's response to Socrates. He asked in the *Eudemian Ethics* whether we would soberly say that a man on the rack was happy. In the *Nicomachean Ethics* he asked whether anyone would say that Priam was happy. He challenged his imaginary interlocutor to make a third-person judgement about the man on the rack or about Priam. My claim has been that the sense of what Aristotle is challenging is such that its assertion can only be in the first-person singular, and that its third-person application amounts to a *refusal* to say that it could not be so with others. In the case of Priam, it amounts to the refusal to say that his sufferings compel one to say that it would have been better if he had never been born, or that he could not express a sense of gratitude for his life. If someone refuses to say this of any human being who is capable of taking an attitude to their life, then it will radically transform their sense of what it is to be a human being.

The second point to be made about Aristotle's misunderstanding of Socrates is that he does not seem to think that the difference between the examples in the *Eudemian Ethics* and the *Nicomachean Ethics* is important (certainly the commentators have not thought it important). It was the first which prompted Hardie's parody that Aristotle believed that a man could be happy on a rack if he were a very good man and it were not a good rack. But there is no particular difficulty in thinking that someone on a rack need not despair of his life, that he need not curse the day he was born. If we say that there will come a point when the pain is so great that anyone will break, then the emphasis is on the fact that such a person has been broken – that he has collapsed – and that this is, therefore, not the right kind of case to present against Socrates. The disintegration of people under torture, if we are thinking only of the pain, is as different from despair as clinical depression is from sorrow. (Thomas More wrote to his daughter from prison, 'I thank God that my case was such in this matter, through the clearness of mine own conscience, that though I might have pain I could not have harm. For a man may in such a case lose his head and have no harm.'[16]) Priam, however, is the right kind of example, because his suffering is the kind that can lead to despair. He lost everything that gave his life sense. If despair drives someone to curse the day he was born, or if we say of someone who suffered as did Priam, that it would be better if he had never been born, then it is not because of the pain in his life, but because we cannot see any meaning left in it. Aristotle seemed to run these together.

We may think that there *was* meaning left in Priam's life and Aristotle might be brought to agree. His point, however, is that there are some lives that have irrevocably lost their meaning. If we deny that for the reasons that I have been suggesting, then we will not do so because our attention has been fixed on the Noble, in whose light we are able to see our life as something for which we may be thankful even though we had lost all that gave it sense. The concept of the Noble is too mediocre. Goodness is the only concept that is appropriate. In *Republic* Plato says that people do not understand the distance between the necessary and the Good.[17] If we take him to mean by 'the necessary' those human goods whose radical absence drives people to despair, then we can see him as saying that there is something in the light of which we need never despair: it is the (indestructible) Good. But we need not read that as an attempt to underpin metaphysically what Socrates meant when he said that a good man cannot be harmed. Rather, we can see what Socrates meant as giving sense to that way of speaking of the Good.

In the *Nicomachean Ethics* Aristotle offered a number of criticisms of the Platonic Form of the Good. Most of them were metaphysical criticisms, but he offered one that he took to be decisive from the point of view of ethics. He said that even if there were such a thing as the Platonic Form of the Good, it would be irrelevant to ethics because it would be beyond the reach of human achievement. Ethics, he said, is concerned with what is humanly achievable.[18] In this criticism he revealed a deep misunderstanding of Plato, for whom the Form of the Good is not an object of pursuit, but in the light of which we and our pursuits are judged.[19] One reason why Aristotle failed to see that was because his sense of the ethical is limited to virtues whose focal concept is nobility, and he failed to see the distance between an ethics centred on nobility, and an ethics centred on the Good and the love of it. What Arendt said of the men of the enlightenment could also be said of Aristotle: he did not realise that there is goodness beyond virtue and evil beyond vice. He therefore failed to see that everything which he thought to be the proper object of pursuit belonged to the realm of what Plato called the 'necessary', and that the important thing is not to look for an object of pursuit which, if acquired, could not be lost. The important thing is to see the realm of the necessary in the light of a love of the Good.

I believe that those three points show that Aristotle misunderstood the character of the Socratic claim. I do not believe, however, that acknowledgement of that fact would close the gap (or even diminish the gap) between him and Socrates. The difficulty is that those for whom there is a need to close it do not feel the need. They believe, as Aristotle did, that what Socrates said is absurd. And in academic philosophy, the gap that needs closing is of an altogether different and less important kind. It is the gap between a reductive and a non-reductive naturalism.

Another difficulty is that what Socrates says is essentially, rather than accidentally, mysterious. Aristotle found it unintelligible and, in a different sense, so (I believe) did Plato. Aristotle's rejection of what Socrates said is internal to his sense of its unintelligibility. Plato, on the other hand, was bound (we might say he was conscience-bound) in testimony to something whose reality he could not deny, but whose nature he found essentially mysterious. I call it *essentially* mysterious because it is not mysterious for us merely on account of our limited epistemic and logical powers.

I have already said that I believe that this is the deepest of Plato's many, sometimes conflicting, reasons for speaking of the form of the Good, particularly when he speaks of it as an object of love rather than as an object of what is, more narrowly, called 'intelligence' or 'thought'. In such moods, Plato is not devising extreme metaphysical remedies for conceptual puzzles concerning moral objectivity. It is true that even in such moods his talk of the Forms is in response to the pressure of a certain kind of perplexity, and it is a pressure that makes him speak in a certain way about the reality of the form of the Good. But we need not think of him, even then, as offering a metaphysical remedy for certain philosophical perplexities. We can read him as expressing a perplexity that is not philosophical and which philosophy has no power to remedy, but has, at best, only the power to display by clearing away misunderstandings. That, of course, merely follows from the category of the essentially mysterious. Philosophy cannot penetrate such mystery. It cannot even prove that there is anything which is mysterious in that way. It can only provide a conceptual space for its acknowledgement. But the point of trying to do even that depends upon the pressure to fill that space.

If philosophy is to leave space for something which is essentially mysterious then three things need to be noted. First, that the concept of what is essentially mysterious is connected with a certain conception of experience. Secondly, that the concept of experience is connected with that of being bound in testimony. Thirdly, that we must give a serious place to the concepts of love, Goodness and purity. It might be thought that the first of these conflicts with my earlier claim that the Socratic claim is not an empirical claim. By the end of the chapter I hope that I will have shown that this is not so. But it may already be apparent that, if I am right, it should be no surprise that Aristotle was so distant from both Socrates and Plato, and no surprise that this conception of absolute value is so foreign to modern moral philosophy. This general way of speaking conveys little. However, I must try to display the pressure to speak as Socrates and Wittgenstein did.

We have the example of Mother Teresa of Calcutta. It has been said that she showed, to those in the most appalling affliction, a 'compassion that was without a trace of condescension'.[20] It was meant, I think, that her compassion was without a trace of the thought that it would have been better if the people for whom she felt it had never been born, even if they suffered affliction of the most protracted, severe and ineradicable sort. Her compassion expressed the denial that affliction could, and at a certain limit *must*, make a person's life worthless. It was a denial of the necessity internal to Aristotle's sense of the absurdity of the Socratic thought. Someone might retract the Aristotelian denial of it in the face of what they take to be revealed by the example of Mother Teresa, but it would not then be retracted in the face of an empirically revised or extended sense of what is humanly possible. The nature of Mother Teresa's compassion, the purity of her love, is not, as we shall see, a counter-example to anything.

As with many loves, what is striking is not so for its drama, but for its purity. We wonder at what we take to be instances of pure love, but it is not wonder at a feat which would excite our admiration. There are many kinds of wonder — wonder at a person's skill, wonder at a person's courage, wonder at the beauty of a mathematical proof, wonder at the beauty of the world. Great talent, great courage and great resilience excite our admiration partly because they are at the limit of an empirically conditioned sense of human powers. The purity of love is, however, of a different order, as is the humility which is inseparable from it. They strike us not as achievements, but as gifts. It is quite natural to speak of feats of courage, but we can only speak satirically of feats of love and humility.

If I am a witness to a great feat of courage it may strike me as so extraordinary that it would be idle for me to wonder whether I were capable of it. Someone else, however, may realistically wonder whether he was. My immediate realisation that I am not, and his conjecture whether he might be, are on the same plane, just as my immediate realisation that a particular athletic feat is beyond my capacity and someone else's conjecture whether it is are on the same plane. But in the face of an instance of a pure love, no one *conjectures* whether it is possible for him.

Our conjectures about what we may be capable of are based upon an assessment of what is within our power to achieve. To be sure, courage is not merely a developed natural capacity, as is athletic prowess. It is also an ethical requirement, and its absence is a proper cause for shame in the way that mere absence of athletic ability is not. But the sense in which courage is an ethical requirement is itself conditioned by the fact that we may properly conjecture whether certain degrees of it are within our power to achieve. It is one of the marks of shame that we may be consoled by an appraisal of where our failure is to be placed on a continuum of empirical possibilities. I have already noted that shame is, in this respect, quite different from remorse.

Some people love better than others, and in relation to the requirement to love better than we do, there is much that may properly be described as the development of certain powers and capacities. A certain dimension of the requirement to love better is analogous to the requirement to be more courageous. We can exert our will, we can practise, we can develop strategies, we can visit therapists, and if, at the end of the day, we are braver even than Achilles, then we need feel no explanatory gap between our efforts and our achievement. But with certain kinds of love we are judged under a conception of perfection, and we call that perfection purity. The concept of perfection has no application, except in a degenerate sense, to courage, and this is because courage, and our sense of a requirement to it, are conditioned by an empirically conditioned sense of what is within human powers to achieve. Aristotle expressed this (as we noted earlier) when, during his discussion of courage, he said that there are terrors beyond a human being's capacity to endure. He thereby set an empirically conditioned limit to accusations of cowardice.

It is hard to know in a discussion such as this which concepts do the work. I spoke, earlier, of the concept of perfection as though purity were an instance of it. If that is so, then we would better understand the concept of a pure love by thinking of it as an instance of a perfect love. But I think it would serve no purpose to think generally about the concept of perfection. The salient points are that pure love is not an achievement and that our sense of its value is not of it as something at the furthest limits of what is humanly achievable. We might say, therefore, that purity is not a virtue if a virtue is a settled disposition of character. That gives a certain sense to talk of perfection in this case, but the conceptual load is carried by the division between what is an intelligible object of human efforts – in the sense that it may be achievable by effort, natural endowment and a fair amount of luck – and what is beyond the direct reach of such efforts even under optimal conditions of natural endowment and luck. That also gives sense to a certain way of speaking of the *absolute value* of purity. We are inescapably judged in its light, but not because it represents the upper limit on a scale of human achievements, not even if that limit is beyond human achievement. People are sometimes edified by the saying (which often appears on desk calendars) that 'a man's reach must extend beyond his grasp, for what else is heaven for'. That has no application to the purity of Mother Teresa's love. And the Platonic Forms are not in that kind of heaven.

The nature of Mother Teresa's compassion is a matter for wonder, but the wonder is not directed at her achievements. Much of what she did was an extraordinary achievement, and we wonder too, although in a different way, at that – at her tireless efforts, her resilience and so on. Our wonder at these is conditioned by our sense of human possibilities and limitations. However, when I speak of a wonder at the quality of her compassion I do not mean that I wonder at the kind of compassion that can issue in such achievements. What I wonder at is a compassion that was without a trace of condescension, even though it was often for people in the most appalling and ineradicable affliction. It was a compassion without a trace of the thought that it would have been better for such people never to have been born. Her compassion is an example of what I have been calling a 'pure' love. I call it that, not because I claim any insight into her motives, but because of what is revealed in its light. Simone Weil remarks, in connection with a discussion of the love of God, that if we wish to know how bright a torch is, then we do not look at the bulb: we look to see what it has the power to illuminate.[21] In the case of Mother Teresa, the point is not that her love issued into many good deeds, nor that her deeds 'shone like a jewel' because of the purity of her motives. The salient point is that her love revealed – taught – what it is to be a human being because of the light it threw on the afflicted. The wonder which is in response to her is not a wonder at her, but a wonder *that human life could be as her love revealed it to be*. That is quite different from a Kantian kind of rejoicing at the purity of a deed. There is a sense in which *she* disappeared from consideration.

I speak personally, as did Wittgenstein. I know there are others who do not see her in this way, and that there are indeed some who have spoken of her as 'that silly woman who encourages the poor to breed'. I speak personally, therefore, when I say that while I understand things in the light of her compassion, I would never say of another human being that it would have been better if they had never been born. That means that I would never say of any human being capable of the expression of gratitude, that there are conditions under which it would be absurd for them to express a gratitude that they had been born. And if someone asks me whether I really mean *never*, and then produces an ever-worsening catalogue of horrors, then I would turn such a question aside, as did Socrates in his discussion with Polus when Polus piled horror upon horror in sarcastic response to Socrates' claim that it was better to suffer evil than to do it. Socrates replied that Polus was trying to 'frighten him with bogeys', because the point of piling horror upon imaginary horror is to see at what point your opponent breaks. But it reveals a superficial understanding of what it is to respond, as I have described, to Mother Teresa to believe that anything but life could make someone say, for example, that it was all high-minded confusion. And if someone does say it in the face of actual suffering, then it will have *proved* nothing, for he will need to recall that to be claimed in testimony is internal to the nature of his original wonder. He will need to recall that the reality to which that wonder had bound him reveals itself only to wonder. Such is its grammar. That is why I said that the nature of Mother Teresa's compassion is not a counter-example to anything.

12

Ethical other-worldliness

R. F. Holland brings out better than any recent philosopher that someone who speaks of absolute goodness does so under pressure – the pressure of what he calls 'marking an encounter'.[1] He marks that encounter Platonically when he says, 'Absolute goodness *is something*.'[2] The pressure is not discursive or dialectical pressure. It cannot be vindicated, therefore, by the thought that it is necessary for the adequacy of any moral theory. There is no demonstrable lack in any theory that neglects to speak of it – no lack that is demonstrable to those who are acknowledged masters of the subject. He says that 'it is more a matter of registering an experience . . . than passing a judgement'.[3]

I would say (I do not know if Holland would) that the 'registering' he speaks of is the kind of testimony I spoke of in the previous chapter. Such testimony, I think, is internal to the character of the 'encounter' or 'experience' of goodness and to the grammar of 'goodness *is something*'. (It would not be going too far to say that, when it is said as Holland means it, the claim that goodness *is something* is a kind of confession, in the sense in which we speak of a confession of faith. It expresses a requirement to be true to something.) Testimony, as I am speaking of it, is not like the 'testimony of the senses' and does not belong to the same logical or analogical family as do 'intuitions'. It is not a unique or privileged epistemic ability or state. It is a feature of such abilities (as they were understood by, for example, Moore and Prichard) that they do not require an altered sense of the ontological grammar of their objects. Indeed, if they did, the visual metaphor underlying intuitionist epistemologies would have done even less work than it did.

What is given to wondering testimony is not, as to its reality, as to its *being something*, an object for the speculative, discursive intelligence. To be sure, people who are at one time claimed in testimony might at another time think that it was an illusion, but the speculative intelligence cannot confirm them in one place or the other (which is not to say that it has no role). In whatever position they may find themselves – whether as someone who is in conscience claimed in testimony or as someone who says it is all illusory – they stand not as (ideally) unlocated rational agents. Necessarily they stand as historical, individual, human beings who are dependent upon those personal and cultural contingencies that condition their capacity, not so much to report their experiences as data, but to find themselves in them and to speak authoritatively out of them.

Holland says: 'A stance has to be taken, unless it goes by default, towards the difference between judgements that are of the highest significance for ethics and judgments that are not.'[4] In another place he says: 'The argument here, then, is what I have called a life-form argument, and arguments of this family are powerful: so powerful that I would credit them with the capability of accounting for 90% of all ethical phenomena . . . they could account, I should think, for every customary and mediocre goodness. It might then look as if this were all the ethical could contain, whereas absolute value is something different and remains unaccounted for.'[5]

When Holland says that 'a stance has to be taken . . . towards the difference between judgments that are of the highest significance for ethics and those that are not', he does not intend to point to argument in the modern practice of the subject *about what that difference amounts to*. That would presuppose a degree of agreement on *what that difference is between* which is manifestly absent between those who speak of absolute goodness as Holland does and those who find no reason to speak that way. Therefore, when he says that something 'remains unaccounted for', he does not mean to present something which has merely been neglected or forgotten, some 'datum' whose neglect would render some theory liable to revision under pain of not being adequate to the 'phenomena', or to the 'appearances', or to our 'pretheoretical intuitions'. It is not that kind of 'something' – not, for example, the kind that can be confirmed or rejected by the speculative, discursive, intelligence in 'reflective equilibrium' with the deliverances of a 'sensitive moral phenomenology'. It is not a hypothetical or speculative 'something', but it is not a proven 'something' either, nor a 'something' so clearly apparent to those who are qualified to philosophise on ethical matters that it needs no proving. But if it is none of these, and not something which is given to self-authenticating moral intuitions, then a question naturally (and, for the most part, rhetorically) arises for most philosophers: what sort of 'something' is it?

In a different way, it arises for Holland too. If it did not, he would not say that goodness is a mystery, although that is not his only, or his first, reason for speaking that way. Those who are inclined to ask the question rhetorically will say that you cannot make something out of nothing by calling it a mystery. As they think of it, they are right. Holland would not deny it. Someone is either constrained to speak this way or he is not. Most philosophers are not. That might not matter were it not that 'a stance has to be taken'. It might still not matter if that on which a stance has to be taken were, however important, something separable from '90% of all ethical phenomena'; something necessary only for the completeness of any ethical philosophy. But it is not so and Holland does not think it is. Even the old example of returning books to the library is caught up in it: 'there could coexist, for at least some people in a society, a concern for truth of an altogether different character, in which not to falsify became a spiritual demeanour'.[6]

'Absolute goodness *is something*' – that is not a report following an intellectual voyage of discovery. Someone cannot be compelled to speak this way merely because others have, because he has read about it, or argued about it, or because he has studied moral philosophy. But he could not speak that way unless others have. That is to emphasise that discussion of it is not a corroborative comparison of the tales of those who have knocked about in strange spiritual places. Those who would speak in this connection of self-authenticating and intersubjectively comparable intuitions tend to think of it like that, thereby distorting both the way in which what Holland says is personal and the way it is public.

209

Holland sometimes uses the expression 'absolute value', but it is absolute *goodness* he speaks of. In the way that he speaks of absolute value, the concept of goodness informs the sense of something absolute. To be sure, absolute goodness is never disclosed *simpliciter*. Other moral concepts (often those of the virtues) enter the descriptions of those actions whose goodness is a matter for wonder. 'For instance, I might say, in the case of a deed that struck me as wonderful, that it was not only the courage but even more the magnanimity of it.' Speaking Platonically (as in this instance Holland does not), we might say that those more specifically described qualities 'partake' or 'participate' in what is absolute when the actions that instance them reveal a goodness that is something to wonder at in the way that Holland so often describes, and as I described it in the previous chapter when I spoke of the goodness of Mother Teresa. The expression of the sense of goodness which is absolute will emerge from the characterisation of a certain kind of wonder – but also (and necessarily), at *goodness* as it is revealed in action.

The idea of absolute goodness is not, for Holland, a formal idea which could be instanced in a plurality of conceptions of absolute value. There are such conceptions (Holland gives examples), but on this understanding of absolute goodness they are false semblances. When I say that absolute goodness is not a formal idea, I mean that one does not arrive at it by noting that morality is *sui generis*, that it does not allow of external justification, that it is an 'additional principle of discrimination supervening on purpose',[7] that it necessarily overrides all other values, or that moral considerations 'silence rather than outweigh other considerations'. Nor is it arrived at by acknowledging what I said about the grammar of what is essentially mysterious, or by anything I said about the kind of depth and seriousness that is internal to moral issues. But it may now be suspected that my claim that goodness is a reality in the light of which we understand evil has (to borrow an expression from Anthony Flew) died a death of a thousand qualifications. Have I just denied myself anything sufficiently substantive to deserve seriously to be called a conception of reality?

'Reality' is, of course, a tricky word in philosophy, as is 'world'. Those who call themselves 'moral realists' tend to say that moral judgements are truth-valued and that they are so 'in virtue of' what

210

is (with occasional embarrassment) called 'the independently exist-ing real world'.[8] Kant rebuked those who would commit suicide in the disdainful spirit of 'leaving the world as though it were a smoke filled room'.[9] When Socrates explained his opposition to suicide he said that the mystics tell us that we are in the world as a soldier is at his guard post.[10] Those are uses of 'world' which bring with them a correlative sense of the world's independence from our will, but which are of no use in sentences such as the one I quoted from Mark Platts ('if a moral judgement is true then it is true in virtue of the independently existing real world').

The point can, perhaps, be made clearer if we attend to the way Iris Murdoch speaks of the ethical task to 'see the world as it is', for she is often quoted by some realists and Platts speaks of her with admiration.[11] She says it is a task to see the world as it is but, for her, the task is one of *love*. Reality is revealed by the patient work of love, she says, and that coming to see the reality of another person is a work of love, justice and pity.[12] She speaks in connection with this task (which is not prompted by love as an investigation might be prompted by curiosity, but which is itself an expression of love) that the sense of the language expressive of it depends upon con-texts of attention whose character is partly determined by the neces-sarily historical character of the individual who is attending. She says (unsurprisingly) that 'the idea of "objective reality" undergoes important modification'.[13] She thereby invites us into a different understanding of the way the distinctions between the personal and the impersonal, the subjective and the objective, invention and discovery, are used in ethical contexts from when they are used in contexts where the sense of the way they contrast is conditioned by a requirement that opinion converge towards agreement, or by an image of a rational agent's progressive disengagement from partial perspectives towards 'seeing the world as from no place within it'.

The 'world' of which Murdoch speaks is, clearly enough there-fore, not the world which scientists discover, nor is it the world 'in virtue of which' moral judgements are made true. That becomes even more evident if we notice what kind of task Murdoch is thinking of when she says that it is a task (ethically) to see the world as it is. The idea that a requirement to lucidity is internal to a certain understanding of life and its meaning is at least as old as Socrates.

211

However, the idea of an ethical requirement to lucidity, of a *task* to see the world as it is, invokes, I think, a conception of 'the world' which is not independently intelligible from the ethical character of the task. It is a conception of the world in the light of which for Socrates, for example, the unexamined life, and in a different way suicide, could be seen as a kind of ingratitude. It is a way of speaking of the world as we do when we say that Job came to see the world as his dwelling-place: a certain ethical or spiritual demeanour is inseparable from it.

I do not wish to dwell on this way of construing the ethical task 'to see the world as it is' except to say that, for Murdoch, it is inseparable from her mystical (that is her word) interpretation of Plato, and that, *a fortiori*, so is her understanding of the way it is 'endless': its endlessness is not contingent, as it is for Platts, upon our epistemic inadequacies – 'The background to morals is properly some sort of mysticism, if by this is meant a non-dogmatic, essentially unformulated faith in the reality of the Good, occasionally connected with experience.'[14]

If we ask how we retain the sense of what is revealed by the love of Mother Teresa, and if we ask it under the pressure, which is internal to the wonder, to protest, as did Aristotle, that it is absurd, then the answer cannot be that we should try to construct a metaphysic which would secure it. What I claim may be understood in the light of Mother Teresa's compassion requires no metaphysical underpinning, let alone the metaphysical underpinning that is often associated with Christianity. It is true that she said that she would not be able to do what she did were it not for her love of Jesus, but I need not even understand what that means, let alone 'believe it', in order to respond as I have described. The answer to the question how we may retain a sense of what is disclosed by her compassion is therefore: by attention to like things. In what respect should they be alike? The only answer, I think, is that they must be absolutely good. We know them only as they are revealed in the light of a pure love.

Speaking in a similar vein Holland says:

> It is the possibility of coming into an inheritance. It has to do with no less a question than whether a man can be at home in the world – whether he can find it a good world despite the ill

... By being brought into contact with forms of understanding and apprehension in which some good is to be encountered, some wonder to be seen, whether in nature or the work of human beings, a person might be helped to see the beauty of reality, helped to live more fully, helped to be glad that he is alive. The expression knocking at my mind is nourishment of the soul.[15]

I suspect that if they were asked what is substantial in that passage, many philosophers would say that it is the idea that a person might find the world a good world despite the ill, and that such a person might be brought to live more fully and to be glad that he is alive. They would not be wrong, but put that way it does not take us beyond Aristotle. But the tone of the passage is clearly not Aristotelian, and in case there is any doubt about it, here is a passage from Pablo Casals that Holland quotes immediately afterwards:

For the past eighty years I have started each day in the same manner. It is not a mechanical routine but something essential to my daily life. I go to the piano and I play two preludes and fugues of Bach. I cannot think of doing otherwise. It is a sort of benediction on the house. But that is not the only meaning it has for me. It is a rediscovery of the world of which I have the joy of being a part. It fills me with awareness of the wonder of life, with a feeling of the incredible marvel of being a human being ... I do not think that a day has passed in my life in which I have failed to look with fresh amazement at the miracle of nature.[16]

I offer this quotation from Casals as an example that reveals connections of a kind between goodness, attention, love and purity that are foreign to Aristotle, but which are found in Plato, and which are fundamental to the difference between them on what sense might be made of what Socrates meant when he said that a good man cannot be harmed. It also reveals that the conception of goodness is not what we ordinarily call *moral* goodness. But neither is it in the case of Mother Teresa. It would be silly to call her an 'extremely moral woman'. Her example reveals, amongst other things, the relative banality of the concept of 'the moral', and the importance of the concept of goodness.

213

I argued earlier (indeed, it is one of the major themes of this book) that the fertile contrast with that understanding of absolute goodness I have been exploring is not a reductive construal of moral value, but a non-reductive naturalism. A non-reductive Aristotelianism, which acknowledged that the serious use of our appreciative vocabulary in which we record our sense of the virtues does not allow of reduction to purpose or function, need include no sense of mystery of the kind to which Holland testified when he said 'absolute goodness *is something*'.

Unfortunately, Holland often contrasts what he wishes to speak for with various reductive accounts of morality and, indeed, he does so in his introduction to *Against Empiricism*: 'Chapters 6 to 9 are variations on the theme of two ways of thinking about value, the two kinds of ethics. Absolute ethics and empiricist ethics are the most appropriate labels I can think of for them.'[17] A paragraph earlier he spoke of 'the two ways of thinking about value': 'The view that there is a value which differs by a world of difference from all other kinds of worth seeks expression in talk of absolute goodness.' That, I think, is badly misrepresented by the contrast between absolute ethics and empiricist ethics. What is at issue is more perspicuously revealed if we consider my earlier quotation against what Holland called the 'life-form argument'. Then he spoke of 'a concern for truth of an altogether different character, in which not to falsify became a spiritual demeanour'. It is the phrase 'spiritual demeanour' that expresses Holland's understanding of absolute value. It would not have been the same if he had spoken of a concern in which not to falsify became a matter of *honour*. But that would have been sufficient to show the 'life-form argument' to be reductive and inadequate.

Holland asks, 'Where could this spirit come from?'[18] That can be asked from different positions and in quite different spirits. It can also be asked by a reductivist of a non-reductivist construal of the virtues. It can be asked by a non-reductivist about what Holland speaks for. The latter may express the way that Aristotle found unintelligible the Socratic claim that a good man cannot be harmed. It is a serious question. The former is not. The reductivist's question, 'Where does it come from?', should be returned to him or cast aside as confused. Some people are incapable of acknowledging the irreducibility of the ethical. For them, as Holland remarks, moral philosophy will be reductively centred on 'a set of notions among which the chief are, function, role, purpose, aim and desire'.[19]

'Where does it come from?' may be asked in response to someone who says that goodness is a reality whose nature is mysterious. When it is asked in response to such an affirmation, then, even if it is asked by a non-reductivist, it misconstrues Holland's way of speaking of absolute goodness to be a matter for corroboration by the speculative, discursive, intellect. But it may also be asked *in the face* of that goodness which is a mystery: it may be asked by someone who is claimed in testimony to its reality. In such a case, given that a certain kind of religious answer is not forthcoming, it is the expression of a religiously unexplained or unsupported ethical other-worldliness. This may be what Murdoch meant when she spoke of a non-dogmatic mysticism.

The non-reductivist's question to the claim that there is an absolute goodness which is a mystery is the expression of the rejection of anything that goes beyond a non-reductive humanism. That shows it to be a serious question in the way the reductivist's was not. The serious contrast is not, as Holland says it is, between absolute ethics and empiricist ethics. It is between a non-reductive humanism and a kind of ethical other-worldliness.

The reason I call it ethical other-worldliness is to emphasise that the sense of other-worldliness is ethically conditioned rather than the other way about, as most who would say they are humanists because they are not religious would think it to be. The way I have spoken of absolute goodness challenges common construals of what is to be related or kept apart when philosophers (and others) ask about the relation between religion and morality. Some may call the way I have spoken of goodness religious. I would not do so. Because the reality of goodness is not a reality that could be unmysterious to an ideal epistemic being, it is not a notion of reality suitable for a religious (really a metaphysical) underwriting of absolute ethics. As I have already emphasised, this way of speaking of mystery is not conditional upon our contingently limited epistemic powers.

The non-reductive naturalism or humanism on which many contemporary philosophers pin their hopes for an understanding of the nature of morality arose from a legitimate dissatisfaction with available varieties of intuitionism and formalistic non-cognitivisms, and a distorting emphasis on the 'moral ought' as something *sui generis*. In some instances, it expressed a mistrust of what was perceived to be a high-minded denigration of considerations of human harm and welfare as they may be understood independently of any moral perspective. The conception of absolute goodness I have tried to articulate in this chapter and the preceding one relocates the concerns of such philosophers in a conceptual and a moral context that reveals a different sense of their significance.

I quoted Holland as saying that 'the view that there is a value which differs by a world of difference from other kinds of worth seeks expression in talk of absolute goodness'. That might bring Kant to mind. Many naturalists are hostile to Kant because they see him as saying what I have just quoted Holland as saying. They argue that there is a necessary relation between morality and human good and harm. As we have seen, some argue that there is no categorical 'ought' and that moral value is a value amongst others and not necessarily overriding of them. I would not deny much of that, and indeed I have emphasised that there are limits to moral or religious construals of what counts as human good and harm if they are to count as moral or religious. Whatever light an ethical conception may cast on death as a natural evil, for example, it cannot make the natural evil of death external to the evil of murder. But the limits are not as Aristotle saw them when he attacked Socrates for saying that a good man cannot he harmed.[20]

It is not contingent that what counts as a moral understanding or 'perspective' is not systematically destructive of our chances for that kind of happiness which is readily intelligible to any human being, independently of their moral perspective and independently, indeed, of whether they have one. Different ethical perspectives will invite us into different understandings of the meaning of those dimensions of human life, and some will go deeper than others. But it is a condition of them having the kind of seriousness necessary for them to be ethical perspectives, that they take seriously those dimensions of human life, the seriousness of which are readily apparent to any human being. It is a conceptual point that they cannot haughtily dismiss them in the name of the ethical. The general point is that anyone, including someone speaking out of an other-worldly understanding of the ethical, must speak as a human being amongst others – that is, out of a sense of fellowship conditioned by a common sympathetic responsiveness to the significance of ordinary human sufferings and joys. That, as I said, is a conceptual remark about anything that is properly called ethical or religious.

What I have just said is at the centre of all naturalisms, but it need not stay there. Far from being incompatible with, it is itself necessary to, there being a 'value which differs by a world of difference from all other kinds of worth'. The contrast between someone who speaks from an other-worldly understanding of the ethical and someone who speaks from a non-reductive humanism is not that the latter speaks for the human world (although, no doubt, that is how he will understand himself). The former speaks for it too, but out of a sense of its twofold determination – by that on to which humanists fasten and which they think to be the basis of their humanism, and by that confessed to by someone who says that absolute goodness *is something*. The best illustration I am able to give of this twofold determination of the ethical is what I said in Chapter 4 concerning the nature of remorse.

There are those who will say that the contrast between non-reductive naturalism and ethical other-worldliness is not a genuine contrast, or that it is a contrast between non-reductive naturalism (or humanism) and a religious ethic which is not prepared to declare itself for what it is. Clearly, I must say something about this, and I shall do it by commenting on something said by David Wiggins. It is interesting in itself and it is also representative of a certain sense of the religious.

Wiggins quotes a letter by Mozart to Padre Martini: 'We live in this world to compel ourselves industriously to enlighten one another by means of reasoning and to apply ourselves always to carrying forward the sciences and the arts.'[21] He comments:

What we envy here is the specificity, and the certainty of purpose. But, even as we feel envy, it is likely that we want to rejoice in our freedom to disbelieve in that which provided the contingent foundation of the specificity and certainty ... The foundation of what we envy was the now (I think) almost unattainable conviction that there exists a God whose purpose ordains certain specific duties for all men, and appoints particular men to particular roles or vocations.[22]

A few paragraphs later he speaks of 'the concept of God championed by modern theologians' and says:

> Whatever gap it is which lies between 1776 and 1976, such notions as *God as the ground of our being* cannot bridge it. For recourse to these exemplifies a tendency towards an *a priori* conception of God which, even if the Eighteenth Century had had it, most of the men of that age would have hastened to amplify with a more hazardous *a posteriori* conception. Faith in God conceived *a posteriori* was precisely the cost of the particularity and definiteness of the certainty that we envy.[23]

Wiggins speaks of a certainty and a specificity which we envy. I am hesitant to speak of what *we* think or feel on this matter. Some people speak enviously of the certainty of others in ways that range quite freely over content. Some people speak of a desire to be able to speak and to act with religious certainty and some speak, more specifically, of, for example, a desire to pray. I agree with Wiggins that religious certainty is specific and that those who envy religious certainty do not desire only to say with conviction and sincerity that God is the ground of our being. They could not relate that in any concrete way to their lives, and if they cannot do that, then I would say (I do not know whether Wiggins would) that theirs is not the God of religion. The language of religion must be more concrete if it is to illuminate our lives. We need to be able to say things like 'We live in this world to . . .', etc., and a Christian or a Jew must be able to pray, to worship in certain ways and to be able to consent to God's will. But the question is: *What is it to be able to do these things?* Wiggins wants to say that it is, amongst other things, to be able to do them because one believes that there exists a God with certain attributes. This much is certainly true: any account of what it is to do these things must speak of a belief in God and of beliefs about God. But then the question is: *What is it to believe in that way?* I do not speak with any confidence about these matters. Is that not exactly Wiggins' point? But I mean that I do not speak with any confidence about what it is to be religious, about what it is to believe in God, or to pray, or to be able to say, 'Thy will be done', or to say that we are all God's creatures and that He created heaven and earth.

218

If someone says that it is honestly possible to do these things if one believes *literally* that there is a God, that He receives our prayers, that everything that happens is an expression of His will and that He created heaven and earth and all things in them, then I want to know what such a person means by 'literally'. A religious person will speak of what God knows and he will say that God knows everything, although, more usually, he will speak of God's knowledge of what is in our hearts, of the good and evil in us, of what we have done and what we have suffered. Does He know my telephone number? Would one have to believe that to believe, literally, that God knows everything? That seems to me to be nonsense. The alternative is not to say that God knows only some things. It is to say, as has been said many times by D. Z. Phillips, that this kind of literal-mindedness misconstrues the grammar of serious religious speech.[24] But to accept the claim that God must know my telephone number if he is to be omniscient as a *reductio ad absurdum* of a certain conception of the religious, is to reject the sense of literalness invoked by those who say that someone like Phillips reduces religion to ethics. Have I begged the question by speaking of the grammar of *serious* religious speech? No, because any account will have to invoke the contrast between what is serious and what is not and between what is deep and what is not. If we are speaking of the 'more hazardous *a posteriori* conception of God', then we are speaking of the God of religion and not of the God of the philosophers, so we cannot get by with notions as limited as 'true', 'false' and the various modes of valid and invalid inference. (We cannot get by without them either, but I assume that is obvious.)

The reason we cannot is because we are concerned with what is spiritual, and the concept of the spiritual is the concept of something that deepens our lives in certain ways. At least, so I think of it. If it is not, then there is nothing to envy in anyone's religious certainty. The difficulty I have with what some people call a literal belief in religious propositions is in connecting them, in their intended sense, with anything spiritual. If someone says that to believe in God is to believe that there is some x with attributes F_1, $F_2, \ldots, F_n$ and that it knows my telephone number, then that is to speak of God in a way that is not yet spiritual.

There are those (perhaps they are many) who would say that it is not internal to religion that it be spiritual in the way I have been speaking of. Perhaps they would say that religion consists of a number of metaphysical propositions which, if true, would have serious consequences for us. Depth and shallowness do not come into it, although, they might add, we ought not to be too high-minded about the 'spiritual' irrelevance of being (literally) resurrected and of having our petitionary prayers answered. It is easy to make rhetorical points about God knowing our telephone numbers, they would say. They may remind me that there are shallow protestations of shallowness: 'Nebuchadnezzar had it forced on his attention that only by God's favour did his wits hold together from one end of a blasphemous sentence to another – and so he saw that there was nothing for him but to bless and glorify the King of Heaven, who is able to abase those who walk in pride.'[25] In that passage, Peter Geach criticises what he takes to be thoughtless denigration of the relation between wisdom, goodness and the fear of God. Worship of God, he says, 'is worship of the Supreme power, and as such is wholly different from, and does not carry with it, a cringing attitude towards earthly power. An earthly potentate does not compete with God, even unsuccessfully.'[26] But if an earthly potentate does not compete with God even unsuccessfully, then we do not speak of God's power in the same sense as we speak of the power of earthly rulers. It is therefore unclear what we are to make of Geach's remarks about Nebuchadnezzar's abasement by the 'Supreme power'.

To return to Wiggins' example. He says that the 'foundation' for Mozart being able to speak as he does was his belief 'that there exists a God whose purpose ordains certain specific duties for all men, and appoints particular men to particular roles or vocations'.[27] Wiggins does not say this only because Mozart saw meaning in what he did, nor because that meaning was perceived by him under the modality of obligation. He says it because both the meaning and the sense of a requirement which is internal to it are given their character by Mozart's belief that 'we live in this world to compel ourselves industriously to enlighten one another by means of reasoning and to apply ourselves always to carrying forward the sciences and the arts'. That is what Wiggins says we envy. It is properly, or at any rate reasonably, described as a religious sense of life's meaning. Humanists could not speak that way without suspecting that it threatened their humanism. But that still leaves us with the question of how we are to understand what we should contrast with humanism. Humanism is an unclear notion because to some – but inexpungeable – degree it defines itself by its rejection of the religious.

Must a person who speaks as Mozart did answer the question, 'Who put you in this world and what are His purposes?' under pain of falling in with demythologising theologians who in their own way make religion as abstract as metaphysicians do? Must he, even if he does not answer in such a way, construe the grammar of how he speaks of God and His purposes as fundamentally the same as when he speaks of human purposes? And if not, are the differences of a kind to undermine the idea that the fact that he speaks as he does rests upon his belief in certain metaphysical propositions?

Wiggins has an interesting footnote to his quotation from Mozart. It is a quotation from Cyril Connolly:

> Do people say such things now? Outside religious writing in the strict sense, the closest I know to a twentieth-century equivalent of Mozart's expressions is: 'As we grow older ... we discover that the lives of most human beings are worthless except insofar as they contribute to the enrichment and emancipation of the human spirit. However attractive in our youth animal graces may be, if in our maturity they have not led us to amend one character in the corrupt text of existence, then our time has been wasted.'[28]

Would Wiggins want to say that the expression 'our time has been wasted' requires metaphysical support? It is that expression which suggests the comparison with Mozart. But I take it that Wiggins' sense of the contrast between religious writing 'in the strict sense' and what Connolly says is that the former requires metaphysical support whereas the latter does not.

The point can be pressed harder by noting something else Wiggins says. He says it would be 'utterly wrong' to say that Mozart had 'thrown his life away' even if we think that there is no God.[29] He goes on: 'But if one doubts that God exists, then it is one form of the problem of life's meaning to justify not wanting to speak of throwing one's life away.'[30] Obviously, he does not think that speaking of 'throwing one's life away' requires metaphysical support. If anything he believes the contrary. But now we could rightly ask why he is so selective in what he believes requires metaphysical support. Why does he not say that the belief that there exists a God to Whom we owe our life as His gift is the 'contingent foundation' for speaking of 'throwing one's life away', in the context in which he does? For notice that the only reason for anyone suggesting that Mozart had thrown his life away is that he believes that he lived it under an aspect that was false. Wiggins does not suggest that this 'error' (if it is one) led to other disasters of a more obvious kind. He wants to say that if we do not believe in God we may still speak of a life as 'thrown away', even though the only reason for saying it is that it was a life lacking in lucidity about its meaning. That is close to saying that life is a gift which we honour and cherish by striving for lucidity. If someone speaks that way, must he answer the question, 'Who gave the gift?' under pain of either muddle or bad faith?

To speak of life as a gift is to see our life as having a certain kind of unity. It is internal to that sense of unity that we feel ourselves to be under certain obligations or requirements which are acknowledged under the aspect of gratitude. Speaking of life as a gift may get its sense from the pressure to speak in tones of gratitude of our relation to the world. Recall the quotation from Pablo Casals. It is something better to compare with what Mozart says than the quotation from Connolly, because what Connolly said has too much disgust in it. Suppose Casals had said, 'I do not think that a day has passed in my life in which I have failed to look with fresh amazement and *gratitude* at the miracle of life.' Would he have passed into a realm where metaphysical justification was required? But Casals does not need to use the word 'gratitude'. What he said *is in the accent* of gratitude. Is he, therefore, already required to give a metaphysical justification of what he said? I cannot see any reason to say that. More strongly, we cannot derive the gratitude expressed by Casals from some general metaphysical propositions. We speak of life as a gift out of the accents of gratitude rather than speaking in accents of gratitude because we (first) believe that life is a gift. And if we speak of life as a gift, then we do so under the pressure of particular occasions – under the pressure of 'marking an encounter'.

Casals does not speak as he does because of eighty years of experiencing the joys of spring. It is not because he felt every day what others might feel only sometimes, say, on a fine spring morning when they say that it is good to be alive. Repetitions of feeling that it is good to be alive are still only that – repetitions – and do not, of themselves, introduce the pressure to speak of life as a gift and of the requirements that go with it. Even eighty years of daily repetitions of feeling that it is good to be alive could not, of itself, lead someone to think of suicide or of living in a cloud-cuckoo land as a species of ingratitude. It need not even lead anyone into a concern for the meaning of their life. Without that concern, a sense of the kind of unity implied in speaking of life as a gift would be impossible.

Such differences locate one kind of conceptual gulf. I do not think that there is a conceptual gulf between speaking as Casals did and speaking as Mozart did. If we see life as a gift, then we cannot look on that as an accidental fact about ourselves. We see ourselves as defined by it. We see ourselves as essentially people who are claimed in response to the gift which is our life. That is naturally expressed in the words 'we live in the world to . . .'. I do not wish to deny an important difference between someone who can speak of life as God's gift and someone who cannot speak that way, although he speaks of life as a gift. I do not, even, wish to deny that the former speaks out of the implicit recognition (or love) of God. What I have been questioning is whether such a way of speaking of the implicit recognition or love of God is the same as saying that someone who speaks of life as a gift, does so rightfully, only if he assents to certain metaphysical propositions.

What is the difference between those who can speak of life as a gift, but who cannot speak of it as God's gift, and those who can? I confess that I do not know. If, however, the first group found in themselves a longing to speak of God, then, I think, they would not be satisfied if they could only assent to the truth of the proposition that 'there exists an x whose purpose ordains certain specific duties for all men and who appoints particular men to particular missions'. That is not to deny that they would describe their longing as a longing to *believe*. Nor is it to deny that they must describe the gap between where they are and where they long to be in terms that are irreducibly epistemic. I am denying only that those terms would be

223

irreducibly epistemic because their constitutive grammar is to be elucidated by reference to truth-valued metaphysical propositions.

Wiggins is right to link a concern with the meaning of life with a concern for truth, but that does not mean that 'truth' here means what philosophers mean by it when they construct theories of truth. It may mean that to be concerned with the meaning of our life is (amongst other things) to strive to 'see things as they are' relative to the categories of meaning under which we see our life and which determine what it is to 'see things as they are'. The epistemic grammar of 'seeing things as they are' is not univocal and it is not always centred on the kind of truth that has interested philosophers. And the love of truth is not the love of truths. The person who speaks of life as a gift, but who cannot speak of it as God's gift, might say that to be religious in the 'strict sense' is to be able to speak of God and to speak His name in prayer. That does not mean that someone who is not religious in the strict sense is not religious at all, or that he is religious in a waffly sense. If such a person may be said to speak out of an implicit recognition or love of God then he speaks religiously even if he would only shrug his shoulders at the claim that he does. There are first- and third-person asymmetries here.

I have tried to show that someone who comes to speak of life as a gift does not speak that way because he derived it from an unacknowledged metaphysical premise. If that is so, then there is no pressure to say that a person who speaks out of implicit recognition or love of God speaks out of the implicit affirmation of a metaphysical premise that asserts the existence of God. The claim that he speaks out of the implicit recognition of love of God is not the claim that he could only be intellectually justified in doing so if he acknowledged a metaphysic implicit in it.

I said earlier that someone who speaks in those accents of gratitude which condition the sense of speaking of life as a gift must speak that way under the pressure of particular occasions. I meant that he must speak in authoritative and authentic response to what has moved him. Such speech is an act of trust that we have not been seduced by what we feel we must be true to. That is part of what I mean when I speak of 'authoritative and authentic response'. It can, perhaps, be captured by saying that moral and spiritual understanding cannot be expressed in cliché. It must, however, be expressed in a form of speech which is vulnerable to cliché. What cannot find its expression in cliché is not 'cognitive' in the way philosophers usually speak of it. The reason I use the (I admit not entirely felicitous) words 'authentic' and 'authoritative' is to draw attention to the fact that we must find our own words or our own place for common expressions in ways that reveal certain virtues of character (a lack of sentimentality, for example) to be internal to what we say. Anything that we think may go deep demands that we strive to be lucid about it. Mostly, perhaps always, that means that we must strive for the right words. Iris Murdoch said:

> We do not simply through being rational and knowing ordinary language 'know' the meaning of all necessary moral words. We may have to learn the meaning; and since we are human historical individuals the movement of understanding is onward into increasing privacy, in the direction of the ideal limit, and not back towards a genesis in the rulings of an impersonal public language.[31]

At another place she says: 'As Plato observes . . . words themselves do not contain wisdom. Words said to particular individuals at particular times may occasion wisdom'.[32] The connections she suggests between moral wisdom and speaking words in the contexts of occasions which are what they are because of the way they are, conditioned by the essential historicity of persons, is part of what I wanted to convey when I spoke of 'authentic and authoritative response'. Moral and religious speech has the power to illuminate what claims us in response. I have invoked this idea before and I argue more directly for it in Chapter 15. For the moment, I want to bring out that the movement from speaking of life as a gift to speaking of it as God's gift *must be a movement of the same kind as led someone to speak of life as a gift*. The movement from speaking of life as a gift to assenting to those metaphysical propositions that assert God's existence and attributes in the manner of, for example, Aquinas' Five Ways, is not of that kind. Metaphysical propositions are not, and cannot be, undermined by cliché.

Not all moral and religious speech is as I have been characterising it. To suggest that it is, or ought to be, would be a sentimental dramatisation of the point I have been making. But if I am right, then it cannot be said against me that I fail to distinguish between asserting that God exists and various other speech acts (such as prayer) which rely on that assertion, for that is the distinction whose application I have been questioning. If I am right, then speaking God's name in prayer is not a speech act in which is embedded or which relies upon a metaphysical assertion.

Even so, moral and religious speech, if it is to be authoritative, is constrained under a discipline which is given in a critical vocabulary that is irreducibly epistemic. I remarked earlier on the fact that Wiggins said that we envied the certainty and specificity that marked the way people of the eighteenth century spoke of what conditioned their sense of life's meaning. I wanted to record my doubts about how he understood what he said we envied, not because I wanted to record what Wiggins himself notes – that there might be a tension between envy at the certainty of others and satisfaction in what we might think of as our intellectual emancipation – but because I am surprised at the confidence with which many philosophers speak of these matters. I want to continue the exploration of that scepticism by focusing on where Wiggins thinks we stand.

Until now my attention has been on how we might understand where those of the eighteenth century stood. Wiggins thinks that we stand at a place marked by our intellectual scepticism of the metaphysical propositions which the people of the eighteenth century believed and which rooted them in their certainty. He believes, I think, that if we do not believe those metaphysical propositions, then our thoughts about morality and the meaning of life must be constrained within humanistic limits. 'Naturalism' is another word for humanism as I am using it. I have not given a precise account of these terms, partly because it would be an exaggeration with point to say that this entire book is an exploration of them. It is an exploration of them through what might be contrasted with them.

Wiggins would be suspicious of what I said about what it may be to speak of life as a gift. So would MacIntyre.[33] It would seem to them an *ersatz* occupation of a conceptual space against which an honest naturalism defines itself. If it is a non-reductive naturalism, informed by a sensitive moral phenomenology and psychology, they might say, then we can have more of what we long for in religion than we might have thought. But not, they will insist, the right to speak of life as a gift. Their suspicion would be sustained by the fact that much of what I said seems to invite completion by explicitly religious assertion. I acknowledge that, but it cuts both ways, for it could lead us to change our sense of the grammar of serious religious speech. However, if someone thinks that religious speech requires to be underwritten by a true metaphysic, then he will be inclined to judge what I have said to be an illusory middle position, structured in its grammar by metaphysical propositions whose truth is dubious, and by certain psychological and social dispositions. If the metaphysical propositions are false, he will say, then naturalism will have its explanation of why they were believed, and if it is a non-reductive naturalism, of why they went deep. Take my discussion of remorse as an example. A naturalist will have plenty to say on how my talk of the radical singularity of those who are claimed in recognition of their guilt is a grammatical shadow shaped by the psychological and social isolation of the guilty. He will also note that what I said invites completion by, for example, speaking of the guilty as alone before God at the last judgement. He will construe that as a truth-valued metaphysical proposition which, as a naturalist, he will think is false but at least honest.

Wiggins said that it would be 'utterly wrong' to say that Mozart had thrown his life away, even if we think the beliefs in the light of which he lived his life are false. That is true, but it depends on our being able to take Mozart's life seriously under some characterisation different from the one he would give. (It depends on it if we think that much of Mozart's life was based on an illusion.) That may be easy enough to do in the case of Mozart, but it is not always so. It is not so in the case of Mother Teresa. More precisely, it is not so easy to give a naturalistic account of our wonder at her compassion which is true to the character of the wonder. Then a naturalist would have to choose between fidelity to the nature of the wonder and his commitment to naturalism. (And commitment is what it is because there is nothing like a proof of naturalism.) That, however, depends on what he believes to be the character of the wonder.

Wiggins says that it would be utterly wrong to say of a life such as Mozart's that it had been thrown away, even if it were 'intimately conditioned by the belief in God'. 'Intimately conditioned' cannot mean that it gives the description under which we (on reflection) take it seriously, because, for a naturalist, that has to be a naturalistic description. But what naturalistic descriptions will satisfy a person that he has done justice to what he takes seriously depends on what he takes seriously and what he dismisses as a shadow cast by it (perhaps together with certain false beliefs). It would be a foolishly brave naturalist who would claim that all he takes seriously is either discursively or empirically underwritten, or sufficiently evident to all normally knowledgeable and intelligent people, that it needs no underwriting. In the face of religious speech and behaviour he must determine what he can extract as worthy of his naturalistic seriousness. If he is a sensitive naturalist then he will push his naturalistic descriptions to their limits. He may then find something between his non-reductive naturalism and what he believed religion to be.

13

'The repudiation of morality'

Socrates said that if we know what evil is then we cannot do it. That was thought to be ridiculous when he said it and has been mostly thought to be so since. More politely, it is said to be one of the 'Socratic paradoxes'.

It is often said that what Socrates said is plainly contradicted by the facts of life. He would, no doubt, reply that his life of asking questions showed him that we are none too clear what the facts of life are. Peter Geach accused him of the 'Socratic fallacy', it being the fallacy of thinking that we cannot know something if we cannot define it.[1] That is a fallacy. Socrates was sometimes guilty of it, although he did not look for definitions as often as people say he did. He was not looking for them in *Gorgias* when he said to Polus that the evildoer is necessarily miserable and pitiable and that anyone who properly understood that could not do evil. But often, even on those occasions when Socrates was hunting for definitions and inclined to say that ignorance was in store for him and his interlocutors if they were not found, his point could be put like this: If we perpetually get into deep confusion when we try to think about good and evil, then we should be less confident than we often are that life teaches us that a person can do evil while fully understanding what he does. If we are confused about the concepts that are deployed in the descriptions of life's lessons, then we cannot be confident about what those lessons are. That is considerably weaker than the claim that we cannot know what we cannot define, but it is strong enough to be a serious objection to anyone who says that life teaches all who are not incorrigibly naive, that people do evil knowing full well what they are doing. When I stated the Socratic claim I spoke of a person *fully understanding* what evil is. Socrates must qualify his claim in some such way if he is to distinguish, as he must and as he does, between a good person tempted and a thug who cares only for himself.

There are four kinds of counter-examples that have been raised against the Socratic claim. The first is a thug who says that he knows what justice is but cares nothing for it. The second is a good person who succumbs to temptation. The third is the position expressed by Cavell when he says that 'morality must leave itself open to repudiation [and that] . . . there [can be] a position whose excellence we cannot deny, taken by persons we are not willing or able to dismiss, but which morally would have to be called wrong'.[2] The fourth is when, through no fault of his own, a person must choose between evils. That last example is not one I will consider. Although there are circumstances when a person, through no fault of his own, must choose between evils and will, therefore, do evil whatever he does, and although it is, strictly, a counter-example to Socrates' claim, his claim thus qualified would still seem paradoxical to many and would still be open to the other objections.

The first two examples, but mainly the second, are what people typically have in mind when they say that Socrates is easily refuted by the facts of life. There are many things wrong with the idea that moral philosophy should be haunted by examples of intelligent thugs, but in this connection it is the evident assumption that they understand what they are saying when they say that they care not a fig for morality. Do they? Only if what makes them a thug is irrelevant to the epistemic grammar of what they claim to understand. The assumption is that there is a 'cognitive' route from where they are to what they claim to understand, and that they need nothing more than certain facts and a good discursive intelligence to travel it. The thought is that if moral understanding is *bona fide* understanding then the epistemic route to it can bypass their callousness. That is a lot to assume. Much of what I have already said has been argument against such an assumption and I will say more in Chapters 14 and 16.

Even if we leave the intelligent thug aside for the remainder of the chapter, is it not evident that a person can understand what evil is, yet be tempted into doing it? I think it is not evident, but I think it is true. In what follows I will not attempt to give an account of temptation, or *akrasia*. Instead, I will try to show why what Socrates says is not evidently false, what would be needed for it to be true and why I suspect that it cannot be true.

Socrates would say that an evildoer always gets more than he bargained for, and that when good people do evil they get something they could not accept as part of a package along with whatever else they get through their deeds. They get themselves as evildoers. Socrates would say that could only seem true but trivially so, if we do not know what it is to be – what it *means* to be – an evildoer. He would say that if good people who have been tempted to do evil try to hide from that knowledge, then they will eventually lose themselves and whatever goodness they have because of their corrupting self-deceptions. The point applies not only to evildoing but also to vice (as I distinguished these in Chapter 4). Cowards flee, as they think, into safety, but they flee also into cowardice. Murderers may aim to get money, but they also get themselves as murderers. It is as though the tempting desire carries only the past self into the future with it; as though the tempted person thinks that everything will be as it is when he is tempted, except that he will also have what he now desires and does not have.

Suppose a good person is tempted to murder to gain some money. Add whatever circumstances you wish to make that temptation consistent with his being a good person or, at any rate, someone who is sufficiently removed from being a thug for him to count as someone tempted. Socrates would say that such a person knows what he is tempted to do only if he understands what harm he does himself in doing it. What, then, must he know if he is to understand what he is tempted to do?

Such people must hope to feel remorse once they have done the deed because that is a condition of their understanding, after the deed, what they did. If they say, before the deed, while they are tempted, that they do not care whether they are remorseful afterwards or not (and if we are to take them as meaning that and understanding it) then they are not merely people who are tempted but people who are selling their souls. They no longer care whether they retain sufficient moral understanding to be repentant. They are handing themselves over to evil. If they *are* remorseful afterwards, then they must relinquish what they gained through evil. They cannot say, 'We know the evil we did, but at least we have the money!'

Must they not understand that before the deed? Must they not, as people who are both tempted and knowledgeable of what they are tempted into, know that they are being tempted into an impossible deed? The purpose of the deed is to secure some money; but their moral understanding tells them that they cannot keep it, unless they lose their moral understanding of what they did.

Suppose someone who is tempted to murder his lover's husband so that he may be with her. Suppose too, that he sincerely believes that he ought not to do it because it would be evil. He does it, nonetheless. Afterwards he is remorseful. How should we characterise his remorse if it is lucid?

I have previously remarked on how natural it is to describe remorse as the pained realisation of the significance of what we did. 'My God! What have I done?' is a natural expression of remorse. It records a shocked awakening to the reality of the evil we did. It is also natural to express a certain kind of incomprehension – 'How could I have done it?' I have emphasised that these expressions of remorse are important and revealing. Rightly understood, they are in conflict with most theories of morality because they reveal them to have an inadequate account, if they have one at all, of what *it means to be wronged.*

'How could I have done it?' Why would the man in my example say that? Is it not obvious why he did it? He killed a man to get him out of the way so he could be with the woman he loved. It is not so simple, however. I described him as seriously believing, before he became a murderer, that he ought not to do what he was tempted to do. I described him as seriously believing that he was tempted to do something evil, and I asked, as I did of the previous examples, what must he understand if he is to understand fully what he is tempted to do?

He must understand that if he murders his lover's husband, then he becomes a murderer and that he must carry the significance of that into the future – that, to put the point Socratically, he must live with a murderer in the future. He must understand that the future will not be like the present except that he will be relieved of his

232

misery because he will be with her. He must understand that if he murders her husband, then their love can never be celebrated except in forgetfulness of the fact that a murdered husband haunts it. He must understand that he can never look at her without cursing his enslavement to his passion for her, because if he murders, understanding what he does, then it can be only in the desperation of despair. He cannot possibly *want* what he gets – a love and a life polluted by murder. What he wants is she with her husband out of the way. He wants what he would have if her husband left her or if he died in an accident and *the desire which tempts him pretends that* that *is the achievable purpose of his deed*. Desire presents his deed to him as 'getting her husband out of the way'. But that is not the most significant thing he gets, and it can only appear to him to be so if he has only a partial understanding of the meaning of what he is tempted to do. He can live with her as though her husband were merely 'out of the way' only if he plunges into a life of radical self-deception, but short of abandoning himself to the evil that will spread through his life, no degree of self-deception could hide his murderous self from him.

I offer this as an example of the Socratic thought that evildoers do not want what they get because they always get more than they bargained for. They get themselves as evildoers, and if they understand what that means they cannot accept it as part of a package along with whatever else they may get. The example could be extended and countless others could be given of the way evil can spread through a life, destroying any intelligible purpose for which the deed was done. The man in my example who murdered his lover's husband was tempted into an impossible deed. The deed into which he was tempted was structured by an illusory teleology. He thought that the murder, evil though it is, would be a means to the achievement of what he most wanted. But that is an illusion, and the realisation that it is an illusion is expressed in the question (which asks for no answer), 'How could I have done it?'

It is an example of the way our understanding of good and evil and our understanding of what we call 'the meaning of our lives' interpenetrate. It also illustrates the way an evildoer is, non-accidentally, 'miserable and pitiable'. But the meaning he came to see in what he did, and which reveals him to have been engaged in an impossible project, could not, had he appreciated it before the deed, furnish him with a motive or a reason for not murdering the husband. If he had said before the deed that he could not do it *because* its purpose was impossible to achieve, then he would have revealed himself to have a corrupt understanding of the evil he was contemplating.

That does not mean, however, that his understanding of what it would be to murder his lover's husband and the way the evil of it would spread through their lives is irrelevant to the characterisation of the fact that he does not do it, if he does not do it, because he fully understands the evil of it. He might say, 'I cannot do this' or even, 'It is impossible', *and his understanding of what he would be doing conditions the character of those modal expressions*. But his full understanding of what he is tempted to do cannot present itself to him as a consideration to be weighed alongside others. The salient description of what he is contemplating is that it is the murder of another human being. It is not that he is contemplating something under an illusory description of what he wants and what he will get. *Considered as a reason for action*, his realisation of how it will be afterwards is irrelevant, but it is not irrelevant to the sense of the modalities that limit his will. It may be for that reason that Simone Weil and Iris Murdoch emphasise that deepened moral understanding is a movement towards necessity, of the world becoming, as Murdoch puts it, 'compulsively present to the will'.[3] The example reveals that a deepened understanding of the nature and reality of evil is not always a deepened understanding of the reasons for not doing it, and why it is a mistake to believe that reflection on the nature of good and evil is always, or even most importantly, reflection on a certain class of reasons for action, of considerations which may have a legitimate speaking-voice in a piece of practical reasoning.

The man in my example did not merely realise, in his remorse, that he did what he ought not to have done, or that he broke a rule or a code of conduct, or that he betrayed his principles. These would be ridiculous descriptions of what he realised (although it is to these kinds of description that most moral philosophies are committed). Nor did he merely realise that he did the sort of thing he ought not to do again, or that he had to make what reparations he could, and so on. He saw other aspects of his life in the light of his understanding of the evil he had done and that furnished standards for the truthful description of them. (Plato would say that evil could furnish no standards, no light, according to which one could truthfully describe anything. He would say that evil itself is seen for what it is only in the light of the Good. I think that he is right, but it does not matter to my point, for I am not saying that the evil furnished the standard, but rather that his understanding of it did so.)

Is what I have said unSocratic? Here is Socrates speaking in *Theaetetus*:

> For they [evildoers] lack knowledge of the punishment of injustice, and that is, in all the world, the thing one should the least lack. This punishment is not what they expect, not the death and the blows which sometimes wicked men do escape, but another punishment which it is impossible to escape . . . There are in fact two patterns, one divine and blessed, the other devoid of God and wretched. But they do not perceive that this is so. Their stupidity, their utter ignorance blinds them to the fact that by their unjust behaviour they resemble the second and differ from the first. They are punished by the fact that they live a life which matches the pattern which they resemble.[4]

Some might say that since it is *Theaetetus* it is likely to be Plato rather than Socrates who is really speaking. But what is said is as fine an expression as we could wish for of the claim that an evildoer is miserable and pitiable only because he is an evildoer and as good an expression as any we will find in the uncontroversially 'Socratic' dialogues.

What I have said does not show that people cannot do evil fully understanding what they are doing if they are thoroughly evil, if, as I put it before, they are prepared to give themselves over to evil. Nor does it show that someone in despair could not do evil fully understanding what they were doing and fully understanding that they had been driven into an impossible deed in the sense I described earlier. But it has not been my intention to show that. I have tried to reveal two things. First, how important the idea of what someone becomes through the evil he has done can be in such a discussion. Secondly, how evil can spread through a life, destroying any intelligible purpose for which it might have been done. Moral cases of temptation are, in this respect, importantly different from non-moral ones. When morality is not at issue we can (at least typically) enjoy the fruits of our weakness without self-deception. That is connected with the fact that reflection on weakness of will in non-moral cases is part of reflection on the nature of practical reasoning.

I think that the only plausible argument in favour of saying that evildoers never fully understand the evil they do would need to show that a full understanding of the evil we would be doing would always so transform our desires and needs that they could no longer be a source of temptation or despair. That is plausible up to a point. What once tempted a person might no longer do so because, in the light of a certain moral understanding, he sees it as squalid, or ridiculous, or perhaps more generally, as ugly. And, of course, that possibility is not restricted to contexts of temptation. An important dimension of Socrates' polemic was his attempt to offer a different understanding of what those whom he engaged in argument cared for and pursued. In *Gorgias*, for example, part of the argument is intended to show that oratory is not at all a manly pursuit, nor one to which someone who cares for freedom and power should be attracted, since orators are people with no centre. They are soft and fragmented because their lives are lived in pandering accommodation to fickle mobs.

That is the kind of example that makes plausible the idea that the temptation is a clouding of our moral perception. Desire often speaks with a charmed and sophistical voice, when our hold on that perspective in whose light something appeared squalid falters. Perhaps it now appears instead (in a romantic light) as daring, or a free and open response to life itself. Thinking of such situations there is much sense in drawing attention, not to spiritual push-ups, but as Simone Weil and Iris Murdoch have done, to the importance of what we attend to.[5] As Plato said, we become like what we love.[6] The emphasis of Plato's 'moral philosophy' is not on what we ought to do but on what we ought to love. I say that is his emphasis, for I do not say that he believed that the two are logically independent (which of course they are not), but it matters where we put the emphasis. It is striking that for all the talk of Plato's 'moral realism', he is not concerned to show that moral judgements correspond to moral facts. And it is striking that for all the talk of his moral absolutism he is never concerned to establish that certain things are impermissible at all times and in all places. With respect to both 'moral realism' and 'moral absolutism' his emphasis is not on our actions, but on the objects of our loves. To put it in his language: the real object of love is the Good and it is the only thing of absolute value.

Not all temptations, however, are redescribable so that they lose their power. We see this if we attend to a mistake made by John McDowell, who is the only recent philosopher I know of who has attempted to defend the idea that, as he puts it, someone who has 'a clear perception of the requirements of virtue'[7] could not be tempted to act against them. McDowell says that 'a clear perception of the requirements of virtue silences rather than outweighs other considerations'. Considerations which would otherwise be tempting '*count for nothing*' (my emphasis). He says that when Jesus asked, 'For what shall it profit a man if he shall gain the whole world but lose his own soul?', he was not inviting us to weigh the loss of our soul against the gains of the world. Against the loss of our soul the world should 'count for nothing'.[8]

I would express my agreement with McDowell this way. If the man I described earlier who was tempted to murder his lover's husband were to think it a consideration, if only a weak one, in favour of the murder, that he could not be with her unless he did it, then we would say that he did not understand what murder is. The consideration that he could not be with her has no *deliberative* voice, no proper voice – not even an extremely weak one – in an inner dialogue. That is a way of understanding the idea that a consideration is 'silenced rather than outweighed'. It points to an important difference between moral and non-moral instances of temptation (when judgements are of what one ought to do 'all things considered'). It means that, in the example I gave, his need of her 'counts for nothing' *in deliberation* if he is deliberating whether to murder her husband. Or, to take another example: if someone is pleading to be exempted from military duty, the fact that they might be killed is a consideration which 'counts for nothing'. It does not follow in the case of the person tempted to murder his lover's husband that there is some redescription of his condition which, if he properly understood it, would ameliorate his crippling need of her.

Nor does it follow in the case of the person pleading to be exempted from military service that there is a redescription of his terror which would leave it powerless over his will.

McDowell says, following Aristotle, that the virtuous person keeps his sights set on 'the noble'. It is true that a perception of the ignobility of certain desires, or of their satisfaction in certain ways, can lead to their death – at least relative to certain forms of their fulfilment. Sexual desire, for example, may dissipate on a particular occasion in a virtuous person if he sees that on that occasion it could only be fulfilled in a squalid affair; and there is at least a case for saying that if, on such an occasion, desire does not dissipate, then it is because the person's 'vision of the requirements of virtue has become clouded'. In some cases we may take it as criterial for a proper understanding that what we acknowledge to be *deliberatively* impotent is also *motivationally impotent*. But that is true of only some cases. A man with a deep, but adulterous, love for a woman need be under no illusion about the blighted nature of that love in order to be continuously tormented and seriously debilitated by his need of her and by his clear sense of the moral impossibility of its fulfilment. His need of her is deliberatively impotent, but it is not thereby motivationally impotent. It is a serious question what the relation is between the role that considerations may play in deliberation and the role they can play in motivation. McDowell does not consider it.

I have wanted to show that what might be 'silenced' in deliberation might nonetheless issue into action. When it does, is it because people have forgotten that the reason for which they act has no deliberative voice? I see no reason to think so, although there may be reason to think they can only do so in despair. The hope that all that is deliberatively silenced might also be motivationally silenced must rest on the assumption that people who understand what evil is will unify their soul – the disparate springs of action – under that knowledge. Socrates thought that was possible, as did Plato (at least some of the time). There are reasons to think that they are deeply wrong, and they are conceptual rather than psychological reasons. They have to do with the fact that what can often conflict with morality is also what conditions it. The point can be put generally like this: what 'counts for nothing' deliberatively will always 'count for nothing' motivationally only if our attachments to one another do not threaten 'the requirements of virtue' when they conflict with it.

The sufferings which lead us into temptation are often connected with our deepest loves, and these determine our self-understanding, not merely as 'human, all too human', but just as human. They are connected with the sense our lives make for us and they condition the unique kind of individuality that I have argued is fundamental to what is disclosed in remorse. The question then is not whether knowledge can overcome weakness, or ignoble desire, or whether it is to be 'dragged about like a slave',[9] but whether there are not deep and irreconcilable tensions between the requirements of morality and what conditions those requirements. Those who have felt the full force of this question have either tied themselves to the mast or spoken of detachment from the world.

Cavell speaks of the 'repudiation of morality'. He says that 'morality must leave itself open to repudiation', and he speaks of 'the salvation of the self through the repudiation of morality'. He also says: 'There are conflicts which can throw morality as a whole into question, but the significance of this question is not, or not necessarily, that the validity of morality is under suspicion, but perhaps that its competence as the judge of conduct and character is limited.'[10] And a little later:

> It [morality] provides *one* possibility of settling conflict, a way of encompassing conflict, which allows the continuance of personal relationships against the hard, and apparently inevitable, fact of misunderstanding, mutually incompatible wishes, commitments, loyalties, interests and needs, a way of mending relationships and maintaining the self in opposition to itself or others. Other ways of settling or encompassing conflict are provided by politics, religion, love and forgiveness, rebellion and withdrawal.[11]

Cavell often speaks as though morality were an instrument with which to settle conflicts. I have already argued that is a misunderstanding. He wants to say that there are situations in which morality finds its limits. 'Mere morality', he says, 'is not designed to evaluate the behaviour and interaction of monsters.' That is true, but not for the reason he thinks. Morality is not designed *for* anything. It is not an artefact. People sometimes feel compelled to say that morality is an 'artefact', or a human creation, or a human 'invention', because they think that is all that is left to us if we deny that it is of natural or supernatural origin. But none of these terms can be taken seriously as descriptions of the origins of morality. If we wish to deny that morality is of natural (biological) origin, or of supernatural origin, then we should simply say that it is of human origin.

To say that there are situations in which morality finds its limits is not to say anything clear, and Cavell did not say it in a context which would give it point or even power. We start too low, I think, to reach the disclosure of what serious point there might be in saying such a thing if we begin by speaking about what morality is designed to do. Situations which might prompt someone to say that morality finds its limits are various and they do not instantiate a single concept, 'the limits of morality'. Nothing, I think, that anyone might seriously mean by it need lead us, under pain of superficiality or naivety, to acknowledge that there are things that human beings do that are above or below the conceptual reach of a sober remorse. But is that not to deny that morality must leave itself open to repudiation?

Consider the example, raised by Bernard Williams, of someone who must choose between leaving his wife and children and living a life he judges to be necessary for his artistic work. Williams calls him 'Gauguin', and he uses the example to discuss the different ways luck may enter the justifications a person finds for his actions.[12] My concern will be different. I will take it as an example of the claim that 'there [can be] positions whose excellence we cannot deny, taken by persons we are not willing or able to dismiss, but which morally would have to be called wrong'.

After he says that, Cavell speaks of the 'repudiation of morality', but why should anyone who repudiates morality be someone who occupies a position 'whose excellence we cannot deny'? If he does anything which should be the occasion for serious remorse, then he must acknowledge it, whatever else he does, if he is to be someone 'we are not willing or able to dismiss'. If Williams' Gauguin leaves his wife and children, it must be with a proper understanding of what it means to do that. He cannot do it in the spirit of 'repudiating

240

morality'. Why should we judge that to be anything but superficial posturing? Could he leave if he fully understood the wrong he would do them yet it not be a case of moral weakness? I think the answer to that is yes, and that Williams is right to press the case for that answer.

Williams also says that Gauguin may be *justified* in leaving, but only if he succeeds as an artist.[13] We need not, however, be concerned with whether he might be justified in what he did. I do not deny the difference it will make to his sense of what he did if he fails as an artist because he did not, after all, have it in him to be a fine painter. It will also make a difference to what he did if his wife kills herself or if one of his children is killed, even if accidentally. He has serious reasons for what he does. They are not moral reasons, but morality need not override them for anyone who is morally serious and who fully understands what he does. Why do we not leave it at that? (Why try to sum it all up?) What would Gauguin, or what would we, be after in asking whether he was justified in leaving his family?

Suppose he succeeds. Williams says that he will be glad that he left. Why should that be so? Why is he not just glad that he succeeded? Is it because he thinks he would not have succeeded if he had not left, and since he is glad that he succeeded, he must be glad that he left? That does not follow. First, he cannot know that he could not have succeeded if he stayed. Perhaps he would have, but perhaps not. He does not know and no one else could either. Secondly, it does not follow that if we are glad of an outcome then we are glad about what was necessary to achieve it.

Williams says that if we are glad to have his paintings, then we must be glad that he did not stay with his family. That does not follow, for the same reason. There is no inconsistency in being glad to have the paintings and not judging whether he should, or should not, have left his family. Nor is there inconsistency in being glad to have the paintings and judging that he should have stayed with his family, or wishing that he had. The paintings are here and we are glad they are here. Should we wish them away because we know how they came to be? If we do not wish them away, should we approach them morosely? Should we not take pleasure in them, or admire them? That would be absurd. But then we will be glad of them.

241

If he is not glad that he left, must he be sorry or indifferent that he left? He cannot be indifferent if he is to be serious, for he did his family a grievous wrong in leaving (whatever happens to them). Must he be sorry? He must be sorry for the wrong he did his family in leaving, and the sorrow is remorse even though he need not think he would act differently next time. (Remorse, as D. Z. Phillips has pointed out, does not always entail repudiation of the deed for which one is remorseful.) Does that mean that he thinks he made the right decision? It means only that he would make the same decision again and that he is glad he had it in him to succeed. If that is thought to *mean* that he judges that he made the *right* decision, then it is too thin to carry a substantial notion of justification. What depends on his success is not whether he was justified in leaving but what is to be said about his leaving and his life. There is no reason why that must concentrate on the question, 'Was he justified?' – not for him, and even less for a spectator. If he fails, will he not wish that he had not left? Possibly he will; but not in the same sense as he might wish that he had not failed, or that he had never been required to make such a decision in the first place. It does not follow that he thinks himself unjustified, and that he would have been justified if he had succeeded.

I have said that his reasons for leaving were serious reasons. Does that mean that they must be weighed as reasons for anyone in a similar situation? They need not. Someone else might find it unthinkable to leave. Does that mean there is something that such a person (who finds it unthinkable) does not see?[14] It does not. It would, however, if they could not understand that someone could understand what they would be doing in leaving, yet leave and it not be a case of weakness. Whether the person who leaves could be rightly judged to be morally serious will depend on the details of the example.

Is this incompatible with the Socratic claim that it is better to suffer evil than to do it? Does Gauguin not show that he would prefer to do evil than to suffer it? Williams describes him as constituted by his relation to his painting. It is not irrelevant that it should be painting, for it is important that what gives sense to his life and conflicts with his obligations to his family does not itself reveal deep deficiencies of character. (Think of Midas and his gold.) It is, therefore, wrong to describe him as someone who would prefer to do

242

evil than to suffer it, or as someone who thinks it is better. He is caught between different kinds of impossibilities.

Those impossibilities are, however, not equal partners. Moral value is not merely one kind of serious value amongst other kinds of serious value. His art could cease to claim him, but morality will not. If he leaves his family, then he lives under that inescapably serious fact and its meaning. Morality is not renounced or repudiated, because a morally serious person, without weakness, does wrong fully knowing what he does. The claims of morality, as I have argued previously, do not express themselves only in what ought to or must be done.

I said earlier, in my discussion of practical necessity, that Gauguin's guilt might undermine what had given sense to his life, denying it the power to continue to do so. It does not follow that he should not have done what he did. Acknowledging that, however, does not mean that, if for the most serious reasons someone does not or cannot renounce doing what would seriously wrong another, the severity of the moral description of what he does should be softened. That is true whether the reasons are of a moral kind (a moral dilemma) or whether, as in the example just discussed, they are not.

It may seem that my argument has depended upon the concept of morality and may therefore be vulnerable to the kind of contrast Williams draws between morality and ethics. In the example of Gauguin we might say that, instead of conceiving of it as a conflict between morality and something else, we should conceive of it as a conflict within the ethical.

There is much to be said for that suggestion, for there is no doubt that the concept of morality is often used in ways that (non-accidentally) trivialise what may come in conflict with it. We could avoid that by characterising it as a conflict within the ethical. Certainly it would not help Gauguin to represent his conflict to himself as between morality and something else, for what greater insight does he achieve into what it would be for him to abandon his wife and children by calling it a moral matter? But by the same token, how would it help him to call it an ethical matter?

Williams believes that what he calls the morality system is a corrupt species of the ethical. It is (in his judgement) corrupt because of the way it distorts substantial ethical concepts like practical necessity into empty notions like the categorical imperative. Part of the point of calling it a *system* is that, if we think about the nature of morality, then there are things which, *non-accidentally*, we think about – virtue, obligation, justice and so on. Williams believes that reflection on the concept of morality tends to distort what it non-accidentally directs us to. Or, to put it another way, reflection on what the concept non-accidentally directs us to is distorted if the thought that they are *moral* matters intrudes to any degree. But suppose we ask, as Williams does not, whether what he calls morality is a distorted species of the ethical or whether it is a corruption of morality. I think that the answer is that it does not matter. It does not matter, for example, whether or not what Aristotle discussed in the *Nicomachean Ethics* is rightly called a morality. The difference that people have noticed between Aristotle's conception of value and certain elements of a post-Christian sense of value is not best captured in the thought that Aristotle did not really have an understanding of *morality*. If what I have been arguing in this book is right, then we capture it better if we say that he was lacking in a certain understanding of goodness and of evil. I have spoken freely of morality and of what it is for something to be a moral matter, but not, I hope, in a way that commits me to what Williams calls 'the morality system'. The word 'morality' is so much with us that it would be extremely difficult and, I believe, artificial to try to stop using it.

It does not matter, then, whether what Williams calls the morality system is a corruption of the ethical or whether it is a corruption of morality. It does matter, however, whether our concepts of good and evil are *sui generis* and whether they are of a kind which, on the one hand and for one kind of purpose, undermines the contrast between the moral and the psychological as that is characteristically drawn by moral philosophers, and whether, on the other hand and for a different purpose, they heighten the sense of contrast between themselves and all other valuations. In the preceding chapters, I have tried to bring out how and why that is so. Although I have spoken freely of morality, and sometimes interchangeably of it and the ethical, I do not think that I have spoken of either, and especially not of morality, in ways which make me vulnerable to one of the main reasons why Williams draws the contrast between morality and the ethical – because 'the morality system' trivialises whatever conflicts with it.

14

Ethics and politics

Since at least the time of Socrates some people have believed that there is an irreconcilable tension between morality (or ethics – the distinction need not concern us for the moment) and politics. Others have not, and some – Aristotle and Marx for example – believed that the ethical requires completion by the political. It is controversial whether Plato was closer to Aristotle and Marx than to Socrates on this point, but anyone who thinks that he was cannot think that it was easy for him. The Platonic Socrates of the earlier dialogues seems to believe that a preparedness to do evil when necessary is internal to serious political commitment and that those who refuse to do it will be judged to be irresponsible by their fellow citizens. Even as late as *Republic* where Plato presents portraits of the perfectly just and the perfectly unjust man, it is the perfectly unjust man who is praised as a benefactor of mankind and is favoured even by the Gods.[1] In modern times Max Weber distinguished between an 'ethics of absolute ends' and an 'ethics of responsibility'.[2] There is much confusion in Weber's essay, but it is deservedly a classic, and that is, partly, because of the way he captures the age-old sense that those who say, as did Socrates, that it is better to suffer evil than to do it, or those who say, as did St Paul, that one must not do evil though good may come of it, are in some sense irresponsible. In this chapter I want to try to understand what that charge of irresponsibility comes to.

One should not say, flatly, that there is a conflict between ethics and politics. Nor should one flatly deny it. What one says will depend on one's conception of the ethical and also of the political.

Consequentialists will see no conflict, because they believe that we ought to manage things for the best, whatever our circumstances.[3] Many philosophers who are not reductive in their ethics tend to think reductively about politics even if they do not think, as Holland does, that 'consequentialism is the ethics of politics'.[4] It is common to think of politics as high-level management, so common, indeed, that some businessmen think that because they have successfully managed large companies they would probably 'run the country' better than most politicians. They may be right. Nonetheless, it is a politically illiterate boast, however effortlessly it may be made and received in a community which speaks quite naturally of politicians 'running the country', and in which it is common to think of them as managing the instruments of power for the sake of certain ends which may be described independently of political activity. The idea that political institutions are not essentially instruments of power serving a particular purpose, and that political activity is *sui generis*, irreducible either to morality or to management or to some combination of both, is foreign to us.[5] A proper exploration of the relations between ethics and politics would require an exploration of that conception of politics and that conception of ethics which generate the conflict. It would be, I believe, a conception of the ethical as absolute and of both as *sui generis*. Such an exploration is a task too large for a chapter in a book, even if I were capable of undertaking it. However, a book on the nature of an absolute conception of good and evil would be radically deficient without at least outlining what the relation is between such a conception and politics.

Does politics *particularly* suggest a consequentialist account of it even to someone who finds it implausible elsewhere? If we think of politics generally rather than the more extreme, or at any rate more dramatic, examples where the consequences of a refusal to do evil are truly terrible, then there is no reason to think that politics is more receptive to consequentialism than is any other realm of value. It is a truism of moral philosophy that consequentialism seems to deliver an inadequate account of justice. If we are inclined to think that is true, then consequentialism will hardly appear to yield an attractive account of politics. How could something be both an attractive account of politics but an unattractive account of justice? One could go on to give countless instances of judgements made concerning the honour and integrity of political action, and indeed of the political realm, which appear to be resistant to consequentialist construals of them. Consequentialism is as inadequate to the values expressed in the normal course of political life as it is to everything else. Clearly, a form of Aristotelianism offers a more serious account of ethics, of politics and of their relation than does consequentialism. Why, then, is it so often thought that politics provides difficulties for those who are not consequentialists? Because, I think, it is tempting to believe that politics is *at the crunch* consequentialist. At certain critical points nearly all people will make the same judgements as would a consequentialist and, if they are inclined to theorise about the matter, in apparent inconsistency with their other judgements. That inclines many people to think that, at certain critical points, consequentialist considerations will override all others, revealing that one was all along a closet consequentialist, or at any rate that politics will bring out the consequentialist in all of us.

It is, of course, the same sleight-of-hand we noticed before. Consequentialists are right in believing that there will come a point at which almost everyone will agree that evil must be done if it is the only means of avoiding certain terrible consequences, and they are also right in thinking that politics provides them with serious examples to press for that agreement in judgement about what ought to be done. But they are wrong to describe those considerations that compel most people to agree with them as *consequentialist* considerations, for they thereby hijack for their own purposes considerations which are common to any serious understanding of ethics and politics.

The sleight-of-hand is crude, but something serious prepares us to be taken in by it. It is that we are almost irresistibly inclined to think that those considerations, because of which we do evil in the political realm, and feel in some sense required to do it, are themselves moral considerations. The reason is because we are inclined to think that anything that looks like a requirement to do evil *must* be a moral requirement. We are inclined to think that because we tend to believe that any consideration that seriously weighs against a moral consideration (which is not advanced self-deceivingly to serve weakness or corruption of character) must be a moral consideration. It is, therefore, tempting to think that the conflict is a conflict *within* morality rather than *between* morality and politics. Consequentialism will then appear to have the merit (in the judgement of those who are looking for a theory of the matter) of giving a consistent account of it. I have been consistently critical of the various phases of Bernard Williams' attack on morality as *sui generis*, but he is importantly right in seeing that considerations for which a morally serious person may do evil are not *ex hypothesi* (because such a person is described as morally serious) moral considerations. He is also right in thinking that the tendency to think that they are trivialises what may come in conflict with morality. But as I have already indicated, I do not believe that his distinction between morality (the 'morality system') and the ethical will help those whose sense of the conflict between ethics or morality and politics turns out to be a sense of the conflict between politics and the kind of conception of absolute value I have been trying to elucidate. The conflict then, as I understand it and will try to describe it in this chapter, is between politics and a certain conception of good and evil.

One naturally thinks of Machiavelli, who said that a prince must learn how not to be good, and who said of himself that he loved his city more than his soul.[6] Machiavelli, however, was concerned mainly with the qualities of character which were needed by one who sought power and hoped to keep it. The same is true of Weber: he was concerned to describe what kind of person is fit to 'venture to lay hands on the spokes of the wheel of history'.[7] My concern will not be with the character of the politician, but rather with an ordinary citizen's sense of what it is to be a citizen. But before turning to that, it is worth noting how seriously both Machiavelli and Weber took politics. They both thought of it (as Weber makes explicit in his title) as a *vocation*. We are more inclined to think of it as a career, partly because we do not tend to think of anything under a serious conception of a vocation, and partly because we are not inclined to think of politics as sufficiently deep to deserve to be called a vocation. We tend to think of it as we do garbage collection – it is important and must be done, and one does it either because one recognises that someone must do it, or for reasons and motives we would discourage in our children. Machiavelli and Weber, however, saw politics as something to which one may be called, to whose discipline one must submit, and whose nature and requirements one is committed to discovering in an ever-deepening exploration.[8]

For someone who takes the concept of vocation seriously, the realisation that politics may be a vocation will reveal the superficiality of the idea of politics as social and economic engineering and also of the idea that it is of the nature of politicians that they seek power for their own enhancement. No doubt power has its attractions which corrupt many politicians, and in many other ways politicians must, as Weber puts it, distinguish whether they are living for their cause or off their cause, but, far from being internal to the political life, such things are corruptions of it. The failure to realise that – the repetition of the banal oversimplification that power corrupts and absolute power corrupts absolutely – has contributed, even amongst politicians, to a cheap cynicism about the character of political life. A shallow and high-minded form of absolutism asserts itself against it.

> It may be protested that without lying the work of the world cannot be done. Some respected Christian figure, I forget who, said that those who do the world's real work cannot hope to keep their hands clean. No doubt, but only to those who have clean hands and a pure heart, who have not sworn deceitfully to their neighbour, is the blessing of the LORD promised. Those who do the world's work have their reward; the world passes away and the plans of the world, but he who does the will of God is God's own child, who can dwell in God's house forever.[9]

Its counterpart is an unsavoury fascination with the evil which is thought to be ineradicable from politics. Thus Croce:

> Machiavelli discovered the necessity and autonomy of politics; politics which is beyond moral good and evil, which has its own laws against which it is futile to rebel, which cannot be exorcised and banished from the world with holy water.[10]

Someone who feels a tension between a politics and an absolute conception of good and evil need not feel that she must choose between Geach and Croce.

My concern is not with someone who seeks power and the means of retaining it. I am concerned with the sense of a conflict between ethics and politics as it may concern anyone who thinks about what it is to have a political *persona*, as that is conditioned by that distinctive mode of human association and practice which is politics.

That *persona* is, in modern times, mostly that of a citizen, and although for convenience I will usually refer to it as that, it need not be citizenship. The sense that there may be an irreconcilable conflict between ethics and politics has most often been voiced by ordinary citizens in our times in two contexts (excluding their concern with the character of politicians). First, when they have protested against the evil done by their governments, mostly in foreign affairs. Secondly, in revolutionary politics where great evil was often done to achieve and secure the revolution. The second has been the source of much discussion because so many intellectuals were sympathetic to the aims and achievements of the revolutionary governments. The most famous argument concerning this was between Jean-Paul Sartre and Maurice Merleau-Ponty on the one hand and Albert Camus, Arthur Koestler and (in a more complicated way) George Orwell on the other.[11]

Thinking of such examples, it is (as we noted earlier) tempting to think that we are presented with a conflict *within* the ethical or between different ethical conceptions (between a conception which refuses to do evil whatever the consequences and one that will not refuse it), and that this has been misunderstood as a conflict *between* ethics and politics because politics has provided the occasion for the conflict and because such conflicts are so dramatic when politics is the occasion for them. That is mistaken on both counts. It is mistaken in thinking that the conflict is really within or between moralities, and, more specifically, in thinking that it is a conflict between those who think that there are certain things that cannot be done whatever the consequences and those who will do evil to secure great good or avoid even worse evil. Isaiah Berlin, for example, said that the mistaken idea that there is a conflict between ethics and politics rather than a conflict between different ethical conceptions is sustained by a conception of political activity as merely the application of technical skills. He says of Machiavelli that his 'values . . . are not instrumental but moral and ultimate . . . For them he rejects the rival scale – the Christian principles of *ozio* and meekness – not as being defective in itself, but as inapplicable to the conditions of real life.'[12] Later he says, 'There are two worlds, that of personal morality and that of public organisation. There are two ethical codes, both ultimate; not two "autonomous" regions, one of "ethics", another of "politics".'[13] That is a bland solution, achieved by a bland conception of morality as a code of 'ultimate ends'[14] and by the attribution of a simplistic conception of politics to those who have felt an irreconcilable tension between ethics and politics. I hope that my previous discussion of the nature of good and evil relieves me of any further need to justify that judgement.

When Bertolt Brecht joined the communist party during Stalin's reign of terror he wrote: 'What vileness would you not commit to root out the vile . . .? Sink down into the slime/Embrace the butcher/ *but change the world*.'[15] As Hannah Arendt brings out, Brecht and many other revolutionaries were driven by the 'passion of compassion' and they acted, in the light of what they saw to be the historically conditioned possibilities, to 'change the world' because of the suffering they could not bear to behold.[16] On another occasion Brecht wrote of 'the fierce temptation to be good', thinking of it as a temptation against compassion.[17] But the good of which he spoke and struggled as against a temptation was not surrounded by sneer quotes, which shows that for Brecht the conflict could not be represented as between consequentialism and absolutism or between consequentialism and anything else. Brecht spoke of good and evil as no consequentialist can. In Chapter 5, I gave some reason for thinking that Brecht's compassion disguised a certain kind of contempt for those for whom he was prepared to 'sink down into the slime/Embrace the butcher', but I do not intend to argue the matter more fully here. My purpose is to point out that nothing in the character of the conflict Brecht expresses suggests that it is a conflict between ethics and politics. If we refuse to do what Brecht did, or if (as so many did) we go some of the way but no further, then whatever else may be said, it cannot be said *merely because* of our refusal that we do not understand the character of politics or what it is to be a political being. If someone decides that she must murder for the sake of the afflicted or the oppressed, then whatever else she says, she may not rightly say that those who refuse to do it are apolitical or politically naive. In Brecht's case, politics was merely the occasion for his asking whether evil may be done because of the good that might come of it. The contexts in which that question may arise are not peculiar to politics, although it is not accidental to politics that it should often throw it up. But not all the occasions when politics throws it up are occasions when a conflict has arisen, or has even appeared to have arisen, between ethics and politics. The fact that it is not accidental to politics that it should often pose that question may mean only that it is not accidental to politics that it should be a source of moral conflict.

The same may be said of many examples in foreign affairs. Two examples from the Second World War are often discussed – the saturation bombing of the German cities and the dropping of the atomic bomb on Hiroshima and Nagasaki. They are often discussed in the same breath, but they are importantly different. If we take the official reasons given at the time as the considerations advanced in favour of both (criminal) acts, then the first is an example of a conflict between ethics and politics, but the second is not. There are good reasons to believe the official reasons were not the actual reasons for the bombings in either case, but I will ignore that for the sake of the argument. They were plausible, and although political actions will seldom be so simple that the motives of their agents could be represented as simply as those official reasons suggest, they are the kind of reason ordinary citizens must sometimes assess if they are to judge the actions of their governments.

The official reason given for dropping the atomic bombs on Hiroshima and Nagasaki is that it would force the Japanese to surrender, thus stopping the war and saving many more lives than were lost in the bombings. I am not concerned to ask whether that is morally a good reason or even whether it is one that should be considered. I am concerned to point out that insofar as someone was moved by such a consideration but was also horrified at what it enjoined her to do, then there is nothing in her conflict, as it has been described, which suggests that it is a conflict between morality and politics. Her question is, 'What is it permissible to do to save lives?' That is, of course, a serious question, but it is not one that refers to politics except as the occasion for moral conflict. Some, of course, did not think there was a conflict. They believed it was out of the question to drop the bomb, that it was quite clearly the murder of the innocent and, therefore, an unjust means of prosecuting the war.[18] Others – consequentialists – believed that, if the calculations about the proportion of lives saved to lives lost could be relied upon, then it was obvious what to do.

Some people thought that it was also out of the question to drop the bombs on the German cities. There is little reason to doubt that it was a war crime according to the Hague Conventions, and no reason to doubt that it was murder. But it was quite different from the dropping of the atomic bombs on Hiroshima and Nagasaki. The official reason for bombing the German cities was not that it would shorten the war and save lives and misery, but that it was necessary to defeat Germany. There would have been two consequences of a German victory. First, many more people would have suffered and been murdered. Secondly (to the extent that the Germans succeeded in their aims), many more *peoples* would have been destroyed – some because they would have been wiped off the face of the earth as the Nazis tried to do with the Jews, and others because they would have had their culture and ways of life destroyed. These are consequences of different kinds. The Third Reich was a threat to mankind in the sense in which Arendt expresses it when she suggests how we should understand the phrase 'a crime against humanity' as it was used in the Nuremberg Trials. Genocide, she says, is a crime against humanity because it is a crime against human diversity. It is part of our understanding of humanity, she argues, that it is non-accidentally composed of many peoples.[19] These are considerations of a different kind from those that refer to the death and suffering of individual human beings, however many they may be.

Grant, for the sake of argument, that the destruction of a people is different from the killing of individuals even if they number more than the people. Grant also that the destruction of a people is an irreducibly *political* crime. Still, it does not follow that doing evil to prevent the destruction of a people is anything other than doing evil to prevent a greater evil. It looks, therefore, as though, for someone for whom it is a problem, it is a problem *within* morality, occasioned by politics. And at this stage we might feel that the question whether something is a conflict within morality, or between moralities, or between morality and something that is not morality, is becoming uninteresting and merely verbal.

I think that it is not merely a verbal matter and that we can see that it is not if we reflect on why treason is such a serious political crime. Treason is a crime against the conditions of political communality. Traitors, by 'aiding and abetting' the enemy of their people, help those who would destroy them as a people. Or, they deliver their people and the conditions that make them a people – which enable them to say 'we' in ways that are not merely enumerative but expressive of their fellowship in a political identity – as a hostage to the improbable good fortune that their enemies will respect their integrity as a people. Therefore, treason is not essentially, or indeed ever at its deepest, a crime against the *state*. It is a crime against a form of civic association which, in modern times, it is the responsibility of states to protect. That does not make treason morally evil. It may or may not be, but whether or not it is is usually politically irrelevant.

E. M. Forster is much quoted as saying that if he had to choose between betraying his country and betraying his friends, he hoped he would have the courage to betray his country.[20] That was, I suspect, a reaction to certain forms of jingoism which, because they express a corrupt conception of the love of one's country, also express a corrupt conception of treason. It ought not to be taken, as it often has been, as a remark which reveals that Forster had no serious understanding of the nature of treason. If, however, he thought it a mitigating plea against the charge of treason that he had to choose between the betrayal of his country and the betrayal of his friends, then he would show that he did not understand what treason is. That someone had good moral reason to commit treason is, generally, as irrelevant to the nature of the crime as the fact that someone does not want to die is to the character of their obligation to fight for their country. There is no inconsistency in sentencing a person to death for treason and admiring his motives for being treasonous. People may sometimes feel a moral obligation to do something treasonous, for two importantly different reasons. First, because they feel a moral obligation of a kind that prevents them from recognising the legitimacy of the state which charges them with treason. The second is of a kind that does not require, or if the person is clear-sighted does not allow, the denial of such legitimacy. Germans who fought with the allies against Germany in the Second World War are an example of the first. Americans or Australians who supported the Viet Cong and the North Vietnamese in the Vietnam War are an example of the second. The difference in these cases reveals the complexity of the relation between the ethical and the political.

Germans who fought in the resistance or who gave other forms of active support to the allies in their war against Germany sometimes said that they were the true patriots, that they fought against the Third Reich out of their love for Germany. That was not mere rhetoric. The evil of the Third Reich was so great that no German who knew what was going on could support it and be even moderately decent. By the early 1940s, no German could fail to know that something terrible was being done by their government unless she was radically self-deceived. Or, at any rate, no one could support the Third Reich without being in the kind of error that makes serious political (or moral) discussion impossible. That means that the evil of the Third Reich was of a kind, and sufficiently public, to destroy the possibility of community between decent human beings. Writing in 1945, Hannah Arendt pointed out how, after their defeat, the Nazis tried to implicate the entire German population in their crimes by, for example, giving Nazis documents which falsely stated that they had been in concentration camps. She says:

> Whether any person in Germany is a Nazi or an anti-Nazi can be determined only by the One who knows the secrets of the human heart ... Those, at any rate, who actively organize an anti-Nazi underground movement in Germany today – and there are such persons in Germany of course – would meet a speedy death if they failed to act and talk precisely like Nazis. In a country where a person attracts immediate attention by failing either to murder other people upon command or to be already an accomplice of murderers, this is no light task. The most extreme slogan which this war has evoked among the allies, that the only 'good German' is a 'dead German', has this much basis in fact: the only way in which we can identify an anti-Nazi is when the Nazis have hanged him.[21]

One cannot commit treason against such a government, except in the trivial sense that one would of course be charged for treason by it. My point is not merely that the state had lost its legitimacy. That may happen and one may still be treasonous against one's community. In the case of the Third Reich, the state was not only illegitimate: the nature of its evil had destroyed the possibility of a decent community under its government. A decent German community could re-emerge

255

only after the destruction of the Third Reich. For that reason it was not double-talk to say that a patriotic German would have done whatever he could do to bring about its destruction.[22]

During the Vietnam War, some people from nations whose armies were fighting in Vietnam against the Viet Cong and the North Vietnamese army gave active support and encouragement to their countries' enemies. They did so because they believed that their countries were waging an unjust war against the Vietnamese people, that the means and the cause were unjust. Some of them also believed that they were conscience-bound to give what support they could to the Viet Cong and the North Vietnamese. They thereby gave active support to those who were killing their fellow countrymen. In this respect they were quite different from those whose opposition to the war at no stage extended to helping the enemy, but which took the form of demonstrating against it, refusing to be conscripted and so on. The difference is between those who committed treason in their opposition to the war and those who did not.

I am not concerned to judge whether those who actively supported the North Vietnamese were morally justified in doing so. The point I wish to make is that if they acted clear-sightedly, they could not believe that their country had lost the legitimacy to try them for treason. The reason is that they could not rightly believe (or even reasonably believe), as could the Germans, that no one could know the facts of the war and still support it without being evil. They could not reasonably believe that the prosecution of the war and its support amongst their fellow countrymen was evidence of either such deceit and self-deceit or such evil that the possibility of communality between moderately decent and knowledgeable people had lapsed. No one can expect to speak and act in fellowship with people whose friends, husbands and children are being killed by an enemy she is supporting unless she has good reason to believe that the war is so evil that a clear-sighted acknowledgement of it by her fellow citizens would restore the conditions of fellowship, even if it is a tragic fellowship.

The example shows, I think, that an act may rightly be judged as treasonous, and therefore amongst the most serious of political crimes, without being judged to be morally wrong. There are many crimes morally worse than some forms of treason but they are not a threat to a people. They do not undermine, as treason does, the conditions which make it possible for a people to speak as a people.[23] That is why the most fitting (though not, any more, practical) punishment for unrepentant traitors who are not also guilty of other crimes, such as the murder of their fellow countrymen, is banishment. But in civilised communities, the punishment for even the most evil of murderers (even when it is death) expresses the fact that they remain one of us.

In Chapter 1, I quoted Polus' sarcastic response to Socrates' saying that it is better to suffer evil than to do it and that it was better for an evildoer to suffer just punishment than to escape it. An important part of what Polus says is that not only will the evildoer suffer 'exquisite torture' he will also 'see his wife and children suffer the same'. The point was often made against Socrates that someone who believes that it is better to suffer evil than to do it will be unable to protect himself and, more importantly, those he cares for. The point can be generalised (as it may well be intended in the dialogue whose bitter political tone has often been noted) to politics. A government constrained by the belief that it is better to suffer evil than to do it, or by the belief that we may not do evil though good may come of it or some terrible evil be averted, will surrender its people as a hostage to the improbable good fortune that they will have no enemy sufficiently wicked or cunning to attack them in ways which leave them with only evil means of defence. That happens, for example, when guerrillas do as Mao Tse Tung advised them to and 'mingle with the people as fish in the ocean', thereby forcing their enemy to choose between defeat or killing more civilians than combatants.

No amount of casuistry on the distinction between intended and unintended consequences can reconcile the killing of two innocent civilians for every soldier with the traditional doctrine of a just war. And, equally importantly, there is no way of 'updating' the traditional doctrine to accommodate modern warfare or such guerrilla tactics in a way that would enable us to defend ourselves both effectively and justly. People sometimes talk of morality as though it were a kind of map to guide us through the perplexities of our times, and they say that, like all maps, it may need updating as the moral terrain changes with the times. Alan Donagan says that adherence to the precept that we must not do evil though good may come of it may lead to *tragedy* but not to *disaster*, because those who formulated it ensured that it would not do so. He seems to believe that the original mapmakers were extremely prescient, although really, he is merely whistling in the dark, as is revealed in the desperate tone of the following: 'Traditional morality ... has been constructed at every point with careful attention to the nature both of human action and the world in which it takes place.'[24] Elizabeth Anscombe also whistles in the dark when she says that we can always be just in the means of our defence and not withdraw from the world.[25]

The impossibility of reconciling the nature of much modern warfare and much guerrilla warfare with any plausible conception of a just war is a clear example of the fact that we cannot necessarily match morality to our needs or commandeer it into our service. There are times when morality and the world are badly mismatched, and not because of a failure of our creative imagination. There are situations in which the evil that needs to be done to avoid a terrible evil suffered is such that it makes nonsense of the idea that it is justified to do it because it is the lesser of two evils. There are, of course, situations in which we are justified in choosing the lesser of two evils – that is, there are situations where the concept of the lesser of two evils applies in such a way as to give sense to a substantial notion of justification. But we cannot employ that idea soberly just to permit ourselves to do evil to avoid suffering it – to guarantee that, although we may be ethically compelled to face tragedy, we need never feel ethically compelled to face disaster. The Socratic ethic and the traditional concept of a just war do not offer such guarantees. And if it is true, as Donagan says, that those who coined the slogan *fiat justitia ruat coelum* did not believe that the heavens could fall because we acted justly, then we have scant reason to agree with them.

Socrates' claim should not be confused with what Weber called 'an ethics of absolute ends', because Weber tended to identify that with Christian pacifism. Socrates was not a pacifist. Nonetheless, the Socratic ethic is, as Holland pointed out, an ethic of forgoing and it is not accidental to politics that forgoing is not its manner. Thus, although there are very important differences between the Socratic ethic and Christian pacifism (taken here, minimally, as a principled refusal to adopt the means of violence in defence of oneself or of anything else), Weber was not entirely confused in thinking that such pacifists were a particularly revealing case to contrast with the acknowledgement of that kind of responsibility he believed to be internal to political seriousness. We may see why if we reflect upon the kind of unease people often feel with them.

The unease is, I think, the expression of an ambivalence. On the one hand pacifists are sometimes thought (I do not say rightly) to represent something extremely fine – at the very least a high, if unrealistic, ideal. On the other hand, they appear to many to refuse to accept a certain kind of burden which is intimately connected with the very nature of human life. Anscombe expressed the kind of intimacy well when she said: 'To think of society's coercive authority as evil is akin to thinking the flesh and family life evil. These things belong to the present constitution of mankind: and if the exercise of coercive power is a manifestation of evil, and not just the means of restraining it, then human nature is totally depraved in a manner never taught by Christianity.'[26]

Orwell said that in the Second World War any decent person, whether or not she was a pacifist, would hope that the Allies would win the war. Since they could not win the war by waving a magic wand, that meant hoping that the Allies would kill enough Germans to win it. He thought that was an argument against pacifism, that it revealed an inconsistency in it. The argument is flawed in much the same way as is Williams' argument concerning Gauguin and his paintings, which I discussed in Chapter 13. But although it is not true that someone who wishes for, or who would applaud, an outcome must will the means to it, Orwell brutally drew attention to the same kind of intimacy between the conditions of human life and the need for human beings sometimes to kill one another, as Anscombe did. The same, I think, is true of the necessity to do evil to protect political communities.

Our unease with pacifists is not, or should not be, that they accept the benefits of a community protected by force without paying the cost. Nor need it be that they are unrealistic, for they may not be (they need not believe that non-violent resistance would secure the means of our defence and other political ends as effectively as violence does). Our unease is, I think, the expression of a feeling that they are not truly amongst us. And if we ask what marks that

259

sense of community from which they are, partly, excluded – what kind of 'we' is it? – then, I think, the answer is that it is a community constituted by the fact that we will do evil when it is necessary in the defence of the conditions of political communality and by the fact that we know that we will do it.

Now I come to a fundamental point that will seem to many people very strange, or even self-contradictory. The qualification 'when necessary' is not meant as a *justification* for doing evil. It does not even signal the possibility of a justification. It functions negatively to condemn the use of evil means when they are not necessary, but it does not work positively to justify their use. Governments will do evil to protect their peoples, and their peoples will, mostly, consent to it. They will look upon those who do not as strangers in their midst. (More often than not, indeed much more often than not, governments will claim that it is necessary to do evil when it is not, and more often than not they will get the support of their peoples, but that is irrelevant to my argument.) Those are facts, but just because they are facts, philosophers have been inclined to think they are not important. A philosopher is likely to say, granted most people will do that, but there is a further question whether they ought to or whether they are justified in doing so. In the same spirit someone might ask, why is that sense of fellowship from which those who refuse to do evil are excluded not the corrupt fellowship of the guilty which I condemned in Chapter 4?

The latter question would be the right one to ask of someone who said that we cannot make omelettes without breaking eggs, or that we must be prepared to dirty our hands and other things like that which are commonly said. I hope that what I have said in other chapters makes it clear that I believe that someone who refuses to do evil in such circumstances need be ignorant of nothing, that she need not mistakenly think that her refusal is a means of achieving something. She need not be vulnerable to the charges of being preciously afraid to dirty her hands or that she has in some way reneged on the (implicit) rules of entry into the political community. I also hope that my discussion of remorse reveals why I would not say, as some have with a romantic thrill, that we must be prepared to shoulder the burden of becoming evildoers – that being the tragic burden of our humanity. I do not wish anything I have said to be misunderstood as being sympathetic to such frivolous romanticism, be it on behalf of a community or, as was suggested at one time by Michael Walzer, on behalf of politicians.[27]

What, then, does constitute that sense of communality from which those who would apply the Socratic precept to political life are excluded? Why is it felt that they are not one of us? It is most likely to exist when a particular people is threatened. But they do not then speak (when they think that some of their fellow citizens are not fully 'one of us') as that particular people even though *that* they are a people is internal to their sense of the kind of fellowship we are exploring. The reason why those who refuse to do evil are judged 'not one of us' is not because they are not prepared to do what is necessary for, say, the English people to survive as a people. The thought is not, how can they call themselves English men or women? The thought is, rather, that the acknowledgement that we must do evil is not merely a condition of the survival of this or that community under these or those contingent circumstances. The acknowledgement, *in advance*, that we will do evil is a condition of political communality as such. It is a condition of the sober acknowledgement of one's political *persona*. Acknowledgement in advance that we will do evil and the absence of a justification for doing it (because, for example, it is the lesser of two evils) distinguishes this from a moral dilemma.[28]

What do I mean when I say that the acknowledgement of the necessity to do evil is not for the survival of this or that political community, but a condition of political communality as such? I mean, primarily, that the evil should not be done for the sake of certain natural goods which we may think it is the business of governments to secure or distribute. The point may be made in a way that might sound brutal. There is a distinction between doing evil to save lives – in the case of the Second World War to save individuals from being murdered in the concentration camps, however great the number – and doing it to avoid the destruction of a people, either by genocide, or by the destruction of the conditions which make them a people (their culture and their language). There is a difference in kind between murdering individuals or interring them in concentration camps and destroying their language or destroying the roots of their culture by suppressing its past.[29] The ancient charge of irresponsibility is not, I think, levelled at those who, individually or collectively, would rather suffer such evils as imprisonment or murder than do evil. It is levelled against those who, because they will not do evil, seriously put at risk the conditions that make communities of human beings a people.

The recognition that those conditions must be defended, certainly by violent and sometimes by evil means, is the recognition that acknowledgement of such necessity is a condition of human plurality, and is, therefore, a kind of loyalty to something fundamental to our humanity. If that is so, then although the Socratic ethic is in non-accidental conflict with politics, it is not, as Berlin thinks, because of the *public* character of politics. The conflict between such an ethic and politics is not a conflict between public and private morality. There are many kinds of public institutions, and some (the Church, for example) may refuse to do evil to protect themselves without being vulnerable to the charge that such refusal is in conflict with a lucid appreciation of their character as public institutions. Pacifists might create a community on an island and have many of the institutions of government, yet refuse to defend the community against aggression by violent means. No one would think that to be radically paradoxical. The leaders of such a pacifist community would not be judged irresponsible if they did not avail themselves of violent means to protect the community against those who would destroy it and murder as many of its members as they could.[30] Or, more accurately, they would not be judged irresponsible in the way that non-pacifists, who refuse to do evil though it is necessary to preserve the conditions of political communality, are judged to be. That is partly because, in renouncing violence completely, pacifist communities are not political communities. They have delivered up the future as a hostage to fortune, and that is the renunciation of politics.

To describe the fact that governments do evil to protect their peoples, and that their peoples generally consent to it as a kind of loyalty to what makes us human, looks like an attempt to justify the evil done or consented to. I do not intend it to be. I say we always have done this and we always will, but that is no justification. There is more to be said, however, about the fact that we always have and always will, which explains our unease with those who

262

systematically refuse, and also explains why the charge against them has so often been that they are irresponsible.

It is by no means always a justification that one did something out of loyalty, but those who are loyal to the same thing feel a sense of communality. It is that which I have been trying to capture. I hope to have shown why such loyalty to the conditions of political communality might be seen as the exercise of a kind of responsibility and, therefore, why the charge of irresponsibility comes so naturally to those who are unable to find their feet with those who refuse to do evil. If, as I am suggesting, it is a kind of loyalty, but a kind that cannot be offered as a justification for the evil done because of it, then we may see why it should sometimes be misunderstood by those who are loyal in that way as a justification and a reason for condemning those who are not. We may also understand why they are tempted to romanticise their loyalty as an expression of their clear-sighted acceptance of the tragic burden of their humanity because of the reasons why they were prepared to do evil. The next step, and it is a very small one, is to speak of the need occasionally to dirty one's hands. Then the evil which is done to protect the conditions of political communality may destroy them.

15

Moral understanding

I have repeatedly spoken of a deepened moral understanding and suggested that, properly understood, it creates difficulties for most ethical theories. It creates difficulties, indeed, for the very idea of a moral *theory* insofar as that brings with it a certain conception of the distinction between appearance and reality as it applies in ethics. A rightly developed account of what it is for moral understanding to deepen will also undermine the visual metaphors so common in ethics and especially favoured by contemporary cognitivists. I suggested, too, that Kant's rejection of the empirical as a determinant of morality was an expression of his failure to see how an understanding of morality – of its nature and the character of its seriousness – was dependent upon a natural language. It is time to deal more directly with these matters.

Much moral thinking is not thinking *what to do*, and even when it is it is also an attempt to understand the *meaning* of what we do, which is rarely thinking about the empirical consequences of what we do, or about how our principles stand in relation to those consequences and to one another. It is, most often, an attempt to achieve a deepened understanding of the *meaning* of our actions. That, as much as conscientiousness, is a mark of moral seriousness and of what we should understand by having arrived at a 'right answer' to a moral question. It is, therefore, important to understanding moral deliberation to look at what it is for moral understanding to deepen. Moral philosophy has paid little attention to this and has mostly assumed that any deepening will be the result of theory, either directly in moral philosophy, or indirectly elsewhere – most likely in psychological or social theory.

The reasons for that neglect are various. Some are banal – a thoughtless scientism, for example, which assumes that only theory really penetrates the appearances. One, however, is as deep as the subject itself and depends upon an assumption about what thought is in its primary and proper sense. The assumption is that a thought is truth-valued and stands in logical relations to other thoughts. The primary terms of critical appraisal, then, are 'true', 'false' and the names of the various modes of valid and invalid inference. Our actual critical vocabulary is far more extensive than that would suggest, but on this understanding of what thought is, of what is properly speaking 'cognitive', our more extensive vocabulary marks out not further *modes* of thought's successes and failures, but, rather, distinctive *causes* of its success or failure in its primary modes. Thus (to take an example which I will discuss more fully later), to criticise someone's thought as sentimental is, on this conception, to offer a causal explanation of why his thought is false or muddled, and when this is not so, then it is judged not to be, strictly speaking, a criticism of his *thought*. According to this conception, sentimentality does not mark a distinctive way in which thought can fail alongside being false or invalid. It marks a distinctive cause of thought's failure in one of its primary modes, rather as, for example, tiredness or drunkenness does. This implicit division of our modes of critical appraisal into primary and secondary is not limited to discussions of value. It pervades philosophy and is as evident in epistemology as it is in ethics. Philosophy, which prides itself on thinking about thinking, is marked throughout by a neglect of most of the terms of the actual critical vocabulary with which we mark our sense of what it is to think well or badly.[1] As a consequence, philosophers have neglected what is necessary to an appreciation of what it is for moral understanding to deepen, in the sense in which Raskolnikov came to a deepened understanding of the meaning of what he did when he murdered the moneylender and her sister.

It is not accidental that there are no moral whizz-kids. That is partly because we cannot acquire moral knowledge in any sense that would make us morally *knowledgeable*. Philosophers often speak of moral knowledge without noticing how unnatural it is in most contexts. It is more natural to speak of a depth of moral understanding or of wisdom, and *it is not accidental to these that their achievement takes time*. I mean that the fact that it takes time is not contingent upon our limited epistemic powers or, as Mark Platts puts it, with a certain relish, on our being 'tawdry, inadequate epistemic creatures'.[2] There could be no ideally epistemic being for whom wisdom did not take time to achieve.[3] That means that such understanding does not deepen towards an epistemic result, a system of true propositions which could, in principle, be granted to an ideal epistemic being in a flash. It means, too, that it could not be something granted by theory, because theory, as it is generally understood, aims at results which are expressed in propositions whose epistemic and general grammar is not conditioned by the fact that it takes maturity to achieve them.

The necessity for the achievement of wisdom to take time is the necessity for it to take time in the life of an individual, and (as I suggested in previous chapters) for that individual to be dialogically rooted in a particular culture. An individual's past is, in its relation to his moral understanding, not merely an epistemic route along which he has gathered information and evidence for a set of propositions which would mark his arrival at what he is seeking in seeking a deeper understanding. Many philosophers see the relation between time and wisdom in that way – that it takes a long time for creatures like us to gather sufficient information, to overcome deficiencies of character which get in the way of clear thinking, and to develop those physical structures which are the material 'realisation' of thought. That is what I call 'accidentally taking time'. Someone who thinks that way will think that our actual past could, in principle, drop away without that affecting our competence to speak on what it had, contingently, provided evidence for. (Think, for example, of Descartes' *res cogitans*, of an individual thinker's relation to a Fregean 'Thought', or of computer models of the mind.) He will also believe that we might intelligibly wish that there were better ways of achieving wisdom than the laborious human way of needing to grow older. But there are no better ways of achieving wisdom than by living the life in which it is achieved. We might wish that we had learnt without so much folly, but we (logically) cannot wish ourselves out of a historical human life without *wishing to be without those concepts which alone allow for the idea of a deepened moral understanding.*

266

In moral matters (though not only in moral matters) the achievement of deeper understanding requires that we have the depth to receive it, and that depth in ourselves is not a depository of propositions in our heads which God could have put there 'in a flash', but an historically *achieved* individuality. Our lives must have a certain kind of unity that involves a truthful responsibility for and to our past – we cannot flee it, for example. There are those who persistently 'start life over again', who disclaim their past anew each time. They are like someone on the run, a refugee from his many 'pasts'. Such people lack 'integrity' in the sense in which Vlastos used that expression in the passage I quoted earlier when he said that Plato had no conception of the love of an individual in the 'integrity of his or her individuality'. 'Integrity' here means a kind of integration in time – not just *through* time (as a person may be unified through time by the single-minded pursuit of a particular project), but *over* time in a way that depends on a truthful concern for the meaning of what is past. And in addition to truthfulness, it requires *fidelity* to what is past. Integrity, here, means being rooted in our life, which is impossible without a truthful acceptance of our past and a degree of lucidity about its meaning. Some people are vagabonds in their own history, and they cannot find a centre out of which they may deservedly trust themselves to speak and respond in ways that are not corrupted by their vices.

The requirements internal to wisdom clearly have no application to a *res cogitans*. It could not seek a deepened moral understanding because it has, and could have, no depth. That is not because it is immaterial and disembodied. Even if it were material and embodied, it represents a conception of thought and its virtues and vices to which history is accidental. Alan Donagan expresses this conception well when he says that 'Reason' is 'a rigid designator, referring to a capacity to perform acts whose contents belong to the domain of logic'.[4] Donagan does not intend this as a minimal conception of thinking, to be supplemented according to the forms which life takes for those who are host to this capacity. He intends it as an account of what thinking essentially and perfectly is; thinking, one might say, *as such*. Ironically, he does so in a book in which he defends what he calls 'traditional morality', but there is nothing in his account of what Reason reveals which suggests that our living in time, and in the form that we do, conditions the epistemic and critical grammar of our moral concepts as distinct from their content. For Donagan, the tradition he defends is the accidental depository of truths accessible to any rational being, which is a being of some determinate form (in our case *Homo sapiens*) and which is host to that capacity 'fixed for all possible worlds, to perform acts whose contents belong to the domain of logic'.

We would not seek moral advice from someone whom we knew to be morally jaded. Being scientifically jaded, however, in the sense of one's interest in science having 'gone dead' on one, is of itself no bar to a scientist's authority to speak in his field, provided only that his memory is good and that he has not been jaded for too long, for if he had been, we would be doubtful whether he had sufficient energy or interest to keep up with his subject. The difference has to do with our sense of what it is to 'have something to say' in each of these cases. We say of some people that they 'have something to say' on moral or spiritual matters, but we do not mean that they have information to impart or a theory to propound. We mean that they speak with an individual voice, but not because they know something that few people know. They are not to be likened to scientists with new discoveries or to travellers from strange places. Indeed, what they say may often be familiar. Novelty is not an important concept under which to understand them, although it need not be excluded. The manner of their presence, their demeanour, we might even say their 'style', *are* important, provided that we do not think of these as separable from what they say.

To have something to say is to be 'present' in what we say and to those to whom we are speaking, and that means that what we say must, at the crux, be taken on trust. It must be taken on trust, not because, contingently, there are no means of checking it, but because what is said is not extractable from the manner of its disclosure. In matters of value we often learn by being moved, and our being moved is not merely the dramatic occasion of our introduction to a proposition which can be assessed according to critical categories whose grammar excludes our being moved because it is extraneous to the cognitive content. None of which means that we must surrender critical judgement. Trust is not surrender. To trust is both to judge something worthy of our trust and ourselves to be worthily trusting. We are often mistaken on both counts. We may have been conned and been too sentimental or too naive to notice. The remedy is not in hankering for an extractable propositional content which can be assessed by a relatively Spartan set of critical concepts consisting of 'true', 'false' and the modes of valid and invalid inference. In the example mentioned, the remedy lies in ridding ourselves of our sentimentality and naivety. That, as Simone Weil and Iris Murdoch have emphasised, depends on the nature of what we attend to and on the quality of our attention.[5] Plato was right to say that we become like what we love.

I shall try to reduce the obscurity of what I have said: first, by contrasting two ways we might criticise a person's thinking as sentimental, and then by illustrating, in a further discussion of moral advice, what I have said about the way a person who has something to say is *present* in his words and to those to whom he is speaking.

Suppose a biologist who is accused (as was Konrad Lorenz) of being sentimental in his description of the behaviour of certain animals. In such a case we can often assess what he said without reference to the concept of sentimentality. We simply check whether what he said is true or false, and there are, for the most part, well-established procedures for this. If we refer to his sentimentality then it will function as a quasi-causal concept explaining why he said something false – why, perhaps, he characteristically says something false of this kind. It is likely that the style in which he made his false claims betrayed his sentimentality, but that is irrelevant to the primary mode of our assessment of what he says, which is whether it is true or false. In this case we do have a 'cognitive content' extractable from the style of its expression and to which the style is irrelevant, because reference to the style is irrelevant to the thought's primary mode of assessment.

Contrast that with the judgement that it is sentimental to think that it can be expressive of something deep in our feelings for a dead dog to light a candle for it on each anniversary of its death. Now sentimentality is not being cited as the *cause* of what is primarily wrong with such a thought: it *is* what is primarily wrong with it. There is an inclination to say that such a person must have some beliefs about dogs which are false. In a sense I agree. They have the sentimental belief that such behaviour may be properly expressive

269

of our relation to a dead dog, and, no doubt, that belief hangs together with other beliefs which are equally sentimental. But that is not the sense of 'belief' that was invoked in the objection. There it meant something that has to be what philosophers call 'truth-valued' if it is to be, strictly speaking, a *belief*; and it implied that its being false is primary over its being sentimental. But I see no reason to emphasise that what is wrong with such a thought is that it is false over its being sentimental, and it would obscure the contrast between this case and that of the scientist, where there is point in saying that we are not interested in whether what they say is sentimental but only whether it is true or false. That contrast has no application when someone lights candles each year for a dead dog. Often enough, people who are sentimental over animals have, in the philosopher's sense, false beliefs about them generally, about their capacities – they might believe, for example, that they can converse with them. However, they need not have beliefs of this kind, and some of their beliefs are such that sentimentality characterises the primary mode of their defect rather than its cause.

What shows that something is sentimental? Finally, only something that is not. Sentimentality needs to be shown up by example. There is, too, discussion and argument, but it should be argument informed by the realisation that it cannot, discursively, yield a standard, or set of standards, in the light of which all examples are to be judged. No example is self-authenticating, but it does not follow that their place in our judgements is merely to guide us to discursively establishable principles of which they are intuited instances. Nor can any example play a role akin to that of the standard metre, for that would distort the *necessarily provisional* place they have for those whose judgements they have inspired and shaped. That is reasonably evident in aesthetic cases, and I think it is the same in ethical ones. When I speak of examples, I am thinking primarily of what has moved us in the speech and actions of others and because of which we stand by certain judgements and reject others. Philosophy has been suspicious of the fact that we learn by being moved because of a mistaken conception of thought that judges this as its desertion.

I hope now to be in a better position to explain why we cannot seek moral advice in the way we seek advice on taxation options, and why we would not seek advice from someone we knew to be morally jaded. Suppose that someone who is deeply bitter over some matter seeks our advice on it, and suppose too that, although we think him to be confused, we are silenced by his bitterness because we are unable to rise to what would be required of us if we were seriously to engage with it. Under such conditions, to speak out our objections to what he is saying would be disrespectful, no matter how deeply we had thought on such matters in the past, and no matter how confident we were that our past thoughts bear relevantly on what he is saying. If we should speak out our objections, then he would be justifiably angry. Why is that so? Should he not consider what we say in relation to what he says, that is, consider the logical bearing of the propositions we utter, however dejectedly, on the propositions he has uttered? Should he not, as Plato jokingly remarks in *Phaedrus*, welcome the truth even if it comes from stones or trees? Are not his bitterness and our failure to rise to it, irrelevant to what might 'cognitively' pass between us?

That sounds like a parody, but I think it is exactly what many philosophers should say, and is implied by what I suspect Nagel takes to be the 'realist claims of ordinary practical reasoning'.[6] The reason that it sounds like a parody is because it makes explicit what is often left implicit, namely: that our inability to be properly responsive to the depth of his bitterness is assumed to be extraneous to what is deemed the 'properly cognitive' content of our interchange. Our weariness of spirit is treated as an external psychological impediment to his being able to accept what we have to say to him. Perhaps we should leave him an article we published on the matter![7]

Mostly when someone needs moral advice he needs not only thoughts to take away with him, but also comfort. It may seem that I have succeeded in making a certain philosophical position seem ridiculous only because I have suggested that it ignores that fact and its bearing on what it is to treat a person with respect. That would be to misunderstand my objection, because it implies that if we suggested to him that we send him a report of our thoughts on his problem, then the only thing wrong with that is that we do not give, in addition to advice, something else he needs, both in itself and as a means to facilitating his preparedness to take seriously what we said.

Our trouble, however, is not that we cannot comfort him, for we may still be able to do that, and it is not that we are cold and indifferent so that he is in no mood to listen to us. Our trouble is that what we have to say about what we take to be his confusions is weary and lifeless; and my point is that the position I am opposing treats our weariness and his response to it as psychological trapping, interfering with his receptivity to the content of whatever advice we have to give. The idea seems to be that all would be well if only we could extract our advice from its jaded expression and get it into his head, or into that part of him where resides that 'capacity to perform acts whose content belongs to the domain of logic', by telepathy, thereby circumventing those human complexities which make its communication so fraught. But our reluctance to speak is not because our words will not be accompanied by a psychological lubricant which would ease the passage of their 'cognitive' content into his head. It is because we are not actively present in our words, and so to him. That deprives what we say of the authority necessary for its serious consideration. It does not matter how pertinent our past thoughts seem to the matter between us. It does not matter if he thinks so too. If we wearily restate them and sincerely profess that we think them to be true and pertinent, then we are, in this situation, someone with nothing to say. Wisdom, and our fitness to offer moral advice, depend upon a kind of energy, a vital responsiveness, quite different from Kant's rational will whose potency to produce actions which would 'shine like a jewel' was undiminished by the kind of spiritual malaise I have been describing. And quite different, too, from the kind of energy necessary for creative thought in science.

What I have just described is external to the content of scientific propositions and indeed all propositions which can be formalised. What can be formalised without loss of cognitive content cannot be corrupted by cliché or spiritual deadness. Not, at any rate, *essentially*. I hope, therefore, that it is clear that what I have called being 'present in our speech' or 'standing behind' our words is not a matter of our resolutely backing what we say. A scientist may resolutely back a new theory, but his doing so is external to the epistemic and more general grammar of its content. It may be helpful to think of poetry and its discipline and of the way poets may lose their voice in exile, or because of a spiritual weariness or certain corruptions of character. I do not say that moral speech aspires to poetry, only that it is closer to it than it is to science or to the kind of reflection that philosophers think will be perfected by theory.

Much of what I have been saying is, I believe, the lesson of the dialogical form of some of Plato's dialogues. In *Gorgias*, Socrates criticises the orators for pandering to the souls of their audience. He does not say they should appeal to the impersonal rational capacities of their audience (although many commentators say that he does say this). He says that they must learn how to *converse* and he means that they must be present, in disciplined sobriety, to their partner.[8] That is why he insists that they speak for themselves. Socrates' point is not merely that they must say what they mean and mean what they say: he is teaching them what that amounts to. His lesson is that the 'part' of us which must be obedient to the 'claim of Reason' and which must 'follow the argument wherever it goes' must be the same part of us which can be a proper respondent to another's call to seriousness. The capacity to answer seriously under Socratic examination requires that the ethical subject – one who understands and is responsive to the requirements of morality – be more than a rational agent.

When Polus gives long speeches and Socrates asks him to keep his answers short and to stick to the point, he is not merely initiating Polus into the method of dialectic: he is recalling Polus from an enchantment with his rhetoric in which he speaks to a crowd and thus to no one in particular. When Socrates ridiculed the power that Polus boasted he displayed in doing this, it was because, in losing himself in his enchantment with the 'power' of his oratory, Polus lost himself as someone who might have anything serious to say and as someone who might have anything serious to learn. When he asks Polus to stick to the point, he asks him to stick with himself and with Socrates, in a conversation in which they must speak as individuals.

A grotesque but instructive example of how we may be lost to ourselves, and to the possibility of any serious understanding of what we are doing because of our enchantment by oratory, is given by Hannah Arendt at the conclusion of her report on the trial of Adolf Eichmann. Eichmann had always been 'elated' by, as he put it, the 'winged words' of oratory. Arendt gives this account of his last moments before his execution:

> He began by stating emphatically that he was a *Gottgläubiger*, to express in common Nazi fashion that he was no Christian and did not believe in life after death. He then proceeded: 'After a short while Gentlemen, *we shall all meet again*. Such is the fate of all men. Long live Germany, long live Argentina, long live Austria. *I shall not forget them*.' In the face of death, he had found the cliché used in funeral oratory. Under the gallows, his memory played him the last trick; he was 'elated' and he forgot that this was his own funeral.[9]

When Callicles meets Socrates, he too is elated by 'winged words' – those of the orator Gorgias.[10] We know of the powerful effect Socrates had on some people from other Platonic dialogues, especially from Alcibiades' speech in *Symposium*. It is clear that the kind of man Socrates was had as much to do with his impact as his arguments did, which is why Plato is concerned to show the difference between Socrates and Gorgias. It is not as easy to distinguish them as it might seem if we are content to say that, whereas Socrates cared for the truth and appealed to logic or to reason, the orators cared not at all for truth and appealed mainly to emotion. Socrates did care for the truth, but it is not clear what that amounts to. It is usually taken to imply that the fact that he said something should have no bearing on an assessment of its worth. We need only notice what the Platonic dialogues would be without Socrates to be suspicious of that.

Socrates rebuked the orators for not caring for the truth. Gorgias did not care whether he persuaded others into truth or into error, provided that he persuaded them to believe whatever was necessary for them to play their part in the realisation of his purposes. But it is strange, or at least it should seem so if we look at it from the standpoint of the conception of truth and reasoning that is commonly attributed to him, that Socrates seemed to think that his dialogical practice was fundamental to what distinguished him from the orators. He rebukes Polus for being good at oratory but bad at conversation because when Polus spoke to Socrates he did not speak for himself and because he spoke as he would to a crowd. Socrates would also have rebuked him if Polus had spoken to Socrates as one instantiation of rational agency to another. He would not count that as Polus speaking to Socrates. Socrates insists that those with whom he discusses philosophy must say what they believe rather than reporting what others had said or proposing hypothetical propositions – what one might or could say. He required the same of himself.

It is often thought that the conditions Socrates imposes on discussion are merely a pedagogical strategy of the kind that makes teachers prefer small classes to large ones. One reason for thinking that there is more to it is that Socrates insists that his partners speak for themselves so that he might learn from them as well as so that they might learn from him. Why, then, should he so restrict the range of propositions available for discussion? Is it because he believes that it will increase the likelihood that his partners will produce propositions of benefit to him? But why should he believe something so implausible? We will misunderstand what Socrates is doing for so long as we think that a partner in philosophical discussion is primarily a source of new propositions or a source of logical correction – that we need to learn from others only because of our limited epistemic and logical powers.

Earlier, I said that Socrates required his partners in discussion to say what they believe. That is not quite right, and I can, perhaps, make myself clearer by explaining why it is not. It is because we can say something which is sincerely expressive of our belief, but it be, nonetheless, 'mere words'. Socrates called his partners in conversation to a kind of seriousness. They could respond to that call only if they spoke in an effort of disciplined lucidity out of what they had made of themselves. That does not mean that he wanted them to voice their sincere personal opinion. Their sincere personal opinions were worthless unless constrained by the discipline of thought and character which conditions the proper contrast between what is personal and what is impersonal in moral thought and discussion.

Socrates presented Polus with an argument whose conclusion was that it was better to suffer evil than to do it. Polus was not convinced; he assented to the premises, to the steps of the argument and to its conclusion, but he suspected that he had been tricked. Suppose, however, that he did accept the conclusion, and that he vigorously professed it to all who would listen. His profession would be mere words, and would be so even if he invented further and better arguments of the same kind. The reason is because he would be essentially unchanged. I do not say that because I assume that his life would not change. It might change dramatically, but if it changed only in conformity with what he deduced to be the implications of this 'principle' (as some philosophers call it), then his deeds, just as much as his words, would not be informed by a Socratic understanding of good and evil. They would be as empty as Eichmann's demeanour at his execution.

I do not deny that Polus could change in a way that would be a result of his having understood what Socrates meant when he said that it is better to suffer evil than to do it. However, if he did, it would be because *Socrates* changed him rather than because he was convinced by an argument that happened to be put to him by Socrates. If Polus came across such an argument written on a blackboard, studied it out of curiosity and was convinced of the truth of its premises and of the validity of its conclusion, then he would not understand what Socrates understood. I do not mean that only Socrates could teach him what it is to do evil as Socrates understood it, but if Socrates did, then it would be internal to Polus' understanding of it (as opposed to his inclination sincerely to believe and profess a 'Socratic proposition') that his teacher was the kind of man he was.

Plato's answer to the question of how Socrates differed from Gorgias is, I think, that Gorgias' charisma was a false semblance of Socrates' presence. His charisma could induce belief but not understanding. Charisma is important to the ability of orators to persuade their audience to believe whatever they want them to believe, but it is evident that it is irrelevant to the cogency of what they say. Their charisma is something to be wary of. We are, therefore, easily tempted by the thought that, with Socrates, it is the argument that counts independently of the fact that he presented it. But charisma or strength of personality are not the concepts with which to characterise the kind of impact Socrates had. If they were, he would be, at least in that respect, indistinguishable from the great orators. Charisma gives no more weight to what we say than shouting it does.

Callicles praises Gorgias for never having failed to answer a question put to him. Gorgias' charisma had, no doubt, much to do with his ability to silence his interlocutors before their questions could become troublesome. Plato's ironical point is not that Gorgias is about to flounder under Socratic examination. It is that Socrates will teach him what it is to ask, and to be properly responsive to, a question and why that is important to the difference between them. Callicles praises Gorgias for being beyond surprise. He does not realise what a terrible condemnation that is.

Conversation promises and threatens surprise. Martin Buber said that 'talking to oneself' is utterly different from talking to someone else, and that the difference is marked by the fact that one cannot be a surprise to oneself in the way that another can be:

> Every attempt to understand monologue as fully valid conver-
> sation, which leaves unclear whether it, or dialogue, is the more
> original, must run aground on the fact that the ontological
> basic presupposition of conversation is missing from it, the
> otherness, or more concretely, the moment of surprise. The
> human person is not in his own mind unpredictable to himself
> as he is to any one of his partners: therefore, he cannot be a
> genuine partner to himself, he can be no real questioner and
> no real answerer.[11]

The surprise Buber speaks of is not conditional upon routine or ignorance. It is a kind of shock at the realisation of how other than, and *other to*, oneself another human being can be. It is the shock of the reality of other human beings and the strange and unique kind of individuality of their presence, which is quite different from the individuality attributed to someone because of his vividly indi-viduating characteristics – a colourful personality, for example. It is in connection with such a sense of the reality of another human being that we should understand Socrates' insistence on conversa-tion and the kind of presence he required of himself and his partners. That is connected with the moral objection to Gorgias' practice – that, as we put it since Kant, he treated others as a means to his ends rather than as ends in themselves.

But it will now seem that I am running together issues that should be kept distinct. Treating our partners in discussion with respect is one thing, someone might object; assessing the content of what they are saying is another. The two are, I think, connected. When we say that we are treating someone as a means to our ends, we mean that his reality as a human being does not limit our will as it should. Or, to put it more accurately: it is part of our sense of the reality of another human being, that he be the kind of limit to our will that we express when we say that he must never be treated merely as a means to an end but as an end in himself. We express this more simply when we say that we must treat him as a human being. To acknowledge the reality of another human being is to have our will engaged and limited.

Is such a way of speaking of the reality of another human being merely a dramatic but obscure way of saying that we must treat others with respect? It is not, for it embodies the claim that the concept of a human being (or of a person) as an object of respect is not available to the static epistemology that limits what may properly be called 'reality' to what is available to a 'cognitive capacity' whose nature may be only that of an observer. It is a 'static' epistemology because it treats the responses that are expressive of our respect for another human being as dependent upon a prior application of the relevant concepts, rather than as a condition of his senses. I argued this in Chapter 10.

The point I have drawn from the Socratic practice is the connection between coming to see another human being as 'other to my one' and that openness required to be a respondent to another's call to seriousness. It is part of what we understand by conversation insofar as we contrast that with oratory. Conversation requires an openness to the other because we must be present in what we say and to those to whom we speak – present as someone who is living their life and no one else's. The Socratic conception of conversation, of what it is to be present to an other in conversation, involves a certain conception of intersubjectivity. We invoke it when we think of a person as another perspective on the world and mean more than that he is a centre of consciousness. David Wiggins invoked it when, after criticising certain conceptions of the Golden Rule, he said that they denied '*alterity*, the otherness of the subjectivity of others'. He seemed to think that the expression 'the otherness of the subjectivity of others' would put some life in the tired expression 'intersubjectivity'.[12]

None of what I have been saying is essential to conversation even makes sense in the case of machines, which is why it is right to say as did (I think) Rush Rhees, that the reason machines cannot speak is because they have nothing to say. The concept of having something to say, as I have been using it, does not apply to what machines may do. The idea of a machine speaking out of a life makes no sense, nor does the idea that it might live under the requirement to live its own life and nobody else's. The belief that it makes sense to speculate on whether machines might converse with us is prevalent amongst philosophers because they believe that it is accidental to one's having 'something to say' that one speaks out of a life that, non-accidentally, takes time to live. They are helped along in this mistake by an ambiguity in the concept of a 'capacity'.

We speak of the human capacity for speech. In one sense of 'capacity', that capacity might be explained by some branch of physical theory, say neurophysiology. It is the same sense of 'capacity' as we mean it when we say that a person lost his capacity for speech after an accident. We mean that he became dumb. There is another sense of 'capacity' in which philosophers sometimes conjecture whether computers have, or could have, the capacity for speech. Could they speak as one person speaks to another? Could they speak to us and we to them? My answer has been that they could not. What could it be for a machine to stand behind its words, for us to call upon it not to be so stupid, or to say to it 'for pity's sake think about what you have just said', or 'surely you can't think that', or 'why do you always think in clichés!'? Those are not possibilities of conversation at a sophisticated level. They are internal to our understanding of what it is to speak, to *say* something at all. If I am right, then there are limits to the way physical theory, which is relevant to the explanation of the 'capacity' for speech in the first sense, can be relevant to our understanding of the 'capacity' for speech in the second.

Suppose someone who, after a car accident, retains a capacity for speech in the first sense, but whose thought and conversation is so fragmented, so confused, that it is 'impossible to speak to him'. Someone might say of him that we can never locate him in his words, that it is as though we were talking to a machine. But expressions like 'we can no longer locate him in his words' are not explanations of his incapacity, nor are they pre-theoretical markers recording a commitment to, or the hope of discovering, an explanatory theory. The fact that there is a physical theory which explains someone's condition, in the sense of 'explains' in which the surgeon explains to his relatives what has happened to him and what hopes there are for him, is not the slightest reason for pinning our hopes on, for example, a functionalist theory of speech of a materialist variety, according to which there can be no principled objection to the idea that machines might converse with us. The physical explanation (again in the sense of how the surgeon might explain his condition to his relatives) of how a human being might lose the 'capacity' to stand behind his words is irrelevant to the understanding of why it may be said of a human being, but not of a machine, that he can stand behind what he is saying, that he can converse with another as 'other to [his] one'.

The point also applies to speculation about whether animals might be said to speak because of the way they communicate as a species – dolphins, for example, or Washoe the chimpanzee. Some people say that dolphins have a language and that they speak to one another. But unless they care for the truth, and are claimed in response to its demands, unless a dolphin can say to another dolphin 'come now, do you really mean that?', unless a dolphin can be asked to stand behind its words and speak out of the life that it must make its own, then dolphins do not do what we do when we speak to one another. They do not do the *kind* of thing we do when we speak to one another if they merely 'communicate' information to one another by means of a complex system of signs. If a dolphin is to do what we do, it must be able to speak out of its life, not merely 'communicate' in ways characteristic of its species. It must be able to converse, and so discover and respond to another dolphin as 'other to its one'. In the absence of that, whatever dolphins do, they do not do *primitively* what we do more complexly when we speak to each other, no more than did Wittgenstein's builders. They might as well have whistled.[13] If that is acknowledged, then it is of little interest whether or not we call what they have a language. Rhees brings out that Wittgenstein's builders do not have a form of life.[14] The same may be said of dolphins, insofar as one means, and surely Wittgenstein did mean, that a form of life is something like *the life of a people*. Dolphins do what they do as a species or, at any rate, they do as a species what prompts philosophers to speculate on whether or not they speak.

Ethical understanding is often coming to see sense where we had not seen it before, or coming to see depth where we had not seen it before. It is seldom learning something completely new (there are no Nobel Prize-winning discoveries in ethics) and it is seldom seeing that there is, after all, a valid argument to support positions we had previously judged to be dubious. It is often seeing what someone has made of something that we had often heard before. But seeing 'what he made of it' is not seeing to what practical purpose he put it in his life. It is seeing what he made of himself through it, or rather, the two – his making something of himself and his making something of it – are interdependent. The ethical and the individuality of which I have been speaking mutually determine each another. Recall my remarks on remorse and the radical singularity of someone who labours under its requirements. The ethical subject is, as Kierkegaard stressed, a human being under the discipline of the ethical requirement to become an individual – to rise to the requirements of the kind of individuality which I have been attempting to characterise and which, I have claimed, is conceptually interdependent with our sense of the ethically conditioned reality of another human being.[15] Both the discipline and the requirement are revealed in the serious use of that more extensive critical vocabulary which, I have argued, is internal to our understanding of what it is to think well or badly in ethics.

I have followed Kierkegaard in thinking that Socrates' requirement that his interlocutors be utterly serious is the requirement that they rise to the individuality, which is not so much a mark of the *dignity* of their humanity, as it is of its *reality*. Socrates required it of them under pain of intellectual irresponsibility. We may become intoxicated with the heady transcendentalism of the conception of reason which Donagan expresses, which deems the grammar of its constitutive categories to be transcendent to our humanity, and indeed, to any particular form of life. That conception of reason provides its own edification, and indeed, its own 'winged words'. Philosophers have been too uncritical of their susceptibility to such edification, especially when it provides, as a model of intellectual purity, of the readiness to yield to the discipline of argument, someone who turns their life upside down after stumbling across an argument written on a blackboard. There is something important in the call to follow an argument wherever it may validly take one from premises which are responsibly held to be true, but there is a question of what it is to do that soberly. I have been trying to say what it might be in ethics.

Understanding in ethical matters is, then, the expression of a life and the grammar of the contrast between appearance and reality in ethical matters reflects that fact. That would seem so obvious as not to be worth stating, were it not for the fact that most philosophers, because of a shared misconception of the nature of ethical understanding, are committed to denying that it is *essentially* so. I have argued that the capacity which Donagan calls 'Reason' and which I have preferred to call understanding, or simply thinking, can only be identified and characterised through the grammar of those critical concepts with which we express our sense of what it is to think well or badly on ethical and other matters. I have suggested a reason for the otherwise extraordinary neglect in philosophy of most of those critical concepts, namely, that it is based upon an assumption of what thinking is in its primary sense and what it is in merely a secondary sense.

16

Truth

There are social commentators (they are sometimes called cultural critics) who believe that scepticism about whether moral judgements are true or false has corrupted many of the most important of our cultural institutions. They usually call the corruption 'relativism', but that is not important. What is important is the connection they make between the decline of moral seriousness and scepticism about whether moral judgements could be true or false. Any philosopher who has thought about the matter will know two things. First, that the arguments outside of philosophy which are intended to show that moral judgements are not either true or false are usually so bad that their prevalent acceptance is itself evidence of cultural decline irrespective of any further effects of their acceptance. Secondly, they will know that although such bad arguments are easily refuted,[1] the question of whether moral judgements are true or false has become so technical that even many professional philosophers rightly see themselves as incompetent to assess the arguments for one side or the other. Even if we think the question has been ill-served by the technical character of its contemporary treatment, we will need to be competent in the technicalities to feel confident of that judgement.

Amongst analytical philosophers, David Wiggins has presented the most serious and subtle case, not only for (most) moral judgements being true or false, but also for the importance of whether they are. He writes:

What I have always been concerned to do myself ... is to identify the least extreme distinctively cognitivist option that preserves for some unsanctimonious, unmysterious species of

283

ordinary morality the main features of the picture that that morality has of itself, refrains from any systematic or philosophical redescription of the actual purport of the claims that it advances, but allows all the room to which they are entitled for certain sorts of doubt that cannot help in real life but impinge upon practice. The beauty of such a philosophical position, if it could attain to verisimilitude, would reside in its effecting a certain kind of closure. With this we should achieve mutual transparency between philosophy and practice, the transparency of practice to itself, and a clear meet between particular philosophical doubts about morality and particular doubts we are actually prone to about how to see the human world.[2]

Wiggins' discussion is highly technical and depends upon discussions which are even more technical.

Those who think that it matters whether moral judgements are true or false usually think that it matters to any reflective person's sense of the seriousness of morality. They are inclined to say that if moral judgements are not true or false then they are *merely* something or other – expressions of feeling, the results of arbitrary decisions, cultural artefacts and so on. The social commentators who deplore the consequences of scepticism about whether moral judgements are true or false believe those consequences are reasonably inferred from such scepticism. Those who believe that it matters whether we believe that moral judgements are true or false ought, therefore, to be dismayed at the prospect that the issue will be settled only in a highly technical philosophical journal and that the result will be delivered to a community that is incompetent to appreciate the reasons for it. The reason they ought to be dismayed is not because an important issue awaits technical resolution – that is often so without it being a reason for dismay. It is because, as we have seen in previous chapters, *moral importance is not of the kind to await that kind of clarification*. Whether or not good and evil are to be taken seriously is not something a culture worthy of respect leaves experts in philosophical logic – or in anything else – to decide.

Fortunately, it does not matter whether moral judgements are true or false in a sense that is more substantial than is suggested by the fact that we naturally say that they are. Someone may call someone else a swine and a third person might say that the judgement is a true one. That is commonplace. Philosophers have been interested in whether this perfectly natural way of speaking of moral judgements as true or false may be underwritten by a philosophical theory of truth, and this philosophical suspicion of our ordinary ways of speaking is usually expressed in the technical question whether moral judgements are 'truth-valued'. But someone who is not interested in this question need not be ashamed for being unreflective, and someone who is interested in it is likely to be so for the wrong reasons. Whether or not moral judgements are true or false is not a question a seriously reflective person need bother himself with, nor is the question important in moral philosophy. So I shall argue. And I shall, indirectly, provide reason for thinking that the importance usually attributed to the question whether moral judgements are true or false is of a kind whose appreciation is not deepened by the technical discussions that are appropriate to philosophical problems concerning truth.

Wiggins writes:

> Even now, in an age not much given to mysticism, there are people who ask 'What is the meaning of life?' Not a few of them make the simple 'unphilosophical' assumption that there is something to be known here. (One might say that they are 'cognitivists' with regard to this sort of question.) And most of these same people make the equally unguarded assumption that the whole issue of life's meaning presupposes a positive answer at least to the question whether it can be plainly and straightforwardly *true* that this or that thing or activity or pursuit is good, has value, or is worth something. And then, what is even harder, they suppose that questions like that of life's meaning must be among the central questions of moral philosophy . . . In what follows, I try to explore the possibility that the question of truth and the question of life's meaning are among the most fundamental questions of moral philosophy . . . My finding will be that the question of life's meaning does, as the untheoretical suppose, lead into the question of truth – and conversely.[3]

Elsewhere he writes, 'it is hard to imagine how human engagement could survive extinction of the belief that value was in some sense to be discovered (out there so to say) in the world'.[4] His thought is that the belief that value is, in some sense, to be discovered could not survive extinction of the belief that most judgements of moral value admit of what he calls 'plain truth'.[5]

The 'plain man', 'the man on the Clapham omnibus', the untheoretical person, the one in possession of 'ordinary moral consciousness' – he is supposed to believe that moral judgements are true or false in a way that is left unspecified but which is taken to be non-trivial – to believe this in a way that amounts to more than the fact that he uses the words 'true' and 'false' and that he would resist any suggestion that he should not. Some philosophers would even say that he believes that values are 'part of the fabric of the universe'.[6]

It is an interesting question why the 'plain man's' opinion on this, one of the most technical issues in philosophy, is found to be so interesting. There is, as one might expect, no one answer to that question. It will be answered differently according to whether he stands in for ordinary language, common sense, pre-theoretical intuition, sobriety and common decency, and so on. But as I noted in Chapter 2, in many of his forms he represents a condescending conception of what life is like before philosophy, which is, basically, that it is inarticulate and unreflective. Even Wiggins, whom one is reluctant to accuse of this (not least because of what he says in the first of my quotations from him in this chapter), says of the 'unphilosophical' that they 'make the unguarded assumption that the whole issue of life's meaning presupposes a positive answer at least to the question whether it can be plainly and straightforwardly true that this or that thing or activity or pursuit is good, has value, or is worth something'. He says that, without showing any uncertainty whether it is so and without bothering to show his reader how he came to such a conclusion. In that way, he insulated himself from the kind of reflection with which he hoped to engage when he said he hoped to achieve a 'mutual transparency between philosophy and practice, a transparency of practice to itself and a clear meet between particular philosophical doubts about morality and particular doubts we are actually prone to about how to see the human world'.

Wiggins says, 'there are people who ask, "What is the meaning of life?" [and that] Not a few of them make the simple "unphilosophical" assumption that there is something to be known here. (One might say that they are "cognitivists" with respect to this sort of question.)' Suppose then, such a person. When Wiggins says he might be called a 'cognitivist' he means, I think, that he (the one making the 'unphilosophical' assumption) believes there is knowledge and truth to be found in an inquiry into morality and the meaning of life and (perhaps) in an inquiry into their connection. Presumably he believes there is knowledge to be found *because* there is truth to be found.

Suppose that we pressed such people by asking them whether 'knowledge' was really the word they were most happy to apply to what they sought in ethical reflection and whether they were happy to say that some people were more knowledgeable about the meaning of life than others. We have already noted that if there is something reasonably called moral knowledge then it is not the kind that can accumulate in the way that knowledge in encyclopaedias can accumulate, that there can be no experts in it, no whizz-kids and no Nobel Laureates. The 'unphilosophical' might be expected to agree that if there is moral knowledge then it is different in kind from what we normally called knowledge, and they might then wonder what point there is in calling it knowledge. But if they became sceptical of the point of talking of moral knowledge, it would not mean that they had become sceptical about whether there is moral *understanding* which may deepen and that some people are wise and others foolish. They might then be less inclined to 'make the equally unguarded assumption that the whole issue of life's meaning presupposes a positive answer, at least to the question, whether it can be plainly or straightforwardly true that this or that thing or activity or pursuit is good, has value, or is worth pursuing'. For although they may readily agree that if someone knows that *p* then *p* is true, they may be less ready to agree that if someone is wise about *p* then he knows the truth about *p*. And if they were asked first, whether it would matter to them whether moral judgements were truth-valued provided that uncertainty about this did not devalue the concepts of 'understanding', 'wisdom' and other epistemic concepts as they applied to moral matters, and secondly, whether they believed that these concepts would be so devalued, is there any justification for being confident about how they would answer? But unless they are pressed in something like that way, what right have we to say that they believe more than that we say that

287

moral judgements are true and false, which is not the same as saying that they believe that we speak *as though* moral judgements are (non-trivially) true or false?

If such people as we have been imagining are not unreflective (if their opinions are not intended as paradigms of 'pre-reflective intuitions') and if they are permitted to be moderately educated and thoughtful, although not philosophical theorists, then they may have read some of the Platonic dialogues. They might have been struck by Socrates' passionate insistence to his interlocutors that the inquiry into how one should live was amongst the most important of human activities. If they were asked whether Socrates thought there might be wise or foolish answers to this question and that some answers to it revealed a deeper understanding than did others, then, assuredly, they would have to answer that he did. A philosopher is likely to continue with these questions. Was it not Socrates who distinguished in this area, as in others, between those who had mere belief and those who had knowledge? Was it not Socrates who said that he who knew what evil was could not do it? Was not Socrates a 'cognitivist' on these matters? Did he not believe that there is a true answer to the question of how one should live, and is it not a fact that he thought there is a true answer to this question basic to any understanding of the character of his intellectual passion? The 'unphilosophical', innocent of philosophical theory and prejudice, will, of course, not answer 'No' to any of these questions. But are we sure they will answer 'Yes', and without hesitation?

We could ask them to consider the following. Gregory Vlastos has also been struck by Socrates' passion and is ambivalent about it. He has written some fine things exploring that ambivalence. Here is one example of his attempts to capture that passion and (I assume) what he finds admirable in it:

> His is the aggressive outreach, the indiscriminate address to all and sundry, of the street evangelist. If you speak Greek and are willing to talk and reason, you can be Socrates' partner in searching, with the prospect that truth undisclosed in countless ages might be discovered here and now, on this spot, in the next forty minutes, between the two of you.[7]

The 'truth', which Vlastos believes may be discovered in 'the next forty minutes', is a system of true propositions which would answer the question, 'How should one live?'

Vlastos tries to whip up a storm, but succeeds only in producing a parody of philosophical passion. He unintentionally achieves something unfortunately similar to Kierkegaard's parody of Hegelian metaphysics, when he (Kierkegaard) said that the word had passed around, even in Copenhagen, that 'the System will be finished next Sunday'.[8] Kierkegaard's point was not, of course, to deny that even a very large book may be finished next Sunday, nor was it to deny that a 'system' could be. On the contrary, it is of the nature of a system such as Hegel's, and of what we call a 'theory', that it may, in principle, be completable at a definite time – next Sunday indeed. The point of Kierkegaard's parody is that anything which may be completed, in the sense in which a 'system' or 'theory' may be completed, will not count as an 'answer' to the Socratic question, 'How should one live?' To respond to such a question by searching for a theory that would provide its answer is to misunderstand what *kind* of question it is. Wittgenstein remarks in a similar spirit:

> If anyone should think that he has solved the problem of life and feel like telling himself that everything is quite easy now, he can see that he is wrong just by realizing that there was a time when this 'solution' had not been discovered; but it must have been possible to live then too and the solution which has now been discovered seems fortuitous in relation to how things were then ... [He goes on to say] And it is the same in the study of logic. If there were a 'solution' to the problems of logic (philosophy) we should only need to caution ourselves that there was a time when they had not been solved (and even at that time people must have known how to live and think).[9]

Vlastos seems to believe that Socrates' questioning of himself (if not his questioning of others) may have come to an end at any time when he had reason to believe that he had found 'the answer', in which case he may have taken early retirement and done something else, or perhaps he would spend the rest of his life checking the details of his answer or responding to criticisms of it. But this should be a *reductio ad absurdum* of any view of Socrates that implied it.

We cannot imagine Socrates saying 'It is finished!' There can, therefore, be no 'truth undisclosed in countless ages' which he might discover 'in the next forty minutes' and which would answer his question, 'How should one live?' If there were such 'truth' and Socrates hit upon it, then even Callicles would acknowledge it to be an extraordinary achievement deserving high honours.

It will have been evident that when I have been speaking of Socrates I have been speaking of the *character* of that name in Plato's dialogues. The essence of the Platonic Socrates is that he lives under a requirement to philosophise and that this requirement is to something which has no end in either of the senses of that term: it cannot finish in an achievement which is the realisation of its end and so there is no time at which the requirement may lapse. The Socratic requirement to philosophise is a requirement to a task which can issue in no result which would be its completion. The general conceptual nature of the point was wittily expressed by Kierkegaard:

> When in a written examination the youth are allotted four hours to develop a theme then it is neither here nor there if an individual student happens to finish before the time is up, or uses the entire time. But when the time itself is a task, it becomes a fault to finish before the time has transpired. Suppose a man were assigned the task of entertaining himself for an entire day, and he finishes the task of self-entertainment as early as noon, then his celerity would not be meritorious. So also when life constitutes the task. To be finished with life, before life has finished with one, is precisely not to have finished the task.[10]

The historical Socrates – the actual man who inspired Plato – might have stopped philosophising for a variety of reasons, of which the most important is that he might have ceased to believe that he could not stop. Or: he might have philosophised in a different spirit, perhaps seeing himself as a humble underlabourer in the great enterprise of building a system or theory which would most likely take generations or even centuries to complete. However, to ask whether the Platonic Socrates might stop philosophising, or even whether he could philosophise in a different spirit, is like asking whether Macbeth might have repented of his murder of Duncan and sought just punishment. When we say that the Platonic Socrates could not stop philosophising we mean that such a Socrates is no Socrates, just as a repentant Macbeth is no Macbeth. But although that is true, it does not take us to the heart of the matter.

The Platonic Socrates is defined by his sense of his task, but the interesting modalities are not those which define him as a character, but rather those which define his task and his relation to it. That can easily be seen if we consider that the actual Socrates may have understood himself in the same way as does the Platonic character, in which case, he would believe that he could not stop philosophising for so long as he was able to continue, under pain of betraying his calling, and so himself. This would give a certain sense to the claim that if he ceased to philosophise then he would no longer be himself, but it is not the sense in which Socrates the *character* would cease to be Socrates. In fact, the Platonic Socrates does say, both in *Apology* and in *Crito*, that if he conceded to the wish of the court that he 'mind his own business'[11] and to the wish of his friends that he escape from prison, then he would no longer be himself. But he is, of course, not speaking of himself as a character in Plato's dialogues.

Two modalities need to be explored. First, why is the 'task' one that cannot be completed in the sense of issuing in results that would count as the realisation of its end(s). Secondly, why *cannot* he relinquish the task? Two, mainly negative, things can be said straightaway to help to focus our inquiry.

The first is that the reason that Socrates could not stop examining himself and others is not of the kind that is usually called 'psychological'. The concept of the psychological, especially as it may be used to contrast with the moral or the ethical, is (as we have noted before) to some degree obscure, but I have in mind things of the same *kind* as a passionate or even compulsive curiosity. Psychoanalytical and other accounts which allegedly display the true nature of such energies through revealing their real origins and objects are concerned with phenomena of such a kind. So, too, are the considerations which come into play when we explain why someone who has been doing something for a very long time might cease to do it only at the cost of a loss of a sense of identity. Neither of the two senses that I cited earlier, in which Socrates would cease to be himself, is of that kind. Neither depends on his having philosophised for a long time. In cases where explanations are of the sort that I am calling 'psychological', a sense of identity is formed from the actual and relatively long-term practice of something, whereas in the case of Socrates, the determining factor is not so much an actual practice, nor the psychological effects on him of its duration: it is his sense of a *requirement* to that practice.

I have given examples of considerations I would call psychological. For our purposes, the salient mark of such considerations is that they display a sense of how someone might say that he *cannot* do something which is (conceptually) open to the suggestion that he should try. Or, if he cannot even try, in the sense of *directly* try because it is not within his immediate power, then he can be invited to participate in a strategy devised to enable him to do what he says he cannot do. However, there is no more sense in thinking that Socrates could try to stop philosophising than there is in thinking that Martin Luther might have tried to do what he said he could not do when he said, 'Here I stand. I can do no other.' That is not because Socrates and Luther were driven by something extremely powerful. It is because the impossibility they express is of a kind which has nothing to do with power. Socrates makes the point to Polus, who had been praising the virtues of great power, when he says that Polus had forgotten his geometry.[12] His point is that there are things which are impossible to do even though no obstacles of the kind which may be overcome by force, efforts of will or ingenious strategies stand in the way. I do not mean that psychological considerations are irrelevant to understanding Socrates and his sense of what it was for him to philosophise. He was a human being, and despite his unworldliness, philosophy was for him a human activity. But the psychological dispositions necessary to philosophise were, in his case, transformed under his sense of a spiritual requirement to lucidity. (That is itself a Platonic way of putting the matter, as may be seen by reflecting on the various transformations of *eros* in its ascent through *categorially* different stages, as that ascent is depicted in *Symposium*.[13])

I come now to the second account of why Socrates could not stop philosophising, which I believe should be rejected. Whereas the first looked inward to the psychological, the second looks outward at the nature of his task and observes that it is a task of such magnitude that no human being could accomplish it in a lifetime. It assumes the Socratic task to be completable only after the labours of generations. I shall call this a conception of the task as only '*accidentally* incompletable' by one person in a lifetime. I shall also call it a conception of the task as only 'accidentally incompletable' if it is a conception according to which it could be completed only by beings of vastly superior epistemic and intellectual capacities than are possessed by human beings. There are those, for example, who say that it is beyond the epistemic powers of human beings to deliver a 'completed science', but who also say that sense can be made of the idea of a complete science. It would reveal the world as God sees it, or to put the same point differently, it would reveal the world as seen 'from no place within it'.[14]

We misunderstand the nature of Socrates' quest or task if we consider it to be only accidentally incompletable and, even at this stage of my argument, it is evident that this has radical implications. It means that the object of his quest or task was not knowledge or theory as these are usually conceived. The object of his quest was not something that even God could grant him such that he could rest in it. Socrates himself brings this out in his playful but also serious remark, that if there is a life beyond this one, he will be found there doing what he does here, namely, asking questions.[15] Wittgenstein made a similar point when he said that it was foolish to think that the meaning of life could be revealed in an after-life because the question of the meaning of an after-life would arise just as it had of this life.[16] His point was that the questions that we call questions about the meaning of life are not difficult for us on account of our limited epistemic vantage point, or on account of our limited epistemic powers.

It may seem, by now, that I have been misusing words like 'task' and 'quest', for it may be objected that the idea of an essentially incompletable task is no longer the idea of a task and, similarly, that the idea of an essentially incompletable quest is no longer the idea of a quest. There is a point in this objection, but it is not a strong one. Or, the point is no stronger than when it is objected that we should not speak too seriously of life as a gift unless we are prepared to say who gives it, or that we should not speak too seriously of teaching as a vocation unless we say who it is who calls. But the serious point to a way of speaking cannot be settled by considerations as thin as these. We must look to see what can be made of it.

To summarise the implications of what I have said about the sense in which there cannot be an end to Socratic philosophising. First, it is not wholly explicable by psychological (let alone social) theory. Secondly, it cannot issue in anything which might be described as a result or an achievement (a theory or a body of knowledge) if these are understood as the ends of inquiry. These are the conclusions reached in Chapter 15 concerning the deepening of moral and spiritual understanding. It should not be surprising that they also apply to the nature of the Socratic necessity to philosophise. It is evident that the Socratic quest for lucidity is a spiritual quest.

What do I claim to have shown? First, that what I said about Socrates is at least plausible and available for critical reflection to someone who is not trained in philosophy. The 'pre-theoretical' landscape is not as uniform, not as simple and not as simplistic as it is often made out to be. Secondly, while what I said about Socrates tends to undermine the place which Wiggins would assign to the concept of 'plain truth' in relation to the Socratic quest, it does not thereby compromise the irreducible role that concepts like 'understanding' and 'wisdom' have in any adequate characterisation of that quest, even though the concept of knowledge may, for reasons I gave earlier, become (at best) marginal. We could not characterise the Socratic quest without the use of the concept of understanding and of its deepening. Is that in conflict with my suspicion that the concept of truth as philosophers are interested in it when they ask whether moral judgements are truth-valued is not the object of the Socratic quest (that his quest is not to be characterised as motivated by 'an aspiration to truth')? Only if we assume that the substantial use of such concepts as understanding and wisdom depends upon their being underpinned by a non-trivial conception of truth.

It is worth reminding ourselves how the cognitivist/non-cognitivist argument usually runs in ethics. It is something like this: Philosophers notice the extent to which words like 'understand', 'reality', 'illusion' and so on occur in our moral speech. They then notice that they do not function as would be expected if their sense were tied to certain paradigms of truth – scientific truth, factual truth or even mathematical truth. Thus far *nothing* suggests that, for example, moral understanding is not really or strictly speaking a *bona fide* form of understanding. Thus far nothing suggests that such words should be placed in inverted commas. The idea that the use of such epistemic expressions in moral contexts ought, strictly speaking, to be put in inverted commas insinuates itself by way of certain mediating notions. They are either semi-technical expressions or terms of art like 'cognitive', or they are ordinary words given a certain philosophical emphasis as when philosophers ask 'Do moral judgements really express *beliefs?*' Such mediating notions set up the connection between the 'strict speech' use of words like 'understanding' and 'wisdom' on the one hand and 'truth' on the other. The following dialectic emerges: Our talk of moral understanding is, strictly speaking, of *understanding* (of *bona fide* understanding) only if it is 'cognitive'. It is, strictly speaking, cognitive only if it is non-trivially truth valued. But (the argument runs) we have already noticed that any non-trivial concept of truth seems inapplicable. Therefore these expressions are not *bona fide* cognitive expressions. Therefore they are not what they give themselves out to be. The innocent (the 'unphilosophical') need to be warned that ordinary speech is systematically misleading about the cognitive status of moral judgements.

The counter-argument goes like this. If the *prima facie* cognitive vocabulary of ordinary language is systematically misleading then moral judgements are merely . . . (the expressions of will, or desire, etc.). But if we were seriously to try to speak the philosophically revisionist strict-speech we would find it ludicrously inadequate. (It is sometimes said that non-cognitivist, 'strict-speech' reductions of the serious use of our moral vocabulary are reductively inadequate to what is revealed by a sensitive moral phenomenology of moral deliberation, as expressed, for example, by Nagel in the quotation in Chapter 7.) The point is even more persuasive when we move from deliberation to what Wiggins called valuational or appreciative judgements and to what Williams called the 'thick' ethical concepts – concepts such as courage, cruelty, meanness, injustice, etc. Therefore, it is concluded, the question of the cognitive status of moral judgements must again be raised. By this it is meant that the question of whether they are true or false must again be raised.

The non-cognitivist moves from the unlikelihood of truth to the plausibility of reduction. The cognitivist moves from the implausibility of reduction to the likelihood of truth. Both assume that the issue between them hangs on whether there is a substantial sense in which moral judgements are truth-valued, and both are helped in this assumption by their uncritical use of certain mediating notions – the central one being that of the 'cognitive' supported by a philosophically emphatic use of epistemic concepts like 'belief', 'understanding' and 'knowledge'. (Recall Bambrough's emphatic use of 'know'.) We should reject the terms of this debate.

If I were asked to give an example of a 'cognitive' expression, I would give 'understanding' as one. The task then is to see what can be said seriously with it. If some of its uses, for example in ethics, are denied to be 'really' cognitive, then the onus is clearly on those who deny it, to give a non-question-begging account of what is 'really cognitive'. The idea seems to be that what we call 'moral understanding' is 'really' understanding only if it is 'cognitive', and that it is 'really cognitive' only if it expresses belief, and that something is 'really' belief only if it is truth-valued, and that something is 'really' truth-valued only if . . ., and so on. This prompts the question, 'Which concepts do the work?'

It does not matter whether moral understanding, wisdom, shrewdness, naivety, stupidity, shallowness and depth are 'really cognitive'. What matters is that these are indispensable critical terms in our moral vocabulary and that serious moral speech is resistant to non-cognitivist reduction. The main substantial point in 'cognitivism' is that 'non-cognitivism' is mistaken – and vice versa. But that does not mean that our actual speech is *prima facie* 'cognitivist', that it clumsily intimates that 'values are in the fabric of the universe'. *It is not* prima facie *anything and it pretends to nothing.* The idea that it *appears* to be cognitive, and the suspicion that it may not be, are both based on the assumption that our actual speech intimates that impoverished conception of thought which I have been criticising, and that serious moral speech is to be measured against it. The suspicion that our actual speech may have false metaphysical implications is the suspicion that our human form of life may have shaped our speech in ways that disguise its serious and pervasive errors from us except at moments of philosophical reflection. But to be prone to that suspicion is not to notice the deepest of Wittgenstein's lessons. That lesson is that our human life conditions not only our beliefs, but also, and more importantly, the only concepts that we have, or could have, with which we can express what it is to believe something – the concepts which require us critically to distance ourselves from our beliefs and the concepts which reveal when we seek a distance beyond the limits of intelligibility. The idea that the serious use of our critical moral vocabulary intimates a possibly false 'ontology of values' and the idea that philosophical reflection is the exercise, *par excellence*, of the 'capacity, fixed for all possible worlds, to perform acts whose content belongs to the domain of logic' are two sides of the same counterfeit coin.

Wiggins writes:

> Against the suggestion that axiological predicates are a species of predicate not clearly marked off from the factual, there is a trick the non-cognitivist always plays and he ought not to be allowed to play. He picks himself a 'central case' of a descriptive predicate and a 'central case' of a valuational predicate. Then he remarks how very different the predicates he has picked are. But what on earth can that show? Nobody thinks you could prove a bat was not an animal by contrasting some bat (a paradigm case of a bat) with some elephant (a paradigm case of an animal). Nothing can come clear from such procedures in advance of explanation of the point of the contrast.[17]

Have I been guilty in what I have thus far said (especially in Chapter 15) of something equivalent to concluding that a bat is not an animal, or that if it is an animal, it is an animal in a different sense than is an elephant? Wiggins has a point, but its rhetorical power is considerably weakened when we ask the obvious question. Why does no one conclude that a bat is not an animal whereas most people are at least troubled by the discrepancy between words like 'true', 'fact', 'knowledge', as they are used in moral contexts and the way they are used in contexts where their legitimacy is incontestable? We have noted how radical the differences are and of what kind they are. That does not show that we should not speak of moral knowledge, of moral facts or of moral truth, or that if we do, then we should appreciate that we speak of knowledge in a different sense from the way we usually do. But someone makes such a point only if he wants to say it *is* knowledge despite appearances to the contrary. It is clear where the onus now lies.

We may get a clearer focus on my disagreement with Wiggins and find its crux if we attend to some interesting remarks he makes on his relation to Peirce. He says:

> For me the main interest of convergence is this: by the use of this idea, which is one of the several that animate the search for the marks of truth, I arrive at a necessary condition for a subject matter's being one that admits of truth. For instance, if I am right to claim ... that if *s* is true then (i) *s* will under favourable conditions command convergence and (ii) the best explanation of the existence of this convergence will require (or be inconsistent with the denial of) the actual truth of *s*, then it follows that a subject matter that admits of truth will need to have the wherewithal to create and sustain (in the favourable cases) the beginnings of a principled agreement; and it will also need to afford materials for us to describe (though not necessarily to determine effectively) the difference between principled and non-principled agreement. Truth is in jeopardy unless things are like that. [But unlike Peirce] On the account of truth offered ... it is still a clear, however remote, possibility that the predestinate opinion of all determined researchers should be false.[18]

He then quotes Peirce:

> Now there are some people, among whom I must suppose that my reader is to be found, who, when they see that any belief of theirs is determined by any circumstance extraneous to the facts, will from that moment not merely admit in words that that belief is doubtful, but will experience a real doubt of it, so that it ceases in some degree at least to be a belief. [These contrast with beliefs] determined by nothing human, but by some external permanency – by something upon which our thinking has no effect ... [but] which affects or might affect every man: [by] Reals whose characters are entirely independent of our opinions about them.[19]

Wiggins comments:

> What we need is the distinction between states of mind proper
> to idle supposition, wishful thinking, telling a good story or
> whatever, for which the third method seems perfectly appro-
> priate, and propositional attitudes like belief that are proper to
> active inquiry and have, on pain of extinction, to see them-
> selves as answerable to something . . . in so far as we want to
> settle opinion and end the irritation of doubt, what we have
> to want is for our belief that *p not* to be determined by 'circum-
> stances that are extraneous to the facts' but to come about
> precisely *because p*. This, however, is a state we can often attain
> without our opinion's being determined by 'external perma-
> nencies' or 'Reals' that affect every inquirer in the same way
> regardless of his history or acculturation so that 'any man if
> he have sufficient experience and he reasons enough about it
> will be led to the one True conclusion'. There are subjects where
> getting a grasp of the sense of the language proprietary to them
> is not at all independent of specific acculturation. In these
> subjects we need not look to such a thing as the 'one true
> conclusion' of *all* inquirers . . . The real mark of a state that is
> truth-oriented . . . is simply that the state should be one which,
> in virtue of being the mental state that it is, seeks to be deter-
> mined by causes that are *not accidental relative to its content.*[20]

I have quoted Wiggins at such length because these interesting
remarks reveal how much both he and Peirce are reacting to reductive treatments of belief and inquiry, of those 'propositional attitudes
like belief that are proper to active inquiry and have, on pain of
extinction, to see themselves as answerable to something'. We know
well enough what it is for a belief to be determined by improper
causes (believing something merely because we want to, for example)
and we understand well enough why someone would wish to assert,
against psychologically or sociologically reductive accounts of
beliefs, that the reason we believe that *p is because p*.

Wiggins is aware of how empty is Peirce's positive suggestion
concerning the proper determination of belief. But when he says that
it is a mark of the proper determination of belief that convergence
on the belief that *p* is best explained *because p*, has he added

anything to the legitimate, negative, anti-reductive points, and the point that inquiry is constrained by disciplines internal to it? He seems to believe that he has. He seems to believe that when he says that 'We believe that 7 + 5 is 12 because 7 + 5 *is* 12. We have no choice',[21] he points to how the anti-reductivist position may be securely underwritten. But when he offers what he takes to be merely a stricter formulation of the conditions of proper convergence (that the best of our explanations of the convergence on the belief that p is inconsistent with our denial that p), he seems to be offering something quite different in kind. We may agree with the latter claim while resisting the former, not because the former is imprecise or a little too restrictive, but because it is not compatible, as Wiggins believes it is, with specifying 'no limits in advance on what can count as a reality, or as the ins and outs of such'.[22] The kind of discipline which constitutes the way mathematical thinking is answerable to something, and which determines what the emphatic 'is' amounts to when Wiggins says that 7 + 5 *is* 12, is internal to the character of mathematical practices – to what a mathematical problem is and to what thinking towards its solution may be. We may, to be sure, speak of mathematical thinking as answerable to something (to some kind of reality, indeed) while not thinking that it is answerable to whatever scientific thinking is answerable to. But if that emphatic '*is*' is to do the kind of work Wiggins wants of it, then the disciplines of thought which condition its sense in that context are of the impersonal kind I described in Chapter 14. If my arguments in that chapter are sound, those disciplines are quite different from the disciplines that characterise moral thought.

All this raises the following important question: what kind of constraint on what kind of thinking subject do we need to have the kind of distinction Wiggins draws between 'states of mind proper to idle supposition, wishful thinking, telling a good story or whatever ... and propositional attitudes like belief that are proper to active inquiry and have, on pain of extinction, to see themselves as answerable'? Some such contrast is necessary to secure the irreducibility of concepts like understanding in characterising, for example, the discipline of the Socratic quest for lucidity. And it is surely right that a substantial conception of understanding requires the idea of belief as something properly arrived at (as 'determined by causes that are not accidental relative to its content') and (although it may amount to the same idea) it requires the idea that thinking, as it is in serious inquiry, is constituted by those disciplines which make it '*answerable*' to something – to 'how things are'. But we need not think that these general truths will be univocally instantiated in different kinds of inquiry, for different kinds of reflectiveness. Our task is to see how they apply in ethics.

In Chapter 15 I quoted Hannah Arendt's description of Eichmann's last moments before his execution. I quoted it as an example with which to understand the nature of Socrates' objections to rhetoric. I argued that Socrates thought that a certain kind of personal collectedness, a certain kind of personal integration, was not merely an aid to, but actually constitutive of, those disciplines and constraints which mark thinking from mere reverie – thinking as we mean it when we call someone to seriousness, as Socrates so often did, by saying, 'Come now, *think* about what you are saying'. This is the kind of thinking Wiggins describes (even if he does not have it in mind) when he speaks of 'propositional attitudes like belief that are proper to active inquiry and have, on pain of extinction, to see themselves as answerable to something'. The point bears fundamentally on our question: what kind of subject can be in that way answerable, and how does his being in that way answerable connect with the epistemic and more general grammar of his subject matter? The question is not innocent of the suspicion that at least some of what is usually thought to be at best an external aid or an external obstacle to thought is, in truth, internal to those modalities which condition thought itself. Indeed, I argued this in Chapter 15.

It is worth recalling Arendt's remarks:

He began by stating emphatically that he was a *Gottgläubiger*, to express in common Nazi fashion that he was no Christian and did not believe in life after death. He then proceeded: 'After a short while gentlemen, *we shall all meet again*. Such is the fate of all men. Long live Germany, long live Argentina . . .' In the face of death, he had found the cliché used in funeral oratory. Under the gallows, his memory played him the last trick; he was 'elated' and he forgot that this was his own funeral.[23]

The banal sentimentality of Eichmann's behaviour is evident. Concepts that philosophers call 'cognitive' would be pre-eminent in any detailed description of it. Arendt spoke of his terrifying thoughtlessness – terrifying because it was, she believed, the same kind of thoughtlessness which explained his conscientious service to Hitler's genocidal policies.[24] One could also speak of how unconstrained his thought was by any discipline internal to it, or by reality.

It may seem at first that Arendt is suggesting that his radical thoughtlessness shows itself in the fact that he could contradict himself within two sentences – when he declares himself to be someone who does not believe in an after-life and then immediately expresses his belief in it – and also by the fact that he forgot that he was at his own funeral. It might seem, then, that this provides a counter-example to the point I made in Chapter 14 about the concept of sentimentality. It might seem that we have here a good example of the way sentimentality is a cause of muddle and false belief and that the fear of death probably underlies it all. However, the 'reality' which had so little power over Eichmann's thought is not naturally described as 'factual', and the lack of rigour in his thought, its internal freedom from constraint, is not the sort which usually interests logicians. Arendt says that he 'forgot' that it was his own funeral. He did not forget that Adolf Eichmann was being executed and that he was Adolf Eichmann. The reality from which he was estranged was not the *fact* of his death but its *meaning*.

Sometimes people speak of their own misery with an eloquence that moves them to tears. We know then that there is something false in the expression of their sorrow. Sometimes the opposite happens: in the face of misery or death, people reject as mere words what they or others have said about their meaning. They may say that it is all *false*, but the emphasis need not be on that word as it interests logicians. They may say that such words offer false consolation, meaning, perhaps, that it is false consolation to see any meaning in death or in human misery. But that is not a factual claim, even though they might say that they are now *facing reality*.

Eichmann tried to die with dignity. (Arendt says that he did die with dignity but I cannot understand why she says this.) He was determined that fear should not make him betray the sense that his infatuation with 'winged words' had given him of how to die nobly.

302

He was determined that those 'winged words' should not seem 'mere' words because of his fear. Sentenced to be executed, he was loyal to them and the high ideals he thought they expressed, just as he had been when he conscientiously administered 'The Final Solution' in the face of the advancing Allied armies. Hence the ease of the apparent contradiction to which Arendt draws attention. But he did not really contradict himself. I do not say that because the words he spoke do not entail belief in an after-life, but rather because he meant nothing determinate by them. The words that came to him had little to do with his belief in their content. They came to him because of his sense of how they should hang together to become 'winged'. He was not interested in saying anything true. He was interested only in saying something 'winged' so that his death would have a quality that he mistook for nobility. He was not sufficiently 'present' in what he said to be able to contradict himself, for he was not sufficiently present to be able seriously to say anything. He was, because of his infatuation with the corrupt edification of his oratory, *absent* from himself in the sense in which Socrates accused orators of being insufficiently present to themselves and to others to enable them to be partners in serious conversation: 'I think it better, my good friend, that my lyre should be discordant and out of tune and any chorus I might train, and that the majority of mankind should disagree with me, than that *I, who am but one man, should be out of tune with and contradict myself*[25] (my emphasis).

Arendt brings out that although Eichmann did not face the reality of his death it was not because of fear. His words were 'mere words', but not because he was overwhelmed by fear and sought consolation in them. He was, as she says, perfectly himself. He acted in character, and his character was not that of a coward. Once he opened his mouth to speak, or rather once he set himself to die nobly, the result was inevitable. His seduction by 'winged words' made him incapable of a lucid response to the meaning of his death, just as it made him incapable of seeing the reality of the evil he had done. He 'forgot' that it was his own funeral in the same sense in which people are out of touch with reality when they move themselves to tears by their own eloquence.

When someone says, in the face of his own death or the death of someone close to him, that the edifying things he had heard and which he had said in the past are now 'mere words' to him, he means that such words come easily when death is merely, as Kierkegaard puts it, 'a something in general'[26] and that they could be said only by someone for whom its reality was distant. But 'the concept of reality' here is the concept of it *as it necessarily claims an individual.* We say that what was said was 'hollow' or 'empty' or that it 'came cheaply'. We also say that it was 'false', but that word is not primary over the others.

The idea of the *meaning* of death includes the idea of a requirement to a lucid personal response. If we say of someone that he speaks as he does of death only because it is so (psychically) distant from him, then we do not mean that he has literally forgotten that he and those he loves will die. But we do imply that the imminence of death may lead to sobriety, that his words may be hollow to him in the face of death. In Eichmann's case, not even the imminence of death, of which he was perfectly factually aware, could make him hear the hollowness of what he was saying. And the hollowness of his speech showed that although death was factually present to him, its significance was as absent to him as it is to the young of whom we say that they believe they are immortal, by which, of course, we do not mean that they have false factual beliefs. Each of them sincerely believes the proposition that he will die, and none of them has the sneaking suspicion that he might be the exception to the rule that all human beings are mortal; nonetheless, what they say about the meaning of death cannot be trusted. Those whom we trust to have spoken with a depth of understanding about the meaning of our mortality are not privy to esoteric information which is naturally called 'factual'. Our trust in those who speak (as we believe) deeply about death is not dependent upon any empirical information they might possess.

Eichmann's failure to understand what he was doing and what was happening to him was inseparable from his failure to see what death meant *for him.* In the case of the factual proposition, that all human beings die, the fact that it applies to ourself is external to our understanding of it. Someone who is not human and who is immortal could understand it perfectly well. But the effort to understand the meaning of death is an effort that can be made only by someone who is mortal, and there is no understanding here without effort. That was one of the lessons of Chapter 15. Facing death and fearing it are not, of themselves, impediments to clear thought about it. An *individually achieved lucidity* in the face of death is internal to what we mean by understanding its meaning and by the idea that thoughts about it are answerable to some reality. Wittgenstein remarks:

> A hero looks death in the face, real death, not just the image of death. Behaving honourably in a crisis doesn't mean being able to act the part of a hero well, as in the theatre, it means rather being able to look death *itself* in the eye. For an actor may play lots of different roles, but at the end of it all, *he himself*, the human being, is the one who has to die.[27]

Wiggins says that 'a subject or an interpreter has to try to see other subjects as constantly adjusting their beliefs to something – as responding constantly to the ins and outs of some reality or other'. Eichmann is clearly not someone responding 'to the ins and outs of some reality or other'. The metaphors of obedience, attunement and correspondence to reality, which are so fundamental to any conception of serious inquiry, find no place in the description of what he said before his execution. And as Wiggins himself seems to believe, undue weight should not be given to the idea of 'correspondence to reality'. The non-philosophical use of such an expression is just another way of speaking of thought's attunement or obedience to reality. The 'correspondence theory of truth' is a distortion of that natural way of speaking which characterises the fact that we distinguish serious thinking from reverie, day-dreaming, etc. by its disciplined obedience to 'how things are' – to 'reality'. But if we ask what it is for thought to be attuned to reality, in keeping with reality, in touch with reality and so on, then we must look to the grammar of the different *kinds* of critical concepts with which we mark our sense of what it is to think well or badly.

In Eichmann's case, if we ask *why* his thought was so lacking in constraint then we must refer to certain failures of character. And if we ask *how* his thought was lacking in constraint – what *kind* of lack of constraint it was – then we must refer to those same failures of character. If we ask why he was so 'out of touch with reality', then we will say (among other things of course) that it is because he was so grotesquely sentimental. But if we take that as a quasi-causal explanation of why his thought failed, then we will look for a characterisation of that failure which makes no necessary reference to his sentimentality. We saw in Chapter 15 that the concept of sentimentality is sometimes deployed in this quasi-causal way. But Eichmann's sentimentality was not the cause of his thought's failure along some more basic dimension (truth/falsehood). It was one of the primary ways in which his thought failed – one of the primary modes of what Arendt called his 'thoughtlessness'.

Thought on any matter is answerable to a set of critical concepts which mark the way it must be attuned to reality – what it is for thought about that kind of subject matter to be 'in tune with reality', or to aspire to grasp things 'as they are', or to be, as Wiggins says, 'truth-oriented' and to 'respond to the ins and outs of some reality or other'. Those critical concepts expressed in a particular critical vocabulary which individuates a particular realm of reflection or inquiry mark the ways we understand what it is for 'a mental state [to be] determined by causes that are accidental to its content'.

Simone Weil said:

> What is sacred in science is truth; what is sacred in art is beauty. Truth and beauty are impersonal. All this is too obvious . . . If a child is doing a sum and does it wrong, the mistake bears the stamp of his personality. If he does the sum exactly right, his personality does not enter into it at all.[28]

In another place she speaks of her intellectual vocation:

> The degree of intellectual honesty which is obligatory for me, by reason of my particular vocation, demands that my thought should be indifferent to all ideas without exception . . . it must be equally welcoming and equally reserved with regard to every one of them. Water is indifferent in this way to the objects which fall into it. It does not weigh them; it is they which weigh themselves, after a certain time of oscillation.[29]

If one leaves aside the religious emphasis, then the image of obedience and submission is close to the way Wiggins speaks. Aurel Kolnai, to whom Wiggins often refers, speaks that way too when he says:

We do constantly overcome our subjective biases and predeterminations, surmount our subjectivity, deliver up the kingdom of our intellect to its lawful Sovereign, the Object; briefly, in a sense give the lie to the dictum that 'nobody can leap over his shadow'.[30]

What Simone Weil means by the impersonal, her comparison of a completely honest mind allowing ideas to weigh themselves as objects weigh themselves in water, Kolnai's talk of 'delivering the intellect up to its lawful Sovereign the Object' and Wiggins' claim that 'the real mark of a state that is truth oriented is simply that the state should be one which, in virtue of being the mental state that it is, seeks to be determined by causes that are not accidental to its object' – are strikingly similar. But, as I remarked earlier, we can have no conception of what any of this comes to with respect to any particular subject matter other than by careful attention to the grammar of the critical vocabulary which conditions our sense of what it is to think well and badly in that subject matter. Combining Weil and Kolnai, we might say that for thought to be impersonal is for it to be delivered up to its Sovereign the Object. Or we could put it the other way around. In the case of Eichmann, his sentimentality got in the way; it was the way his thought failed to be impersonal. But as Wiggins himself would acknowledge, the remedy for that cannot be conditioned by the ideal of an epistemic subject to whom feeling is accidental. The purification of the epistemic subject in an effort to achieve the obedience to those disciplines which mark a particular mode of thought should not be an effort towards becoming a mere thinking thing, a *res cogitans*, or, to adapt Kierkegaard's remark, a thinking thing *in general*, transparent to truth. We can, therefore, acknowledge the permanent point of the metaphors of obedience and submission in the characterisation of the states of mind necessary for serious inquiry, and we can acknowledge the point it gives to a certain conception of the necessarily impersonal character of all serious thought, while at the same time resisting the temptation to think that such general truths about the nature of thought and reality are univocally instantiated. We should also resist the temptation to say, flatly, either that moral thought is personal or that it is impersonal.

307

17

---❧---

Fearless thinkers and
evil thoughts

We think it is a good thing to be a fearless thinker. That is not merely because we admire courage. It is because we think a *true* thinker is a fearless thinker. Orwell said of Gandhi: 'One feels of him that there was much that he did not understand, but not that there was anything that he was frightened of saying or thinking.'[1] That is offered and taken as high praise. If Orwell had said that there were only *some* things that Gandhi feared to think, then the effect would have been lost. Yet that is the truth, not only about Gandhi, but about anyone who is not a crank, insane or evil.

There are things which anyone would fear to think because even to entertain them would be a sure sign that he could no longer trust his ability to think. Some things we could think only if we were going mad, and the terror of madness lies partly in the fact that we cannot think our way out of it. If we suspect that we are going mad, then we cannot trust our thoughts. Less dramatically, there are some things that only cranks could seriously entertain – for example, that the world is flat, or that they can read their future in the stars, or that the Holocaust is a fiction invented and sustained by a Zionist conspiracy.

We often say that no rational person could believe such things, but it really has little to do with rationality. Such people need not be deficient in the various critical skills. They are deficient in something that is a *condition of their proper exercise*. Descartes called it 'sense' when he said in the Synopsis to the *Meditations* that he did not consider his arguments to be 'very useful in establishing that which they prove, to wit, that there is in truth a world, that men possess bodies and other such things which never have been doubted by anyone of sense'.[2] The trouble with cranks is not that they hold radically unconventional beliefs on insufficient evidence, nor is it that they cannot reason. We call them cranks because we recognise that the proper exercise of our critical concepts – the concept of sufficient evidence, for example – depends upon them not being exercised by cranks and madmen. When they are, we are sometimes presented with the remorseless parody of reason which prompted Chesterton to say that 'the madman is not the man who has lost his reason; the madman is the man who has lost everything except his reason'.[3]

If someone insanely believes that his food is poisoned, you cannot prove otherwise to him, because anything that would count, for us, as a proof is vulnerable to his paranoid ingenuity. Something is a proof only within the ranks of the sane and the sober, those who, as the colloquial expression has it, 'are in tune with reality'. That belongs to the concept of a proof. Being, in this sense, 'in tune with reality' is not a matter of having mostly true beliefs of reasonable genesis. Normally, if we ask someone his name and he tells us, then we believe him, but not because it is *reasonable* to believe him. It would not be unreasonable not to believe him: it would be insane. No doubt we believe him because people normally tell the truth in such circumstances, but that is not the inductive basis for our believing that it is *highly probable* that they are telling us the truth when they tell us their name. Indeed, if we think it is merely highly probable that they are telling us the truth, then we already have one foot in the asylum and we cannot get it out by raising the probabilities, which would anyhow be an idle exercise since we have no idea what they are. Similarly, when we go to a restaurant for dinner we do not believe that it is extremely improbable that the cooks will try to poison us. If it should occur to us that they might, then we will quite rightly fear for our sanity and we will not be consoled by the thought that it is, 'strictly speaking', possible that they intend to murder us, but not very likely. Again, it is important that cooks in restaurants seldom try to poison their customers, but, as Wittgenstein has suggested in another connection, we misunderstand the significance of the generality of facts such as these if we think that in examples such as I have just given they are the evidence for justified beliefs.[4]

If we are sane such thoughts never occur to us, not because for practical purposes (for 'all intents and purposes') we treat what is improbable as being impossible, but because the fact that it does not occur to us if we are sane conditions the sense of such concepts as 'it is possible that . . .', or 'probable that . . .', or 'impossible that . . .'. Such facts are not consequent upon our (implicit) belief in probabilities. They condition the intelligible deployment of such concepts whose philosophical refinement cannot, therefore, furnish the basis for a 'strict-speech' redescription of our practices. The difference between the paranoid and someone who is sane is not that the paranoid thinks that the cooks are trying to poison him or that it is highly likely that they are, while someone who is sane thinks that it is possible but extremely unlikely. The difference lies in the fact that someone who is sane 'rules it out of consideration' while someone who is mad does not.

Such examples, however, were not the kind that Orwell had in mind when he praised Gandhi for being a fearless thinker. He had in mind moral and political examples, and although he praised Gandhi against a background of what he judged to be the moral cant and hypocrisy of British pacifists during the Second World War, the idea of an absolute fearlessness of thought seems more attractive when morality is at issue. That is because the fear of thinking something evil seems to be a fear which would put a stop to thinking for reasons which are external to it, rather as does fear of thinking something that would conflict with the opinion of the majority, or as does fear of thinking something that would conflict with a theory we had spent a lifetime developing. In such cases we feel that a fearless and real thinker will simply ask whether something is true or valid. But if we fear to think something evil, then what we fear is not error or muddle, but the evil of it.

Our practice, it is true, is not quite so simple. It is generally accepted that an argument will have found its *reductio ad absurdum* if it yields a conclusion which is generally agreed to be evil, whereas no one accepts that an argument is defeated if it entails a conclusion unfavourable to a pet theory or to one which is merely unpopular. Arguments which entail conclusions that run contrary to common wisdom *are* often rejected, but never merely because they are contrary to common wisdom. But arguments which lead to what are agreed to be evil conclusions *are* often rejected merely because the conclusion is judged to be evil.

However, that does not show that we have a serious place for the idea of fearing to think something evil. We see this if we consider what happens when what functioned as a *reductio* because it was judged to be evil no longer does so. As recently as the 1970s it was believed that the conclusion that infanticide is permissible would be a *reductio* of any argument that led to it. In particular, it was agreed by all that abortion would be inconceivable if it were shown to be (morally) the same as the killing of a perfectly healthy infant of, say, three weeks. Today there are philosophers who believe that infanticide of that kind is permissible under much the same conditions as abortion. Philosophy students the Western world over who are taking courses in practical ethics think that it is at least arguable. Amongst philosophers it is thought to be perfectly proper to argue that infanticide of that kind is an evil, but it is thought to be improper to say that conjecturing whether it is permissible is *itself* an evil to be feared. If a philosopher were to say that students are liable to be corrupted by those who invite them seriously to consider whether they may kill healthy three-week-old babies for the same kinds of reasons that will procure an abortion, then most of his colleagues would judge that he had shown himself to be less than a real philosopher, less than a real thinker.

If someone finds something arguable then there is no point in anyone telling them that it is not arguable. There is now an entire generation of philosophy students who have been taught to believe that it is arguable whether infanticide is permissible under much the same conditions as is abortion. What is interesting is that, often, they have been taught this by people who, as recently as the 1970s, believed that it constituted the *reductio* of any argument that led to it. How should we describe their change?

They would say that argument had shown them to be wrong. It is natural to ask how argument could reveal a conclusion to be acceptable when that conclusion had constituted a *reductio* of any argument that could lead to it. That question is not merely rhetorical. It opens an area of inquiry, but it does not take us far into it, for the nature of such informal uses of *reductio ad absurdum* is not clear. Even so, it should put a stop to the complacent assumption

that someone has yielded to prejudice if he is not prepared to reconsider the matter. The questions which should be to the fore are these:
how should we understand the various ways in which we 'rule
things out of consideration'?, and what is it for an argument to be
compelling? Of course much has been done since the dawn of philosophy to answer the second question, but it has been on the
assumption that any answer to the first awaits an adequate answer
to the second. My argument will be that the two are interdependent: that we need a better understanding of the ways we rule things
out of consideration so that we may achieve a better understanding
of what it is for an argument to be compelling, indeed, for what it
is for something to *be* an argument.

Since the 1970s many things which had been thought to be
'unthinkable' are now seriously entertained, but there has been little
thought about how this should be understood. Those who argue
about what had previously been unthinkable, and especially those
who have been in the forefront of the argument, think of themselves
as exposing old taboos or at least putting them under critical
scrutiny. Their perception accords with what might appear to be the
'objective' view of someone who is not a participant in the argument (a sociologist, for example) and who would describe the
changes in society when *reductio*s lose their power as changes in
beliefs which were fundamental to the 'old' society. Neither of these
perspectives accords any serious role to the idea of the morally
unthinkable as it might appear to someone for whom something
is morally unthinkable. *Reductio*s are not absolute, but neither are
they merely expressive of beliefs which are basic and which are
thought to be well grounded. They mark out what a community
treats as 'beyond consideration', and they invite more specific
descriptions, relative to the topic under discussion, of the disposition to be moved by them – that one is a crank, for example, or
incorrigibly gullible, or that one 'shows a corrupt mind.'[5]

It is sometimes said that those who argue that nothing should be
morally unthinkable are courageously prepared to follow reason
wherever it compels them to go. That is often self-congratulatory
cant and needs to be recognised as such if there is to be serious
discussion of the issue. No one is compelled by argument to reconsider what he had thought to be morally unthinkable. No argument

in ethics could be so compelling except to someone who was so simple-minded that he failed to see the complexity and difficulty which lies not far below the surface of any argument in this area, and which therefore provides many and ample loopholes. Also, arguments in ethics can take us only to what we had already entertained as a morally thinkable conclusion. When something which has generally been thought to be morally unthinkable becomes widely discussed, it is because of shifts in the culture at large rather than because people were compelled by arguments. The arguments are persuasive only because their conclusion had become morally thinkable, if not acceptable, in advance of the arguments. Or more precisely, the arguments are persuasive only because of other elements in the broader culture which predisposed people to find morally thinkable what they had previously found unthinkable. Philosophers and others who present arguments which are described as shattering deep taboos are almost always children of their time. If the times had not already eroded the taboo then the philosopher's arguments could have no force, because the conclusions to which he tended would always be treated as *reductio*s. If your conclusions are those of a child of the times, then you risk making a fool of yourself if you present them as the result of your courageous devotion to reason and yourself as a true heir to Socrates. Philosophers seem particularly prone to this, for reasons which are seldom edifying.

It seems almost tautologous to say that a morally serious person will fear to fall into evil. He may do this by losing his sense of which things are evil or, more generally, by losing his sense of the reality of evil. Kierkegaard said that just as the logician most fears a fallacy, so the ethical thinker most fears to fall away from the ethical.[6] By 'falling away from the ethical' he meant losing one's sense of its reality, which means losing a sense of the *kind of seriousness* which is internal to it. It is also close to tautologous to say that ethical considerations are necessarily serious considerations. Someone who said that such and such was merely *morally* terrible, and therefore not to be seriously counterbalanced against his pleasure, would have shown that he did not understand what it was for something to be a moral consideration, in much the same way as he would were he to say, 'I know that it is shallow, sentimental and irredeemably banal, but there it is, my morality.' But, as we have seen in previous chapters, it is controversial how to characterise the kind of seriousness it is. The fear of thinking something evil is an important part of it.

Philosophers sometimes express a scepticism about morality which suggests that it should be an open question whether we ought to fear doing or being evil. Not all forms of moral scepticism are like this, but some are. The idea seems to be that our sense of the terribleness of being an evildoer may be an illusion. Some philosophers say that we should seriously consider the argument that morality may be a fraud perpetrated by the weak against the strong. They mean that we should be open to its conclusion being true, which means that we should be open to the possibility of being the kind of person who believes it and lives accordingly. Some even say that this is the only real form of moral scepticism and they are thrilled that they dare to express it.

This kind of scepticism, however, is itself a fraud, for no one puts it forward in his own name. It is always someone else who is represented as seriously entertaining it, and he is either a fictional character, such as Thrasymachus, or a mere sketch of a character – someone 'neither timid nor stupid and committed to rationality', for example.[7] No philosopher will seriously say, '*I* believe that our sense of good and evil may be an illusion' and no philosopher would accept responsibility for one of his students seriously believing it because of his teaching. One who did would be at best morally frivolous, and no one would take seriously his protest that such a judgement begs the question against him. Yet the game goes on, and within the terms of the game the accusation that the serious profession of this kind of scepticism is itself a form of moral corruption is treated as question-begging. Perhaps that is why there is no serious discussion of it in the mainstream of the subject.

Moral scepticism falls under the moral judgements it would suspend, not only at the end of the day, but in the very act of announcing itself. The fraudulent kind that I have been discussing, which titillates itself with the pretence of thinking dangerous thoughts, is a tasteless form of intellectual and moral irresponsibility. If it were not fraudulent it would be corrupt. To see this quite clearly one need only imagine a tutorial in which one of its members had been a victim of terrible evil of which all the other members were aware, and in which the tutor invited them to consider whether our sense of the terribleness of evil was not an illusion. Everyone would be outraged if the tutor were not serious and struck by unbelieving horror if he was.

The example brings out that scepticism of this kind is itself an act against those who have been the victims of evil. The victim need not be directly before us as in the example. If people find themselves thinking that Jews are swine who deserved what the Nazis did to them, then that is itself something for which they should be ashamed, not merely because of what it shows about them, but also for the sake of those who suffered under the Nazis. In thinking what they did they placed themselves in a concrete moral relation to those who suffered. If they said that theirs was, after all, *merely a thought*, they would betray their moral coarseness.

When we say that we must never forget such evils as the Jews suffered in the death camps of the Third Reich it is not primarily because we must prepare ourselves against the recurrence of such evils, but because we owe it to the victims to remember the evil done to them. Such 'acts of remembrance' often take public forms, as, for example, visiting Yad Vashem in Jerusalem, but they may take the form of a private ritual which, from one perspective, consists only of 'mere thoughts'. Yet hardly anyone would deny that such acts of remembrance place a person in a concrete moral relation to those remembered. And what we remember, what we are *obliged* to remember, is not that six million people died and suffered, but the *evil* done to them. That is the context in which to place nihilistic forms of moral scepticism. The person who says that we must consider the argument that morality may be an illusion says that *we must in intellectual conscience question, and if the argument goes a certain way have the courage to deny, the reality of the evil which at other times we think it our duty to remember*. Of course no one is really serious about it. But who would confidently say that such frivolity is without consequence?

What would it be like to be seriously sceptical? That is not at all clear, which is why, as Roy Holland remarked, this (nihilistic) kind of moral scepticism seems such a trumped-up affair.[8] It is not that we do not have examples of a loss of the sense of the reality of evil.

315

We have only too many. What we lack are examples of people who have *thought* themselves from a serious sense of good and evil into a seriously professed scepticism. But to say that we have no examples of such people is to understate the difficulty. We do not even know how to describe them, which is why they appear in philosophy as no more than sketches of characters. When detail is added it becomes impossible to take them seriously. Thrasymachus is an example. He is little more than a moderately clever and brazen thug who sulks when the argument gets difficult. That, no doubt, is part of Plato's point. Thrasymachus is not an example of someone with a serious understanding of the good and evil which he claims to be a fraud, nor is his challenge an example of the serious and persistent intellectual inquiry which scepticism is meant to represent.

A certain kind of philosopher is inclined to say that although that may be true, Thrasymachus surely has a point?[9] The answer is that *he* does not have a point. We can of course extract arguments from what Thrasymachus says and write them on a blackboard, and we can try to improve on them, but until someone is prepared to assert them seriously in his own name, then they are arguments only in inverted commas for they yield only inverted commas conclusions – 'conclusions', that is, which no one is seriously prepared to conclude. The fact that blackboards can be filled with what are called sceptical arguments is what sustains the illusion that it is a serious intellectual option. If someone seriously asserted them in his own name we would judge him to be wicked and we would believe his wickedness to have been the reason such arguments carried any weight with him. But then he would not be someone whom we credit to have come to this conclusion simply by following an argument where it took him. He would not be credited as someone who had reached his destination merely by thought.

It seems that we cannot take seriously the idea that people could reject or even question the reality of evil, in the manner of someone like Thrasymachus, merely because they have thought themselves to such a position – no more than we can take seriously the idea that genuine despair could issue merely from an argument that concluded that life is meaningless. There are many different *kinds* of propositions that cannot be seriously asserted, or seriously asserted as the conclusion of a process of reasoning. I have called them, disparagingly, 'blackboard conclusions', because a proposition which cannot seriously be asserted, or one which we take to be asserted seriously only when we see that it was not and could not be the outcome only of thought, is a conclusion in a secondary sense. Philosophers, for reasons which go very deep, have constructed and found edifying an ideal of intellectual purity which takes as its exemplar someone who would turn his life upside down after stumbling across an argument with just such a conclusion, even if it were written in the sand by the wind.

Someone under the sway of the idea that scepticism is not only an intellectual possibility, but also an intellectual requirement, will say that all that I have said is from the moral perspective which all sceptics challenge, and is therefore no answer to him. He is right. It is no answer if answering the sceptic requires meeting him on his own ground. He wishes to stand in a place where moral judgement is suspended until what he understands to be a purely intellectual judgement has been passed on it.

Many philosophers have argued that morality cannot be undermined or underwritten from a perspective outside of itself. That is sometimes expressed in the slogan that morality does not admit of an external justification. In this kind of argument it is deployed to show that the reasons for being just, for example, are not the kind that a sceptic wants, and that the reasons a sceptic wants are not the reasons a just person could have for being just. Someone who believes this will question the intellectual coherence of scepticism. My emphasis has been not on the incoherence of scepticism, but on its wickedness, and I wish to say that rejection of scepticism because it is wicked does not await a justification on the grounds that it is incoherent.

The idea that morality does not admit of an external justification can itself take many forms, but arguments for it are usually of a kind that a sceptic may be expected to accept as revealing the incoherence of his sceptical project. He wanted an argument and he got an argument. True, it was not the kind he expected. He usually does assume that if morality has a 'justification', then it will be an external one. But the possibility that his scepticism is incoherent is a possibility he must accept, and so he must be prepared to argue on those grounds. And although, as I said, it is not the argument he expected, it is an argument he must accept as being a proper response to the initial formulation of his scepticism. But he will not accept that he is wicked even to raise his (nihilistic) sceptical questions. He will not acknowledge the claim that the entire game is at best intellectually and morally irresponsible to be a move in the game. He will say that scepticism is an option unless it is intellectually defeated.

My argument has not been that there is nothing outside of morality which could justify it. It has been that our answerability to moral judgement cannot be suspended while we question the reality of good and evil. If that is true, then I have not begged the question against the sceptic by calling his scepticism corrupt. The judgement that he is corrupt is not a move in an argument against him, and something which is not intended as a move in an argument cannot beg any questions. My discussion has not been an argument to the conclusion that the sceptic is corrupt, but rather an attempt to *place* that (rather obvious) judgement amongst the various reactions to scepticism, some of which are arguments. I have claimed that there is nothing which can be called a requirement of Reason, an intellectual requirement, to suspend moral judgement, including moral judgement of the activity of thinking about morality. To put the point very simply: no matter what we do, we remain human beings who are answerable to moral judgement when such judgement is appropriate, and it is obviously appropriate if we are questioning the reality of good and evil. There are different ways of questioning the reality of good and evil, but there is no way of doing it that permits this protest: 'Tell me, if you wish, that I am muddled. Tell me if you wish that what I say is false. Tell me if you wish that what I say is incoherent. But keep your moral judgements out of it.'

In Chapter 2, I commented on Elizabeth Anscombe saying that anyone who thought '*in advance*, that it is open to question whether such an action as procuring the judicial execution of the innocent should be quite excluded from consideration [shows] a corrupt mind'. She makes clear in a footnote what she means by 'in advance'[10]: she means in advance of actually being in a situation in which we might be tempted to do it for the kinds of reason which are often rehearsed in discussions of consequentialism. Nearly all philosophers do not think that 'it should be ruled out of consideration' whether an innocent person should in certain circumstances

318

be judicially executed. The subject would be hardly recognisable if they did. Anscombe knew this. She condemned modern moral philosophy as a corrupt subject.

Most academics would think Anscombe had acted disgracefully when she implied that most of her colleagues showed corrupt minds, and they must think that this is obvious because they have not bothered to discuss it. But it takes only a moment's reflection to see that it cannot be so simple. How should we describe the disposition to accept as at least worthy of consideration a manifestly evil proposal, offered as a *reductio* of any argument that supported it? The expression 'a corrupt mind' is not without meaning. It is not merely a bullying ejaculation expressing disapproval. It denotes, amongst other things, a disposition to accept, or even to entertain, the evil conclusions of certain arguments. It is a more specific description of the disposition to accept this kind of *reductio*. Nonetheless, the idea persists that proper academic practice and accusing one's colleagues of showing corrupt minds are deeply incompatible. There are different reasons for this. The least interesting is that people are usually angered by being told they have corrupt minds and that this gets in the way of cool and sober discussion. That makes no distinction in kind between accusing a colleague of showing a corrupt mind and accusing them of hair-raising ignorance and muddle. That too is likely to inflame tempers. Also, as this last example shows, many of the conventions of academic propriety depend on academic practices not deteriorating to the point where a sober and truthful description of them sounds like abuse.

We get at a deeper reason if we note something which those who are unfamiliar with academic life would find very strange. Someone who agreed with Anscombe need not think that having a corrupt mind should be an obstacle to deserved distinction in moral philosophy – no obstacle, for example, to being appointed to a distinguished chair in moral philosophy; nor to election to a learned society; nor even to becoming a philosophical knight. Such an observation could be merely an expression of cynicism, but it need not be. It can remind us of something important about the nature of philosophy as a subject, or perhaps more accurately, it may remind us that I have been speaking of philosophy as a subject, as we mean it when we speak of students reading a subject and of their being initiated into its mastery by those whose authority to teach and to examine it does not require wisdom (insofar as that is something different in kind from high competence or knowledgeableness). It is possible to become a philosophical knight for services to moral philosophy while being foolish, shallow and wicked and after having corrupted the minds of the youth for thirty or forty years. *And, up to a point, rightly so.* The intellectual character of the academic community is determined by the fact that its members are primarily answerable to one another as servants of their subjects. Academics are answerable to their colleagues for their ignorance, their errors and their confusions, but not for their corrupt minds.

It is therefore quite ambiguous to say that which critical terms are appropriate in philosophy depends upon the nature of a philosophical problem, for it ignores the difference between philosophy as we do it and philosophy as Socrates did it. It was not and could not have been a subject for him. Academics, especially philosophers, are usually not sufficiently observant of this distinction and its implication because they are inclined to ignore the social and historical conditions of their practice. They tend to ignore not only the social and historical determinants of the content of their subjects, but also the nature and scope of the critical vocabularies which partly define and individuate them. It is not the relatively ahistorical character of philosophical inquiry as determined by the nature of its problems, insofar as they may be thought to be common between us and Socrates, which has determined that it is appropriate to say that such and such is false or invalid, but not that it shows a corrupt mind. That has been determined by the historically and socially conditioned character of philosophy as a subject or a discipline.

Philosophers, unconsciously or unwittingly, exploit the ambiguity in the sense in which philosophy is a subject when they appeal to the example of Socrates to justify the recent growth in practical ethics. It is the institutional dimension of the subject (its character as a subject in the sense to which we have been attending) which protects philosophers who say that it might be permissible to kill healthy babies or to experiment on them in much the same circumstances which make it permissible to experiment on chimpanzees, from those outside the academy who would call for (at least) their resignation. But that which makes it proper for the university to protect them – indeed that which makes it obligatory for a university to protect them if it is to be true to its nature as a university – should also make them see that having a chair in practical ethics does not qualify anyone to sit on committees which decide who amongst us should be killed if the going gets tough. Socrates philosophised in the market place. He was convicted of corrupting the youth and was executed for it. His example is invoked whenever people wish to stop any talk of academics having corrupt thoughts, but it is forgotten that at no stage in his defence did Socrates plead that the charge was irrelevant to the nature of what he had been doing.[11]

It is common, not only amongst philosophers, to lament the fact that philosophers in the analytical tradition did not direct their skills to what are called substantive or first-order moral questions, and it is said they failed to do this because of the sharp distinction they had drawn between meta- and normative ethics. I have been arguing that the issue is considerably more complicated than that. I have not argued that when philosophers comment on substantive political and moral issues they go beyond being philosophers. I have argued only that they ought not to appeal to the authority they have by virtue of being competent, or even eminent in a subject. Nobody, for example, should be thought to be particularly well placed to decide whether to switch off a life support machine merely because he is a professor of medical ethics, not even if he is the director of an internationally famous bio-ethics centre.

G. E. Moore said that life had presented him with no philosophical problems, that these had come to him entirely from the writings of other philosophers.[12] There are those who sneer at this as an example of degenerate academic practice, and believe they are entitled to do so because they think they are true to Socrates. But as Wittgenstein, who had an uneasy relation to academic practice, appreciated, Moore was not an example of academic degeneracy. He was an example of academic purity. His remark captures something fundamental to philosophy as an academic subject – no academic honours are awarded on the basis of an assessment of what life taught their recipients.

It is true it is not quite so simple. Nonetheless Socrates cannot be unproblematically invoked as a standard by which to judge a philosopher like Moore. There is a permanent tension between academic practice and the example of Socrates, which is why philosophers cannot simply appeal to their authority as people who have mastered a subject to justify their entry into a discussion that requires some depth and wisdom. If they do enter it then they must not only expect, but also accept as proper, the extension of the critical vocabulary in which their remarks are to be assessed – that, for example, they are shallow, naive, callow, fatuous, or even corrupt. As things stand, those practical philosophers who have been in the forefront of the argument to relax the conditions under which it is permissible to kill people and who have created a new genre called 'practical ethics' have not made academic philosophy less insular. Quite the contrary. They have extended the arrogance and insularity of the worst kind of academic professionalism beyond the academy. Generally they show no fear or even slight anxiety at the responsibility they have assumed. They have no sense of awe in the face of the questions they have raised, and no sense of humility in the face of the traditions they condescendingly dismiss. They are aggressively without a sense of mystery and without a suspicion that anything might be too deep for their narrowly professional competence. They mistake these vices for the virtues of thinking radically, courageously and with an unremitting hostility to obscurantism.[13]

Someone will protest that the critical concepts which are relevant to the assessment of a philosophical claim ought, in the first instance, to be determined by the conceptual character of philosophical problems, and that if the conceptual character of the problems are the same for Socrates and for an academic philosopher, then the critical concepts which mark what it is to think well or badly about such problems will apply in the same way to both. He will say there may be dispute about what those critical concepts are, but it is clear at the outset that they must mark out species of *intellectual* failing, as do, for example, the concepts 'true' and 'false' and the ones that mark the various modes of valid and invalid inference. He will acknowledge that there are, of course, other considerations which bear on academic practice, more fully described as the practice of a community, but they will generate criticisms of conduct rather than thought and they must be criticisms in service to thought. He may even acknowledge that there are corrupt thoughts, but he will remark that there are books which do not make good door stops and composers who are not much good for making plants grow. Anyone, he will say, can see that these are criticisms which are secondary to the primary dimension along which books and musical compositions are judged. If this means anything, however, it means that if he suspects that his own thought is leading him to a corrupt conclusion, then that suspicion should have no weight with him. That seems to show that either he does not take the concept of corruption seriously or he thinks himself immune to it, which is just another way of not taking it seriously. He seems to want to say that, *qua* philosopher, thinking something evil or falling into corruption holds no terrors for him except insofar as it is thinking something false. But now one wants to ask, as Kierkegaard did, 'Who, or better, *what* does he think he is?'[14]

Is not that the kind of question an inquisitor would ask? The answer is no, but it cannot be flatly 'no' for I have not intended what I have said to advance an argument with the sceptic. I have wanted to stop the argument just as Anscombe wanted to stop the argument with consequentialists. That should go without saying, except that it is often objected, in a highminded tone, that saying this sort of thing does not help matters, that it is not a contribution to the discussion, or that it is not very interesting – which is true, but beside the point. Yet it would be wrong, or at any rate misleading, for me to say that I have not intended to offer anything intellectually or philosophically to the discussion of a certain kind of scepticism, that I have attacked it on another plane – the moral plane. I have intended my discussion to be an invitation to reflect on what it is to have such discussions, and on what is intellectually or philosophically relevant to them.

My question, 'What does he think he is?', was not intended rhetorically. There is an answer to it which is important and not at all obvious. I think that he believes that, *qua* philosopher, he is essentially a *res cogitans*, a mere thinking thing, but I do not mean that he believes that he is essentially a non-material substance. He may be a materialist. I mean that his understanding of what it is to think philosophically is determined by an idealisation of thinking as such, thinking abstracted from the form which life takes for any thinking thing. It is thinking as it would be for any rational being as Donagan expressed when he said that 'Reason is a rigid designator, fixed for all possible worlds, which refers to a capacity to perform acts whose contents belong to the domain of logic.'[15] The capacity to which Donagan thinks 'Reason' refers is the capacity of which I was thinking when I spoke of the capacity to draw conclusions which were merely 'blackboard conclusions'. When a philosopher says that, *qua* philosopher, he most fears error, he speaks as one who seeks to distil the *res cogitans* in himself from the impure mess which is his humanity. A *res cogitans* can no more have a corrupt mind than it can be a crank. The judgement that a thought is corrupt is external to the set of critical categories which are constitutive of it. Anscombe was trailing her humanity.

We may now see what lies behind the idea that, whatever else the sceptics may be, they are intellectually serious because they are prepared to follow reason wherever it takes them. Those who say this either do not remember, or do not notice, that the only sceptics we have who are not mere ciphers of an unargued assumption concerning the nature of intellectual seriousness are, like Thrasymachus, far from being intellectually serious. Callicles is not much better when seen in action. He is completely unworthy of the great speech with which Plato introduces him. It takes him a little longer than Thrasymachus to go off in a sulk, but not much longer. Polus is not even worth considering. And if all we have is someone described as being 'committed to rationality and who is neither timid nor stupid', then we may as well just write the arguments on a blackboard and shrug our shoulders when we are asked who would seriously put them forward.

The idea of being seriously responsive to the claims of reason means nothing unless people can seriously and without equivocation stand behind what they claim reason compels them to conclude. That is why a conclusion must be someone's conclusion in a sense more substantial than is suggested by the fact that he feels compelled to write it at the end of a piece of reasoning on a blackboard. The indivisible human being, rather than merely that part of him which has the capacity to tell what must appear at the end of the argument on the blackboard, must be able to say in all seriousness: this is what I believe. In the case of (nihilistic) moral scepticism no one has been prepared to do it. It is, therefore, nonsense to say that we have in moral scepticism a pure instance of intellectual seriousness, of a fearless commitment to seek the truth. All this might have been learnt from the Platonic dialogues in which Socrates persistently demands of his interlocutors that they stand behind their words, that they say what they seriously believe rather than what might be said, or even what they believe must be said, by someone 'committed to rationality'. Thought which issues into a mere 'blackboard conclusion', that is, a conclusion which seems inescapable when we write an argument on a blackboard, but which is a conclusion that we cannot seriously assert or even *wish* to assert, is thought that can have only the appearance of rigour. That is the lesson of the dialogical form of Plato's Socratic dialogues.

When we think of obedience to the claims of Reason we often think of Socrates. He often insisted that he and his interlocutors must follow the argument wherever it takes them. Such insistence would be pointless if the argument did not sometimes take them where they would rather not go, if it did not sometimes take them beyond what they cared to believe, beyond what was judged to be common sense and beyond what was 'ordinarily said'. It took Socrates to a place where Callicles could say without hyperbole, 'If you are serious and what you say is true then we will have human life turned completely upside down.'[16] But it never took Socrates to a place where he could not be unequivocally serious in what he said. The *res cogitans* by contrast is, amongst other things, a device used precisely to ameliorate the effect of the equivocation in anyone's profession of the sceptical conclusions of the *First Meditation*. Descartes equivocates on whether he is serious when he says that one may seriously doubt whether one is awake, for example, because he does not see clearly that he should say that Descartes the human being could not doubt it but the *res cogitans*, the *persona* of the *Meditations*, can. (The *res cogitans* is not so much a discovery of the *Second Meditation* as it is a presupposition of the project announced in the first.) The deep lesson of the dialogical form of Plato's dialogues is that the 'part of us' that is obedient to the claims of reason must be the same part of us that can be the proper respondent of another's call to seriousness – 'Tell me Socrates, are we to suppose that you are joking or in earnest?'[17]

Why is no one seriously prepared to say that justice and our sense of good and evil may be a fraud? It is not because it is false. Nor is it because it is incoherent. If these were the important categories, then there would be many people who were serious sceptics until they discovered that it was false or incoherent, and there would be at least some who are still sceptics because they do not believe that it is false or incoherent. It is interesting in this respect that there have been and still are people who would claim to be sceptical of the existence of the external world or of the existence of other minds. There is, as I have already implied, a problem about how these forms of scepticism could be seriously asserted, but it is important that people have, at least, claimed that they were sceptical about these matters. (Never mind for the moment that in the most famous first-person profession of scepticism it is unclear who or what the 'I' is.)[18] But I know of no case (I do not exclude Nietzsche) of anyone seriously asserting, in his own name, that our talk of good and evil may be through and through a fraud, even though morality seems much more vulnerable to scepticism than does 'the external world' or other minds. Moral scepticism has never found its Descartes, and even he, who ventured to doubt everything, found it 'prudent' to continue to believe the ordinary moral precepts of his day.

The reason for this should, by now, be obvious. Only someone who is corrupt can say seriously that our sense of good and evil is a fraud, and although the sceptic says only that *perhaps* it is a fraud, this 'perhaps' means nothing unless he is prepared to conclude, if the argument 'compels' him to, that it is a fraud. Philosophers could at least appear (even to themselves) to be professing a serious scepticism about the external world because of the familiar contrast they draw between a concern for truth and those concerns which make up the rest of our lives. Moral sceptics also appeal to that contrast, but its relatively transparent inadequacy is revealed in the fact that they will not use it to explain why they will not profess such scepticism in their own name.

Does this mean that we fear being wicked more than we fear being the victims of an illusion? The opposition is a bogus one. But that is not because the sceptical proposal is obviously false. That is why I emphasised that scepticism is to be rejected, not because it is false or muddled or incoherent, but because, seriously entertained,

326

it is a corruption. If we wish to emphasise that scepticism is *false* because we wish to deny the opposition the sceptic proposes between a concern for truth and a fear of thinking corrupt thoughts, then the sceptic would be right to say that this needs to be shown, and that it is not shown by saying that scepticism of this kind is corrupt. And if someone says that scepticism is *obviously* false in order to explain why we do not even seriously consider it, then he is whistling in the dark. If the sceptical arguments do anything, they show that scepticism is not obviously false. To say that the sceptic's proposal is obviously false is to step onto his ground only to refuse, stubbornly, to engage him. We may be tempted by this because it is hard to shake off the fear that the sceptic's ground is the intellectual high ground, and that he will take possession of it if we merely say that he is corrupt. The idea that he is obviously mistaken is appealing because it seems to place us on that intellectual high ground where only intellectual categories are used, while relieving us of the obligation actually to argue with him.

I said earlier that the fear of losing our sense of the reality of good and evil is a fear internal to a serious understanding of good and evil. It is therefore quite unlike the fear of having our pet theory overturned or the fear of having our prejudices undermined. These latter examples inform our sense of fears that may be in opposition to truth. The fear of having our pet theory overturned is a psychological state external to theoretical inquiry, and it is a psychological state of the same kind as the fear of admitting that we are really ill, or that the person we love no longer returns that love. But if someone says that he fears his tendency to think that morality is an illusion, then we misunderstand the nature of his fear, if we say that he must have the courage to think it through and face the fact that it might be so. His fear is not the fear of facing a painful truth. Yet that is how it is constantly represented.

There is a final consideration which at first seems close to those advanced in defence of scepticism, but which is really quite different. It appeals to a powerful inclination to say that the pursuit of truth *cannot* be evil and that a pure concern for truth cannot lead us into evil. That is not even plausible if we are thinking of a passionate drive to discover certain truths, for some of the doctors who operated on living human beings in the Nazi concentration camps may

327

have been in the grip of such a passion. To make it appear plausible we must speak of truth in the singular and perhaps even with a capital 'T'. But then we may have achieved a degree of plausibility at the expense of obscurantism.

In Chapter 15, I quoted Simone Weil speaking of her intellectual vocation. I shall quote it again here so we have it before us:

> The degree of intellectual honesty which is obligatory for me, by reason of my particular vocation, demands that my thought should be indifferent to all ideas without exception – it must be equally welcoming and equally reserved with regard to every one of them. Water is indifferent in this way to the objects which fall into it. It does not weigh them; it is they which weigh themselves, after a certain time of oscillation.[19]

The image is beautiful, but the thought, though edifying, can no more be taken literally than Orwell's unqualified praise for Gandhi. If Weil were 'equally welcoming and equally reserved with regard to every idea', then she would seriously consider things which could only be seriously considered by a crank, or by someone incorrigibly gullible. Then she would not be fit for the intellectual vocation to which she was called.

Why are we edified by the absolute versions of such statements? Because, I think, they represent a certain picture of purity. Their power usually depends on images of obedience and submission – to Truth, to the claims of Reason, to the Argument wherever it may lead us. Listen again to Kolnai:

> In our rational operations . . . we do constantly overcome our subjective biases and predeterminations, surmount our subjectivity, deliver up the kingdom of our intellect to its lawful Sovereign, the Object; briefly, in a sense, give the lie to the dictum that 'nobody can leap over his own shadow'.[20]

But the question we need to ask is how much of what Kolnai counts as part of our shadow conditions our understanding of those disciplines which constitute our sense of what it is to 'deliver up the Kingdom of our intellect to its lawful Sovereign, the Object'. Or, to make the same point in connection with a contemporary philosopher: when David Wiggins says that 'the real mark of a state that is truth oriented is simply that the state should be one which in virtue of being the mental state that it is, seeks to be determined by causes that are not accidental relative to its content', then we want to know what counts as being accidental to its content. That question partners another one: how thin can our conception of such a 'truth oriented' subject be? One would like to say: as thin as the Object allows. That seems to put the emphasis in the right place – on the determination of the thinking subject by the nature of thought and its object. Is that not what lies behind the images of obedience?

At one level, it is – the level at which the metaphor of obedience has permanent relevance to the characterisation of the intellect and the forms of its discipline. At another level of reflection, however, we must say that it is not so simple, that (as Wittgenstein showed us) any intelligible conception of the subject (the thinker), the object (what he is thinking about) and the range of critical concepts under which he judges whether he thinks well or badly are mutually interdependent. At least, so I suggested when I criticised the conception of a thinking subject fit to draw only blackboard conclusions.

Plato gives an example of a 'state of mind' being determined by causes accidental to its object, and also of what it is to 'deliver up our kingdom of the intellect to its lawful Sovereign, the Object'. The passage I have in mind is so fine I shall quote it at length. Socrates is speaking to Callicles:

> Each one of us is in love with two objects – I with Alcibiades, son of Cleinias, and philosophy, and you also with two, the Athenian demos and Demos son of Pyrilampes. Now I notice on every occasion that, clever though you may be, whatever your favourite says and however he describes things to be, you cannot contradict him, but constantly shift to and fro. In the assembly, if any statement of yours is contradicted by the Athenian demos, you change about and say what it wishes, and you behave much the same towards the handsome young son of Pyrilampes. For you are incapable of resisting the words and designs of your favourite, with the result that if anyone should be astonished at the absurdities that you utter again and again under their spell, you would probably say if you were willing to tell the truth that unless someone stops your favourites from saying as they do, you yourself too will never stop speaking thus.

329

You must think yourself bound then to hear much the same things from me, and do not be astonished at my speaking thus, but stop my love philosophy, from saying what she does. It is she, my friend, who says what you now hear from me, and she is far less unstable than my other love, for the son of Cleinias is at the mercy now of one argument, now of another, but philosophy holds always to the same and she says what now astonishes you, and you were here when the words were spoken. You must either prove against her . . . or if you leave this [previous argument] unrefuted, then by the dog that is god in Egypt, Callicles himself will not agree with you, Callicles, but will be at variance with you throughout your life. And yet, I think it better, my good friend, that my lyre should be discordant and out of tune, and any chorus I might train, and that the majority of mankind should disagree with me, rather than that I, who am but one man, should be out of tune with and contradict myself.[21]

The image of obedience is there. He will do as his love bids him, and he will be true to her 'though the mass of mankind should disagree with and contradict him'. His obedience is a kind of fidelity. Not anything intelligent can be faithful. A human being can be, but a *res cogitans* could no more be faithful than it could be sober. Are these merely picturesque ways of speaking?

The answer depends on what non-rhetorical sense we make of the ways in which people have spoken of the love of truth throughout our tradition since Socrates. Descartes appealed to it to explain the extraordinary nature of his project, and it underlies the edifying power of the quotations from Weil and Orwell. It all depends on how seriously we mean to speak of a *love* of truth and what we take its object to be (it obviously cannot be *truths*). Plato took it seriously but hardly anyone has after him. Someone who really means to speak of love rather than merely a passion or a concern or a drive (we mostly speak of these interchangeably) will find his way to different conceptions of purity, obedience and impersonality, than those which are interdependent with the conception of thinking idealised in the *res cogitans*. But that is another project. It might offer a deepened understanding of the thought that the love of truth is incompatible with evil, but it will be far from anything proposed by those who urge that Thrasymachus has a point.

330

Afterword

In the chapter entitled 'Individuality' I tried to explain why I believe it is right to say that many of the slave owners in the Southern States of the USA saw their slaves as 'less than fully human'. I was not then concerned to give an account of racially based slavery. Rather, I wanted to illustrate the role that the concept of a human being should play in our efforts to understand some of the most basic of our moral concepts.

When I wrote that chapter, however, I was only partially aware of how rich and also how radical the lessons of an analysis (conceptual) of a certain kind of racism can be for moral philosophy. In other works, particularly in *A Common Humanity*, I have tried to show how truly radical those lessons are, but my attempts, I must confess, appear to have failed to radicalise most of my readers. I persist with that attempt here because I hope that, more fully articulated, it will enable the reader to understand better what is at issue in the chapter on individuality and also in my discussion of Peter Singer in Chapter 4. I hope to show more clearly something about the epistemic and conceptual space which enables some of my satirical remarks to work as they do and in which we may be moved to change quite radically our beliefs about our moral obligations, in the one case towards people who have been the victims of racial denigration, in the other towards people who are destitute but who live far from us, in other countries. If I succeed, I will also have succeeded in showing the interdependencies between our sense of what it is seriously to wrong someone and our sense of someone who, as I put it in the last paragraph of this afterword, is capable

331

of an ever deepening, individuating responsiveness to the defining facts of the human condition.

In *A Common Humanity* I discussed the example of a woman whom I called 'M'. It is a (true) story of a woman whose son had recently fallen to his death from a cliff. Only a few days after his death she was watching television, where she saw a documentary that showed Vietnamese mothers grieving over their children who had been killed in American bombing raids. At first she leaned forward in her chair towards the television as though to express her sense that she and the Vietnamese mothers shared a common affliction. After a minute or two she sat back and said, 'But it's different for them. They can just have more.'

By themselves, her words will not tell us what she meant. To understand that, we need to know some things she did not mean. She did not mean that she was physically incapable of having more children. Nor did she mean that, because the Vietnamese had for many years suffered the traumas of war, they had become brutalised, losing the sense they had (and that 'we' have) of what it means to lose one's child. Had she meant that, she would have believed that when life returned to normal for them, they might recover an understanding of what it means to love and to lose a child. Fully in possession of that understanding, they could not have more, just as she cannot. Or, she might have accepted that she should not have generalised so hastily, that only some of them had been brutalised to such a degree. But her remark, intended to apply to all Vietnamese, is not what we normally think of as an empirical generalisation. It expressed a certain kind of racism. She meant that the *differences* between 'us' and 'them' went much deeper than could be accounted for by the effects on 'them' of even terrible misfortune. That is what informs her sense of the *difference* between 'us' and 'them'.[1]

The grammar (if I might put it that way) of her (mis)perception is common to a certain kind of racism – racism directed against those whose skin colour is different, especially when it is under no pressure to rationalise those misperceptions by appeal to the kind of stereotypes that take the form of empirical generalisations. James Isdell was Protector of Aborigines in Western Australia in the 1930s. There he administered a programme in which children of mixed blood were taken (usually forcibly) from their Aboriginal mothers and placed in circumstances in which (it was hoped) most of them would have children with lower-class whites. The architects of his programme believed that Aborigines were genetically such that there would never be 'throw backs' – that no black baby would appear in later generations. At that time the idea behind the programme was, as one of its architects put it, to 'breed out the color'. Brutally administered, it was, for the most part, saturated with racist contempt for the Aborigines. Responding to the question, how did he feel taking children from their mothers, Isdell answered that he 'would not hesitate for a moment to separate any half caste from its Aboriginal mother, no matter how frantic her momentary grief might be at the time'. They 'soon forget their offspring', he explained.

Again, those words – 'they soon forget their offspring' – can mean different things in different mouths. Coming from Isdell, they were an expression of his racist disdain for the Aborigines and, as with M, they marked his sense of the kind of gulf that existed between 'them' and 'us'. 'Our' children are irreplaceable; 'theirs' are not. Taking their remarks as expressions of a certain kind of racism, we can see that the attitude they betrayed extends to virtually every aspect of the lives of the Aborigines and the Vietnamese. Nothing, M and Isdell thought, goes deep with 'them'; not their loves, nor their griefs, nor their joys. In a perfectly natural sense of the expression, they saw the victims of their racism as 'less than fully human'.

They knew, however, that Aborigines and Vietnamese form attachments, are mortal and vulnerable to misfortune, that they are rational, have interests, that indeed they are persons (as philosophers tend to define them when they discuss whether machines or dolphins or foetuses are persons). Isdell did not suffer from ignorance of the facts about the victims of their denigration. (I have in mind that workaday conception of facts that a judge appeals to when she says to a witness who is perhaps too emotional, or who is given to literary embellishment, 'Stick to the facts, please!') Like M, he suffered a kind of blindness to the meaning of what they did and suffered. Although the grief of the women who had lost their children was visible and audible to him, he did not see in the women's faces or hear in their voices grief that could lacerate their souls and mark them for the rest of their days. It was literally unintelligible to M and Isdell that sexuality, death and the fact that at any moment we may lose all that gives sense to our lives could mean to 'them' what it does it us – unintelligible in the same way that it is unintelligible that a face that looked like the Black and White Minstrel Show's caricature of an Afro-American face could express the magnificence and misery of Othello. The impossibility we encounter when we realise that we cannot cast a face that looks like the Black and White Minstrel Show face to play Othello, because it is *unintelligible* that such a face could express the necessary depth of feeling, is neither a moral nor a logical impossibility. Nor, however, is it merely psychological impossibility, even if it is true that to see actual black faces like that is always the expression of (an unconscious) psychological motive. Not even God could see in the Black and White Minstrel Show's face the expressive possibilities needed to play Othello. To see that is to see that the generality expressed in the belief that faces like that cannot play Othello is not an empirical generalisation. For the same reason, it is to see that insofar as he saw the expressive possibilities in an Aborigine's face as being limited in the way they are in a Black and White Minstrel Show face, Isdell did not give voice to an empirical generalisation when he said that Aborigines 'soon forget their offspring'.

People like M and Isdell can change. When they do, it is often because they have lived with the people they denigrated, perhaps because one of their children married one of 'them'. If experiences of that kind made them realise that they had been terribly mistaken, does that not show that they did, after all, intend their denigratory remarks as empirical generalisations? I do not want to argue about the meanings of the words 'empirical' and 'experience'. I do, however, want to draw attention to an important distinction. It is the distinction between how racists like Isdell come to think of themselves as having been mistaken about what losing a child can mean to the victims of their denigration, and how they might come to acknowledge that they were mistaken in believing that blacks have significantly lower IQs, are lazy, have inordinate sexual appetites, are promiscuous, have rhythm in their blood and are cruel to animals (to list an arbitrary number of stereotypes). Those stereotypes do have the grammar of empirical generalisations. Even when they are, in ways characteristic of racists, psychologically so entrenched as to be beyond rational correction, they are like beliefs that Germans are efficient, that Italians are good lovers and that it is hard to get a decent meal in an English restaurant. But coming, through living with a people, to see dignity in faces that had all looked alike to us, to see the full range of human expressiveness in them, to hear suffering that lacerates the soul in someone's cry or in their music, or to see it in their art, to hear all the depth of language in sounds that had seemed merely comical to us – all or any of that is quite different from coming to acknowledge that, for example, they score well on IQ tests. We do not discover the full humanity of a racially denigrated people in books by social scientists, not, at any rate, if those books merely contain knowledge of the kind that might be included in encyclopaedias. If we discover it by reading, then it is in plays, novels and poetry – not in science but in art. That, at any rate, is part of the argument of Chapter 9.

I have elaborated at some length the conceptual structure (as I would put it, rather than, say, the phenomenology) of a certain kind of racist perception because I believe it has radical implications for moral philosophy. For ease of exposition, I will restrict myself to M in drawing out those implications.

It is clear, I hope, that M's belief (if 'belief' is the right word) that she cannot quickly have more children whereas 'they' can, and the further differences that implies, is fundamental to her sense of who she is. My point is not that for psychological reasons she must define herself against an alien 'other' (though that may be true). It is that her sense of who she is has been formed within the conceptual space from which she excludes the Vietnamese. It is a space in which she explores – and may think of herself as obliged, under pain of superficiality, to explore – what it really means to love, to grieve, to be courageous in the face of misfortune, to face death with lucidity, and so on. With an effort of imagination, M might acknowledge that protracted suffering could brutalise her to the point where she no longer saw her children, or anyone else, as irreplaceable. Or, she might acknowledge that an accident could leave her feeble-minded, as it did her neighbour who did have a second child after her first died, in much the same spirit as she bought another pup when her dog died. Such acknowledgements are within the reach of her powers of imagination because they depend only on an imaginative sympathy with those who would have been like her had they not been struck by misfortune. But the Vietnamese are not, in her eyes, as they are because they have suffered misfortune. She could no more imagine how, in different circumstances, they could be like her than she could imagine herself to be the kind of person she sees as appropriately caricatured by the Black and White Minstrel face. Though it may at first seem strange, it is important to see that M does not see the Vietnamese as shallow. Rather, from her perspective, they do not exist in the conceptual space in which attributions of depth and shallowness make sense.

Essential, therefore, to her sense of her self is her understanding of what it means to be 'one of us'. That, of course, is a determination of herself as a person of a certain kind (one whose extension is necessarily indeterminate, I think), but the kind is distinguished from the one to which she thinks the Vietnamese belong by the fact that (barring misfortune) its members can rise to an individuating responsiveness to the meaning of what they do and suffer. That, I think, is an important part of what we mean when we say that each person is a unique perspective on the world, and means more than that each person is a centre of consciousness.

I must now try to explain what I mean when I speak of an 'individuating responsiveness'. Weary perhaps of condolences offered by people whose words, though generous and well intentioned, mean little to her, M may come across someone who causes her to exclaim, 'At last someone to talk to!' The joy of finding 'someone to talk to' is the joy of conversation that is open to the independent reality of the other, in which its participants speak as individuals from their experiences, having, as Kierkegaard put it, lived their own lives and nobody else's. Each has something to say in a sense that implies that each has found the voice in which to say it. In a number of places in *Good and Evil*, I try to show why pleasure of such conversation is not the pleasure we often find in novelty or in hearing something we had never heard before. It is especially wrong to think of scintillating personalities, bent on distinguishing themselves. One gets more of the hang of it if one thinks of the times when one says that though one had heard certain words many times before, it was only when so and so spoke, that one sat up and listened, and for the first time understood what they meant. Such experiences can be transforming, but the concepts we need to articulate why are quite different from those that articulate the excitement of hearing new theories, or the charm and power of charismatic personalities.

When we find wisdom in words or deeds because a particular person has spoken or done them; when the authority of someone's speech or practical example moves us to take seriously something we had perhaps not taken seriously before, or to find depth where we had not before, then, usually over time and sometimes not even very consciously, we critically assess whether we were right to believe the words to be wise words, right to have been moved as we were. Then we must try to assure ourselves that we did not yield our assent only because we were naive, or callow, or sentimental, or liable to pathos, or gullible and so on. To try to be lucid about these matters is to make our thought answerable to a range of critical concepts that is more extensive than those to which factual thought or conceptual analysis (neutrally conceived) is answerable, and that is also impersonal in a way that is different from the impersonality of thought about facts (again as conceived by judges) or thoughts about the grammar (the logic, the conceptual structure) of various ethical positions. It is the kind of impersonality that is achieved when we have submitted to the disciplines with which we try to rid our thought of banality, of second-hand opinions, of cliché, of sentimentality, of our vulnerability to pathos and so on. In what only appears to be a paradox, that kind of un-selfing requires one to become an individual who is truly responsive to the demands of conversation.

In order to be critically true to what moves us we must be properly responsive to the disciplined individuality of the Other as he or she is present in the speech or actions that move us. To speak here of the Other as present to us in ways that are internal to the authoritative force of what he or she has said or done is to say that necessarily the authority and our critical acceptance of it are personal. The truism that something moves us, to the extent that it 'speaks to us', is an expression of it. Something speaks to us insofar as we hear in it the disciplined individuality of its speaker. But of course, in rising to that, in responding to what moves me, I must acknowledge and submit to the same individualising disciplines which made the Other authoritatively present in her words or deeds and which gave them her 'voice'.

337

There is only one way to do that. It is by submitting to the disciplines demanded by the critical categories that both tell us and determine what it is to be rightly moved. This is true whether we think in the presence of what moves us or in remembrance of it. If I am right, then the public character of that thought is best conceived as a dialogical engagement between people who must speak personally in ways I have tried to make clear, here and in the main body of the book. To put the point in the idiom of the philosopher who was one of the first to see this and who has been much misunderstood: in responding properly to what moves me, I must make myself I to someone's Thou. That is an essential part of what determines the common-ness of the conceptual space from which M excluded the Vietnamese.[2] It is, I think, what we mean by 'experience' when we say that M and Isdell may change when they live with the people whom they have denigrated, and thus learn from experience that these people are not as they had previously believed them to be. And it is to the concept of experience that we appeal when we say that wisdom comes only through the experience of a life seriously reflected upon.

If M could see the Vietnamese as possible participants in the kind of conversation I described just now, her perception of them would no longer be distorted by racism. Excluded, in her eyes, from living their lives in such a conversational space, the Vietnamese do not appear to her to have 'a life' in the sense we mean when we say that biography aims to disclose the identity of the subject whose life-story it tells. Unless we thought we could, by revealing the nature of their individuated responsiveness to the big facts of human life, reveal the distinctive presence in the world of their subjects, we would not, I think, write biographies. We do not write biographies of animals, though we tell stories about them, because it makes no sense to speak of an animal taking the wrong turning in life, facing life honestly, without consoling fantasies, despairing of life, or rejoicing in it, cursing the day it was born and so on. From M's perspective the animals are on one side. 'We' are on the other. In between, in a conceptual twilight zone, marked as such by the inverted commas with which she qualifies what they do and suffer, are the Vietnamese.

Much (perhaps most) of our reflection on life and morality occurs in a conceptual space of the kind I have been trying to delineate as the one in which M develops her sense of who she is. In *Good and Evil* (and more explicitly in *The Philosopher's Dog*) I call it 'the realm of meaning'. Because that realm is partly defined by the fact that reflection in it is in idioms in which form and content cannot be separated, understanding of meaning (as I have been speaking of it) is more like understanding in literature than in science or metaphysics.

Now I am in a position to outline the implications of M's example for moral philosophy.

For so long as M perceives the Vietnamese as she does, she cannot, I think, believe 'they' can be wronged as 'we' can, which is not to say that she believes that they cannot be wronged at all. She might deplore cruelty done to them, but if she did, it would be as some white slave owners in the USA deplored the cruelty of their slave-owning neighbours while finding it unintelligible that slavery it-self constituted an injustice. Compassion (or sympathy, as Hume thought of it), M's example makes clear, depends for its character on a person's conception of what elicits it in her. Elicited by those whom we regard as less than fully human, compassion is one (kind of) thing. Elicited by those whom we regard (whom we would never dream of not regarding) as fully human, it is another. If that is so, compassion cannot take us to a sense of a common humanity with others, for it depends on it.

Earlier I observed that M and Isdell saw quite clearly that the victims of their denigration are rational agents, are persons, have interests, are vulnerable to misfortune, have sympathies, are mortal and so on. Why then should we not say that they saw all they needed to realise how terribly mistaken they were? If M were a philoso-pher, might she not have realised that, because the Vietnamese were rational agents, one could deduce in, Kantian fashion, moral imper-atives prescribing duties and obligations owed to them of the same kind as are owed to us?

Given the history of philosophy, that question is irresistible, because M and Isdell readily attribute to the victims of their racist condescension all the raw materials from which philosophers have, for the most part, constructed theories of morality. But, if I am right, their example puts that philosophical tradition seriously to the ques-tion. To think that one could construct, from what M attributes to the Vietnamese, rules of conduct or a list of virtues, consistent with our sense of what it means to wrong someone, and therefore consistent with the distinctive kind of authority and seriousness morality has for us, is to think that one can bypass all that, for M, marks the difference in kind between 'us' and 'them'. The point is not that she thinks they cannot be wronged. If that were all we need not be especially troubled by what is so obviously a mistake. The point is that we can see – or, at any rate, it looks so plausible to us – that while she sees the Vietnamese as she does, she cannot think they can be wronged as we can be.

Even if it were true, therefore, that merely from the premise that someone is a rational agent one could derive imperatives that would be binding on all rational agents and that coincide with the imperatives we call 'moral', one would still not have conveyed what it means to fail (morally) to rise to them. What it means to wrong someone, in a way that M finds unintelligible that 'we' could wrong 'them', will still be – I suspect *entirely* – unaccounted for. That is why it is probably no accident that philosophers who operate only with what M can grant to the Vietnamese constantly appeal, despite themselves, to expressions whose associations in natural language go far beyond the conceptual resources allowed by their theories. Instead of speaking only of persons or rational agents, for example, they will avail themselves of the rich associations that attach to our ways of speaking of human beings and of our common humanity. Naturally one wonders what is really doing the conceptual work.

When Wittgenstein expressed his doubts about the possibility of private ostensive definition he remarked, 'When one says "he gave a name to his sensation" one forgets that a great deal of stage setting in the language is presupposed if the mere act of naming is to make sense'.[3] I am making a similar point about many philosophical accounts of morality: we forget what sets the stage for our sense of what it means to wrong someone, of the kind of seriousness morality has for us and, therefore, of what makes a principle a moral principle and what we prize in the virtues. To be sure, we disagree about the kind of seriousness distinctive to morality. Socrates believed that nothing mattered more than to live virtuously – and for him, nothing really meant nothing. Few people believe that. But we all understand, I think, that when a person grievously wrongs someone, she might feel that she could no longer live with herself. Remorse might haunt her all her days. Shame for one's vices can be devastating and we can think about good and evil, virtue and vice, in ways that appear to be capable of deepening without limit.

Aristotle advised those who wanted to know what justice is to look to the just man. But of course, one had to have eyes to see. In detailing the difference between the conceptual space M takes herself to inhabit from that which she believes the Vietnamese inhabit, I have been trying to detail what is involved in 'having eyes to see'. To 'have eyes to see', one must live and think in conceptual space in which examples of what others say and do can speak authoritatively to us, can deepen our sense of the virtues, of good and evil and, more generally, of what it means to live a human life. To do that, one must live and think in a conceptual space in which attributions of depth and shallowness make sense. For that reason, none of the Vietnamese could be an example to M in the sense that Aristotle assumed his audience to understand when he told them to look to the example of the just man if they wanted to understand what justice is.

To see others as capable of a reflective, ever deepening, individuating responsiveness to the defining facts of the human condition – our mortality, our sexuality, our vulnerability to misfortune – is to see them as inhabiting with us the space of the kind of common understanding that we often take to be necessary if we are to treat others justly. It is the kind we have in mind when we urge upon others and ourselves an acknowledgement of our common humanity with all the peoples of the earth. When, as philosophers, we discuss the variety of ways human beings live and value, we often assume they live and value in the space of that kind of common understanding.

Notes

Preface to the second edition

1 R. F. Holland, *Against Empiricism* (Oxford: Blackwell, 1980), ii.
2 Christopher Hitchens, *The Missionary Position: Mother Teresa in Theory and Practice* (London: Verso, 1995).
3 Raimond Gaita, *A Common Humanity: Thinking about Love and Truth and Justice* (London and New York: Routledge, 2000).
4 Hannah Arendt, *Eichmann in Jersusalem: A Report on the Banality of Evil* (New York: The Viking Press 1964).
5 Peter Winch, *Ethics and Action* (London: Routledge & Kegan Paul, 1972), p. 172.
6 Simone Weil, 'The Love of God and Affliction' in *Science, Necessity and the Love of God* (Oxford: Oxford University Press, 1869) p.81.
7 Simone Weil, 'Forms of the Implicit Love of God' in *Waiting on God* (Glasgow: Collins Fountain Books, 1977) p. 100.
8 Alan Donagan, *The Theory of Morality*, (Chicago, Ill.: University of Chicago Press, 1971) p. 240.
9 Rush Rhees, *Moral Questions*, edited by D. Z. Phillips (Basingstoke: Macmillan, 1999).
10 Raimond Gaita, *The Philosopher's Dog*, (London: Routledge, 2002).
11 Phillipa Foot, *Natural Goodness*, (Oxford: Clarendon Press, 2001).
12 Simone Weil, *First and Last Notebooks*, (New York: Oxford University Press, 1970) p. 211.

1 Evil and unconditional respect

1 Quoted from George Steiner, *Language and Silence* (Harmondsworth: Penguin, 1969), p. 191.
2 Plato, *Gorgias*, 473c, trans. Walter Hamilton (Harmondsworth: Penguin, 1976).

3 The sense in which I think it is mysterious will emerge more clearly later in the book, especially in Chapter 4. It is worth noting at this stage that it can be a dangerous idea. It becomes so sometimes (in my judgement) in the hands of Elie Wiesel: 'I have always placed the Holocaust on a mystical level, beyond human understanding' (*A Jew Today* (New York: Vintage Books, 1979, p. 46)). He goes on to say: 'I have quarrelled with friends for making easy apologies and comparisons in that domain. The concentration-camp phenomenon eludes the philosopher as much as it does the novelist, and it may not be dealt with lightly.' It is the choice of the word 'mystical' that troubles me.

4 Simone Weil, 'Human Personality', in G. A. Panichas (ed.), *The Simone Weil Reader* (New York: David McKay Co. Inc., 1977), p. 325.

5 Hannah Arendt, *Eichmann in Jerusalem: A Report on the Banality of Evil* (New York: The Viking Press, 1964), p. 5.

2 The scope of academic moral philosophy

1 Mark Platts, *Ways of Meaning* (London: Routledge & Kegan Paul, 1979), p. 243.

2 Because of the influence of J. L. Mackie's *Ethics: Inventing Right and Wrong* (Harmondsworth: Penguin Books, 1977), moral scepticism is often taken to be, at least, scepticism about whether moral judgements are true or false. I shall argue, in Chapter 16, that this is not an important issue and that it is no serious form of scepticism.

3 Renford Bambrough, *Moral Scepticism and Moral Knowledge* (London: Routledge & Kegan Paul, 1979), p. 15.

4 Stanley Cavell, *The Claim of Reason* (Oxford: Clarendon Press, 1979), p. 269.

5 Stuart Hampshire, *Morality and Conflict* (Oxford: Blackwell, 1983), p. 153.

6 F. R. Leavis, *Nor Shall My Sword* (London: Chatto & Windus, 1972).

7 G. E. M. Anscombe, *Collected Philosophical Papers* (Oxford: Blackwell, 1981), vol. III. By 'in advance' she meant in advance of actually being in a situation that inclined one to that belief. To think in the situation, she said, is just to be an understandably 'tempted' human being.

8 Bernard Williams, *Ethics and the Limits of Philosophy* (London: Fontana, 1985), chapter 10.

9 *Ibid.*, p. 19. The point is also made by John McDowell, 'The Role of Eudaimonia in Aristotle's Ethics', in A. Rorty (ed.), *Essays on Aristotle's Ethics* (Berkeley: University of California Press, 1980). Peter Winch makes a similar point in a way which is not, I think, vulnerable to my objection to Williams, in 'Universalizability', in *Ethics and Action* (London: Routledge & Kegan Paul, 1972).

10 Williams, *Ethics*, p. 20.
11 Plato, *Gorgias*, 481c, trans. Walter Hamilton (Harmondsworth: Penguin, 1976).
12 *Ibid.*, 485 a–e.
13 *Ibid.*, 487e. This is not inconsistent with my earlier claim that Socrates did not take seriously the question 'How should one live?' as often as he asked it. Sometimes he did, and I think this is one of those occasions. I do not, however, believe that it was a serious question for him whether it is better to suffer evil than to do it.

3 Mortal men and rational beings

1 Gregory Vlastos, 'The Individual as an Object of Love', in *Platonic Studies* (Princeton: Princeton University Press, 1973), p. 31.
2 Alan Donagan, *The Theory of Morality* (Chicago: University of Chicago Press, 1977), p. 240.
3 Aristotle, *Eudemian Ethics*, Book I.
4 Donagan, *Theory*, pp. 65–6.
5 *Ibid.*, p. 232.
6 *Ibid.*, p. 235.
7 Augustine, *Confessions*, trans. E. B. Pudsey (London: Dent & Sons, 1975), p. 270.
8 Simone Weil, *The Need for Roots* (London: Routledge & Kegan Paul, 1976), p. 242.
9 John Passmore, for example, misunderstands this when he says of Weil's view: 'To love a subject, singling it out as love does, is on this view, a threat to the love of God.' See his *The Philosophy of Teaching* (London: Duckworth, 1980), p. 195.
10 It would be fruitful to go through Donagan's entire discussion to see which concepts really do the work. When he discusses suicide, for example, he says that 'one may not hold one's life cheap' (*Theory*, p. 76). That way of putting it has many resonances and could be developed in a number of ways, but it is not clear why killing oneself while knowing oneself to be a rational creature should count as 'holding one's life cheap'.
11 John Rawls, *A Theory of Justice* (Oxford: Oxford University Press, 1973), p. 47.
12 I have already indicated the direction in Chapter 2. For further discussion see Chapter 15.
13 Stuart Hampshire, *Morality and Conflict* (Oxford: Blackwell, 1983), p. 23.
14 *Ibid.*, p. 28.
15 *Ibid.*, p. 106.
16 Plato, in a number of dialogues but see especially *Gorgias*.

17 Stanley Cavell, *The Claim of Reason* (Oxford: Clarendon Press, 1979), p. 269.
18 Plato, *Gorgias*, 469.
19 *Ibid.*, 481c.
20 R. F. Hare, *Freedom and Reason* (Oxford: Oxford University Press, 1963).
21 Rush Rhees, *Without Answers* (London: Routledge & Kegan Paul, 1969), p. 56.
22 Chapter 8.
23 Bernard Williams, *Ethics and the Limits of Philosophy* (London: Fontana, 1985), Chapter 10.
24 D. H. Lawrence, 'Pornography and Obscenity' in *Phoenix* (London, 1966), p. 675.
25 See Chapters 15 and 16.
26 Immanuel Kant, *Groundwork of the Metaphysics of Morals,* trans. H. J. Paton (London: Hutchinson, 1969), p. 89.

4 Remorse and its lessons

1 The matter is sometimes discussed in relation to Oedipus. It is clear in Sophocles' play that Oedipus feels remorse when he discovers that he murdered his father and married his mother. Yet he did both unintentionally and because of non-culpable ignorance. To be sure, the chorus does not blame him: it pities him, but it pities him for what he has morally become. There are many who would say that if he acted in non-culpable ignorance, then remorse is rationally inappropriate. But if we ask why that should be so, I know of no answer which does not, in the end, beg the question about the connection between responsibility and blame.
2 Immanuel Kant, *The Groundwork of the Metaphysic of Morals*, trans. H. J. Paton (London: Hutchinson, 1958), p. 294.
3 Aristotle, *Nicomachean Ethics*, trans. W. D. Ross, Book 6, chapters 8–12.
4 Simone Weil, 'The Love of God and Affliction', in *On Science, Necessity and the Love of God* (London: Oxford University Press, 1968).
5 Isak Dinesen, quoted in Hannah Arendt, *The Human Condition* (Chicago: University of Chicago Press, 1958).
6 Brian O'Shaughnessy, 'Observation and the Will', *Journal of Philosophy* 60 (14) (1963), p. 368.
7 Iris Murdoch, *The Sovereignty of Good* (London: Routledge & Kegan Paul, 1970).
8 Bernard Williams, 'Moral Luck', in *Moral Luck* (Cambridge: Cambridge University Press, 1981).

9 See, for example, 'War and Massacre' or 'Ruthlessness in Public Life',
   in Thomas Nagel, *Mortal Questions* (Cambridge: Cambridge University
   Press, 1979).
10 Ludwig Wittgenstein, *Philosophical Investigations* (Oxford: Basil
   Blackwell, 1963), Part 1, § 287.
11 Peter Singer, *Practical Ethics* (Cambridge: Cambridge University Press,
   1979), p. 162.
12 *Ibid.*, p. 167.
13 Søren Kierkegaard, *Purity of Heart Is to Will One Thing*, trans. Douglas
   V. Steere (New York: Harper Torchbook, 1956), p. 42.
14 In what follows, I shall explore what I think Socrates is saying.
   Although I shall say 'Socrates said this' and 'Socrates thought that', I
   do not claim exegetical authority for my remarks. Moreover, what I say
   goes contrary to most current scholarly opinion. I would, however, offer
   the following considerations in support of my interpretation. First, it
   treats Socrates as though he meant what he said – that it is better to
   suffer evil than to do it and that the worst thing that could befall
   someone is to become an evildoer – and he was not merely trying to
   point to hitherto unexpected consequences of evildoing. If Socrates
   meant what, for example, Terry Irwin – *Plato's Moral Theory* (Oxford:
   Clarendon Press, 1977) – says he does (that virtue is needed to achieve
   independently desirable goods), then it is only in a gratuitously
   misleading sense that Socrates claims that the worst thing someone can
   suffer is the evil of their own deeds. On Irwin's account, the worst thing
   someone can suffer is the loss of those independently desirable goods.
   I would say that the pathos of the discussion with Polus depends on
   that not being so. Secondly, what I say does justice to the moral and
   spiritual distance between Polus and Socrates – the moral and spiritual
   distance between their understandings of life, its meaning and morality's
   place in it. If I understand many of the commentators, they think that
   distance could be bridged if Polus assented unequivocally to an argument of a purely discursive kind. Polus convinced that way would, I
   think, not be very different from Polus unconvinced (see Chapter 15).
   But what a difference there is between Polus thus convinced and
   Socrates! I acknowledge that raises the question: 'What role, then, does
   that kind of argument have?' But that should be a genuine question
   rather than a rhetorical one.
      Irwin said that Socrates was concerned to find a 'rational justifica-
   tion' for morality. Gregory Vlastos said that 'Socrates lived by a faith
   that he mistook for knowledge' (Gregory Vlastos, 'Socrates' in *Socrates*
   (New York: Anchor Books, 1971)). I shall deal with these points in
   turn. To my knowledge, Socrates does not say that he is concerned with
   a 'rational justification' of virtue, nor does he accuse Polus or Callicles
   of irrationality. He says that there is something they do not *understand*,

and that is different. No doubt Irwin would say that the search for a rational justification is the evident assumption of Socrates' practice. I think it is not evident. What Socrates is doing must be determined by an overall understanding of what he is saying. Irwin agrees with Polus in thinking that you can know what evil is and yet dispute whether the evildoer is harmed in doing it. Similarly, Polus thinks that you can understand what evil is yet not pity the evildoer. I think that Socrates denies both. If that is right, then you cannot be brought to pity the evildoer through discursive argument. It depends where one thinks the centre of gravity lies in the argument with Polus – whether one thinks it lies in his incredulity when he exclaims 'What? Does happiness depend entirely on that!' [whether or not one is just] (*Gorgias* 470e) or in the curious argument at 474cff.

Did Socrates misunderstand himself, then, when he argued as he did with Polus? That is what I say should be a genuine and not a rhetorical question. Vlastos thinks that he did. That is why he said that 'Socrates lived by a faith that he mistook for knowledge.' He is right to say that there are problems to do with the relation between the *persona(e)* of Socrates as a character given to us in Plato's dialogues and Socratic philosophy. But these two – the *persona* and the 'arguments' – must both figure in an interpretative dialectic. Their relation must emerge in the inevitably controversial testing of one against the other, as must Plato's relation to them.

That introduces the third consideration that I would advance for what I say about Socrates. He said at his trial, 'But you too, my judges, must face death with good hope and remember the one truth, that a good man cannot suffer any evil in life or after death' (*Apology* 41D). The problem is how to place that in an understanding of his philosophy. Perhaps Vlastos would not place it. Perhaps he would say it belongs not with the philosophy but with the *persona*. I would place it centrally.

Socrates says that 'it is the one truth'. Perhaps not too much should be made of that, but I would make at least this of it: it seems close to what he said in *Gorgias*. Yet it is hard to see how a functional understanding of the virtues will take one even near to it, for it speaks of a certain demeanour in the face of affliction and of the light that an understanding of the ethical can throw on our sufferings if they threaten despair. A functional construal of the virtues is concerned with what virtue can get, with what virtue can bring about. It centres on the idea that the exercise of practical intelligence should be the intelligent direction of the instrumental power inherent in action, with a view to placing limits around our vulnerability to misfortune. Clearly we cannot hope for too much. Certainly not that 'a good man [should] not suffer any evil in this life or the next'. Virtue is no guarantee against misfortune, and a functional understanding of virtue cannot teach us to consent to it, nor even to accept it, except as a species of sitting things out.

15 Aurel Kolnai, *Ethics, Value and Reality* (London: Athlone Press, 1977), p. 87.

16 Is it ridiculous or sentimental to say this? Some have said it, and have also said that it is in the same sense ridiculous to say it. Simone Weil said that it was 'foolish', even that it was 'crazy'. See, for example, various essays in *Intimations of Christianity amongst the Ancient Greeks* (London: Routledge & Kegan Paul, 1957). She meant that it went against everything in nature and human nature, against everything that had a proper title to be called reasonable. She would call it 'Christian foolishness' and if she saw it in Socrates she would call it an 'intimation of Christianity'. When some people think of intimations they think of antennae. It is an image conditioned by the extensional dimension of perception. If someone sees a person in a fog, but mistakes him for a tree, then though he misperceives, his perception is structured by something real, by what in fact he sees. Visual metaphors in ethics are often attractive for just that reason. We need not understand what Simone Weil says in the light of such an image, however. She means, I think, that Christianity is the best expression of the thoughts which she calls 'intimations' of it. Could this be said of Socratic pity? I do not know.

5 Evil done and evil suffered

1 R. F. Holland, 'Absolute Ethics, Mathematics and the Impossibility of Politics', in *Against Empiricism* (Oxford: Blackwell, 1980).

2 The point is actually made in such words by G. H. von Wright, *The Varieties of Goodness* (London: Routledge & Kegan Paul, 1963), p. 119.

3 Geoffrey Warnock, *The Object of Morality* (London: Methuen, 1971), chapter 2.

4 Plato, *Gorgias*, 448c.

5 Stuart Hampshire writes in *Morality and Conflict* (Oxford: Blackwell, 1983): 'When lecturing in Moral Philosophy, I used often to tell a true story of a wartime experience to illustrate moral conflict . . . The theoretical interest in the story-telling was always in the selection of the circumstances surrounding the interrogation which should be included in the story if the complexity of the original moral problem was to be fully reproduced. I noticed that on different occasions and without any clear intention, I tended to stress different features in the situation as relevant to the problem, and that I did not always even include the same elements of the situation as belonging to the story. Even to speak of "elements of the situation" and "features" as included in the story is to oversimplify by false individuation' (p. 114).

6 Bernard Williams and J. C. Smart, *Utilitarianism: For and Against* (Cambridge: Cambridge University Press, 1973), p. 99. On the tone of Williams' discussion see Holland, 'Absolute Ethics', p. 139.

7 See Chapters 6 and 7.

8 Williams, *Ethics*, p. 99.

9 Hannah Arendt, *On Revolution* (Harmondsworth: Penguin Books, 1965).

10 Che Guevara, *Guerrilla Warfare*, trans. P. J. Murray (London: Cassell, 1962).

11 Jack Smart says (Williams and Smart, *Utilitarianism*), 'There is a *prima facie* necessity for the deontologist to defend himself against the charge of heartlessness.' He is being polite when he says the necessity is only *prima facie*. Like many consequentialists, he seems to think that consequentialism is the ethics of compassion.

6 Naturalism

1 Bernard Williams, *Morality* (Harmondsworth: Penguin, 1973), p. 25.

2 *Ibid.*, p. 25.

3 Plato, *Gorgias*, 476e.

4 Simone Weil, 'Forms of the Implicit Love of God', in *Waiting on God* (Glasgow: Collins, 1978), p. 97.

5 Sophocles, *Electra*, 243–6, trans. E. F. Watling (Harmondsworth: Penguin, 1973), p. 76.

6 Plato, *Gorgias*, 471 a–d.

7 Philippa Foot expressed the former position in 'Moral Beliefs' and, as far as I am able to judge, the latter in 'Morality as a System of Hypothetical Imperatives'. Both papers are reprinted in *Virtues and Vices* (Berkeley: University of California Press, 1978).

8 See J. L. Stocks, *Morality and Purpose* (London: Routledge & Kegan Paul, 1969), chapter 1.

9 G. E. M. Anscombe, 'Modern Moral Philosophy', in *Collected Philosophical Papers* (Oxford: Blackwell, 1981), vol. III.

10 Iris Murdoch, *The Sovereignty of Good* (London: Routledge & Kegan Paul, 1970). R. F. Holland, *Against Empiricism* (Oxford: Blackwell, 1980).

11 Peter Geach, *The Virtues* (Cambridge: Cambridge University Press, 1977), p. 17.

12 Alasdair MacIntyre, *After Virtue* (London: Duckworth, 1981), chapter 15.

13 Practices have goods internal to them; often one cannot appreciate those goods unless one is a participant in the practice; 'practices have a goal or goals fixed for all time . . . but the goals themselves are transmuted by the

history of the activity'; they have standards of excellence disclosed in part and authoritatively, by the tradition of those practices and they require certain virtues (*ibid.*, pp. 180–1).

14 *Ibid.*, p. 116.
15 *Ibid.*, p. 175.
16 *Ibid.*, p. 217.
17 Aurel Kolnai, *Ethics, Value and Reality* (London: Athlone Press, 1977).
18 Terence Irwin, *Plato's Moral Theory* (Oxford: Clarendon Press, 1977).
19 See MacIntyre, *After Virtue*; Holland, 'Education and Values'; S. Weil, *The Need for Roots* (London: Routledge & Kegan Paul, 1952).
20 Aristotle, *Nicomachean Ethics*, 1169a, 33–6.
21 The difference between Plato and Aristotle on this matter is important, and only to be expected if we think of Plato as trying to be true to Socrates, for Socrates denied the internal connection between virtue and appearance. In *Republic* (Book 2, 361b) Plato draws a portrait of the 'perfectly just man'. He is:

> A simple and noble man who, in the phrase of Aeschylus, 'does not wish to seem but to be good' but who must be 'deprived of all seeming' and stripped of 'everything but justice ... though doing no wrong he must have the repute of the greatest in justice ... He will have to endure the rack, chains, the branding iron in his eyes and finally, after enduring every extreme form of suffering, he will be crucified and so will learn his lesson that not to be, but to seem just is what we ought to desire.

Here, as so often, Socrates' fate shapes Plato's thought. To be sure, Socrates did not suffer in any way that is seriously comparable to the 'perfectly just man', and although Plato was vulnerable to an indulgent (self-)dramatisation of his own vocation, it is striking that he does not exclude even the gentle, conventionally moral and conventionally pious Cephalus from amongst those who would clamour for the crucifixion of the perfectly just man. We may now see how radical are its implications. The question it raises is not only, as it first appears, how justice can be a good to a just man if he is tortured and crucified, with the rhetorical implication that everyone would choose the appearance rather than the reality of justice, if they could. The more radical question is how justice (or any virtue) can be said to be a good to its possessor if, *ex hypothesi*, it is invisible ('deprived of all seeming'), if there is no internal connection between, as it were, the virtue of a virtue and its being visible to the appreciative judgement of one's peers? Even Kant, who amongst the great philosophers seems as far as one may be from Aristotle, and who wondered whether there had been a pure instance of goodness throughout human history, said of the good will that it 'shines like a jewel'.

22 J. L. Ackrill, *Aristotle's Ethics* (London: Faber & Faber, 1973), p. 24.
23 Simone Weil, *Notebooks*, trans. A. Wills (London: Routledge & Kegan Paul, 1976), p. 7.
24 Hannah Arendt, *The Human Condition* (Chicago: University of Chicago Press, 1958).
25 Friedrich Nietzsche, *Thus Spake Zarathustra* (New York: The Viking Press, 1954).
26 Richard Hare, *Freedom and Reason* (Oxford: Oxford University Press, 1963).
27 Stuart Hampshire, *The Freedom of the Individual* (New York: Harper & Row, 1965), p. 106.

7 Modalities

1 Immanuel Kant, *Groundwork of the Metaphysic of Morals*, trans. H. J. Paton (London: Hutchinson, 1958).
2 For example, by Philippa Foot in 'Morality as a System of Hypothetical Imperatives', in *Virtues and Vices* (Berkeley: University of California Press, 1978), and by Bernard Williams in 'Internal and External Reasons', in *Moral Luck* (Cambridge: Cambridge University Press, 1981).
3 Bernard Williams, 'Practical Necessity', in *Moral Luck*.
4 Thomas Nagel, 'The Limits of Objectivity', in *The Tanner Lectures on Human Values, 1980* (Cambridge: Cambridge University Press, 1980), p. 100.
5 Rush Rhees, *Without Answers* (London: Routledge & Kegan Paul, 1969), p. 175.
6 Simone Weil, 'Human Personality', in G. A. Panichas (ed.), *The Simone Weil Reader* (New York: David McKay, 1977).
7 Peter Winch, 'Universalizability', in *Ethics and Action* (London: Routledge & Kegan Paul, 1972), p. 165.
8 *Ibid.*, pp. 164–5.
9 *Ibid.*, p. 165.
10 *Ibid.*, p. 168.
11 David Wiggins, *Needs, Values, Truth* (Oxford: Blackwell, 1987), seriously misunderstands Winch when he says in a footnote to a sympathetic discussion of Winch's paper:

> I note . . . that Winch spoke of self-*discovery*, in preference to self-*determination*. But he deliberately blurs the effect of this by refusing to distinguish the process of discovery from that of decision – and in a manner presumably most unwelcome to unrestricted cognitivists. In dialogue with these or moral realists it is better I believe to say that the place where self-discovery

comes in is that it supervenes on the deliberated decision and need not be part of the build-up to that decision. (p. 182, n. 44)

That leads him to suggest why universalisation need not be necessary, but his suggestion goes less deep than does Winch's:

Human interests and concerns are as indefinitely various and heterogeneous as are human predicaments. Even moral interests and concerns are indefinitely various and heterogeneous. Therefore, in a world which was not made for us, and is in any case replete with economic and social conflicts . . . there is simply no general reason to expect that a common moral consciousness will issue in some rational disposition to single out just one from among all the moral/practical alternatives apparently available in any situation. (p. 174)

I do not say that what Wiggins says is unimportant or even that it is irrelevant to an account of why universalisability must fail. But just as Winch's emphasis on decision leaves the difference between the personal character of moral deliberation and other forms of deliberation unaccounted for, so does Wiggins' emphasis on conflicting and incommensurable interests.

12 Williams, 'Practical Necessity', p. 128.
13 *Ibid.*, p. 127.
14 *Ibid.*, p. 127.
15 Winch, 'Universalizability', p. 169.
16 The phrase is Vere's, quoted by Winch, *ibid.*, p. 157.
17 John McDowell, 'Are Moral Requirements Hypothetical Imperatives?', *Proceedings of the Aristotelian Society*, suppl. vol. (1978).
18 See Chapter 13.
19 Bernard Williams, 'Persons, Character and Morality', in *Moral Luck*, p. 14.
20 See Chapter 13.

8 Meaning

1 Cora Diamond, 'Eating Meat and Eating People', *Philosophy* 53 (1978).
2 See, for example, Peter Singer, *Animal Liberation* (New York: Random House, 1975).
3 See Ilham Dilman, *Morality and the Inner Life: A Study in Plato's Gorgias* (London and Basingstoke: Macmillan, 1979).
4 Hannah Arendt, *The Human Condition* (Chicago: University of Chicago Press, 1958), p. 181.
5 Most discussions of abortion are like this. It is often said that such descriptions are 'emotional'. I hope to reveal both what is right and

what is wrong about the way of putting it. My main discussion of it is in Chapter 15.

6 Rush Rhees, *Without Answers* (London: Routledge & Kegan Paul, 1969), pp. 121ff.

7 I wish to emphasise that the language of love depends on certain practices, indeed on a culture.

8 See Chapter 10.

9 David Wiggins, *Needs, Values, Truth* (Oxford: Blackwell, 1987), p. 106.

10 Immanuel Kant, *Groundwork of the Metaphysic of Morals*, trans. H. J. Paton (London: Hutchinson, 1958).

11 It is interesting that people who have been adopted may seek their natural parents even though they know that they slept with one another only once and under squalid circumstances. Even so, they believe this to be important to an understanding of who they are. I do not think that anyone would seek, in the same spirit, someone who donated their sperm to a sperm bank. I do not believe they would think that seeking such a person is seeking their father, although they might have prudential reasons for seeking him as the sperm donor.

12 The analogy with secondary properties which has been the focus of much recent moral philosophy has at least this point: once we acknowledge 'red' as an anthropocentric predicate while not wishing to say that colour is not part of the world, then we are left with the possibility of other anthropocentric predicates in some ways importantly different from red but which are also of 'things as they are'.

13 Plato, *Crito*.

14 Aristotle, *Nicomachean Ethics*, Book 1.

15 *Ibid.*, 1100b 30–33.

16 Alasdair MacIntyre, *After Virtue* (London: Duckworth, 1981).

17 Aristotle, *Nicomachean Ethics*, Book 1.

18 *Ibid.*, Book 1.

19 John McDowell, 'The Role of Eudaimonia in Aristotle's Ethics', in A. Rorty (ed.), *Essays on Aristotle's Ethics* (Berkeley: University of California Press, 1980), p. 366.

20 MacIntyre, *After Virtue*, Chapters 15, 16.

21 *Ibid.*, p. 203.

22 *Ibid.*, p. 203.

23 *Ibid.*, pp. 172–4.

24 *Ibid.*, p. 201.

25 See Raimond Gaita, 'Integrity', *Proceedings of the Aristotelian Society*, suppl. vol. 15 (1981). Also Chapter 11.

26 I mean that although any substantial use of an epistemic vocabulary requires that a contrast be drawn between 'how things are' and 'how we feel about them', it does not follow that 'how things are' is always (ideally) characterisable independently of feeling and character.

27 Iris Murdoch, *The Sovereignty of Good* (London: Routledge & Kegan Paul, 1970).
28 *Ibid.*, p. 32.

9 Individuality

1 See R. F. Holland, 'Absolute Ethics, Mathematics and the Impossibility of Politics', in *Against Empiricism* (Oxford: Blackwell, 1980).
2 Stanley Cavell, *The Claim of Reason* (Oxford: Clarendon Press, 1979).
3 By, for example, Philippa Foot, 'Morality as a System of Hypothetical Imperatives', in *Virtues and Vices* (Berkeley: University of California Press, 1978).
4 R. M. Hare, 'Universalizability', in *Essays on the Moral Concepts* (London and Basingstoke: Macmillan, 1972).
5 Hannah Arendt, *The Human Condition* (Chicago: University of Chicago Press, 1958), p. 181.
6 Bernard Williams, *Moral Luck* (Cambridge: Cambridge University Press, 1981), p. 14.
7 *Ibid.*, p. 15.
8 *Ibid.*, p. 14.
9 Cora Diamond, 'Eating Meat and Eating People', *Philosophy* 53 (1978).
10 Williams, *Moral Luck*, p. 16.
11 *Ibid.*, p. 16.
12 Cavell, *The Claim of Reason*, p. 376.
13 *Ibid.*, p. 376.
14 We encountered a similar problem with consequentialists in Chapter 5.
15 Peter Singer, *Animal Liberation* (New York, 1979).

10 'An attitude towards a soul'

1 David Wiggins, *Needs, Values, Truth* (Oxford: Blackwell, 1987), p. 106.
2 Rush Rhees, 'Wittgenstein's Builders', in *Discussions of Wittgenstein* (London: Routledge & Kegan Paul, 1969).
3 Stanley Cavell, *The Claim of Reason* (Oxford: Clarendon Press, 1979), Section 1.
4 Ludwig Wittgenstein, *Philosophical Investigations*, trans. G. E. M. Anscombe (Oxford: Blackwell, 1963), § 283.
5 *Ibid.*, Pt 2 IV.
6 *Ibid.*, § 281.
7 Wiggins, *Needs, Values, Truth*, p. 173.
8 Thomas Nagel, 'Subjective and Objective', in *Mortal Questions* (Cambridge: Cambridge University Press, 1979), p. 206.
9 Stuart Hampshire, *Thought and Action* (London: Chatto and Windus, 1965).

10 Often for ill. So I would judge the impact of Richard Rorty's *Philosophy and the Mirror of Nature* (Oxford: Blackwell, 1980).

11 David Hume, *Enquiry Concerning the Principles of Morals*, Appendix 1.

12 For example, John McDowell, 'Are Moral Requirements Hypothetical Imperatives', *Proceedings of the Aristotelian Society*, suppl. vol. (1978).

13 See McDowell, but also Wiggins 'Truth, Invention and the Meaning of Life' in his *Needs, Values and Truth*, and Iris Murdoch, *The Sovereignty of Good* (London: Routledge & Kegan Paul, 1970), chapter 1. But not dialogical as Rorty (*Philosophy*) thinks of it.

14 Cavell, *The Claim of Reason*, p. 395.

15 Wiggins, *Needs, Values, Truth*, p. 70.

16 Peter Winch, 'Eine Einstellung zur Seele', in *Trying to Make Sense* (Oxford: Blackwell, 1987), p. 146.

17 Simone Weil, 'The Iliad: A Poem of Might', in *Intimations of Christianity amongst the Ancient Greeks* (London: Routledge & Kegan Paul, 1957), p. 28.

18 *Ibid.*, p. 28.

19 In many of her writings, but see, for example, Simone Weil, 'Forms of the Implicit Love of God', in *Waiting on God* (Glasgow: Collins, 1977), p. 103.

20 Wittgenstein, *Philosophical Investigations*, § 287.

21 Ludwig Wittgenstein, *The Blue Book* (Oxford: Blackwell, 1958), p. 24.

22 Aristotle, *De Anima*, Book III, 433b.

23 Walter Bonnatti, *On Great Heights* (London: Hart-Davis, 1964).

24 Cf. Cora Diamond, 'Eating Meat and Eating People', *Philosophy* 53 (1978).

25 I say this despite Wittgenstein's remark (*Philosophical Investigations*) § 284.

26 Simone Weil, *Notebooks*, vol. 1, trans. A. Wills (London: Routledge & Kegan Paul, 1976).

27 Wittgenstein, *Philosophical Investigations*, § 286.

28 Nagel, 'What Is It Like to Be a Bat?', in *Mortal Questions*.

29 Wittgenstein, *Philosophical Investigations*, § 287.

30 Cf. Diamond, 'Eating Meat'.

31 See Winch, 'Who Is My Neighbour', in *Trying To Make Sense*.

32 We cannot be *in that way* unrelenting in our struggle against the under-growth – as Diamond ('Eating Meat') pointed out, to be unrelenting in this way is to be unrelenting in the face of a plea even though it may be only in her eyes.

11 Goodness

1 Aurel Kolnai, *Ethics, Value and Reality* (London: Athlone Press, 1977), p. 85.

2 *Ibid.*, p. 85.

NOTES

3 Although Terence Irwin believes that Plato's talk of the Forms as separately existing was an extravagantly mistaken way of saying that 'moral predicates were not reducible to observational predicates'. See *Plato's Moral Theory* (Oxford: Clarendon Press, 1977), chapter 3.
4 Plato, *Apology*, 41 c–d.
5 That seems to be the lesson of the ascent. *Symposium*, 210a–211c.
6 Aristotle, *Nicomachean Ethics*, Book 1 and *Eudemian Ethics*, Book 1.
7 W. F. Hardie, *Aristotle's Moral Theory* (Oxford: Clarendon Press, 1968), p. 27.
8 Aristotle, *Eudemian Ethics*, Book 1.
9 Aristotle, *Nicomachean Ethics*, 1100b.
10 George Orwell, 'Reflections on Gandhi', in *The Collected Essays, Journalism and Letters of George Orwell* (Harmondsworth: Penguin, 1968), vol. IV.
11 Simone Weil, 'Forms of the Implicit Love of God', in *Waiting on God* (Glasgow: Collins Fountain Books, 1977), p. 100.
12 Simone Weil, 'The Love of God and Affliction', in *Science, Necessity and the Love of God* (Oxford: Oxford University Press, 1968), p. 173.
13 *Ibid.*, p. 172.
14 Norman Malcolm, *Wittgenstein: A Memoir* (London: Oxford University Press, 1978), p. 100.
15 Ludwig Wittgenstein, 'Lecture on Ethics', *Philosophical Review* 78 (1965).
16 Thomas More, 'Letters to Margaret, June 1535', in A. L. Rowse (ed.), *A Man of Singular Virtue: A Life of Sir Thomas More by his son-in-law William Roper and a Selection of More's Letters* (London: Folio Society, 1980), p. 126.
17 Plato, *Republic*, 493c.
18 Aristotle, *Nicomachean Ethics*, 1096b.
19 I discuss this in 'Integrity', *Proceedings of the Aristotelian Society*, suppl. vol. 15 (1981).
20 As reported on television programme.
21 Simone Weil, *First and Last Notebooks*, ed. R. Rees (London: Oxford University Press, 1970), p. 147.

12 Ethical other-worldliness

1 R. F. Holland, *Against Empiricism* (Oxford: Blackwell, 1980), p. 2.
2 *Ibid.*, p. 128.
3 *Ibid.*, p. 2.
4 *Ibid.*, p. 2.
5 *Ibid.*, p. 186.
6 *Ibid.*, p. 107.
7 J. L. Stocks, *Morality and Purpose* (London: Routledge & Kegan Paul, 1969), p. 69.

8 See Mark Platts, *Ways of Meaning* (London: Routledge & Kegan Paul, 1979), p. 243.
9 Immanuel Kant, *Lecture on Ethics* (New York: Harper Torchbooks, 1963).
10 Plato, *Phaedo*, 61c.
11 Iris Murdoch, *The Sovereignty of Good* (London: Routledge & Kegan Paul, 1970), p. 40. In a footnote Platts says: 'These and ensuing remarks, are meant as preliminary ruminations about the theory of moral language implicit in Miss Murdoch's brilliantly thought-provoking book, *The Sovereignty of Good*; the detailed development of that theory of language seems to me a matter of great importance' (*Ways of Meaning*, p. 262, n. 6). It will be clear, when the reader reaches Chapter 15, that I believe that the development of Murdoch's remarks about 'moral language' would not be in the direction suggested by Platts.
12 Murdoch, *The Sovereignty of Good*.
13 *Ibid.*, p. 26. This is in marked contrast with many of those who, like Platts, have taken the wrong cue from her emphasis on the importance of the metaphor of vision in ethics. Platts, for example, says: 'moral judgments are viewed [by him] as factually cognitive, as presenting claims about the world, which can be assessed (like any other factual belief) as true or false, and whose truth or falsity are as much possible objects of human knowledge as any other factual claims about the world' (*Ways of Meaning*, p. 243).
14 Murdoch, *The Sovereignty of Good*, p. 74.
15 Holland, *Against Empiricism*, p. 59.
16 *Ibid.*, pp. 59–60.
17 *Ibid.*, p. 3.
18 *Ibid.*, p. 107.
19 *Ibid.*, p. 98.
20 Socrates sometimes came at least close to adopting the highminded tone which I have suggested Aristotle found offensive. For example, the tone in which he questions whether death is an evil in *Apology*, 40b–c.
21 David Wiggins, 'Truth, Invention, and the Meaning of Life', in *Needs, Values, Truth* (Oxford: Blackwell, 1987), p. 89.
22 *Ibid.*, p. 89.
23 *Ibid.*, p. 90.
24 See, for example, D. Z. Phillips, *The Concept of Prayer* (London: Routledge & Kegan Paul, 1958).
25 P. T. Geach, *God and the Soul* (London: Routledge & Kegan Paul, 1969), p. 126.
26 *Ibid.*, p. 126.
27 Wiggins, 'Truth, Invention, and The Meaning of Life', p. 89.
28 This quotation is from a footnote to Wiggins' original British Academy text, but which he deleted from the revised version in *Needs, Values, Truth*. See *Proceedings of the British Academy* (1976) p. 332.

29 Wiggins, 'Truth, Invention, and The Meaning of Life', p. 89.
30 *Ibid.*, p. 89.
31 Murdoch, *The Sovereignty of Good*, p. 29.
32 *Ibid.*, p. 32.
33 See Alasdair MacIntyre, *After Virtue* (London: Duckworth, 1981).

13 'The repudiation of morality'

1 Peter Geach, *God and the Soul* (London: Routledge & Kegan Paul, 1969), p. 40.
2 Stanley Cavell, *The Claim of Reason* (Oxford: Clarendon Press, 1979), p. 268.
3 Simone Weil in many of her writings, but for example: 'We should do only those actions which we cannot stop ourselves from doing, which we are unable not to do, but through well-directed attention, we should always keep on increasing the number of those we are unable not to do': *Gravity and Grace* (London: Routledge & Kegan Paul, 1972), p. 39. Iris Murdoch, *The Sovereignty of Good* (London: Routledge & Kegan Paul, 1970), p. 39.
4 Plato, *Theaetetus*, 176d–177a.
5 Simone Weil in nearly all her writings and Murdoch, *The Sovereignty of Good*.
6 Plato, *Republic*, Book 5, 480.
7 John McDowell, 'Are Moral Requirements Hypothetical Imperatives?', *Proceedings of the Aristotelian Society*, suppl. vol. 52 (1978), p. 27.
8 *Ibid.*, p. 28.
9 Plato, *Protagoras*, 352a.
10 Cavell, *The Claim of Reason*, p. 268.
11 *Ibid.*, p. 269.
12 Bernard Williams, 'Moral Luck', in *Moral Luck* (Cambridge: Cambridge University Press, 1981).
13 Provided that his failure is not caused by ill luck of a kind Williams calls 'extrinsic' to his project. But this point is not important to my discussion.
14 Except, perhaps, in the sense already discussed earlier in this chapter.

14 Ethics and politics

1 Plato, *Republic*, Book 2, 362c.
2 Max Weber, 'Politics as a Vocation', in E. Runciman (ed.), *Weber: Selections in Translation* (Cambridge: Cambridge University Press, 1978).
3 For example, Richard Hare said that he did not understand what anyone could mean who claimed there was a deep tension between

ethics and politics. That is because he collapsed both into consequentialism. See 'Reasons of State', in *Applications of Moral Philosophy* (London and Basingstoke: Macmillan, 1972).

4 R. F. Holland, 'Absolute Ethics, Mathematics and the Impossibility of Politics', in *Against Empiricism* (Oxford: Blackwell, 1980) p. 135.

5 By way of eloquent contrast see Michael Oakeshott, *Human Conduct* (Oxford: Clarendon Press, 1975), Parts II and III. Also Rush Rhees, *Without Answers* (London: Routledge & Kegan Paul, 1969), chapters 4, 5 and 6.

6 Machiavelli, *Prince*, chapter 15.

7 Weber, 'Politics as a Vocation', p. 212.

8 Plato, too, taught this lesson in *Republic*, 342e, in the first instance to Thrasymachus.

9 Peter Geach, *The Virtues* (Cambridge: Cambridge University Press, 1977), p. 114.

10 Quoted in Isaiah Berlin, 'The Originality of Machiavelli', in *Against the Current* (New York: Viking Press, 1978), p. 53.

11 See Jean-Paul Sartre, 'Reply to Albert Camus' and 'Merleau-Ponty', in *Situations* (London: Hamish Hamilton, 1965); Maurice Merleau-Ponty, *Humanism and Terror* (Boston: Beacon Press, 1969); Albert Camus, *The Rebel* (Harmondsworth: Penguin, 1965); George Orwell, *The Collected Essays, Journalism and Letters* (Harmondsworth: Penguin, 1970).

12 Berlin, 'The Originality of Machiavelli', p. 54.

13 *Ibid.*, p. 58.

14 'Ultimate ends, in this sense, whether or not they are those of the Judeo-Christian tradition, are what is usually meant by moral values', *ibid.*, p. 45.

15 Quoted by Hannah Arendt, 'Bertolt Brecht', in *Men in Dark Times* (Harmondsworth: Penguin, 1968), p. 237.

16 *Ibid.*

17 *Ibid.*

18 See, for example, G. E. M. Anscombe, 'Mr. Truman's Degree', in *Collected Philosophical Papers* (Oxford: Blackwell, 1981), vol. III.

19 'Genocide . . . is an attack upon human diversity as such, that is, upon a characteristic of the "human status" without which the very words "mankind" or "humanity" would be devoid of meaning.' Hannah Arendt, *Eichmann in Jerusalem: A Report on the Banality of Evil* (New York: The Viking Press, 1967), p. 269.

20 E. M. Forster, 'What I Believe', in *Two Cheers for Democracy* (London: Edward Arnold, 1939).

21 Hannah Arendt, 'Organized Guilt and Universal Responsibility', in R. H. Feldman (ed.), *The Jew as Pariah* (New York: Grove Press, 1978), pp. 227–8.

22 The de-Nazification of German institutions immediately after the war appeared to be principally concerned to establish and to maintain the conditions which would enable Germany to become a peaceful and democratic member of the community of European nations. That was an understandable response to what were, according to traditional political categories, the most salient features of the Third Reich – that it had again started a terrible war and that it was totalitarian. However, the most distinctive feature of Germany under Hitler was not that it was totalitarian, nor even that its armies had marched through Europe: it was its genocidal practice against those people who were judged not to be fit to inhabit the earth with the master race. This terrible evil was not readily politically classifiable (as was revealed in the difficulty the Nuremberg court had in finding and interpreting a description of it); nor was there a readily discernible appropriate political response to it. The difficulty was compounded by the degree to which ordinary Germans were suspected of complicity in a crime the character and enormity of which seemed then, as now, to defy comprehension. Even if one makes a generous allowance for exaggeration, the passage I quoted from Arendt reveals the impossibility of a coherent political response to what is now called 'the Holocaust' which would be commensurate with the moral sense of its evil. Herman Glaser reports Senator Landahl Glaser as saying immediately after the war:

> We Germans want to face the bitter truth courageously, avoiding the lure of self-deception. Only in this way will we be able to find and preserve our bearing and our dignity in the face of collapse. Defeated in two wars due to the dilettante and irresponsible nature of our political leadership, we stand here not only in the midst of the rubble of our cities, but also of our Reich and of our spirit.
> *The Rubble Years* (New York: Paragon House, 1980), pp. 74–5

There was a lot of such talk about, but it is common knowledge that the most bitter truth of all – concerning the degree of complicity of ordinary people in the Holocaust – was not faced. But that is partly because it was politically impossible to do so. Whatever one's moral judgement on this, it would evidently be politically insane to require every child to interrogate their parents about what they knew of the Holocaust and what they did, while at the same time attempting to rebuild Germany. But this is a political point with no moral implications for any individual German, nor indeed for the attitude of anyone else to the Germans. It is therefore hardly surprising that the Allied de-Nazification programme was not a coherent response to the unique and distinctive evil of the Holocaust. The Allies concerned themselves with the relatively tractable problem of how to rebuild a German nation which would be democratic and which would not again threaten the peace of Europe.

This tension between the moral and the political response to the evil of the Third Reich and of the relations between them showed itself in many ways in German life, and one would expect it to have affected high culture and those institutions which served it. Sigrid Undset, a Norwegian novelist and Nobel Prize winner who fled to the United States during the war, said in 1945:

> There must be millions of German children whose fathers took part in the atrocities against civilian women and children in Russia, Poland, Yugoslavia, Greece, France or Norway! Countless German children have parents who experienced a fleeting prosperity as a result of the plunder of Europe, or who took part in the murder of 4 million Jews, pocketing some of the booty which had been taken from the dead! There must be millions of children whose mothers have made the German woman almost more loathsome than the German man, as they gleefully took over the homes and property of people in occupied territories, even keeping family portraits which they occasionally offered to sell back to their owners at a high price! ... *The greatest hindrance to German re-education is not German thinking, but rather the actual deeds which have been committed as a result of this thinking.*
> Glaser, *The Rubble Years*, p. 76 [My italics]

She was surely right in the judgement that I have emphasised.

The reasons one would expect this conflict to be felt in the institutions of high culture are twofold. First, it does not matter to mathematical or scientific truth if it is proposed by people who are radically evil or who have been implicated in radical evil: $2 + 2 = 4$ no matter who says it and even Hitler would have to acknowledge that $E = mc^2$ although no doubt he would have preferred that it had not been discovered by a Jew. The matter is far more complex in the humanities, as is evidenced by the crisis many writers felt in relation, not only to their native culture, but also indeed to their native tongue. The point may be seen not to be as obscure or rhetorical as it may at first appear if we remember that the health of a natural language, its capacity to remain vital and to resist deadening cliché, is dependent on the way those who keep it alive and vital are rooted in it. It is a common phenomenon (even if it is not fully understood) that writers may dry up in exile, and there are many ways in which a writer may be uprooted. It was the common testimony of many writers whose mother tongue was German that the evil of the Third Reich uprooted them from their native culture and tongue. The difficulty German artists and writers had (and some still have) in re-establishing a living relation to their cultural past is of a different order from the difficulty faced by writers whose past has been denied them through its suppression and falsification by totalitarian or dictatorial governments.

Reflection on the plight of high culture after the Third Reich reveals two broad truths about value which we have already had occasion to note: each generation has to find its way of expressing what it takes to be the truths of the past; and its capacity to do that depends, to a large degree, on the fertility and the moral accessibility of its cultural roots. Whatever we may make of the idea of universal moral or spiritual truths about the human condition as they may be expressed in art, they are unlike mathematical or scientific truth: each generation does not need to find its own way of expressing that $2 + 2 = 4$ or that $E = mc^2$. But it is a commonplace in aesthetics that we must find our own voice no matter how much we may love the style of past architects, painters, poets or musicians, and it is so in all matters of the spirit. The evil of the Third Reich estranged many Germans from the finest parts of German culture.

It is true that Germany is the Germany of Goethe, Schiller, Beethoven and Bach and not merely the Germany of Hitler, and it is true that the evils of the extermination camps cannot diminish the glories of German cultural achievement. But the problem felt even by those Germans who pointed this out (against, for example, others who refused even to speak German again) was not how to remain appreciative of German cultural achievement, but rather, how to remain in a living and creative relation to it.

23 Although murderers may be a threat to what we call 'society', although they may threaten the stability of a political community, and although murder as a crime is a crime against a community, neither in its aspect as an evil deed nor in its aspect as a crime is murder an act against a people.

24 Alan Donagan, *The Theory of Morality* (Chicago: University of Chicago Press, 1977), p. 206.

25 Anscombe, 'Mr. Truman's Degree', p. 51. But cf., 'We may not commit any sin, however small, for the sake of any good, however great, and if the choice is between our total destruction and the commission of sin, then we must choose to be destroyed', *ibid.*, p. 79.

26 *Ibid.*, p. 52.

27 Michael Walzer, 'Political Action: The Problem of Dirty Hands', *Philosophy and Public Affairs* 2, (1972–3).

28 I do not mean this merely as a prediction. It is tempting to speak of our 'preparedness' to do evil. I am reluctant to do so because of the resonances of saying of those who will not do evil that they are not 'prepared to do it'. Such voluntaristic modal expressions are too close to saying that they are not prepared to shoulder the burden of their humanity, or that they are not prepared to dirty their hands, and so on.

29 Which means that a people are not always threatened by a foreign enemy.

30 The discussion of these matters has in recent philosophy been couched in terms of the contrast between public and private morality, as in the essays in S. Hampshire (ed.), *Public and Private Morality* (Cambridge: Cambridge University Press, 1978). The distinction between the public and the private is more complex than is suggested by the points I make about the Church and about a pacifist community. But the points I make are, I think, points against what is made of the contrast by modern philosophers. Also, the way the distinction between the public and the private is typically drawn gives insufficient (if any) emphasis to the historical character of political life and institutions. A community which had the normal range of political institutions would not, I think, be so ready to do evil to protect itself, or if it did we would have to give a different account of it, if it knew that it would not survive for another generation.

15 Moral understanding

1 In case this should seem to be an exaggeration, I would point out that there is, in the subject, no mainstream discussion of good judgement, common sense (whatever Moore was defending, it was not common sense as we speak of it when we praise those who were not taken in by Uri Geller for their common sense), gullibility, sanity and madness, superstition and many other such 'workaday' critical concepts. Most students go through an entire philosophy course without so much as an inkling that these concepts matter to an understanding of the nature of critical thinking.

2 Mark Platts, *Ways of Meaning* (London: Routledge & Kegan Paul, 1979), p. 252.

3 This might seem to imply that I believe that God cannot be wise. I would make the same point here, as I did in Chapter 12, concerning the claim that God must know my telephone number if He is to be omniscient.

4 Alan Donagan, *The Theory of Morality* (Chicago: University of Chicago Press, 1977), p. 235.

5 Simone Weil in almost all her writings. Iris Murdoch, *The Sovereignty of Good* (London: Routledge & Kegan Paul, 1970). See also Chapter 13.

6 See Chapter 7.

7 Cf. the example of a teacher and his student discussed in Chapter 9.

8 Plato, *Gorgias*, 471d.

9 Hannah Arendt, *Eichmann in Jerusalem: A Report on the Banality of Evil* (New York: The Viking Press, 1964), p. 252.

10 Plato, *Gorgias*, 447a.

NOTES

11 Martin Buber, 'The Word That Is Spoken', in *The Knowledge of Man* (London: George Allen & Unwin, 1965), p. 113.
12 As it does, although Wiggins did little with it. See David Wiggins, *Needs, Values, Truth* (Oxford: Blackwell, 1987), pp. 70ff. See also Chapter 10.
13 Ludwig Wittgenstein, *Philosophical Investigations*, trans. G. E. M. Anscombe (Oxford: Blackwell, 1963) § 2.
14 Rush Rhees, 'Wittgenstein's Builders', in *Discussions of Wittgenstein* (London: Routledge & Kegan Paul, 1969).
15 Søren Kierkegaard, *Concluding Unscientific Postscript*, trans. D. F. Swenson (Princeton: Princeton University Press, 1941), Part 2, chapters 1–3.

16 Truth

1 Most excellently in a little book by Renford Bambrough, *Moral Scepticism and Moral Knowledge* (London: Routledge & Kegan Paul, 1979), which should be a primer for all who think on the matter.
2 David Wiggins, *Needs, Values, Truth* (Oxford: Blackwell, 1987), p. 330.
3 *Ibid.*, pp. 87–8.
4 David Wiggins, *Sameness and Substance* (Oxford: Blackwell, 1980), p. 186.
5 The qualification is over what Wiggins calls 'deliberative' judgements, such as 'I must/ought to do x.'
6 J. L. Mackie, *Ethics: Inventing Right and Wrong* (Harmondsworth: Penguin, 1977), p. 15.
7 Gregory Vlastos, 'The Socratic Elenchus', *Oxford Studies in Ancient Philosophy*, vol. I (Oxford: Oxford University Press, 1983), p. 34.
8 Søren Kierkegaard, *Concluding Unscientific Postscripts*, trans. D. F. Swenson (Princeton: Princeton University Press, 1941).
9 Ludwig Wittgenstein, *Culture and Value*, ed. G. H. Von Wright, trans. P. Winch (Oxford: Blackwell, 1980). As is indicated in the quotation, when Wittgenstein wrote this, 'logic' and 'philosophy' were virtually interchangeable terms for him.
10 Kierkegaard, *Concluding Unscientific Postscripts*, p. 147.
11 Plato, *Apology*, 37e.
12 Plato, *Gorgias*, 508A. I owe the recognition of the significance of Socrates' reply to Polus to R. F. Holland, *Against Empiricism* (Oxford: Blackwell, 1980), p. 131.
13 Plato, *Symposium*, 210a–211e.
14 The expression is Thomas Nagel's. See 'Subjective and Objective', in *Mortal Questions* (Cambridge: Cambridge University Press, 1981), p. 206. Bernard Williams speaks in a similar way of an 'absolute conception of knowledge', in *Descartes: The Project of Pure Inquiry* (Harmondsworth: Penguin, 1978).

364

15 Plato, *Apology*, 41b.
16 Ludwig Wittgenstein, *Tractatus Logico-Philosophicus* (London: Routledge and Kegan Paul, 1961), 6.4312.
17 Wiggins, *Needs, Values, Truth*, p. 107, n. 20.
18 *Ibid.*, p. 340.
19 *Ibid.*, p. 342.
20 *Ibid.*, pp. 344–5.
21 *Ibid.*, p. 153.
22 *Ibid.*, p. 150, n. 13.
23 Hannah Arendt, *Eichmann in Jerusalem: A Report on the Banality of Evil* (New York: The Viking Press, 1964), p. 252.
24 'There was no sign in him [Eichmann] of firm ideological convictions or of specific evil motives, and the only notable characteristic one could detect in his past behaviour as well as in his behaviour during the trial and throughout the pre-trial police examination was something entirely negative: it was not stupidity but thoughtlessness.' Hannah Arendt, *The Life of the Mind* (London: Secker & Warburg, 1978), vol. I, p. 4.
25 Plato, *Gorgias*, 482c.
26 Kierkegaard, *Concluding Unscientific Postscripts*, p. 149.
27 Wittgenstein, *Culture and Value*, p. 50. I am grateful to Peter Winch for drawing my attention to this passage.
28 Simone Weil, 'Human Personality', in George A. Panichas (ed.), *The Simone Weil Reader* (New York: David McKay Co. Inc., 1977), p. 318.
29 Simone Weil, *Waiting on God* (Glasgow: Collins, 1977), p. 50.
30 Aurel Kolnai, *Ethics, Value and Reality* (London: Athlone Press, 1977), p. 27.

17 Fearless thinkers and evil thoughts

1 George Orwell, 'Reflections on Gandhi', in *Collected Essays, Journalism and Letters of George Orwell* (Harmondsworth: Penguin, 1970), vol. IV, p. 530.
2 René Descartes, 'Synopsis', *Meditations*, 'Meditation on First Philosophies'.
3 G. K. Chesterton, *Orthodoxy* (New York: Doubleday Image Books, 1959), p. 19.
4 Ludwig Wittgenstein, *Remarks on the Foundations of Mathematics*, ed. G. H. von Wright and Rush Rhees, trans. G. E. M. Anscombe (Oxford: Blackwell, 1974), 50e. I am grateful to Rush Rhees for drawing attention to the importance of this point of Wittgenstein's in seminars he gave at King's College, London, in 1980.
5 See G. E. M. Anscombe, 'Modern Moral Philosophy', in *Collected Philosophical Papers* (Oxford: Blackwell, 1981), vol. III, p. 40.

6 Søren Kierkegaard, *Concluding Unscientific Postscripts*, trans. D. F. Swenson (Princeton: Princeton University Press, 1968), p. 121.

7 The expression comes from Philippa Foot, 'Moral Beliefs', in *Virtues and Vices* (Berkeley: University of California Press, 1978).

8 R. F. Holland, 'Moral Scepticism', *Proceedings of the Aristotelian Society*, suppl. vol. (1967).

9 Foot, 'Moral beliefs', for example.

10 Anscombe, 'Modern Moral Philosophy', p. 40.

11 I am speaking of the Platonic Socrates. It is a controversial matter why the historical Socrates was executed.

12 G. E. Moore, 'An Autobiography', in P. A. Schilpp (ed.), *The Philosophy of G. E. Moore* (Wisconsin: George Banta Publishing Co., 1942).

13 See Michael Tooley, 'A Defence of Abortion and Infanticide', in J. Feinberg (ed.), *The Problem of Abortion* (Belmont: Wadsworth, 1984), and P. Singer, *Practical Ethics* (Cambridge: Cambridge University Press, 1979).

14 Kierkegaard, *Concluding Unscientific Postscripts*, p. 175.

15 Alan Donagan, *The Theory of Morality* (Chicago: University of Chicago Press, 1977), p. 235.

16 Plato, *Gorgias*, 481c.

17 *Ibid.*, 481b.

18 The interesting discoveries by philosophers that they have not said anything or that they are unable to say something in all seriousness are never the discovery that they were insincere in saying it.

19 Simone Weil, *Waiting on God* (Glasgow: Collins, 1977), p. 50.

20 Aurel Kolnai, *Ethics, Value and Reality* (London: Athlone Press), p. 27.

21 Plato, *Gorgias*, 481c–482c.

Afterword

1 Cora Diamond drew this distinction in another connection in 'Eating Meat, Eating People' in her *The Realistic Spirit* (Cambridge, MA: MIT Press, 1991).

2 That is, I believe, why Iris Murdoch was wrong to contrast the impersonality of a public language with the increasingly private determination of meaning. She ran together a distinction between the public and the private with a distinction between the personal and the impersonal in ways that were unhelpful.

3 Ludwig Wittgenstein, *Philosophical Investigations*, trans, G. E. M. Anscombe (Oxford: Blackwell, 1997), § 257.

Index

367

eBooks – at www.eBookstore.tandf.co.uk

A library at your fingertips!

eBooks are electronic versions of printed books. You can store them on your PC/laptop or browse them online.

They have advantages for anyone needing rapid access to a wide variety of published, copyright information.

eBooks can help your research by enabling you to bookmark chapters, annotate text and use instant searches to find specific words or phrases. Several eBook files would fit on even a small laptop or PDA.

NEW: Save money by eSubscribing: cheap, online access to any eBook for as long as you need it.

Annual subscription packages

We now offer special low-cost bulk subscriptions to packages of eBooks in certain subject areas. These are available to libraries or to individuals.

For more information please contact webmaster.ebooks@tandf.co.uk

We're continually developing the eBook concept, so keep up to date by visiting the website.

www.eBookstore.tandf.co.uk